REVELS STUDENT EDITIONS

PLAYS ON WOMEN

Manchester University Press

REVELS STUDENT EDITIONS

Based on the highly respected Revels Plays, which provide a wide range of
scholarly critical editions of plays by Shakespeare's contemporaries, the Revels
Student Editions offer readable and competitively priced introductions, text and
commentary designed to distil the erudition and insights of the Revels Plays, while
focusing on matters of clarity and interpretation. These editions are aimed at
undergraduates, graduate teachers of Renaissance drama and all those who enjoy
the vitality and humour of one of the world's greatest periods of drama.

GENERAL EDITOR David Bevington

Dekker/Rowley/Ford *The Witch of Edmonton*
Fletcher *The Tamer Tamed; or, The Woman's Prize*
Ford *'Tis Pity She's a Whore*
Jonson *Bartholomew Fair*
Jonson *Volpone*
Jonson *Masques of Difference: Four Court Masques*
Kyd *The Spanish Tragedy*
Marlowe *The Jew of Malta*
Marlowe *Tamburlaine the Great*
Marston *The Malcontent*
Middleton *Women Beware Women*
Middleton/Rowley *The Changeling*
Middleton/Tourneur *The Revenger's Tragedy*
Webster *The Duchess of Malfi*
Webster *The White Devil*

Plays on Women: An Anthology
Middleton *A Chaste Maid in Cheapside*
Middleton/Dekker *The Roaring Girl*
Anon. *Arden of Faversham*
Heywood *A Woman Killed with Kindness*

PLAYS ON WOMEN

A CHASTE MAID IN CHEAPSIDE
Thomas Middleton

THE ROARING GIRL
Thomas Middleton and Thomas Dekker

ARDEN OF FAVERSHAM
anon.

A WOMAN KILLED WITH KINDNESS
Thomas Heywood

Edited by Kathleen E. McLuskie
and David Bevington
with commentary and introduction by Kathleen E. McLuskie

based on The Revels Plays edition
edited by R. B. Parker (Methuen 1969)
Paul A. Mulholland (Manchester University Press 1987)
M. L. Wine (Methuen 1963)
and R. W. van Fossen (Methuen 1961)

MANCHESTER
UNIVERSITY PRESS
Manchester and New York

distributed in the United States exclusively by
Palgrave Macmillan

Introduction, critical apparatus, etc.
© Kathleen E. McLuskie and David Bevington 1999

The right of Kathleen E. McLuskie and David Bevington to be identified
as the editors of this work has been asserted by them in accordance with the
Copyright, Designs and Patents Act 1988.

Published by Manchester University Press
Oxford Road, Manchester M13 9NR, UK
and Room 400, 175 Fifth Avenue, New York, NY 10010, USA
www.manchesteruniversitypress.co.uk

Distributed in the United States exclusively by
Palgrave Macmillan, 175 Fifth Avenue, New York,
NY 10010, USA

Distributed in Canada exclusively by
UBC Press, University of British Columbia, 2029 West Mall,
Vancouver, BC, Canada V6T 1Z2

British Library Cataloguing-in-Publication Data
A catalogue record for this book is available from the British Library

Library of Congress Cataloging-in-Publication Data applied for

ISBN 978 0 7190 1646 2 *paperback*

First published 1999

First reprinted 2009

Typeset
by Best-set Typesetter Ltd, Hong Kong

Printed in Great Britain
by Bell & Bain Ltd, Glasgow

Contents

List of illustrations   *page* vi
Acknowledgements   vii

Introduction   I

A Chaste Maid in Cheapside   67

The Roaring Girl   151

Arden of Faversham   269

A Woman Killed with Kindness   349

List of illustrations

Map of London c. A.D. 1613. Drawing by Patrick Holloway   61

Johannes De Witt's drawing of the Swan Theatre c. 1596   62

Title page of the 1611 Quarto of The Roaring Girl (reproduced
by courtesy of the President and Fellows of Corpus Christi
College, Oxford)   63

Detail from Saxton's Map of Kent, Sussex, Surrey and
Middlesex, 1575 (reproduced by permission of the British
Library, Maps C.7.c.a—Map of Kent)   64

Frontispiece to the 1633 Quarto of Arden of Faversham,
illustrating the murder of Arden at the 'game of tables'   65

Acknowledgements

This edition is truly a work of collaboration. The series general editor, David Bevington, must be given the credit for watching over its development at every stage. He revised the texts, suggested additional commentary notes, refined my arguments and finally helped me let it go with the most generous support and encouragement. His energy, rigour, patience and meticulous high standards reminded me that only the best is good enough for students.

Other friends helped me to live up to those demands. Jean Howard took time from her own busy life to read the introduction at an early stage. Her encouragement and example kept me going. Mike Bristol, Regenia Gagnier, Peter Holland, Diana Henderson, Dennis Kennedy and Shankar Raman kept the ideas fresh and the spirit sane by inviting me to talk about other things. My colleagues in the English Department at the University of Southampton generously bore the burdens of my research leave. John McGavin talked to me about medieval drama and Jonathan Sawday about early modern science. David, Anna, Hilary and Celia kept the rest of my life in place.

The whole thing was Anita Roy's idea. If a copy ever reaches her in India, I hope she likes it.

Kathleen E. McLuskie

Introduction

The connection between plays and women in the early modern theatre aroused a good deal of excited contemporary comment. Those who condemned the theatre homed in on women as the group most in moral danger from this new form of entertainment; those who defended the theatre deplored the way women's tastes undermined its potential as high art. The theatre, they said, was a place where women would be exposed to sexual harassment, and the plays themselves offered them 'a compendious way to warn to be sinful'.[1] For the playwrights and the theatre companies, the presence of women in the theatres offered a marketing opportunity. Stories of domestic life and from the life of the city provided the possibility of pleasing a wider audience and extending the market for a new form of entertainment. The new dramatic genres of domestic tragedy and city comedy turned on relations between men and women. By rendering them pathetic and laughable, the plays turned social relationships into theatrical pleasure.[2] The plays in this anthology, two domestic tragedies and two city comedies, illustrate the ways in which both theatrical pleasures and social relations complicate the connection between women and plays in early modern drama.

The four plays were performed in the London public theatres between 1592 and 1613.[3] Their narratives focus in different ways on central women figures, Alice Arden, Anne Frankford, Moll Cutpurse and Moll Yellowhammer, the Chaste Maid. In both comedy and tragedy these plays established the ways of representing women in contemporary settings which were to become the hallmark of the public theatres. Each of the plays was written for a different adult theatre company and they were produced at a time of rapid change in the London theatrical markets. The theatre seems to have been at its most profitable, and there was frequent pressure, stoutly resisted by the Privy Council and the City Fathers, to allow new companies to perform in London. In particular, the adult companies were facing competition from the exclusive new theatres of the boy players set up in private venues in the liberties of Blackfriars and Paul's.[4]

In focusing their plays on women, the playwrights explicitly offered their audiences theatrical novelty, rejecting the high bombast of Elizabethan tragedy in favour of a more direct appeal to their audience's experience and sensibilities. 'Look for no glorious state; our Muse is bent / Upon a barren subject,' says the prologue to *A Woman Killed with Kindness*. The idea of a 'barren subject' carries with it the implications of unvarnished truth as the dramatists tried to forge a new kind of drama in which recognizable men and women enacted stories in contemporary settings.

1

Contemporary settings did not, of course, exclude extraordinary characters. One of the women in these plays, Moll Cutpurse, was far from ordinary: dressed in men's clothes, she went to taverns and playhouses, smoking her pipe and playing her viol with the same freedom as the young aristocratic roaring boys. Nevertheless, in presenting her in their play, Dekker and Middleton insist on their right to offer their version of the truth which is, again, the antithesis of the high style in drama:

> Only we entreat you think our scene
> Cannot speak high, the subject being but mean.
>   . . . tragic passion,
> And such grave stuff, is this day out of fashion.
>   (*The Roaring Girl*, Prologue, 7–8, 11–12)

In the same prologue, they reject the theatrical pleasure of gross physical comedy, of moral tales of outrageous prostitutes or the familiar trope of the wife who ruins her husband by her extravagance. Dekker and Middleton use their prologue to clear a space for their particular version of a play on women, defining their audience's taste, both creating and satisfying the market for a new kind of theatre, shifting the modes of representation in a new direction.

The dramatists' emphasis on fashion indicates how their plays on women involved a set of choices, all designed to tune an audience to accept a particular version of reality, to develop their taste for one type of drama rather than another. The epilogue to *A Woman Killed with Kindness* offers a merry fable of gentlemen disagreeing on the quality of a wine and concludes, 'good wine may be disgraced / When every several mouth hath sundry taste' (Epilogue, 17–18). More pointedly, the epilogue to *The Roaring Girl* compares the appreciation of the play to controversy about 'The picture of a woman' (Epilogue, 2). The painter, and by analogy the playwrights, offer the image of a woman for sale. It might not please every taste, but the Epilogue pleads that the writers and the actors have done their best and can only offer the recompense of the real Roaring Girl, Moll Cutpurse, appearing soon on the stage of the Fortune Theatre.[5] The Epilogue suggests that in creating a comedy the playwrights have had to pay attention to plot (line 17) and scene (line 18). They have also had to deal with an audience's knowledge of other versions of the stories they enacted. A play can deal only with the writers' version of reality, and the audience might be best pleased with the reality itself.

In defining the characteristics of plays on women, which an audience is encouraged to enjoy, these dramatists also lay down the boundaries of activity for women characters in their drama. They offer the theatrical pleasure which comes from stories of women involved in emotional and conjugal relations with men. In order to make the stories interesting, those relations have to be complicated and insecure: the narratives of these plays all involve adultery and resistance to harmonious patriarchal rule. But those very acts of transgression, whether they lead to comic reinforcement or tragic fracturing of domestic relations, provide theatrical pleasures which have dominated the representation of women to this day.[6] To be sure, the drama of the time offered other roles for women: the wicked queen, the dangerous seductress, the heroic religious martyr.[7] But these roles existed in the worlds of history and romance. The chief woman playwright of the time, Elizabeth Cary, chose a queen from biblical times as the heroine of her play, *Mariam, Fair Queen of Jewry*.[8] Cary, however, was writing a private drama to be read by a coterie. In the world of public theatre performance, there were no plays written by women. Instead, plays on women offered a space in which contemporary ideas and narratives about women were transformed into theatrical pleasure.

AUTHORS AND PLAYING COMPANIES

The authors of these plays present the full variety of kinds of authorship found in the early modern theatre profession. In the early texts, playing companies were identified as often as authors, for the play belonged to the company which had commissioned it, and the companies used authors in a variety of different combinations. For them, authorship was less important than the need to fill the repertory. Plays were provided by individual authors, as in the case of Middleton and Heywood, or by collaborating groups of authors, like Dekker and Middleton for *The Roaring Girl*. Many of the plays remain anonymous, like *Arden of Faversham*. By the end of the sixteenth century, it becomes easier to connect play titles to authors, largely because of references to them in an account book kept between 1592 and 1604 by the theatrical entrepreneur Philip Henslowe.[9] Henslowe recorded payments to authors and groups of authors on behalf of the playing companies who occupied the theatre buildings which he owned. He also listed, quite separately, the plays performed in his theatres and the payments made in connection with their production. The idea of a play as the creative work of an individual was a later development and in the seventeenth century was applied only to a few playwrights.[10]

Modern scholars have nevertheless sought to connect plays with authors, and *Arden of Faversham* has presented them with a particularly intractable problem. The play has been linked with Marlowe, Kyd and Shakespeare, since these were the best-known figures writing at the time of the play's publication. Readers of Shakespeare, in particular, have found in the Arden play a recognizable theatrical terrain. The complexity of the characterization and the recurring poetic images echo the dramatic techniques found in Shakespeare's early work; Black Will and Shakebag, the sinister if incompetent murderers, undergo the same anxieties of conscience as the assassins of Clarence in Shakespeare's *Richard III* (1.4) and are given similarly startling lyrical invocations of changing weather as the unnamed murderers of Banquo in *Macbeth* (3.4.5–8). Recent views on the authorship question, however, have taken a more sceptical view, pointing to the importance of common sources and shared dramatic conventions

rather than the idiosyncrasies of a particular writer. External evidence for
Shakespeare's involvement in the play is found only in a play-list compiled
half a century after the play's first publication, and the sole firm attribution
to Shakespeare occurred in the late eighteenth century when Shakespeare
had come to stand in for the whole of early modern drama.[11]

In the case of Thomas Heywood, the author of *A Woman Killed with
Kindness*, the evidence is on firmer ground. Payments for 'a womones
gowne of blacke velvett for the playe of a womon kylld wth kyndnes' were
recorded by Henslowe, along with two payments of £3 each 'unto thomas
Hewwod' for writing the play.[12] Heywood was active in the theatre from
1596, when he first appears in Henslowe's records, almost until his death
in 1641. This unusually long career was given stability by his long connection with a major theatre company. Worcester's Men, for whom Heywood wrote *A Woman Killed*, were granted royal patronage to become the
Queen's Men in 1604, and Heywood helped the company develop the
popular repertory which made their theatre, the Red Bull, famous. He
experimented with all the genres of early modern drama, writing chronicle
histories, romantic tales of citizen adventure and city comedies as well as
pageants for the city companies and masque-like entertainments for the
royal court. In the contemporary (and subsequent) debates over popular
and elite theatre, the productions at the Red Bull were often dismissed as
opportunist and out of date, but the extraordinary range of Heywood's
work suggests rather a kind of professionalism which both responded to
and redirected the changing needs of the new commercial theatre, which
he also defended in the highest moral and intellectual terms in his polemic,
An Apology for Actors (1613).

Plays on women were an important part of Heywood's contribution to
the developing repertory. He created one of the most famous sentimental
female icons in Jane Shore, the heroine of his two-part historical play,
Edward IV. The combination of pathos and moral crisis which he dramatized in that play established a style which he and other playwrights
developed, and he was equally alert to the potential of comedic fashion in
his representation of women. In *The Fair Maid of the West* he presented a
comic, cross-dressed heroine who, like Moll in *The Roaring Girl*, humiliates a sexual bully, and thirty years later he adapted the same character in
a very different narrative of sexual adventures to suit the changing sexual
ideologies and dramatic styles.[13]

Like Heywood, Thomas Middleton recognized the theatrical potential
of plays on women. The wit and the folly as well as the horror and the
betrayal of heterosexual relations drive his plays' action, and the dramatic
power of his tragedies, *The Changeling* and *Women Beware Women*, can be
seen as the culmination of the different strands of wit and sentiment which
separately animate the plays in this anthology. His extraordinary dramatic
achievements may have developed in part from the different challenges
thrown up by the different theatrical contexts in which he worked. He was
associated with the adult companies financed by Henslowe, writing plays

for them in collaboration with Munday, Drayton and Webster and marrying the sister of one of the actors from the Admiral's Men. However, unlike Heywood, Middleton also took up the new opportunities created by the establishment of the fashionable boy-players companies, writing witty satirical city comedies for Paul's Boys, who played in a tiny theatre in the precinct of St Paul's Cathedral. These iconoclastic and sexually and politically daring plays created new theatrical styles and fashions. Middleton's innovation was to adapt the new material for an adult company theatre, collaborating with Dekker on the first part of *The Honest Whore* and on *The Roaring Girl*. Both plays were performed, at the Fortune Theatre, by Prince Henry's Men, another of the companies taken into royal patronage. The boys' companies were disbanded in 1606 in the wake of political scandal, but in their brief existence they had extended the boundaries of what could be represented on the stage, and they had also changed the relationship between writers, performers and theatrical entrepreneurs.[14] A residue of the disbanded Children of the Queens Revels joined with adult actors to form the Lady Elizabeth's Men, again financed by Henslowe, and it was for this company that Middleton wrote *A Chaste Maid in Cheapside*.

Middleton's freelance relationship with a variety of theatre companies echoes the instability of his social situation. His father was a substantial, property-owning bricklayer at whose death Middleton's mother remarried an impoverished adventurer. The family's subsequent debts involved legal squabbles, and Middleton had to abandon his studies at Queen's College, Oxford in order to help his mother with one of the lawsuits. His profession of playwright and pamphleteer would have placed him on the edge of respectable society, while at the same time providing him with a vantage point from which to celebrate as well as satirize the London scene. His pamphlets place the theatre at the heart of fashionable London, a venue for mischief as well as entertainment. In the *Black Book* one of his city dwellers describes the new private theatres as 'a nest of boys able to ravish a man', and in the same pamphlet he presents a vignette of the adulterous woman, dismissing her chaperoning servant, instructed by her lover to 'give him leave to see *The Merry Devil of Edmonton*, or *A Woman Killed with Kindness*'.[15]

Thomas Dekker inhabited the same London world as Middleton and Heywood but was rather less successful at making money out of it. His first mention in Henslowe's accounts was for a loan to release him from prison, and his life was dogged by debt, most seriously from 1613 onward when he spent six years in the debtor's prison of the King's Bench. On that occasion, his debt seems to have been the result of a bad investment in a city pageant.[16] The commercial possibilities of a writing career did not always produce success.

At the turn of the century, however, his profile was very high. He was writing plays in collaboration for a Henslowe company, the Admiral's Men, and in the year 1599–1600 worked on no less than fourteen plays. One of these was *The Shoemaker's Holiday* whose artisan hero, Simon Eyre, created a new dramatic type and brought a new kind of narrative from folk material to the stage. The cheerful, honest and successful shopkeeper was imitated by Heywood in Hobson from *If You Know Not Me You Know Nobody* and then turned satirically on its head in the sour opportunist citizens of Middleton's boy-player comedies, *Michaelmas Term* and *A Trick to Catch the Old One*.

Dekker was equally influential when writing satire. His *Westward Ho!*, written in collaboration with Webster for a children's company, was imitated in Jonson, Chapman and Marston's *Eastward Ho!* for a rival company. Dekker then returned to the motif with *Northward Ho* for Paul's Boys. His ability to use the closed, self-referential world of the London theatre scene to attract attention and generate controversy was also evident in the case of the so-called 'Poetomachia' in which he, Marston and Jonson exchanged insults in a run of plays from Jonson's *Cynthia's Revels* and *Poetaster* to Dekker's *Satiromastix*. Each playwright made jokes about the other's appearance and wittily denounced the other's writing as no more than vanity and self-seeking, but behind the dispute lay genuine differences about the role of the writer in contemporary culture. Both Jonson and Dekker were concerned with the bargain between entertainment and instruction which the commercial theatre had struck with its patrons and supporters. However, they had different views about the relative authority of writers and players in maintaining the balance between the two. The debate had begun when Dekker collaborated with Jonson on the scripts for James I's royal entry into the city of London. Jonson wanted to present the King with the most learned instruction available while Dekker was much more aware of the pleasure of the citizen spectators. He explicitly refused 'to make a false flourish here with the borrowed weapons of the old Masters of the noble Science of Poesie' (55–8), recognizing that, at least in the case of city pageants, 'the multitude is now to be our Audience' (65–8).[17]

The same serious concern for all of London's people is evident in Dekker's pamphlet-writing. He writes passionately about the plight of the poor, and his 'picture of London lying sick of the Plague'[18] presents with angry clarity the ability of the rich to escape pestilence as well as all other ills. His pamphlet-writing, like his plays, is informed by the high moral seriousness of reformed religion, often presented in old-fashioned allegorical and emblematic terms. Consequently his writing has been more often condescended to than admired. In the collaborative plays, where the question of authorship is just as complex as in anonymous ones, Dekker has often been assigned the moralizing rather than the witty portions. Yet the acute social analysis evident in *The Gulls' Hornbook* and its devastating mockery of empty pretension could equally easily have transferred into Dekker's dramatic writing, and it certainly informs his collaboration with Middleton in *The Roaring Girl*.

The wide range of these authors' work shows something of the extraordinary potential of the new commercial theatre. This theatre offered a new kind of employment for literate men and soon established a set of stories and conventions through which women and their concerns could be constructed for the stage. These tropes could be turned to comic or sentimental account, building on a familiar repertory to offer a multiplicity of theatrical pleasures.

STAGES

The ability of these plays to represent women, to play on and so create a persuasive version of women's lives, depended upon the conditions and circumstances of their staged theatricality. The parts of women were generally, of course, played by boy actors, but once their costumed figures entered on to the stage they became part of a play-world with a complex, shifting relationship to the life world of their spectators.[19]

The plays whose original venues are known (*Arden* is again the odd one out) were first performed in open-air theatres, custom-built for play performance: *A Woman Killed* at Henslowe's Rose, *The Roaring Girl* at The Fortune Theatre—commissioned by Henslowe to be the grandest theatre and a competitor to the Globe on the Bankside—and *A Chaste Maid* at the Swan. The Swan features in the only contemporary drawing of an outdoor stage (p. 62); the contract for building the Fortune provides valuable evidence for the dimensions and construction of its stage and auditorium. The Rose Theatre was uncovered and partially excavated in 1988–89, revealing the remains of a stage which was on an unexpectedly small scale and which was located on the north-north-west side of a thirteen-sided building so that it faced and was lit directly by the afternoon sun.[20]

Although scholars have emphasized important differences between the playing places in which the early modern repertory was staged,[21] a basic structural feature common to all these stages was an open architectural space on and around which the plays' action was built. The two (as at the Swan) or three doors in the back wall of the stage (the so-called tiring-house wall) provided a space in which to place the '*shop being discovered*' as *A Chaste Maid* begins, or the '*three shops open in a rank*' in the long second act of *The Roaring Girl*, or the shuttered stall shut up so decisively by the prentice in *Arden*, scene 3. One door could have framed 'MASTER FRANKFORD *in a study*' when he enters to soliloquize on the joys of matrimony (*A Woman Killed*, scene 4).

The door in the tiring-house wall marked the boundary between interior and exterior space, and the stage could represent both. When Sebastian shuts the doors in the first scene of *The Roaring Girl* (line 58), he indicates the intimacy and privacy of the exchange with the disguised Mary Fitzallard. The doors in *Arden*, scene 4, which Michael leaves open and Arden locks again, are seen from both inside and outside the house in contiguous scenes. The stage roof which protected the actors (but not the spectators) from the weather, and which was added to the Rose stage in the refurbishment of 1592, was held up by pillars which could have provided a hiding place for Black Will and Shakebag in *Arden*, 9.50. The floor of the stage would have needed a trap door for the villains to fall through in scene 12 when they are lost in the fog and Shakebag falls into a ditch. Above the stage (at least at the Swan) was a 'music room' in which a 'sad song' was played for the funeral of Moll and Touchwood Junior.

The stages of the public theatres, in other words, provided the basic theatrical architecture in which the plays could be performed. Yet that architecture did not impose location or setting: it functioned entirely in terms of the relationships among and between the human figures on stage. The physical relations between the figures on stage could be elaborately formal, using the stage architecture as an organizing framework, as in the fully documented stage picture of Moll's funeral procession in *A Chaste Maid*, 5.4. Alternatively the figures could use the stage space more neutrally. Conversations in one imagined location could move easily into action in another, as when the two plots and their characters in *A Woman Killed* come together in a single scene for the play's finale. The stage space could be completely filled by a soliloquy from a single character (e.g. *A Chaste Maid*, 1.2.12–57), by the location of an intimate dialogue in an unlocalized space (see *Arden*, scene 1), or by opening out into a location in which different groups of characters are on stage together but the spaces between them open and close to establish different kinds of relationships (see *A Woman Killed*, scene 16).

Stage directions indicating location were generally absent from the original texts of these plays. A single scene can move seamlessly from one location to another when there is some continuity of characters within it. One of the most theatrically complex examples occurs in *A Chaste Maid*, 2.2, where the action moves across all the plot groups in the play and deals with the play's whole range of social locations. The scene begins with Allwit's soliloquy, moves into a discussion with Sir Walter in which he is presented with his new baby and ends with the action involving the promoters. Since the stage is never emptied of people, there is no need to list a new scene. The focus of action is on Allwit's interactions first with Sir Walter and then with the promoters. The promoters then provide the continuity which carries the scene's momentum through the interplay with the country wench and the final joke with another illegitimate baby, palmed off on the promoters as Lenten meat. The elegant symmetry of the scene is far more striking than its shifts of location; to dwell on questions about indoors and outdoors or different parts of the city would be to hold up the trajectory of the action. The speed of that action links the different plots and generates the witty parallels, both comic and thematic, between different ways of dealing with a baby, different forms of illegitimacy and different ways in which women trade on their fertility.

When location and setting are significant, they are indicated in the dialogue and play a dynamic role in the theatrical meaning generated on stage. In the street scene of *The Roaring Girl*, 2.1, the stage is formally organized around the three shops which are visited in turn by the group of gentlemen and by Moll Cutpurse. The organization of this space, indicated by some precise locational stage directions, creates a sense of a peopled social world but it also indicates the demarcations within it. The shopkeepers and their wives are all held close to their shops with little range of movement. The gentlemen consumers, on the other hand, are free to move among them, beginning with the assignations of the plot between Laxton and Mrs Gallipot, or indicating character and social status by the things they buy. The patterning and interweaving of characters is complex and a good deal of its energy is provided by Moll herself. Unlike the other women onstage, she can move easily and rapidly between the gentlemen and the shopkeepers, saying three times in the course of twenty lines of dialogue that she cannot stay (2.1.166, 184, 198). She, more than any of the other women in these plays, is associated with the street rather than with the interior scenes of women's domestic domain. That movement, and the freedom which it offers, is nonetheless constrained and sexualized in the men's observations:

> Goshawk. 'Tis the maddest, fantastical'st girl! I never knew so much flesh and so much nimbleness put together.
> Laxton. She slips from one company to another like a fat eel between a Dutchman's fingers. [Aside] I'll watch my time for her.   (2.1.186–9)

When groups are kept more separate on stage, the space between them is impermeable so that each group is unheard or unseen by the other (see Arden, scene 3). That stage pattern too can be played upon to create effects of comedy or suspense. When Sir Walter converses with the Welsh Gentlewoman about their former affair at the beginning of A Chaste Maid (1.1.96–112), Yellowhammer is also on stage, in front of his shop, selling a gold chain to a passing gentleman. It is too early in the story for Yellowhammer to find out about Sir Walter's past, and he does not notice the exchange. Yellowhammer's lines nevertheless cut across the dialogue between Sir Walter and the Welsh Gentlewoman, which interweaves the two sequences very tightly together. The counterpoint of actual trading in gold with Sir Walter's plans to trade-in his former mistress marks an ironic commentary on the connection between city dealing and the marriage market.

When the scene shifts to the furnished, interior space of the early modern household, the stage directions and the dialogue in the earliest texts make some of the most detailed demands for stage furniture and properties in early modern drama. In both A Woman Killed and Arden, the stage was strewn with rushes, for dancing in one case and to hide the blood of murder in another. In A Woman Killed, scene 11, the table is set for dinner 'with a tablecloth, bread, trenchers, and salt', indicating that this is a household too rustic to use plate or china for meals. In the christening party at the heart of A Chaste Maid, on the other hand, the excess of company, seated on low stools, the cups of wine, the supply of comfits and Sir Walter Whorehound's present of 'a fair high standing-cup / And two great 'postle-spoons, one of them gilt' (3.2.45–6), all indicate metropolitan affluence and the social milieu of the successful city merchant with aristocratic connections. These physical objects provide local colour and a setting for the action, while at the same time marking the connections between the early modern stage and the social world. The furniture and fittings of early modern houses were undergoing material change as increased trade and affluence brought a greater variety of goods on to the domestic market. That process was the subject of anxious moral commentary as yet another sign of unwelcome social and economic change. In its staging of the affluent household, the theatre brought the material and the moral together. The physical objects on stage were part of the material detail of the setting, and at the same time their presence indicated the way that status and social relationships were marked on people's surroundings. The frequent gap between that carefully maintained appearance and the narrative which unfolds within it is an important dynamic of the play which depends upon the physical detail of the staging to make the contrast felt.[22]

That physical detail and the commentary on it are often provided with great economy. The settings for Mrs Allwit's childbed in *A Chaste Maid* (3.2) and Anne Frankford's deathbed in *A Woman Killed* (scene 17) are established by pushing a bed on to the stage, probably through the large entrance doors in the tiring-house wall. The bed provides a physical focus for a scene's action, creating a centrepiece which holds together most of the rest of the cast. At the same time the beds also carry symbolic meaning as the place of birth and death. By isolating and restricting the women characters' movements, they turn their occupants into icons of womanhood in all its fecundity and all its frailty. This iconic abstraction is not insisted on in Middleton's scene, but in *A Woman Killed* Anne asks, quite literally, to be observed and interpreted:

> Raise me a little higher in my bed.
> Blush I not, brother Acton? Blush I not, Sir Charles?
> Can you not read my fault writ in my cheek?
> Is not my crime there? Tell me, gentlemen.   (17.54–7)

Anne's physical condition, her physical presence on stage, is to be read as an emblem of her past conduct and her moral state.

This potential for staging the plays' meanings in their physical representation is especially visible in the games of chess and cards played in *Arden* and in *A Woman Killed*. Jenkin in *A Woman Killed* provides 'cards, carpet, stools, and other necessaries' (8.113.2), and in *Arden*, scene 14, the backgammon board is brought out, as illustrated in the frontispiece of the third Quarto text of the play (see p. 65). The dialogue in both cases insists on the more sinister significance of the action, playing on the contrast between game and earnest, deepening the suspense leading up to the actions of adultery and murder. The focus of the staging around a central piece of stage furniture, the shop or the bed or the gaming table, ensures the audience's attention while the dialogue moves more widely to make the symbolic as well as the narrative meaning clear.

Iconographic traditions of emblem and allegory, connecting images to moral or theological meaning, are used to turn the stage into a symbolic as well as a physical location. With characters, props and furniture always physically present, the stage organization and the language extend physical into moral meaning, while the stage action gains momentum and rhythm from that interaction. The moment-by-moment construction of that relationship can be charted through scene 13 of *A Woman Killed*. At the end of scene 12, the servants exit through one stage door to go to bed; Frankford and Nick enter immediately through the other indicating that they have come from outside the house. Frankford then asks for his keys:

> This is the key that opes my outward gate,
> This is the hall door, this my withdrawing chamber.
> But this, that door that's bawd unto my shame . . .
> It leads to my polluted bedchamber,
> Once my terrestrial heaven, now my earth's hell. (13.8–15)

The lines focus the audience's attention on the doors at the rear of the stage and on the action which is taking place beyond them. They indicate the spatial organization of the household and its distinction between public and private space, which is to be constructed both on the stage and in the imagination. Although the original text gives no exit direction, Frankford is given lines which suggest he exits and then re-enters:

> *Frankford.* But I forget myself. Now to my gate.
> *Nicholas.* It must ope with far less noise than Cripplegate, or your plot's dashed.
> *Frankford.* So, reach me my dark-lantern to the rest.
> Tread softly, softly.
> *Nicholas.*   I will walk on eggs this pace.
> *Frankford.* A general silence hath surprised the house,
> And this is the last door. (13.17–23)

A simple exit and re-entry changes the stage location from outside to inside the house while the same stage door drawn to the audience's attention changes from being the gate to the estate to being the door to Frankford's bedchamber where the adulterous lovers are in bed.

A further exit and re-entry redoubles the suspense. Frankford goes in and returns with his heartbroken account of the sight of them 'lying / Close in each others arms, and fast asleep' (13.42–3). He is given time to mourn the loss of his perfect marriage before the door is once again used for his final entry into the bedchamber, followed by the explosion on to the stage of the tableau of revenge:

> *Enter* WENDOLL, *running over the stage in a nightgown* [*and exit*], *he*
> [FRANKFORD] *after him with his sword drawn; the* Maid *in her smock*
> *stays his hand and clasps hold on him. He pauses awhile.* (13.67.1–3)

This dumb-show provides the narrative economically without any need for explanatory dialogue. It echoes the action of medieval plays on the biblical story of 'the woman taken in adultery'. The maid's physical gesture, which Frankford compares to an angel who 'stayed me from a bloody sacrifice' (13.69), also shares in the biblical iconography in its reminder of the triumphant finale of the story of Abraham's sacrifice of his son Isaac. These images are picked up in Frankford's reference to Judas hanging on the elder tree and Anne's to Lucifer's agonized longing for heaven.[23] Meaning is made by the dynamic relationship between physical action, poetic imagery and narrative. Its theatrical impact shows Heywood's skilful deployment of the full range of staging conventions built around a simple stage door generating movement, meaning and suspense at the turning point of the play.

The physical action on the stage is directly experienced by the audience in the auditorium, and their co-presence can be directly acknowledged in the dialogue. Heywood's stage clowns, for example, often step out of the dramatic fiction to address the audience, and he often (as at scene 2) leaves space for them to ad lib.[24] Jenkin extends this go-between role when he ends scene 4 of *A Woman Killed* by explaining to the audience the difference between their time-frame in which it is already afternoon and that of the play world where they are just about to take the midday meal. This joking acknowledgement of the audience's presence is elaborated in *The Roaring Girl* when Sir Alexander includes the audience as part of the decoration of his parlour. He invites his guests to admire his pictures which show

> Stories of men and women, mixed together,
> Fair ones with foul, like sunshine in wet weather.
> Within one square a thousand heads are laid
> So close that all of heads the room seems made.   (1.2.17–20)

This metathetrical gesture incorporates the audience into the play's world, and the differences between them are further blurred when the speech is extended to describe a cutpurse at work. The setting in the parlour and the description of pictures is forgotten as the moving mass of people standing below the stage and surrounded by the galleried seats is evoked in the images of a 'floating island . . . Upon a sea bound in with shores above' (1.2.31–2). The sense that audience and characters share the same social world is invoked again at the end of the play, when Moll traps two cutpurses in order to reveal their tricks to her gentry friends. She claims that she has previously caught one of them 'i' the twopenny gallery at the Fortune' (5.1.265–6), the very theatre in which the play was being performed and in which, according to the play's epilogue, Mary Frith herself would soon appear.

This shifting relationship between the audience and the stage is another of the tools with which the plays orchestrate meaning and emotion. After Anne's adultery has been discovered in *A Woman Killed* she turns directly to the women in the audience, pleading with those who have 'kept / Your holy matrimonial vow unstained' (13.141–2) to be warned by Anne's experience and to take a direct message from the play. The staged bourgeois world of the Frankford household is extended to the pit and galleries of the Rose playhouse. This connection to the audience makes the scene emblematic. Frankford's accusatory list of all that he has given Anne summarizes the conduct-manual paradigm of a good husband's behaviour. Then two children, whose birth is not included in the narrative or the time-frame of the play, are brought in to emblematize the purpose of marriage as stated in contemporary social thought. The sequence draws on existing ideas about marriage, but it also turns them into usable dramatic form. Anne's masochistic plea that her scandal be physically removed from her body by dismembering torture presents a powerful image of the physicality of her sin, an image which would be taken up and adapted in later plays on women.[25] Anne and Frankford lose the particularity of their situation and become the archetypal wronged husband and guilty wife. Their staged action, however, takes place in and interacts with the social and moral world shared with the audience at the Rose.

PLACES

When Frankford punishes Anne's adultery with banishment, he is quite precise about where she is to go:

Choose thee a bed and hanging for a chamber,
Take with thee everything that hath thy mark,
And get thee to my manor seven mile off,
Where live.   (13.163–6)

Like the scenes where characters enter in riding clothes, referring to horses left a little way off (see *A Woman Killed* 13.1–2; *Arden*, 9.51–4; *The Roaring Girl*, 3.1.47–54), this speech creates the sense that the action on stage is only the immediately visible part of a larger world. That larger social and geographical world is clearly indicated in all these plays and is an important part of their theatrical effect. The conspirators follow Arden from Faversham to London, plot to catch him as he crosses Rainham Downs, or when he visits Lord Cheyne's estates on the Isle of Sheppey (see map, p. 64); the guests at Anne and Frankford's wedding plan to go hawking on Chevy Chase, setting the action both in the northern country and in the literary context of the ballad; and *The Roaring Girl* and *A Chaste Maid* invoke a London scene whose landmarks were known in city tales, and were identified on contemporary maps (see map, p. 61).

These geographical references were an important endorsement of the plays' claims to authenticity, to be dealing with the here and now, with a recognizable, identifiable world. That world both framed and constructed the narratives which took place within it. The London settings in particular consisted of venues which were topographically real but which together created an iconic version of the city consisting of recurring place names: Tyburn Hill where the gallows stood, Turnbull Street for the whores, Holborn as the main thoroughfare into the city, and through it all the river Thames where the watermen plied their trade, linking the city to the bankside and to the southern suburbs beyond. The metropolitan area of London, although one of the largest cities in the known world, was sufficiently small to include quite countrified neighbourhoods round its edges—Hoxton ponds to the north, Gray's Inn Fields to the west—to which citizens could resort for sport and leisure of both a legitimate and an illegitimate kind. Beyond the metropolitan area itself lay the even more exciting leisure prospects of a trip up the river to Brentford and Staines, or north to Ware. Sequences such as the river chases in *A Chaste Maid* (4.1.271ff.) and *The Roaring Girl* (5.2.6–16) animate the London scene into a narrative connecting character to place. At the finale of the long shopping scene in *The Roaring Girl* (2.1), the bell rings, indicating the end of the working day. The gallants go with the befeathered Jack Dapper for dinner at 'Parker's Ordinary', the name suggesting familiarity. The citizens, on the other hand, exit separately to their games and duck hunting at Parlous Pond in Hoxton. Their preparation for holiday provides a charming vignette of the fondness for animals and male uxoriousness which characterize the sentimental version of citizen social existence.

The mention of a few well-known venues conceptualize London as a set of overlapping territories, marked out by different functions and with clear associations. In this the playwrights follow the pattern of city governance, which differentiated areas in order to regulate markets and control the hygiene of activities such as butchery and different kinds of manufacture. These functional demarcations were notoriously breaking down in early modern London, as the city heaved under an influx of population and unauthorized building and marketing. Discussing these changes, modern social historians have emphasized the achievements of local authorities in sustaining an orderly and well-managed city in the face of the enormous social problems involved in feeding, policing and maintaining the hygiene of a growing metropolis. The organization into parishes created workable communities, even in the notorious suburbs; the evidence of legislation and litigation, enforcing the collection of poor relief and church attendance as well as controlling public disorder, suggests a city which had its problems well under control.[26]

Literary representations of the city, on the other hand, were concerned less with social analysis than the projection of urban myths. In plays, pamphlets and books of jokes, London was presented as both a matron and a monster; the city's traditions of governance were celebrated and their failures condemned; the population of the metropolis was both hardworking and entrepreneurial and greedy and corrupt. The plays set boundaries round London, making the metropolis manageable, controlling the movement through different locations by the narrative. They acknowledge the interconnection between city and country—Master

Gallipot is concerned about his barns at Hockley Hole and the fate of his children out at nurse (*The Roaring Girl*, 3.2.91–4) and Allwit disguises himself as a country cousin (*A Chaste Maid*, 4.1.186)—but they equally insist upon the city's special role as the location of action, the place to which the characters come and without which the stories could not take place. In presenting these contradictory images of the city, this literature turned the complexities of demographic and social crisis into narratives of opposition between country and city, gallants and tradesmen, and acted them out through the relations of women and men. In the process, they made change seem manageable and articulated the terms by which the city's inhabitants could relate to their urban world.[27]

CITIZEN STORIES I: *A CHASTE MAID IN CHEAPSIDE*

In *A Chaste Maid*, Middleton presents city dwellers who adapt to social change by learning to exploit it. Touchwood Senior, for example, soliloquizes on the 'religious, wholesome laws . . . erected / For common good' and his regret that they are subverted by 'corruption of promoters / And other poisonous officers' (2.1.113–17). However, there is no neat fit between his approval of good governance and his exploitative relationship with others. Sir Oliver Kix, too, confirms his role as a city benefactor, 'In the erecting of bridewells and spittlehouses' (2.1.145), but presents his civic generosity simply as another investment. He is quite willing to transfer a thousand pounds from those activities to the task of getting his wife pregnant, taking literally the religious commonplace that good deeds and children are equally profitable moral investments. When Allwit salvages what he can from the debacle of his arrangement with Sir Walter Whorehound, his plan to turn the house in the Strand into an upmarket brothel shows a calm awareness of the investment potential of housing and leisure services in the new fashionable areas west of the city. At the other end of the market, Trapdoor can use his knowledge of London and the suburbs, the familiarity with which he can 'sift all the taverns i' th' city, and drink half-pots with all the watermen o' th' Bankside', as marketable credentials for the job of spy to Sir Alexander Wengrave in *The Roaring Girl* (1.2.205–6). Consorting with the watermen of the bankside, however, was not exclusively a pastime for the lowlife characters. The watermen help Moll to elope with Touchwood Junior in *A Chaste Maid*, and Touchwood Senior reminds him of the time that watermen saved a gentleman from the Blackfriars Theatre. He presents the relationship between the watermen and their clients as one of mutual advantage:

> They are the most requitefull'st people living,
> For, as they get their means by gentlemen,
> They are still the forwardest to help gentlemen. (4.3.3–5)

Mutual support, based on commerce, he suggests, is replacing traditional distinctions between gentlemen and artisans, between high-class and lower-class citizens.

By focusing on different ways of inhabiting the city and new kinds of relationships which it has created, Middleton also complicates the conventional conflict between those who live in the city and those for whom it is merely a place of resort. In his plays written for the boys' companies, Middleton had played variations on the story of a gullible young heir to a landed fortunes who wasted his inheritance on city luxuries and was ruined by grasping merchants. That story worked through a set of oppositions between land and money, the country and the city, the gentry and the citizens. By the turn of the century those oppositions had come to seem too simple, both because affluent citizens were increasingly investing in land and because the stories had hardened into clichés; the jokes had become tired. Those deep comic structures remain in, for example, the mockery of Tim Yellowhammer, whose inappropriate education has rendered him a tourist in the city of his birth (see 4.4.54–8) and who is humiliated in traditional city comedy manner by being married off to Sir Walter's cast-off mistress. Yet by making Tim a citizen and not an aristocrat, Middleton varies the traditional city comedy narrative while also turning the plot around by refusing to allow Sir Walter any comic triumph in his plan to bring his whore to London.

The ability to play with these city stories also gives the comic heroes their dramatic authority. Early in *A Chaste Maid*, Allwit gleefully explains to the audience his mutually beneficial relationship with Sir Walter (1.2.12–57): Sir Walter is provided with sexual services by Allwit's wife and Allwit's family and household are paid for in return. Allwit compares this arrangement favourably with the

> merchants [who] would in soul kiss hell
> To buy a paradise for their wives, and dye
> Their conscience in the bloods of prodigal heirs
> To deck their night-piece.   (1.2.42–5)

In this complex moment, Middleton undermines the moral certainty implied in the familiar narrative of the merchant and the prodigal heir. Allwit is presented instead as a different kind of city-dweller whose exploitation of the landed aristocrat is at once more witty and more scandalous than the clichéd opposition between citizen and gallant.

For Middleton's comic heroes, knowledge of city narratives is as important as knowledge of city locations. When the Country Wench confronts Touchwood Senior with a paternity suit for her child, he proposes comic solutions which come from adapting the traditional city story of the foundling child to her case:

> There's tricks enough to rid thy hand on 't, wench:
> Some rich man's porch, tomorrow before day,
> Or else anon i' the evening; twenty devices.   (2.1.97–9)

He is equally unfazed at the threat of a law suit from the Country Wench's cousin, saying that he will find a husband for her from among the 'two or three gulls in pickle' (2.1.81) he keeps for the purpose.

These comic narratives of trickery traditionally presented control over the city as a male prerogative. Women, for the most part, are the instruments of the tricks and the prizes for men's success. Touchwood Senior can help his brother to elope with Moll Yellowhammer, trick Sir Oliver Kix into paying to be cuckolded, and use his own fertile sexuality to thwart Sir Walter's own efforts to be a city comedy trickster. When Middleton reworks these stories for the adult theatre companies, on the other hand, he extends the dramatic space available to women. *A Chaste Maid*, however, is at its most original in extending the roles of city women, both in the christening scene and in the comic vignette of the Country Wench. Mrs Allwit's gossips bring on stage the social life of the London Puritan community which is as much a part of the city as its markets in gold or land or whores. The women's little fusses over precedence in going through the door (2.4.9–14), their chatter over the baby and the course of the labour, their greedy taste for wine and sweets, dramatize a social world which is comfortable and affluent and secure; a community of women held together by both domesticity and Puritanism.[28] One woman is glad that the child has been well 'kursened, i' the right way, / Without idolatry or superstition, / After the pure manner of Amsterdam' (3.2.3–5); another urges Mrs Allwit to have more children 'like a true sister, / With motherly bearing' (3.2.78–9); and they welcome young Tim from Cambridge, noted for its development of Puritan theology, as 'from the wellspring of discipline that waters all the brethren!' (3.2.181–2).

Allwit's controlling commentary invites the audience to view these gossips and their women's world from the standpoint of satiric misogyny. He is appalled by the sticky permeability of the women's bodies, the wetness of their kisses and of their involuntary pissing after their over-indulgence in his wine. Yet the sheer comic energy of the women counterbalances his commentary and offers an alternative vision of a women's community, confident in its religious and social standing. This is particularly evident in the women's treatment of Tim, entering their world from the exclusively male one of a Cambridge college. Tim is comically unable to sustain his male dignity in the face of the women's sense that, though children must be petted and fed, they are ultimately under women's control. They humiliatingly remind him of how he was whipped as a schoolboy at Paul's (3.2.147–8), and reduce the tutor's intellectual pretension with a reminder that he enjoyed goose pies. The gap between the women's world and the world of young upwardly mobile men is summed up in Tim's outraged 'Come I from Cambridge, and offer me six plums?' (3.2.143). It is a comic line which could unite an audience in mockery, both of the women so bound up with food and eating but equally of the young man, blind to the inappropriateness of his education and the folly of his empty intellectualizing.

The scenes with the gossips present the play at its most apparently documentary. Each of the features of the gossips' social world, their involvement in the rituals of childbearing, their commitment to reformed religion and their admiration for Mrs Allwit's luxury, could be authenticated in the life world of early modern society. Nevertheless the scene's comic structure and its characterization of the women is equally a product of familiar literary and satiric tropes. The 'gossips' meeting' in which women are presented as drinking together and revealing the secrets of their defiance of men provided the setting for a number of medieval and early modern poems.[29] It is possible to read such accounts of women—and indeed Middleton's play—as a delightful celebration of women's transgression, but they equally present the familiar and perennial anxiety about women's behaviour when it is free from male control. In *A Chaste Maid*, Middleton blurs the edges of this device and integrates it into the play's action by combining it with the equally conventional trope of the 'Latin lesson' in which a proud mother admires her son's learning and comically exposes her own ignorance by misconstruing his Latin to comic, and usually bawdy, effect. The comic Latin lesson occurs in full in 4.1, where Tim and his tutor rehearse a disputation and Maudlin questions the power of logic to prove a whore an honest woman; and its deep structural relationship between women and their children is echoed in the christening scene. Middleton's adaptation of these devices draws on reliable sources of comic pleasure, but it also reinforces conventional images of women's gendered relations to their social world. The structure of women's roles in the play places them firmly in the arena of marriage and children: their social relations with men ensure only that those social relations can continue. Lady Kix's desire for a child, for example, is comically connected to her desire to inherit Sir Walter's 'goodly lands and livings', but, as her bitterness at Mrs Allwit's childbirth shows (2.1.154–72), her need for children is also crucial to her sense of her social status in the city community.

The gossips' comic world exists around and outside the action of the play; the scenes in which they appear take place entirely indoors in the communal solidarity of a woman's domain. The Country Wench's story, on the other hand, is placed in the male domain of the city streets. In early modern London, increasing numbers of women were bringing cases of marriage contracts dishonoured, or seduction betrayed, to the church courts,[30] using the public space of the streets and the institutional framework of the courts to claim their own authority in the legislation of sexual conduct. The Country Wench's challenge to Touchwood Senior is not that of a victim but rather of a woman who is aware of her power to 'cry' Touchwood's fornication 'through the streets and follow you' (2.1.67) and her cousin's power to take him to 'a law bout' (2.1.78). The Country Wench's potential social power is translated into theatrical power by her wicked trick on the promoters, the enforcers of Lenten regulations against buying meat.

The regulations against selling meat during Lent were a standard feature of early modern social legislation, enforced by controlling the abattoirs and markets and searching the premises of butchers for illegal meat. In the complex commercial world of early modern London, however, Lenten regulation was not simply a matter of obeying a just law or resisting corruption. The conflicting interests of butchers and fishmongers were also involved, and the relative strengths of their livery companies in city governance bore upon the question.[31] Searches to detect the infringement of Lenten regulations were a routine and necessary part of urban administration—a circumstance that is ignored in Middleton's treatment of the case. The scenes with the promoters show them profiting both from the fines imposed on those whom they are able to convict of the offence of eating meat in Lent and from the bribes which they receive for turning a blind eye to particular violations. These scenes arise partly from social observation but equally from a long comic tradition in which any official is mocked and feared in proportion to his power to restrict the venial pleasures of eating or sex. In the resulting conflict, officials exploit the power given to them by the city authorities but prove to be no match for the city tricksters' comic authority.

Allwit's comic power comes from his ability to understand perfectly how the city works and to tease the promoters by pretending naivety, secure in the knowledge that he is protected by an exclusion from the regulation provided by his wife's childbearing. He is distinguished from the corruption of Master Beggarland's man, the wealthy merchant, and the fool who gets caught. He is within the law, and from that secure position can mock its potential for corruption.

The Country Wench's successful trick puts her in the same comic position as Allwit. In the city world of the play, comic effect depends upon the power of the witty over the stupid. The Country Wench, in an aside, shows that this division depends neither on gender nor on citizenship:

> Women had need of wit, if they'll shift here,
> And she that hath wit may shift anywhere. (2.2.147–8)

Nevertheless, by effecting her trick, the Country Wench gains male comic authority, while those who lack wit are feminized by the rhetoric of the play. Though Allwit gets the better of the Lenten promoters and triumphs over Walter Whorehound, he is also a wittol, denied his masculinity by his acquiescence in humiliating cuckoldry. The Lenten promoters, moreover, are turned into nursemaids in the touching detail of their dismayed apprehension of what it will mean to be responsible for a child:

> Half our gettings must run in sugar-sops and nurses' wages now, besides many a pound of soap and tallow. We have need to get loins of mutton still, to save suet to change for candles. (2.2.194–7)

Their knowledge of the city ways is reduced to sending the child to a wet nurse up the river in Brentford. The losers, the fall-guys, the patsies in the world of city scams, are feminized even when, like Tim Yellowhammer or Oliver Kix the infertile cuckolded husband, they are men. At the end of the play, Tim Yellowhammer is dismayed to discover that his new Welsh wife is no heiress but a cast-off whore. However, his male learning allows him to prove a whore an honest woman: *Uxor non est meretrix, ergo falleris* (5.4.116). Having been feminized and infantilized throughout the action, Tim is gradually learning the tricks and the stories which will allow him a place in the world of male citizens. With her more practical bent, the Welsh Gentlewoman reminds him 'There's a thing called marriage, and that makes me honest' (5.4.118). The comic finale is assured by the discursive legerdemain which can turn *meretrix* into *uxor*. The Welsh Gentlewoman's extension of that discursive solution into a social one merely incorporates social conflict into generic resolution. Maleness and femaleness in these plays are connected as much to theatrical power as they are to the sex of the characters.

CITIZEN STORIES II: *THE ROARING GIRL*

The intricate relationship between sex, gender and theatrical power is equally part of the dramatic dynamic of *The Roaring Girl*, Middleton's collaboration with Dekker. As we have seen above (p. 2), the Prologue to the play draws attention to the different kinds of stories that could be told about roaring girls and the effect this could have on the theatrical pleasure they offer. The end of the Prologue connects those stories to the real-life Moll Frith, declaring 'her life our acts proclaim' (Prologue, 30). In the case of the historical Moll Frith, 'life' and 'acting' were also connected to the way sex and gender were performed and perceived. The record in the *Consistory of London Correction Book* refers to Moll Frith confessing to dressing 'in the habit of a man' as she 'resorted to taverns, tobacco shops and also to playhouses'. This behaviour and the assumptions behind the accusation were based on the assumption that the public arenas of the city were a male domain. Yet Moll was not so much pretending to be a man as playing on gender as a game or an act. When she appeared 'at the Fortune in man's apparel, and in her boots and with a sword by her side', she drew attention to that game with the mocking challenge to the audience 'that she thought many of them were of the opinion that she was a man, but if any of them would come to her lodging they should find that she is a woman'. The suggestion is both that she would behave more like a woman when indoors and that she might give a more intimate view of her woman-liness in private. That public statement, however, seems to have been merely an act. The magistrates of the Consistory Court pressed Moll Frith 'to declare whether she had not been dishonest of her body and hath not also drawn other women to lewdness by her persuasion and by carrying herself like a bawd'. Moll 'absolutely denied that she was chargeable with either of these imputations', distancing herself, in effect, from the female-gendered crimes of prostitution and soliciting, though she accepted the indictments of the male-gendered sins of unruly behaviour and disturbing the peace.

Moll claimed that she had been punished for these misdemeanours in Bridewell and that she was 'heartily sorry for her foresaid licentious and dissolute life, and giveth her earnest promise to carry and behave herself ever from henceforward honestly, soberly and womanly'. Yet this performance of womanliness was also part of the 'acts' of the Consistory Court. When Moll was forced to do penance at Paul's Cross, one observer shrewdly noticed that 'she wept bitterly and seemed very penitent but it is since doubted she was maudlin drunk'.[32] For the Bishop of London presiding over the Consistory Court, such behaviour would have seemed licentious and dissolute; for John Chamberlain, writing a witty letter on current affairs, it was a source of wry amusement; for Middleton and Dekker, the stories of Moll Frith were a way of extending the range of city comedy and further complicating the dramatic roles of women and men.

In creating a fictional character out of a historical one, Middleton and Dekker played on the familiar conventions of cross-dressing boy players as women. This convention had built up a routine series of jokes about sexual identity which the playwrights exploit in the episode where Mary Fitzallard comes in disguise to see Sebastian (4.1.43). Her page outfit, supplied by Moll's tailor, is necessary to protect her from discovery by Sebastian's father. This was the standard function of cross-dressing in romantic comedy, and the dramatists also use it as a trigger for bawdy jokes about sexuality. Sebastian claims that kissing a woman dressed as a man provides a special sexual pleasure (4.1.51, 59–60), and Moll can play on jokes about men's breath and cross-dressed bawds.[33] Moll's cross-dressing, however, is of a rather different kind. When she first comes on stage, she is wearing a skirt with a '*safeguard*' or protective over-garment (2.1.158.1), and a '*frieze jerkin*'. These are not the clothes of a lady or a citizen, but they are not men's clothes either: they indicate a woman who has not adopted women's work or a woman's way of moving and relating to others. Still, this behaviour does not make her a man. Rather, it separates her clothes from her character, allowing them to be the source of humour and comic action. When she is fitted for a 'Dutch slop' (wide baggy breeches) by a tailor, the scene is built around the convention that ladies' tailors were intrinsically comic,[34] partly because they had privileged access to women's bodies and partly because the association with women's clothes left them open to imputations of homosexuality. References to tailors conventionally brought out a predictable string of jokes and comic business. So Moll objects to the tailor's 'fiddling' (2.2.76), and he insists that her breeches will have to accommodate an additional 'yard' (2.2.81)—referring to the measure of cloth, a tailor's measuring rod and the cant word for a penis. This utterly conventional theatrical repartee is here given a new comic twist from the fact that the tailor is measuring Moll for breeches, not a dress.

Moll appears unambiguously in full male dress in the assignation with Laxton in Gray's Inn Fields (3.1). Here, too, the dramatists are using cross-dressing to give a novel twist to theatrical convention. When Laxton first flirts with Moll, she is not cross-dressed, and he offers her the conventional seduction of a trip to the outlying towns of Brentford, Staines or Ware in a coach. She suggests that a nearer city location of Tyburn Hill is a more likely destination, and that, far from being taken in a coach, she is capable of riding a stone horse or stallion, or at the very least 'playing the jade'. When they meet in Gray's Inn Fields, Laxton initially fails to recognize her but is then excited by what he takes to be her sexual overtures. His complete misunderstanding of the situation gives Moll the theatrical power to instruct him in the basic feminist maxim that 'she that has wit and spirit / May scorn to live beholding to her body for meat' (3.1.132–3), but she also warns him as a gallant to stay clear of the victims of a decline in the city, the 'Distressèd needlewomen and trade-fall'n wives' (3.1.92). Since she is dressed as a man, Moll is not including herself with the victims of male lechery. Her long speech anatomizing the fall of women at the hands of the 'golden lecher', money, establishes her as the guardian of women's chastity, but her male dress and her triumph over her lecherous opponent turn the moralizing into witty theatrical power.

An encounter between a braggart and an unexpectedly fierce opponent[35] was a familiar comic device, drawn from *commedia dell'arte*. By making the opponent a woman, Dekker and Middleton use the scene to explore the connection between gender, clothes and conduct, exposing the rigidity of those who make judgements based on external appearances. Moll is described by Sir Alexander, before she ever comes on stage, as a monstrous combination of both sexes (1.2.129–33). Yet Sir Alexander's knowledge of her sexuality can only be based on her clothes, and he confuses women's clothes with their sex and their actions. When he observes the tailor measuring Moll for her breeches, the confusion between clothes and persona is complete: 'I have brought up my son to marry a Dutch slop and a French doublet: a codpiece daughter' (2.2.87–9).

Centring a city comedy on a woman was a significant innovation, and it had wider implications for the comic roles of the men. Laxton's plot to exploit Mrs Gallipot's favours for cash and to seduce Moll at an assignation in Gray's Inn Fields, as well as his cool contempt for the other gallants' idle consumption of tobacco and feathers, mark him out as the clever man about town. This is certainly his reputation among the gallants themselves. Goshawk envies his secret sex life—'I think he commits venery forty foot deep; no man's aware on 't' (2.1.22–3)—and their very sneering shows how they admire his ability to thrive in the city without money or land (2.1.62–7). The gallants' double-edged mockery presents a paradigm of the new man, celebrated in city comedy precisely for his freedom from the constraining conventions of an older social order. At the heart of this social order lay assumptions about heterosexuality and marriage. Laxton gains theatrical status not merely by undermining marriage—all the gallants do that—but by his witty, if cruel, manipulation of Mrs Gallipot's desires. He teases her by refusing to consummate their affair and amuses his audience, both on and off the stage, by mocking the stratagems she employs to get him into bed (2.1.118–29). The dubious pleasures of a mere heterosexual encounter are subordinated to the greater pleasure of male solidarity:

> I know she cozens her husband to keep me, and I'll keep her honest, as long as
> I can, to make the poor man some part of amends.   (2.1.127–9)

Editors and critics have noted the fact that Laxton's name could be pronounced 'Lacks stones'. He lacks 'stones' in the sense of lacking land, but equally of lacking testicles, also called 'stones' in contemporary slang. Thus he wishes he could 'stand' (1.2.57), and he has, apparently, no interest in women.[36] The pun is insisted on, however, only by the tedious Alexander Wengrave (1.2.56–8). Laxton's own account of his sexual orientation is more delicately ambiguous. He asserts

> Their good parts are so rare, their bad so common,
> I will have naught to do with any woman.   (1.2.156–7)

But 'naught' could mean both 'nothing' and 'an ill deed': Laxton may be denying an interest in women, or he may be insisting that their only use is for sex. It is not that Laxton lacks the ability to have sex. It is that heterosexuality is a weakness for the city trickster whose opportunism is such that he will only indulge in sex when real advantage is to be had. Unlike the other gallants, he cannot afford simply to consume sex as one of the city's pleasures. He has to use it for the market, which makes him more like a citizen than a gallant.

For the citizen women, sex is also part of the market. Their flirtations with the gallants involve setting the pleasure of seduction by an outsider against the secure social position of a citizen woman. The contest involves more than chastity and marriage. It also defines the significance of the different public and private worlds inhabited by men and women, and by citizens and gallants. When Mrs Openwork flirts with Goshawk, she is torn between comically compromising her citizen status in order to seem grander and insisting on it in her outrage at her husband's alleged betrayal:

> I had my Latin tongue and a spice of the French before I came to him, and now
> doth he keep a suburbian whore under my nostrils.   (2.1.308–10)

She is as much put out by the non-citizen origins of her husband's alleged whore as she is by his adultery. Her own attempts to claim cosmopolitan sophistication revel in the familiar connections between Latin and French and deviant sexual practices and venereal disease.

So deep-rooted were these citizen assumptions and values that they are often embedded in quite simple lines. Searching for a way to find £30 to pay Laxton, Mrs Gallipot briefly considers pawning her childbed linen but immediately rejects the idea (3.2.66–8). Her childbed linen, brought to her marriage as part of her dowry, is hers to dispose of, but it is connected to her social status. Although part of her private possessions, it is linked to the public world of her claim to respectability. It figures in the public event of childbirth (compare *A Chaste Maid*) and is implicated in her husband's credit in the city: 'if my mark / Be known, I am undone! It may be thought / My husband's bankrupt' (3.2.67–9). Mrs

Gallipot's marriage has brought her social standing—not a trivial consideration. Gallipot's list of the disasters which might have upset his wife illustrates the couple's extensive connections, reaching beyond the city to a wet nurse, barns and houses, and an agent dealing with foreign trade and investment in shipping. The alternative elaborate story Mrs Gallipot composes to get the money also turns on her credit in the social world which regulates the exchange of women in marriage. In suggesting that Laxton had a precontract to marry her, Mrs Gallipot invokes the complexity of marriage law of the time, the tension between different public and private arrangements and the extent to which they were binding.[37] A precontract suit could have consequences that were both financially and socially devastating, and Gallipot is prepared to forgo money rather than that his wife should lose any social standing.

In theatrical terms Gallipot's status is undermined by his irritating uxoriousness. His fussy, if affectionate, concern for his wife suggests that he is not securely placed in the world of men and deserves to be deceived. The gallants, too, are ultimately unsatisfactory to the citizen wives because their merely sexual interest indicates an emasculating weakness. When the women get together to expose their erstwhile suitors, their solidarity, like that of the citizen women in *A Chaste Maid* (see above, p. 17), depends on their communal identity as citizens and as women. They mock the predictable sexual moves of the 'whisking gallants' (4.2.44), wryly aware that if they succumb to their advances they will, in the end, be 'but frumped at and libelled upon' (4.2.59). The outcome of this subplot, in which the citizens reassert their control over their womenfolk and challenge the effeminate gallants with swords and beatings, reasserts distinctions both of status and of gender groups. For the wives' mockery of their husbands stems not from an assertion of their own individuality or any sense of egalitarian aspiration but from a rooted sense of the appropriateness of existing social boundaries. They are loyal to their husbands as citizens even though they may mock them as men.

The boundaries of both gender and status are most fundamentally challenged by the figures of Laxton and Moll. They challenge fixed definitions of gender (see above, pp. 22–3) and they also have no fixed place in the contested hierarchy of citizens and gallants. Instead they compete over which of them will rule the city world, and that competition is enacted in sexual terms. When Laxton first sees Moll, he admires her as the embodiment of all the energy of the city:

> Life, sh' has the spirit of four great parishes, and a voice that will drown all the city! Methinks a brave captain might get all his soldiers upon her, and ne'er be beholding to a company of Mile End milksops. (2.1.171–4)

Laxton recognizes that Moll's is not the city of luxury consumption or the playground of gallants, but the traditional city of the trained bands and the regulated social life of the traditional craftsmen, sentimentalized in so much citizen lore and literature. Laxton knows that he himself is part of the class which exploits and undermines that city world, metonomized in his desire to possess Moll like an alien force from outside it:

> I'll lay hard siege to her. Money is that *aquafortis* that eats into many a maiden-head: where the walls are flesh and blood, I'll ever pierce through with a golden auger.   (2.1.177–9)

Moll's physical presence and style are as much marked by these citizen traits as by gender. She is presented as the type of the idealized young citizen who is not afraid of a fight, especially when it is with someone foreign. Her bout (2.1.222–39) with the 'Fellow *with a long rapier*' signals the triumph of the robust city boy over the effete upper-class fencer who is content to bear blows if he has witnesses to support a law suit. When she trips up Trapdoor to test out his boasting, she comforts him with the assurance that she has 'struck up the heels of the high German's size' (2.1.339), another triumph over a foreigner, armed in a newfangled way, unable to fight with hands and feet like an honest Englishman.[38]

Moll's robust citizen maleness also informs her sexual attitudes. She is contemptuous of Mrs Openwork's affected sexual jealousy (2.1.216–22), but she is equally dismayed by the androgyne gallants whose obsession with style is infecting the robust energy of city sexual relations:

> the gallants of these times are shallow lechers. They put not their courtship home enough to a wench . . . Many a poor soul would down, and there's nobody will push 'em!   (2.1.292–8)

Moll's ability to traverse the social territory between the citizens and the gallants gives her the theatrical power associated with the traditional city comedy hero. She acts as the guide to the city and its ways, using her perspicacity about the city underworld to rescue Jack Dapper from the sergeants (3.3.205–20) and to expose Trapdoor's disguise as a cashiered soldier (5.1.60–106). These episodes are set pieces, recycling tropes from other city comedy (compare *A Chaste Maid*, 4.3) and from Dekker's pamphlet accounts of low-life London; they also dramatize a complex relationship between the city and the different classes of people who inhabit it. Moll defends her 'knowledge in those villainies' (5.1.318) as a kind of prudent self-defence, a worldly wisdom like the intelligence passed from one foreign traveller to another (5.1.312–20). In other words, she is putting her knowledge at the disposal of gentlemen whose ignorance of the city might expose them to danger and loss. The class of gentlemen is further differentiated into the older and younger generation. Dapper has to be rescued from the sergeants because his father, Sir Davy, has plotted to have him arrested, using the prison system to fulfil his parental responsi-bilities to discipline his son (3.3.55–106). However there is no question of associating Jack with the real criminal underclass. He must be integrated with the older generation of aristocrats who understand their role in London life. So, when Moll takes Jack Dapper around the city in 5.1, they are accompanied by Lord Noland and Sir Beauteous Ganymede, friends of Dapper's father but with a more open attitude to the new city world. With Moll's help, they can all see the city for what it is and fulfil their appropriate role as responsible consumers of all the entertainment which the city has to offer.

Moll's reassuring vision of the city as a playground for her aristocratic friends depends upon denying its social inequities and neutralizing its potential for violence. When Jack Dapper asks after Trapdoor, Moll announces that 'He struts up and down the suburbs, I think, and eats up whores, feeds upon a bawd's garbage' (5.1.18–19). Trapdoor's perfidious betrayal of his mistress legitimates her unconcern and absolves her of any responsibility for his degradation. When she encounters him late in the scene, her initial reaction is sympathetic charity—'let's give 'em something . . . I love a soldier with my soul' (5.1.74–6)—but Trapdoor's subterfuge is soon comically exposed as a transparent fiction. Trapdoor and Tearcat act out the alien behaviour and language of the underworld gangs who live on the margins of ordered society. Both their poverty and their social exclusion are presented as a performance which is distanced from the possibility of any real engagement with the problems of the urban poor. The performance is also enclosed by Moll's editorializing translation. She tells Lord Nolan

> they have their orders, offices,
> Circuits, and circles, unto which they are bound,
> To raise their own damnation in. (5.1.308–10)

She reiterates the commonplace of canting literature that it was merely a mirror image of the hierarchically organized legitimate world. The terrible fate of the urban poor, the casualties of war and social upheaval, are translated into a comic performance. That performance enacts the exotic difference of style and language between the rich and poor; the drinking song and the jokes about sex completely occlude the more significant differences of wealth and material comfort. Even the language of anti-social derelicts is translatable: once the barrier of language is crossed, information about their world can be passed from one knowledgeable person to another (5.1.310–11), like the other services the city has to offer.

The comic pleasures of this scene ensured that the audience at the Fortune Theatre was explicitly included in this knowing elite. When Moll exposes some disguised cutpurses in spite of their gallant clothes, she recounts how she took one of the them 'i' the twopenny gallery at the Fortune' (5.1.265–6). The threat to the theatre audience is soon allayed when she makes the criminals promise to call a meeting to recover her friend's purse, lost 'at the last new play i' the Swan' (5.1.284). The theatre audience is reassured that the threat of violence and social instability in the city is not serious: like the law-abiding characters in the play, they might enjoy an urban world which is alien enough to be interesting and familiar enough to be reassuring.

Moll's special role as both a cross-dressed woman and a citizen hero offers the same theatrical pleasure. Like Long Meg of Westminster and other legendary cross-dressed women,[39] she has the freedom of the male city hero but the sentiments of a chaste woman; she supports aristocracy and hierarchy but can defend a younger generation from their injustices. She is in all a utopian figure who promises to become fully integrated into society only when the city itself becomes utopian:

> When you shall hear
> Gallants void from sergeants' fear,
> Honesty and truth unslandered,
> Woman manned but never pandered,
> Cheaters booted but not coached,
> Vessels older ere they're broached;
> If my mind be then not varied,
> Next day following, I'll be married. (5.2.217–24)

The utopia which would bring Moll Cutpurse and all the diverse inhabitants of the city into a harmonious social world could exist only in the theatre. The theatre was the place where the fantasies of urban harmony could be enacted, but even as those fantasies were played out, the spectators were reminded that they were watching a play. When Openwork catches his wife and Mrs Gallipot running off with Goshawk, he asks 'what's the comedy?'. They reply '' 'Tis *Westward Ho*' (4.2.131–2), citing the name of another comedy by Dekker and Middleton in which gallants also plot to seduce citizen women on a trip up-river to Brentford. This awareness that every plot or situation could come from another play draws attention to the theatricality with which the women strike poses of tragic distress (3.2.120–9) or outraged chastity (4.2.145–63) in order to deceive both their husbands and the gallants. Mrs Gallipot's story of the abandoned woman, reclaimed by her long-lost lover, echoes many real church court cases, but the high rhetoric of Mrs Gallipot's delivery wittily underscores her theatrical skill. The most outrageously comic play with well-known stories comes when Laxton pretends that his affair with Mrs Gallipot had been a chastity test (4.2.305–37).[40] So farfetched is his romantic story that even Gallipot is not completely convinced (see 4.2.316). However, once he has his money back, Gallipot concedes, 'If this no gullery be, sir', to which the remainder of the cast on stage chorus, 'No, no, on my life!' (4.2.338).

The possible range of tones in this exchange, from reassurance to cynicism, offers everything to a director and determines the satisfaction of the end of this plot. Gallipot assures the comic conclusion by forgiving Laxton for 'want of doing ill' (4.2.340) and the scene ends with the traditional comedic invitation to supper and a sharing of jests (4.2.341–3). Laxton had insisted that 'What's done is merriment' (4.2.335); in order to be accepted into the social world of the play, Gallipot has to overcome his suspicion about the stories he has spun. That opposition between 'merriment' and 'gullery' sums up both the pleasures and the anxieties about the theatre. Theatre performances offer the illusion that conflict can be resolved, but they also show that this resolution is the product of clever fictions.

By the end of the story, however, the conflict is not completely resolved. Gallipot excludes his wife from the general celebration: 'Wife, brag no more / Of holding out. Who most brags is most whore' (4.2.344–5). Even though the citizen women have shown equal skill in theatrical performance and storytelling, Gallipot prefers to accept Laxton's story, and Openwork similarly forgives Goshawk's connivance as a fault in nature. Like plays on women, the narratives of thwarted cuckoldry ensure the sociability of men. Conflict between social groups can be resolved by good humour and conviviality; conflict between men and women requires the reassertion of men's control. The citizen women are absorbed back into the social solutions of marriage, but the Roaring Girl, like the Country Wench, who challenged male spaces in the action and the streets, remains outside.

COUNTRY MATTERS I: *ARDEN OF FAVERSHAM*

In city comedy, the place of women is effectively subordinated to the competition between men for status and power. The love plots are moved to the margins of the action, and the women's concerns are circumscribed within the arena of marriage. The dangerous emotions of love and sexual passion are suppressed in comedy with bawdy mockery and witty devices. In tragedy, similar competitive forces explode in violence and death. They are brought to the forefront of the action, offering a tragic mirror image of the comic interaction between women, men and the changing social world.

Arden of Faversham builds its action around a domestic narrative of unhappy marriage and adultery in which the couple's personal difficulties are intertwined with one of the major social and economic upheavals of the early modern period. The opening scene places Arden's unhappy marriage alongside his newly established ownership of 'All the lands of the Abbey of Faversham' (1.5). The sixteenth-century redistribution of land seized by the Crown after the dissolution of the monasteries[41] created not only new landowners but different kinds of landholding which significantly shifted social relationships throughout England. As Franklin explains in the opening scene, Arden has been granted a portion of Abbey lands through the patronage of the Duke of Somerset, the Lord Protector, but both Mosby (1.293–4) and Greene (1.460–3) have some claim on the land. Arden's ownership of the land is, as Greene complains, 'generally intitled' (1.461), meaning that Arden has been granted total ownership without regard for the traditional arrangements established over time between the Abbey and its tenants. The seizure of church lands replaced varieties of grants and tenancies with a market in land, creating much clearer distinctions between owners and tenants as land became a commodity to be bought and sold. As a result Arden feels no responsibility for Greene, who has lost his grant of land (1.461), or Reede, whose right to leave his family to work and live off the land is denied when Arden buys the land from him (13.10–25). Reede is resentful that Arden should assume total ownership of the land 'Although the rent of it be very small' (13.14). From the new owners' perspective, however, it was more profitable to buy the land and be able to dispose of it in the market, than to continue with a low traditional rent.

Such disputes were the common stock of rural litigation.[42] They represented the markers of a gradual shift in the economy from traditional rights and privileges, not calculated in monetary terms, to a greater control by landowners over their lands and an insistence that their economic value be met in full and in cash. The long view of modern social history emphasizes the ways in which these moves made for more efficient farming which evened out the cycles of famine and dearth and produced a more stable economy, but the process of change was bitterly resented, and in some cases resisted, by those who bore its effects as changes in a traditional way of life.

These changing economic and social relationships appear, as it were, on the edges of the play's focus. For example, part of the accusation against the historical Arden was that he moved the traditional St Valentine's Day fair from the town, where its dues would be paid to the townspeople, to the Abbey grounds where the fair-holders would have to pay their dues to him.[43] When Arden's assassins plot to 'dog him through the fair' (14.72), nothing is said of Arden's profiteering. The social connections and the anger which they might arouse are buried in the narrative. The narrative uses Greene's grudge against Arden to motivate his involvement in Arden's murder, but neither he nor Reede has a major role in the play. The links from the social to the narrative have less to do with cause and effect, motive and action, than with a set of telling coincidences. Reede's curse on Arden (13.30–8), that the disputed land should prove fatal to him, is fulfilled, but it is mentioned only in passing in the Epilogue (10–13).

The play's occlusion of this social dimension[44] is part of the process of turning a historical narrative into drama. Competition between men over wealth and status and the complex social change attendant on changes in landholding are subsumed within a narrative of adultery and murder. The chronicle source for the play includes marginal glosses which both mark the main episodes of the story (often those chosen by the Arden dramatist) and read off the appropriate moral response. Alice is seen as an 'importunate and bloody minded strumpet' (154), but the murder is also presented as the unwitting instrument of God's vengeance for 'the tears of the oppressed'. Arden is presented both as a willing cuckold who 'winketh at his wife's lewdness' (149) and 'as a covetous man and a preferrer of private profit before common gain' (157). The title page of the play's printed text creates instead a onesided effect by commenting that Arden's murder 'showed the great malice and dissimulation of a wicked woman, the unsatiable desire of filthy lust and the shameful end of all murderers'. Nevertheless, the accumulation of dramatic episodes denies any such neat teleology of vengeance or retribution or justice.

Arden's resentment at Mosby's impertinent advances to his wife is put in terms of his rival's social advancement. Like Arden, Mosby has owed his improved social standing to gentry patronage, but Arden presents Mosby's rise in most unflattering terms. He describes how Mosby has made a profit in his tailoring business and has 'Crept into service of a nobleman' (1.27). Mosby's social progress is marked in his clothes. He 'bravely jets it in his silken gown' (1.30). Arden humiliates him (1.310) by seizing his sword and insisting that the markers of his trade, 'Your Spanish needle, and your pressing iron' (1.313), would be more appropriate sartorial accoutrements. In doing so, Arden reminds Mosby of the legislation which tried, unsuccessfully, to control the effects of social change by regulating social behaviour and physical displays of wealth.[45]

The conflict between Arden and Mosby is dramatized in terms of dress and accoutrements because those were the terms in which social existence was lived. They also picked up for theatrical effect some of the ironies which had been insisted upon in the chronicle version of the story. Both Holinshed's chronicle and the Warmote Book of Faversham note that Mosby murdered Arden with a blow to the head from a pressing iron.[46] Both sources may have been responding more to the demands of narrative irony than to reportage: 'a pressing iron of fourteen pounds weight' seems an unlikely accessory for a man who had given up tailoring. In the play the irony is more economically and theatrically handled. When Mosby stabs Arden, the rancour over Arden's earlier insult explodes in 'There's for the pressing iron you told me of' (14.232), and begins the crescendo of violence in which Alice and Shakebag join.

The disastrous conclusion of *Arden of Faversham* imposes retribution on a group of people who are culpable to varying degrees: Alice, who planned the murder from the beginning, Mosby, Shakebag and Black Will, who stabbed the victim, Michael and Susan, who were accessories to the event, are all dead at the end of the play. However, Bradshaw, who knew nothing of the plan, is also executed, and Greene, who was present at the death, suffers no punishment. Bradshaw protests his innocence to Alice but, though she swears that he knew nothing of the plot, she cannot save him from the final execution. The social mechanism of retributive justice is shown to be confused and partial, complicating the generic coherence of tragic closure. There is a sense throughout the action that the necessary patterning of tragedy, the move from motive to action to consequence, is only partially achieved.

The play's generic incoherence is in large part a consequence of the curious roles played by Black Will and Shakebag. In their incompetence, this villainous pair seem curiously ineffective examples of what the chronicler calls 'organs or instruments' of the devil. However, by developing their roles, the *Arden* dramatist extends the social range of the story, moving part of the action from the country to the city. When the villains are introduced on their way to London, their opening conversation turns on their acquaintance with the villainous Jack Fitten who had stolen Lord

Cheyne's plate. This discussion of the London underworld has no direct
connection with the plot, but it provides a vignette of low-life existence
which underpins the comically casual violence of Black Will's and
Shakebag's roles in the play. They, like Trapdoor in *The Roaring Girl*, are
discharged soldiers, figures with no secure place in the social world. Their
potential for both upward and downward social mobility is seen in Black
Will's resentment that Bradshaw has moved up in the world because he is
a goldsmith and has 'a little plate' (2.21) in his shop. Bradshaw's set-piece
account of Jack Fitten epitomizes the opposite slide out of respectability in
the tattered remnants of an upper servant's clothes:

> A watchet satin doublet all to-torn
> (The inner side did bear the greater show),
> A pair of threadbare velvet hose, seam rent,
> A worsted stocking rent above the shoe,
> A livery cloak, but all the lace was off.   (2.53–7)

Such characters use the opportunistic violence learned on the battlefield
to survive, though their model of survival, as in the underworld literature
of the cony-catching pamphlets, is a pathetic inverse model of respectable
society. Black Will wishes 'that murder would grow to an occupation'
(2.104–5) and is confident that in that case he 'should be warden of the
company' (2.106). The legitimate authority of those who control the city is
mirrored in the power which violence affords. Black Will claims that he has
run a protection racket among the city whores and the 'tenpenny alehouses' (14.22). His comic account of attacks on the brewer's clerk or the
sergeant and the constable echoes the resistances to authority which animate city comedy, but here the insubordination culminates in violence
unmitigated by wit. At the end of the play, Shakebag tells the grisly story
of how he had been refused his customary sanctuary with the widow
Chambley and had 'broke her neck, and cut her tapster's throat' (15.9).
Black Will escapes to Flushing but is burnt at the stake for some other
unexplained offence. Neither of them is included in any orderly exercise of
justice.

Black Will and Shakebag bring a crazy inconsequentiality to the play's
action. There is no reason, other than Greene's opportunism, for their
involvement in Arden's murder. Their comic incompetence and the series
of accidents and misfortune which dogs their attempts to kill Arden are in
part a residue of the clowning tradition associated with low-life characters
on the stage.[47] The physical comedy of the accident with the prentice's stall
(3.47–52), or the slapstick double act at the ferry which ends with Shakebag falling into a ditch (12.1–19), are clowning set pieces. The would-be
assassins' speeches of demented aggression when their plans are thwarted
(see 5.42–5; 14.5–27) leave a comic gap between intention and action. Will
has a moment of anxiety as they approach the door of Arden's London
lodging (5.15–17), but it is soon silenced by Shakebag's sneering. When
they find that Michael has double-crossed them, Will's rallying pledge to

'Lop . . . away his leg, his arm, or both' (5.45) is both comically empty and chillingly precise. Their juxtaposition of grotesque comedy and an action of murder heightens the sense that the characters inhabit a world of random malice, the antithesis of the moral certainty invoked by the play's stated didactic aims.

The theatrical power of this juxtaposition may be a fortuitous effect created by the dramatist's use of the working tools of dramatic convention at his disposal. The instabilities and shifts in tone which characterize the play as a whole also suggest that the dramatist is drawing eclectically from a range of different dramatic scenarios to turn the chronicle narrative into drama. The structure of those scenarios, and the interaction of events and reflection upon them, shape ideas about sexual and social relations in the process of creating character and dramatic episodes.

LOVE STORIES

In the chronicle account of the story, the chronicler demurs at including 'a private matter, and therefore as it were impertinent to this history' (148) in a public document. Though the chronicler describes the story as a 'private matter', early modern marriage and sexual relations were very much matters of public concern, regulated both by the courts and by social opinion. Alice's adultery with Mosby not only wounds Arden personally but affects what Franklin calls 'the speech of men, / Upon whose general bruit all honour hangs' (1.346–7). Arden tells Mosby that his anger was because 'all the knights and gentlemen of Kent / Made common table-talk of her and thee' (1.343–4). This common table-talk refers to more than gossip: it indicates the means whereby social status and personal conduct were regulated at all levels of society.[48] The lovers violate those codes of behaviour in dangerous ways but do so with a measure of defiance which suggests a keen awareness of their regulatory power. Alice is fearful that Mosby will not see her because 'these my narrow-prying neighbours blab' (1.135). When she wishes to force a confrontation between her lover and her husband, she does so by walking arm-in-arm with him in the street (12.62–5; 13.73.1).

Early modern commentators did nevertheless recognize that sexual relations involved more than social status and economic advantage. Next to the chronicle's initial description of Mosby's appearance, there appears a cryptic marginal note: 'Love and lust'. It suggests an acknowledgement of the tension between passion, desire and the social requirements of early modern marriage. This tension offered the early modern dramatist a rich variety of moral and theatrical possibilities. Arden's opening dialogue with Franklin describes the misery which his wife's adultery has brought him. His speech is fuelled by his violent rage at Mosby's upstart impertinence: 'that injurious ribald that attempts / To violate my dear wife's chastity' (1.37–8), but he notes (in parentheses) 'For dear I hold her love, as dear as heaven' (39). Arden's version of married love, 'as dear as heaven', depends upon female chastity and is based on ideas of the godly family, bound in love to one another and to God.[49] It is the version of love one might expect a member of the rural gentry to invoke, though it sits oddly with Arden's violent fantasy of dismembering his rival. Later in the same scene, however, Arden refers to their love in quite different terms. Alice enters and coyly suggests that Arden would not have risen so early if she had been awake. He responds:

> Sweet love, thou know'st that we two, Ovid-like,
> Have often chid the morning when it 'gan to peep,
> And often wished that dark Night's purblind steeds
> Would pull her by the purple mantle back
> And cast her in the ocean to her love.   (1.60–4)

These lines echo the poetic tradition of the *aubade*, in which lovers lament the untimely arrival of the morning which will put an end to their love-making. Both their passion and their high literary origin seem out of place at that moment of the play, particularly as Arden is about to accuse Alice of calling on Mosby in her sleep. The lines hint at a passionate sexual relationship between the couple which gives a poignant twist to their present misery, but this hint is never built on to create a consistency for the action or the characters.

A different image of love is presented in Franklin's advice to Arden about ways 'To ease thy grief and save her chastity' (1.45):

> Entreat her fair; sweet words are fittest engines
> To raze the flint walls of a woman's breast.   (1.46–7)

Franklin's image comes from the Petrarchan sonnets, in which the chaste beloved is a castle to be besieged, or one of the prizes of a chivalric contest. This clash of images from different poetic styles may be the result of careless appropriation of poetic conventions by the anonymous dramatist. Nevertheless it also draws attention to a disjuncture between the authenticity of character and situation and the recognizable artifice of the language being used. It sets up a dissonance between the characters' emotional and psychological struggles and the social relationship of marriage which provided the only acceptable outcome of sexual passion.

The emotional cost of that dissonance is tellingly dramatized in the triangle of love between Michael, Susan and the painter. Alice and Mosby, as social superiors and family members, are entrusted with disposing of Susan in marriage. They abuse this social responsibility for their own ends, offering Susan as the prize for murder to each suitor in turn. This marriage, however, is not simply in the hands of the family. The young men compete with one another over Susan, a competition which reveals both the confusion of motives for love and the difficulties of finding ways to express them. Michael at first fears that Susan will not marry him and that she prefers the painter because she keeps a token from him, a picture of 'a dagger sticking in a heart, / With a verse or two stolen from a painted cloth' (1.152–3). His response is to find an amanuensis for his passion, 'a fellow / That can both read and write and make rhyme too' (1.155–6). This clownish emulation of elite forms of love-making is pathetic but it is also confused with financial considerations and their potential for violent resolution:

> I'll make her more worth than twenty painters can;
> For I will rid mine elder brother away,
> And then the farm of Bolton is mine own.
> Who would not venture upon house and land
> When he might have it for a right-down blow? (1.171–5)

The painter, too, confuses the abstract poetic expressions of love with the violence he is prepared to perpetrate. He agrees to provide poison for Arden's murder and then justifies it by invoking the conventional connection between love and art:

> So we that are the poets' favourites
> Must have a love. Ay, Love is the painter's Muse,
> That makes him frame a speaking countenance,
> A weeping eye that witnesses heart's grief. (1.255–8)

The painter's passion for Susan is irrelevant to the central narrative thrust of the play, and this elaborate justification knocks the emotional balance askew. The mockery of overpoeticized love was a commonplace of contemporary comedy. Here, the comic emulation of elite forms of love-making seem to have tragically infected the rural world.

When Michael goes to London he feels in a superior position to compete with the painter's poetic rhetoric of love. The letter he acquires is a travesty of euphuistic love language, comically using the bathos of inappropriate comparison to mock Michael's aspiration (3.3–16). When Arden finds Michael with his precious letter, he denounces the whole story. The poetic discourses of love are inappropriate for servants and artisans, and Arden dismisses the passion that they call love as a silly attempt to aggrandize 'A crew of harlots, all in love, forsooth' (3.26). Yet the dissonance between the conventions of representing low-life loving and the seriousness of the consequences for Michael create an uneasy sense of real conflict. Michael's aspiration to love is, after all, no more or less contemptible than Alice's, and yet the class relations of the play make it a source of mockery.

The instability of these discourses of love creates a number of puzzles in the play. Alice and Mosby frequently lose confidence in their desire to murder Arden, and their quarrels over both their plots and their emotions are fuelled by confusions over the nature of love and the impossibility of expressing it in a single, consistent way. Again and again, Mosby tries to escape from the affair but is drawn back into it by the passion of Alice's protestations. Before he even appears, Mosby sends a message telling Alice not to visit him, and in the lovers' initial dialogue there is a passionate falling out. The passion of that quarrel is then dismissed as a trial of constancy, and the scene ends with a reaffirmation of their love and the plot to poison Arden. Similarly Alice insists that she will see Mosby, 'Were he as mad as raving Hercules' (1.116), and threatens to tear down the inn where he is lodging. Yet before the end of the scene she denounces him for having made a 'shipwreck of [her] honour' (189), presenting herself as a victim of his advances:

> Before I saw that falsehood look of thine,
> 'Fore I was tangled with thy 'ticing speech,
> Arden to me was dearer than my soul.   (1.195–7)

The apparent inconsistencies stem from the fact that each position is rhetorically coherent, familiar from the poetic and dramatic sources and only tangentially connected to the development of the narrative. Yet they also reveal a sense of love as an overwhelming, uncontrollable force. Mosby renounces responsibility for his passion: 'I could not choose; her beauty fired my heart' (1.331) and he describes 'A woman's love . . . as the lightning flame / Which even in bursting forth consumes itself' (1.207–8).

In the most extended quarrel scene (scene 8), it is as though the dramatist has juxtaposed characters from quite different rhetorical and dramatic traditions in ways which demonstrate the uneasy tension between different models of heterosexual relations. The scene is strategically placed to create suspense between the plot to murder Arden on Rainham Downs and the news that the attempts in London have failed (8.157–60). It sets up the ironic possibility that the murder may prove unnecessary but carries the emotional momentum of the action forward. The confrontation between Mosby and Alice demonstrates both the conflict between the social and the personal in sexual relations and the strain on a conventional rhetoric in expressing them. A rhetoric opposing true love to wealth overlaps with one in which relations between people of appropriate status are approved. Mosby's opening soliloquy presents him as the conventional upstart villain, plotting to use the affair with Alice as a means to acquire Arden's wealth, a motive which appears nowhere else in the play. As the scene continues, the social dimension of their relationship supersedes the personal. Alice regrets not only the loss of her own social reputation— the 'title of an odious strumpet's name' (8.72)—but the further degradation of being associated with 'A mean artificer' (8.77). Mosby in turn insists that he has forsaken 'Fortune's right hand' (8.86) in taking on a whore when he could have married 'an honest maid / Whose dowry would have weighed down all thy wealth' (8.88–9). The language of the quarrel confuses the morality of adultery with the social stigma associated with unequal marriage; a rhetoric which opposes true love to mere wealth is set against the tensions around social mobility. The final reconciliation, too, is expressed in proverbial terms:

> Flowers do sometimes spring in fallow lands,
> Weeds in gardens, roses grow on thorns;

So, whatsoe'er my Mosby's father was,
Himself is valued gentle by his worth.   (8.142–5)

The commonplace language of value can deal only with social status, not
with sentiment or sexual attraction, so that the metaphors of the proverbs
simply gloss over the emotional and social tensions involved in Alice
and Mosby's affair. There is a powerful contradiction between an idea of
gentility dependent on birth and one which depends on the moral worth of
the individual; a notion of love which transcends wealth and social status
is at odds with the love that ensures the stability of a society based on
marriage and the family. The exchanges between Mosby and Alice provide
extraordinary dramatic insight into the emotional costs and confusions
which lie beneath changes in sexual and social relations.

By allowing the characters to express coherent but inconsistent positions, the *Arden* playwright creates a powerful sense of their emotional
complexity. Alice, in particular, is an extraordinary dramatic creation. She
enacts a kind of crazy, intemperate, unpredictable sexiness which gives
the impression of an entirely authentic and idiosyncratic personality. The
swoops and turns of her passion for Mosby, her willingness to denounce
him as 'base peasant' (1.198) with the same social derogation as her
husband, her flagrant violation of all social bonds with the conviction that
'Oaths are words, and words is wind, / And wind is mutable' (1.436–7), as
well as her extraordinary ability to make men do what she wants, all
portray her as the ultimate monstrous, unruly woman. She is the defining
opposite of the idealized chaste, silent and obedient woman; she achieves
her ends by rhetorical manipulation, opportunistically exploiting all the
sources of social resentment against Arden, while remaining herself completely socially isolated and outrageously unconcerned for the opinion of
the social world. That impression of authenticity is created by interweaving the roles of the whore, the misunderstood wife and the lover into the
same theatrical persona.

There is a seductive, self-dramatizing quality to all of Alice's dealings
with the men whom she enlists in her plots. She tells Black Will that if he
had killed Arden 'I would have crammed in angels in thy fist, / And kissed
thee, too, and hugged thee in my arms' (14.69–70). When she is instructing
him in the final murder plans she promises 'My hands shall play you
golden harmony', continuing with 'How like you this?', a line which
requires some accompanying sexual gesture (14.112–13). Her approach to
Greene plays on his existing grievance, reinforcing it with a conventional
account of marital unhappiness, complaining that her husband mistreats
her with 'froward looks, / Hard words, and blows to mend the match
withal' (1.494–5). She readily adopts the posture of the wronged wife when
Arden complains about the taste of the poisoned broth (1.368–71) and
when he leaves her to visit Lord Cheyne (10.13–20). Even after Arden has
retaliated against Mosby's public humiliation of him by wounding him in
a fight, she defends herself in a speech which complains how her husband

misinterprets her every action (13.106–13). She blames their incompatibil-
ity, however, on her husband's 'misgovernment', conventionally relying on
patriarchal government to deal with the ills of the heterosexual domestic
relationship.

Alice's protestations might be regarded as disingenuous, since it is her
adultery that has undermined the fundamental basis of companionate
marriage. Her speeches, on the other hand, also dramatize the emotional
power of contemporary myths about marriage which fuels both her defiant
transgression and her awareness of socially sanctioned conduct. In an
analysis of church court marital disputes, Laura Gowing has shown that
domestic conflict, publicly articulated in the church courts, was organized
around what she calls 'Narratives of Litigation'. These stories told in court
were, as she puts it,

> liable to be inflected by gender. In marital disputes, witnesses had to ally them-
> selves either with a man's story or a woman's; and very often, both sides were
> telling an archetypal version, a man's tale of the betrayals of adultery or a
> woman's tale of the drama of violence.[50]

Alice's account of her failed marriage is one such set of stories; Arden's is
another.

The *Arden* dramatist gives less dramatic attention to Arden's emotional
engagement with his marriage than he does to Alice's. Arden's confidant,
Franklin, draws on conventional misogynist wisdom to encourage Arden
to take the generalized condescending view that 'women will be false and
wavering' (1.21). He dismisses Arden's concerns as weak uxoriousness
(1.52–3) and is obviously impatient with the 'dallying' that holds up their
departure for London. Nevertheless, he provides the most extended insight into the emotional toll taken by unhappy marriage and the ways that
it is expressed in action:

> Now will he shake his care-oppressèd head,
> Then fix his sad eyes on the sullen earth,
> Ashamed to gaze upon the open world;
> Now will he cast his eyes up towards the heavens,
> Looking that ways for redress of wrong.   (4.43–7)

This set speech reads like instructions to the actor playing Arden and
illustrates the process of turning emotion into action. When Franklin
recounts a story of an adulterous woman as he and Arden cross Rainham
Down on their return from London, he gives the guilty woman gestures
which are uncannily similar to those he has assigned to the innocent man:

> First did she cast her eyes down to the earth,
> Watching the drops that fell amain from thence;
> Then softly draws she forth her handkercher,
> And modestly she wipes her tear-stained face;
> Then hemmed she out, to clear her voice should seem,
> And with a majesty addressed herself
> To encounter all their accusations.   (9.82–8)

The rights and wrongs of a failed marriage do not affect the pain which it brings to both parties. Franklin's two descriptions formalize that pain into a set of gestures to be read by the judging audience, dramatizing the emotional expectations which marriage involves. In one of the most poignant moments in the play, Arden shows how his conventional expectations of marriage are sustained in the face of all the evidence of Alice's evil intent. Cheered by Alice's reluctance to see him leave to visit Lord Cheyne, he tells Franklin that her humour seems to have improved and proposes that they hurry home to 'take her unawares playing the cook' (13.73). The ensuing scene, where he encounters Alice and Mosby brazenly flaunting their physical passion, overturns any fantasy about marriage. Its impact has been carefully placed in and against the ideals of marriage.

After Arden is dead, all of the characters lament their part in the terrible deed in terms which once again echo the moral commonplaces about relations between men and women. Mosby denounces Alice as a strumpet. She reminds him that 'but for thee I had never been strumpet' (18.14) and claims that she was 'too young to sound thy villainies' (18.17). Susan remains an innocent victim, and Michael regrets that he has been involved by the offer of marriage from those more powerful than he (18.23–5). Each of them has been seduced by ideas about the possibilities of love which offer appealing alternatives to the conventions of patriarchal marriage. The play sets the conventions of marriage against the conventions of love poetry and the narrative of adultery against the narrative of betrayal. The effect is to dramatize the enormous emotional investment demanded by love and marriage and adultery, the crises which were generated by their failure and the theatrical potential of the clashes between them.

LOVE STORIES II: *A WOMAN KILLED WITH KINDNESS*

The daring innovation of domestic tragedy lay in taking the narratives of adultery and exploring the social damage and personal pain consequent upon it. It turned cuckoldry from comedy to pathos and dramatized both the social importance of marriage and its terrifying fragility. The genre offered artistic opportunities to create theatrical pleasure out of sentiment, to develop the feelings as much as the moral attitudes which adultery might invoke. In *Arden of Faversham* theatrical pleasures were precariously balanced against moral attitudes in a juxtaposition of different ways of talking about marriage and sexual relations. In *A Woman Killed with Kindness*, written a decade later, the equilibrium of these forces seems more firmly in the dramatist's control.

As we have seen (pp. 11–12 above), Heywood manages the staging of the scene in which the adultery is discovered so as to wring the most emotion out of the structurally comic scenario. The emotion is firmly centred on Frankford. He is the physical focus of the audience's attention as he moves about the stage. At the end of the sequence, he apportions blame in his final chilling condemnation: 'It was thy hand cut two hearts out of one' (13.185). In order to show that he has suffered a deep wrong, the action carefully focuses the attention on his sorrow and loss. In the following scene, Frankford systematically empties the house of any reminder of his wife so that he will not suffer further torment. The list of objects by which Anne is represented—'a bodkin or a cuff, / A bracelet, necklace, or rebato wire' (15.7–8)—are all signs of female frippery that need not hold Frankford's attention. Any sense of his ruthlessness is allayed, however, when he comes upon her lute. As his sorrowful musing makes clear, the lute symbolizes not only femininity but also the harmony of idealized marriage.[51] Frankford's speech puns on the divisions and harmony of both music and marriage, extending the analogy to the strings of his heart. Although Nicholas and Cranwell are on stage at the time, Frankford and his feelings command total dramatic attention. What Laura Gowing calls 'the man's tale of the betrayals of adultery' (see above p. 37) is centre stage.

The lute that acted as the focus of this emotion is delivered to Anne in the following scene. When she plays on it she echoes Frankford's punning with 'We both are out of tune, both out of time' (16.18). Her performance on the lute makes her the centre of attention, but now the attention is mediated by the other figures on stage. Wendoll notes that her music, like Orpheus's, makes the carters weep; Nicholas, who had exposed her adultery, also finds that he cannot speak for weeping. Anne is overcome with a sense of her own unworthiness, either to speak Frankford's name or to have her name spoken by her children. She is 'A woman made of tears' (16.77), but her 'inward grief' (16.78) has to be articulated by the men on stage.

Wendoll's commentary, in particular, blurs the focus on Anne. He is aware that he has 'made her husbandless and childless too' (16.91), but his sense of wrongdoing is equally tied up with his debt to Frankford. He claims to suffer the 'horror of a guilty soul' (16.31) (though he blames it on his parents and the stars), and his sorrow comes from thinking on 'Master Frankford's love' (16.36). His final soliloquy begins with a repentant sense of his responsibility for Anne's 'life, her sins, and all' (16.123), but, having accepted his self-imposed banishment, he is sanguine about his future possibilities as a courtier. In this speech, Wendoll reverts to the role of witty gallant, confident that relations with men—his 'worth and parts being by some great man praised' (16.133)—are more significant in his world than relations with women.

The cuckold plot, even when treated tragically, takes place in a world of men. Its dramatic structures isolate the women, excluding them from any sense of the community of women which exists in city comedy. Anne appeals to the women in the audience, but only after she has fallen. As an adulterous woman, she is separated from the wives of the audience, warning them against fellow-feeling with her. In the seduction scene, she turns in ten lines from asserting that her love for her husband 'is as precious / As my soul's health (6.140–1) to a desperate inarticulateness:

> What shall I say?
> My soul is wand'ring and hath lost her way.
> [*To him*] Oh, Master Wendoll, oh!   (6.149–51)

She succumbs to the affair, she says, through 'want of wit' (11.112), and continues it through fear of disgrace. Wendoll's feelings, on the other hand, are fully articulated in soliloquy in which he actively chooses the role of villain. His subjectivity comes from outside himself, generated by the sight of Anne, and dragged into sin by 'some fury' and the 'Fates' (6.99–100). He experiences the struggle with his conscience as a conflict between his soul and his reluctant body. His soul 'Lies drenched and drownèd in red tears of blood' (6.7); he tries to drag his eyes away from Anne 'until my eyestrings crack' (6.15), and he records his debt to Frankford 'Within the red-leaved table of my heart' (6.126), knowing that the title of villain would be printed in his face (6.84–6). His rhetoric of tragic conflict is somewhat undermined by Jenkin's comic asides, but the emotional and dramatic attention of the scene is focused upon it. Frankford similarly assumes that Anne's adultery must be a reflection on him. When he interrogates her about it, he goes through a list which reveals the limits of all a woman could expect in return for her chaste loyalty:

>   Was it for want
> Thou played'st the strumpet? Wast thou not supplied
> With every pleasure, fashion, and new toy . . . ?
> Was it then disability in me,
> Or in thine eye seemed he a properer man?
> . . . Did I not lodge thee in my bosom?
> Wear thee here in my heart?   (13.107–14)

Anne then accepts the terms of Frankford's denunciation, referring to herself as a 'strumpet' (13.132), though she had initially not known 'by what word, what title, or what name' (13.78) to entreat Frankford's pardon. Her repentance, however, hints at a more complex view of women's subjectivity when she expresses the contradictory desire both to preserve the integrity of her body and to be physically dismembered as a way of ridding her body of sin. She first begs Frankford:

>   mark not my face
> Nor hack me with your sword, but let me go
> Perfect and undeformèd to my tomb.   (13.98–100)

and then exclaims:

>   Oh, to redeem my honour
> I would have this hand cut off, these my breasts seared,
> Be racked, strappadoed, put to any torment;
> Nay, to whip but this scandal out, I would hazard
> The rich and dear redemption of my soul.   (13.134–8)

These contradictory impulses do not arise from a coherent interiorized character. Like many other sexualized women in early modern drama,[52]

Anne is constructed both as a beautiful woman and as an anatomy, a body which has to be opened and explored in order to reveal its truth. Her physical presence on stage calls forth the men's passion and grief. She initiates no action and so acts as the mirror in which men's concerns about marriage can be viewed.

Those concerns are partly about the closed emotional and sexual relationships between women and men and partly about the wider social relationships in which those relationships are placed. In addition to the Frankfords and their servants, the adultery plot of *A Woman Killed* has a sub-cast of figures—Cranwell, Tydy, Sandy and Roder. They make no contribution to the action but they fill out the stage, creating the sense of an inhabited social world with capillaries of social relationships extending well beyond the immediate household and family. In early modern England, marriage, as well as involving a couple, also formed the basis of the household, which included servants, kin and friends. The servants in *A Woman Killed* provide a traditional comic chorus, wryly noting their betters' lack of simple moral common sense. They also dramatize the continuities of the Frankford household which the marriage and its crisis are disrupting. When Nicholas reports Anne's adultery to Frankford, he prefaces the accusation with an account of his credentials:

> Sir, I have served you long; you entertained me seven years before your beard. You knew me, sir, before you knew my mistress . . . 'Sblood, sir, I love you better than your wife.　　　　　　　　　　　　　　　　　　　(8.32–42)

For Nicholas, the arrival of a woman in the household disrupts the more stable and long-term relationships between men. Jenkin too defines his mistress in relation to his master, and when his new master Wendoll asks for his mistress, he affects not to know whom he is referring to (6.57–62). Mistresses are extensions of masters. The well-managed household allows no ambiguities in their definition.

It is precisely the crisis of the well-managed household that creates the dramatic action of the play as a whole. Heywood uses the two plots to explore different kinds of domestic catastrophe, one in which a marriage is destroyed and another in which marriage provides an uneasy resolution. The two actions both exist in the same social world. Yet where the Frankford story deals primarily with affect and feelings in marriage, the story of Mountford and Susan deals with the connections between marriage and contemporary economic relations. Lorna Hutson has described how domestic narratives in the sixteenth century emerged from a tension between a discourse of the economical household, self-sufficient and restrained in its credit relations, and a discourse of friendship in which credit, of both a social and economic kind, was felt to be unlimited.[53] Frankford embodies this all-embracing notion of friendship when he offers Wendoll all the resources of his household:

> Please you to use my table and my purse
> They are yours . . .

Choose of my men which shall attend on you,
And he is yours. I will allow you, sir,
Your man, your gelding, and your table, all
At my own charge; be my companion.   (4.63-4, 67-70)

By seducing Anne, Wendoll violates that credit, 'hatching treason to so
true a friend' (6.86). Frankford's generosity gives an economic as well as an
affective dimension to that treachery.

When Wendoll enters the domestic space of Frankford's household
bringing news of the disastrous quarrel between Mountford and Acton,
Frankford is summing up the virtues of his household and the happiness
which marriage has brought him (4.1-14). The contrast between his domestic world and the more dangerous world of aristocratic men is marked.
From the beginning of the play, this group of men has distanced itself from
the domestic world, involving women and servants and young people. The
men joke about the restrictions which marriage will impose on Frankford,
and their plan to wager on their hawks' performance is explicitly contrasted with the lower-class and young people's country pastime:

Now, gallants, while the town musicians
Finger their frets within, and the mad lads
And country lasses, every mother's child
With nosegays and bride-laces in their hats,
Dance all their country measures, rounds, and jigs,
What shall we do?   (1.80-5)

These men identify themselves by an effortless expertise in gallant sports,
dramatized in the technical language of hawking,[54] and in the concentrated
attention given to the offstage competition. The sport, however, is taken
more seriously than the friendly wager suggests: the rules cannot be
unambiguously applied, and the men cannot agree to accept the outcome.
One of Sir Francis's servants is killed in the ensuing quarrel, but the
subsequent action pays less attention to his fate than to the terrible rupture
in gentlemen's social relationships.

The resulting action in which Sir Charles loses his land and household
reveals the fissures in male social relations and the threats to them created
by changing economic and social relations. The murder of Sir Charles's
servant brings Mountford not moral but economic disaster. His wealth
allows him to be released from prison, but it leaves him unable to maintain
his previous social standing. This relationship between wealth and status,
which will drive the whole of the ensuing action, is articulated in unusually
precise terms. Mountford is, he says,

The poorest knight in England . . .
My life hath cost me all the patrimony
My father left his son.   (5.17-19)

He then confides in Shafton:

Two thousand and five hundred pound a year
My father at his death possessed me of,
. . .

And I have now only a house of pleasure,
With some five hundred pounds, reserved
Both to maintain me and my loving sister.   (5.41–2, 46–8)

The drop from one figure to another leaves Sir Charles well above the income of a tenant farmer, but it does move him quite clearly out of the economic stratum of the gentry. The issue is not only economic; it is a question of the social relationships which wealth will allow. The change in his finances deprives Sir Charles of the ability to move in circles where wealth will allow him take part in relations of friendship. This relationship between friendship and wealth is not calculated in mercenary terms of exchange. Rather, it involves a circle of mutual indebtedness in which the reciprocity of friendship cannot be calculated by exact sums, nor assured by legal agreements, nor wiped out by repayment.[55]

The quarrel with Sir Charles Acton abruptly excludes Mountford from this circle of reciprocity and embroils him in the new world of contracts and legal agreements. When he comes out of prison and accepts Shafton's offer of a loan, he assumes that Shafton is lending money as a friend. He is appalled that he has moved into the legal world of bonds and obligations that can only be discharged by money. Shafton's role in this transaction is especially interesting. He is an outsider to the world of the play's action in that he has no narrative role. He is necessary to isolate the world of money-making which, much more than the initial act of murder, brings about Sir Charles's downfall. Like a number of similar figures in early modern drama,[56] he acts as catalyst for action, representing the social change which commutes social into financial relations, but he can be given no dramatic relationships in an action which is organized around men linked by relations of kinship and shared social status.

This tension between social and economic relations is tested throughout the Acton/Mountford plot. It is summed up, almost proverbially, when Susan approaches Old Mountford to save her brother, and he retorts:

Money I cannot spare; men should take heed.
He lost my kindred when he fell to need.   (9.16–17)

Old Mountford and a chorus of Sir Charles's tenants and former friends reiterate the values of an order in which relations of friendship and kin are bound by the expectations that they will never be commuted into actual requests for money. But there is a pat, proverbial quality in the rhyming couplets with which her kin reject Susan's plea. It suggests ideas which have hardened into cliché. Susan responds, equally conventionally, by crying, 'O Charity, why art thou fled to heaven?' (9.37). The idea that Charity had fled, leaving the world to economic calculation, involved Christian ideas about the virtue of poverty and the importance of alms-giving which were equally a part of current ideas about the significance of wealth.[57]

These complex relations between wealth, money and friendship are complicated further when Malby offers Susan Sir Francis's gold. Again misunderstanding the world she is living in, Susan assumes it is an act of friendship, to be rewarded by gratitude and a sense of social obligation: 'God make me able to requite this favour' (9.49). When, however, the terms are explained to her she rejects the money as an offer from a 'bawd' and 'broker', using the language of financial exchange. She was willing to accept Sir Francis's money as a gift but not as an exchange for her sexual favours. It is precisely this exclusion of herself from the world of commerce that gives Susan the standing which makes Sir Francis recognize her worth to be his wife:

> The more she hates me and disdains my love,
> The more I am rapt in admiration
> Of her divine and chaste perfections.   (9.59–61)

In later melodrama, these negotiations around money and status would solidify into a crude opposition between true love and money or true friendship and money. In the early modern period this process was beginning, but older and more complex interconnections between money and wealth and love and honour remained as a complicating factor in the plays' structure of feeling. Sufficiency of wealth was itself a marker of gentry status since it provided an opportunity for charity and friendship. Money was more than a neutral currency of exchange since its source was as important as the sums involved. In the new economy, on the other hand, networks of obligation were commuted into money payments, allowing a more precise calculation of indebtedness, even when the debt was as much moral as financial. When Sir Charles finds that Sir Francis's bounty, not his kin's, has released him from prison, his dismay stems not from ingratitude but from a sense of the burden of obligation which this imposes on him. His decision to give Susan to Francis in return is an attempt to seize control once more of the relations between him and another man. Though these relations are expressed in financial terms, notions of more abstract indebtedness are bound in with them. There is a cold crudeness in the apparent calculation of his plea to Susan:

> A thousand pound! I but five hundred owe;
> Grant him your bed, he's paid with interest so.   (14.45–6)

Yet his desire to pay Sir Francis more than he owes is part of the interaction of money and honour:

> His kindness like a burden hath surchargèd me,
> And under his good deeds I stooping go,
> Not with an upright soul.   (14.63–5)

Susan, for her part, accepts that she is equally involved in the relations of debt and obligation, and concedes 'These arguments come from an honoured mind' (14.77). The gift of Susan, however, is so much greater than the debt which Sir Francis has paid for Sir Charles that the burden of obligation is transferred to him, and he must requite it by making Susan his wife. The language of debt and recompense, of gift and obligation, are complexly interwoven in Sir Francis's speech of acceptance (14.133–46). In accepting Sir Charles's gift of Susan, Sir Francis accepts the obligation that implies and requites it by his gift of marriage. Susan in turn will have to make good that gift by loving him, for, as she says, 'You still exceed us' (14.147). As a result, she has to give not just her body but her love:

> I will yield to fate,
> And learn to love where I till now did hate. (14.147–8)

The marriage, moreover, does more than repay the debt. By making Sir Charles and Sir Francis kin, it removes the need to calculate the levels of indebtedness:

> I pay no debt, but am indebted more;
> Rich in your love, I never can be poor. (14.151–2)

Susan has fulfilled the key woman's role of sealing the bonds between men and has accepted the requirements of love, meaning chastity and loyalty, that go with it. The play does not address her views on the matter.

These fine distinctions between financial and social relations are dramatized not only in the language of exchange but also in its physical representation on stage. When Susan asks her brother's tenants and friends to help him, one of them, Sandy, reminds Susan of her past:

> Then you were mistress Sue, tricked up with jewels;
> Then you sung well, played sweetly on the flute;
> But now I neither know you nor your suit. (9.23–5)

Sandy cruelly emphasizes the signs, not only of wealth but of leisure and accomplishment which characterized Susan's former life. These signs were as important to gentry status as the network of obligations. Their loss is also marked by the stage direction indicating 'SIR CHARLES *in prison, with irons; his feet bare, his garments all ragged and torn*' (10.0.1–2). When Sir Charles hands Susan over in return for his debt to Sir Francis, the stage directions, once again, indicate the value of the gift and the status it will confer:

> *Enter* SIR CHARLES, *gentlemanlike, and* [SUSAN] *his sister, gentlewomanlike.*
> (14.0.1–2)

Their persons, their identity, depend on their position in society, and their clothes are essential indicators of that position, determining their actions and behaviour.

The antithesis of contrasting physical images is matched by the balance and alternations of the two plots with which Heywood dramatizes the tension between heterosexual and homosocial relations. Alternating the scenes increases suspense by holding up the development of each plot; it also brings into focus the importance of the two women. As we have seen, Wendoll enters the Frankford household as Frankford enumerates the sources of his happiness. He lists his estate, his gentry standing, his education:

> But the chief
> Of all the sweet felicities on earth,
> I have a fair, a chaste, and loving wife,
> Perfection all, all truth, all ornament. (4.9–12)

His uxorious dependence on a woman's chastity weakens his position in the world of men with disastrous consequences. The contrast between his emotional vulnerability and the other men's control over women is made evident by placing the discovery of the adultery between the scenes where Sir Charles plans to hand over Susan and the encounter with Sir Francis. Anne's adultery, its motivation entirely unexplored, has destroyed her husband's household and friendship both. The return to the Acton plot offers the more satisfactory alternative in which a woman agrees, again without considering her motives, to act as the seal on male negotiations.

COMICAL DEFLECTIONS: *A CHASTE MAID IN CHEAPSIDE*

These ideals of honour and male friendship are insistently rehearsed and asserted in the drama of the time, perhaps because of the sense that they are passing. The tragic versions of these stories turn abstract social questions into the theatrical pleasures of suspense and loss and complex emotional engagement with the characters. However, the social changes which put these relationships under pressure can equally be viewed more cynically. Heywood's refined distinctions between money and obligation, between accomplishments and status, melt down in *A Chaste Maid* in the comic furnace of a world governed entirely by opportunism and the quest for financial gain. The only possible relations between men and women are sexual; the only point of sexual relations is economic advantage. At the beginning of the play, Mrs Yellowhammer catechizes her daughter about the accomplishments of music and dancing—the same accomplishments which had marked Susan Mountford's gentility and symbolized Anne Frankford's harmonious marriage. Mrs Yellowhammer's references to playing on the virginals are caught in an undertow of bawdy. The entirely financial and sexual basis for social relations has superseded the more subtle structures of debt and obligation which inform the language of gentry interaction.

Sexual relations can also, of course, bring economic disadvantage, as in the case of the overly sexualized Touchwood Senior and his fecund wife. Again, the complex moral discourse with which these issues were discussed in contemporary culture is comically reduced. The Touchwoods' discussion of their situation at the beginning of Act 2, playing on 'barrenness' and 'fruitfulness', travesties the language of both the marriage ceremony and the handbooks on marriage. Touchwood's admiration for 'The perfect treasure' of his wife, his sense that 'A man's happy . . . that has matched his soul / As rightly as his body' (2.1.22–5), rehearse the same ideals about marriage which inform Frankford's celebration of his marital bliss. Touchwood's soliloquy on his wife's discretion and judgement is a comic parody of the unctuous uxoriousness of Puritan marriage theory. In another context, his statement that 'The feast of marriage is not lust, but love' (2.1.50) could have summed up the conduct books' discussions about the role of sexual compatibility in marriage. Here it comically explodes the contradiction between money and love which was so anxiously theorized in those discussions.

The writers of marriage handbooks were, of course, serious-minded Puritan clergy who were profoundly concerned with the importance of building the godly family as part of a godly commonwealth with an equal place for the souls of men and women.[58] Their serious concern with social regulation, the fate of bastards and abandoned women and the right relations between social groupings was easily mocked by city comedy, which spoke primarily to individualistic young men for whom pleasure and social advantage were paramount. The travesty of marriage in the Touchwood Senior plot, and the travesty of patronage relations in the connections between Whorehound and the Allwits, instead expose the potential for hypocrisy in which high-sounding social theory and moral commonplaces could be used to justify atavistic personal advantage. When Allwit abandons Whorehound, he piously announces, 'I tell you truly / I thought you had been familiar with my wife once' (5.1.148–9). When moral outrage is advantageous, it can be deployed with breathtaking comic hypocrisy. It has also been prepared for in the opening scene, where the basis for Allwit and Sir Walter's relationship is presented as a comic travesty of accepted social relations. Allwit, who should be master of the house, holds his status as a result of Sir Walter's generosity. Even his servants recognize that he is not the master 'but our mistress's husband' (1.2.66). Where Jenkin in *A Woman Killed* makes that distinction into a serious point about Wendoll's impertinence, here it is a comic reminder that everyone in the household is conniving at adultery. Sir Walter, in turn, exercises all the proprietorial jealousy which might be expected of the legitimate patriarch, while at the same time showing due awareness of the importance of his blood line in his determination that his children with Mrs Allwit must on no account, 'mingle / Amongst my children that I get in wedlock' (1.2.132–3).

In the play's finale, the trope of the deathbed repentance, so affectingly used in Heywood's play, is mocked. When Sir Walter Whorehound lies wounded in Allwit's house, Allwit does his best to turn Sir Walter's thoughts away from repentance, for fear of the financial consequences. He brings in not his own legitimate children but Sir Walter's illegitimate children. The rich comedy in the contrast between Sir Walter Whorehound and the uxorious husbands of domestic tragedy is increased by a reference to the tradition of moral drama. Sir Walter complains that Mrs Allwit's solicitude 'shows like / The fruitless sorrow of a careless mother / That brings her son with dalliance to the gallows / And then stands by and weeps to see him suffer' (5.1.64–7). The reference to the final pathetic scene of *Nice Wanton*,[59] a morality play of the previous century, may not be explicit. Nevertheless it suggests that the scene is playing with genre as much as with morality. A good deal of the wit in *A Chaste Maid* depends on its overturning of social values. But the comic pleasure those overturnings afford is increased by the sense that they are also a travesty of theatrical narratives. The innovation of domestic tragedy had been to turn cuckoldry from comedy to pathos. In the creative turmoil of the early modern theatre, the reversal could be made in the opposite direction, lampooning the styles of moral tragedy and mocking the paraphernalia of bourgeois marriage and its potential for hypocrisy.

LANGUAGE AND STYLE

These stories of love betrayed, adultery risked and honour sustained have, in modern times, become the commonplaces of romance. Their connection to the argument over social change has been loosened as the repeated oppositions between love and money, or between the rights of husbands and wives, or the power of parents over children settled into narrative formulae. The commercial theatre of early modern London contributed to that process, drawing on stories from history and collections of romances, as well as the traditions of theatre, turning them from comedy to tragedy and back again to meet the demands of a growing theatrical profession. At the same time, the lines of connection between the plays and the social world which produced them can still be traced in the densely metaphorical language used to articulate the conflicts and relationships in which they engaged.

Language in early modern theatre had not yet been naturalized as the direct expression of character. It had a self-conscious quality which could be used to set a scene, or to complicate a social encounter, or to extend the frame of reference in a routine dialogue. Just as the plays recycled theatrical conventions, so they quoted from a rich tradition of language which included proverbs and sermons as well as poetry, offering artistic pleasure in itself. Arden, announcing the morning as he prepares to set off for Lord Cheyne's estate, speaks of 'the Hours, the guardant of heaven's gate' and personifes the sun as Sol, driving his chariot across the heavens (*Arden*, 10.1–5). It is the language we might expect in a different style of play, a residue from classically influenced drama. More startlingly, Shakebag uses a similar strain of extended personification in his description of oncoming night as he waits to go and murder Arden (see 5.1–9). The association between darkness and foul deeds was conventional, but the sudden jerk into a more formal style of poetic language is surprising in a play where, we are assured, 'no filèd points are foisted in / To make it gracious to the ear or eye' (Epilogue, 15–16).

As with the invocation of Petrarchan and Ovidian love poetry (see above pp. 33), it is impossible to tell how far these poetic effusions are to be connected to the particular circumstances of the scene, how far they are the residue of style inappropriately applied and how far they draw attention to the gap between language and character. As we have seen, Michael's poetic aspirations in his love letter to Susan are presented as comic and explicitly mocked by Arden. His language in that instance draws attention to his character and social situation. The same character, however, is given highly charged allegorical poetry with which to dramatize his moral conflict:

> Conflicting thoughts encampèd in my breast
> Awake me with the echo of their strokes;
> And I, a judge to censure either side,
> Can give to neither wishèd victory. (4.58–61)

The Petrarchan trope which presented emotions as combatants in a tournament has been elegantly turned from love to murder, and there is nothing to suggest that this imagery or style is inappropriate for the character. The speech develops from this rather formal allegorization of Michael's feelings to the terrified fantasy of Black Will and Shakebag's vengeance and culminates in his cry of horror which awakens Arden and Franklin. It reads as though the *Arden* dramatist has drawn from the quite different literary traditions of Petrarchanism and the comic-grotesque of contemporary pamphlets. The speech opens up for a moment the possibility of a complex interiority for Michael, but this is not sustained in the action as a whole. The effect, striking though it is, may be no more than a fortuitous result of clashing poetic styles, not completely under control.

Fine writing and the social resonances of style had themselves become the subject of intellectual debate and were reflected in the common connection between poetry and falsehood. When Mosby, for example, expatiates on the instability of 'love without true constancy' (10.91–9), he extends the idea into a metaphor of a pillar built without mortar which, 'being touched, straight falls unto the earth / And buries all his haughty pride in dust' (10.96–7). The image is proverbial, an extension of Christ's parable of the house built on a rock, and Mosby confuses the issue by mixing that metaphor with a comparison between their love and 'rocks of adamant'. A mixed metaphor is not in itself a sign of duplicity, but Greene's impatient advice to concentrate on the matter in hand suggests some distrust of Mosby's eloquent protestation. Similarly, just before the scene of Arden's death, Alice soliloquizes on her passion for Mosby:

> There is no nectar but in Mosby's lips!
> Had Chaste Diana kissed him, she like me
> Would grow lovesick and from her wat'ry bower
> Fling down Endymion and snatch him up.
> Then blame not me that slay a silly man
> Not half so lovely as Endymion. (14.145–50)

The inappropriateness of the comparison between Mosby and Endymion is obvious. Endymion was the type of beautiful boy inducing helpless passion even in the chaste moon goddess. Mosby is described by Holinshed as 'a black swart man'; Diana, emblem of chastity, is not an obvious role for Alice Arden. The incongruity between this language of love and the sordid murder plan draws attention to the gap between Alice's actions and her fantasies about them. Alice's self-delusion is both pathetic and morally culpable; the tension between the two, which has animated the whole play, is held in place by this use of language.

The use of high-flown language to obfuscate the immorality of sexual relations is treated more self-consciously in the comedies. Laxton's letter to Mrs Gallipot, full of references to classical love stories, is obviously insincere. The comedy comes from Mrs Gallipot's inability to read the unfamiliar names, far less understand the allusions. Her ignorance means that she does not understand that Pandarus was not Cressida's lover but her pimp, and that the 'man beneath the silver moon' (*The Roaring Girl*, 3.2.57) (Endymion again) did not love Diana as much as she him. The joke goes completely over her head, creating a bond of comic collusion between Laxton and the witty young men of the implied audience. Mrs Gallipot, however, is not too stupid to see that the letter is a plea for money. Her down-to-earth understanding turns the joke back on Laxton, making for a much more complex comic dynamic which mocks Laxton as much as the citizen women. Mrs Gallipot, too, is able to turn linguistic style to her own account. Her lament to her husband evokes the metaphors of tragedy, comparing herself to 'a fixèd star / Placed only in the heaven of thine arms' (3.2.100–1), and the daring fiction of her precontract with Laxton is couched in the rhetorical elaborations of classical narratives (3.2.120–5). The simple distinction between plain truth and false poetry cannot be sustained. What is at issue is the comic clash of different rhetorical styles. When Openwork moralizes on the evils of wearing masks in 4.2, the abstractions of his speech, the long-winded comparisons and analogies and the commonplace examples all mark it out as part of a tradition of moralizing found in ballads and moral books. The sentiments are in keeping with conventional citizen morality, but the tedium of their expression reminds us that Openwork is playing a part. Mrs Openwork has already (4.2.35–9) told him of the plot to sail to Brentford, and his interception is planned. As the scene develops, however, it is hard to keep that subterfuge in mind. Openwork's expressions of astonishment at his wife's passion could, in a different context, be presented as perfectly sincere. All the characters use language as a way of obfuscating their real positions in a style which is part of the rich comic texture of the play.

Language and style, then, set up a hierarchy of knowledge and power on the stage. Those who could use language most subtly and at the expense of others' misunderstanding set up a connection to the audience which transcends the action of the plot, or the lines of moral approval. This is particularly the case in the comedies' knowing, witty use of sexual innuendo. The plays' language harps constantly on the physical appearance of the male and female genitals and their connection in sex, together with the most obvious variations and failures of intercourse. Understanding this bawdy requires no more than the perfervid imagination of a smutty school-boy, for every reference to a rod or a hole or a ball, or anything similarly shaped, can lend itself to sexualized innuendo. Similarly the actions of lying or standing or rubbing or rocking or beating, swelling or standing, can almost always, in comedy, be read with a sexual meaning. As with all dramatic meaning, however, these puns and innuendoes are not unambiguously present. To unpack a sexual metaphor into other language, to gloss, for example, 'dart' as 'prick' or 'penis',[60] only invokes a different sexual discourse, the slang or the medical, itself involving buried metaphors. For example in *A Chaste Maid* the Fourth Gossip, exiting in procession, remarks, 'There comes as proud behind as goes before', and her friend agrees 'Every inch, i' faith' (2.4.19–20). The exchange is one of platitudes which have characterized the gossips all along, but Allwit's presence and the fact that 'proud' can mean 'sexually erect' opens up a penumbra of surrounding meaning to do with anal intercourse and the sexual voracity of citizen women. We cannot know if the connection was in Middleton's mind or in the original performance. It is one of the potentialities of the scene's comedy, available for, but not necessarily insisted on, in performance.

All through the plays, the bawdy provides localized pleasure of humour. At the same time, it also draws attention to particular moments in the narrative. When Touchwood Junior tricks Yellowhammer into making a ring for his own daughter (1.1.183–220), the question of the size and shape of her finger produces a string of bawdy innuendo on the connection between fingers and penises, sexualizing the act of putting a ring on a finger. Touchwood Junior cannot find the ring measurement and exclaims:

Good faith, 'tis down; I cannot show 't you,
I must pull too many things out to be certain.   (1.1.193–4)

Yellowhammer picks up the bawdy joke in his suggestion that Touchwood will have to 'venture by [Moll's] finger' (1.1.200). Even so, his greed for the commission blinds him to the larger joke of his implication in his own daughter's unauthorized wedding. Bawdy establishes a comic hierarchy between those who understand the joke and those who do not; Middleton takes this further in mocking those who are knowing about sexual jokes but ignorant of the larger action.

Bawdy can be activated in reading and performance. At the same time, its effects are more than a local double entendre; they will inflect the overall tone and dynamic of the scenes in which they appear, deflating pomposity and affectation, giving an edge of violence or danger to other kinds of encounter or just reminding the audience of the physicality of characters which underlies their social status and relationship to power.

The extent to which these innuendoes work in the dynamics of performance depends on the decisions of actors and directors. At worst, they can be underscored with leering and nudging; more subtly, they can provide an undercurrent which make an alert audience aware of how sexualized the social world of the play is, particularly when the stage is full of groups of men. Sexual innuendo is not restricted to the individual pun or joke. It is part of social exchange and is used to characterize the weighty bonhomie of such old bores as Sir Alexander Wengrave with his tedious witticisms about chairs and standing (*The Roaring Girl*, 1.2.55–8), or the low-level sexual harassment of female servants in the dancing scenes of *A Woman Killed*.

In *The Roaring Girl*, Moll Cutpurse's use of sexual language is not only original in coming from a woman, it also gives Moll particular theatrical power, making her not only the equal but superior to the men. Where Goshawk and Greenwit's bawdy language is a matter of clichéd analogies and laboured puns (see especially 2.1.61–7), Moll's is densely and wittily textured with an undertow of bawdy which is never insisted on but always present. She is quick-tempered with Mrs Openwork's rudeness and retorts with a diatribe of witty terms for prostitution (2.1.216–22). She uses the same quick wit against the 'Fellow *with a long rapier*', challenging his maleness by taking on his clichéd oath, 'by this light', literally and metaphorically contrasting the light of day with the candlelight of the night when he insulted her (2.1.230–4). Her quick wit and openness to sexual banter are shown most effectively when Laxton suggests the assignation out of town (2.1.250–76). By punning and playing on all his suggestions, she both transcends narrow-minded moralizing and escapes any commitment to his plans.

The sexualized culture which produced the constant drive to bawdy was informed also by the contemporary science of the human body and by an attempt to understand the processes of procreation in scientific terms. The common scientific understanding of the body was, at this time, informed both by the Galenic science of governing humours—the idea that the balance of bodily fluids determined the physical and psychological aspects of human behaviour—and by an awareness of physiology, informed by the emergent art of dissection.[61] Nonetheless, scientific discourse was not completely separated off from other kinds of language. Images of the body as an organism informed non-scientific ways of talking about the vulnerability and volatility of early modern people. These images were only partly metaphorical. Before the circulation of the blood and the role of the lymph system was understood, the humours theory offered a view of the body in which the whole interior was teeming with fluids (blood, bile, water). These fluids had to be kept in balance in order to lead a healthy life. Women's wombs could wander up to the heart, causing a sensation of suffocation, called 'the mother', and young women, like Moll in *A Chaste Maid*, suffered from a vegetable kind of condition called greensickness which could be cured by sexual intercourse and the filling of their bodies with reviving and strengthening male sperm. Allwit refers to the cuckold's horror that he should 'feed the wife plump for another's veins' (1.2.48) and laughs that Sir Walter's 'marrow melts' with jealousy. The early modern theory of humours envisaged all bodily fluids as interchangeable. Blood, semen, tears and urine came from the same source and had their effects on psychological as well as physical characteristics. So Lady Kix's tears dry up her fertility, not merely because she was depressed but because losing vital juices in the form of tears reduced those available for procreation, weeping her 'to a dry ground' (3.3.13).[62]

The supposed influence of the humours on both the physical and the psychological informs the language used to express and describe emotions. Psychological states are articulated in physical terms without any constraining sense of mixed metaphor. The disturbed Mosby complains:

> Disturbèd thoughts drives me from company
> And dries my marrow with their watchfulness.   (*Arden*, 8.1–2)

His thoughts are both personified in 'watchfulness' and also have a direct drying effect on his marrow. At the same time, these ways of talking about emotions and moods are also folded into and intercut with other images, often to startling effect. Mosby continues:

> Continual trouble of my moody brain
> Feebles my body by excess of drink
> And nips me as the bitter northeast wind
> Doth check the tender blossoms in the spring.   (8.3–6)

The confusion of these lines illustrates the way that different styles of language and clusters of metaphors can run into one another as the writers draw eclectically from a huge variety of sources. The fluids of the brain slide into a reference to the enfeebling dangers of drink (both metaphorically drinking sorrow but with a buried reference to alcoholic drinking), and then the image shifts entirely to the simile connecting the nipping of conscience to the northeast wind.

Scientific discourse similarly slides into bawdy, especially when questions of sexuality and sexual behaviour are involved. In *The Roaring Girl*, the figure of Moll Cutpurse, in particular, generates a rich mix of sexual, scientific and moral language. Moll does not abide by feminine decorum, and so she is described as both monstrously hermaphrodite and also sexually available and exciting to all the men she encounters. Sir Alexander, as befits his age and social standing, describes her most scientifically but also most superstitiously:

>   It is a thing
> One knows not how to name: her birth began
> Ere she was all made. 'Tis woman more than man,
> Man more than woman, and—which to none can hap—
> The sun gives her two shadows to one shape.   (1.2.129–33)

Dissection showed that the vagina was a sheath, shaped in some diagrams as an inverted penis; this combined with the Galenic view that girls were formed when there was insufficient bodily heat (or a deficiency of hot humours) to complete the process of generation to form a boy. In Sir Alexander's view, Moll's generation had stopped after a cold woman would have been produced but did not proceed all the way to being a man. The notion that the sun would produce two separate shadows is a fanciful expression of Sir Alexander's sense of the prodigious nature of the phenomenon.

The language used to describe Moll seems to generate images out of itself without necessarily touching down on any clear point of reference. When Sir Alexander describes Moll as 'a mermaid / Has tolled my son to shipwreck', he connects the idea that mermaids are half fish, half human both to his view that Moll is a hermaphrodite, half man, half woman (1.2.215–16), and to the image of mermaids luring men to their doom. The simple implication is that Moll is a whore—or at the least the ruin of young Sebastian. Trapdoor, however, replies 'I'll cut her comb for you' (1.2.217). He goes beyond the slang connections between mermaids, or sirens, and whores to play on the image of a mermaid's comb and the practice of castrating cockerels by cutting off their combs. He implies that he can castrate Moll since she is imagined to have both sets of genitals. Each joke and reference cannot be appreciated separately. They serve rather to reinforce a normative view of sexuality and at the same time to acknowledge the impossibility of doing so. Every relationship between men and women is potentially sexualized. The different discourses of sex cut across and undermine any simple moral or social definition of sexual relations and, in the case of Moll Cutpurse, even call into question the biological differences between the sexes.

Trapdoor's versatility with language dramatizes the instability of early modern concepts of sexuality. It is also a bravura set piece of linguistic play which is witty in itself, offered as one of the multifarious pleasures of theatrical performance. Language in these set pieces slides away from its social referent and becomes a kind of game. When Trapdoor comes to tell Sir Alexander of the assignation between Moll and Sebastian (3.3.5–48), he spins out this simple information into another explosion of puns. He says that Moll will come in a 'shirt of mail' (3.3.19) which he immediately glosses as 'a male shirt, that's to say, in man's apparel' (3.3.21). When Sir Alexander asks after his son, Trapdoor puns on 'son' and 'sun', with 'your son and her moon will be in conjunction, if all almanacs lie not' (3.3.23–4). He continues with an extended account of the transformation of Moll's women's clothes to men's, ending with the bawdy suggestion that both sets of clothing are metaphors for sex: 'you shall take 'em both with standing collars' (3.3.27). The sequence derives from the play's preoccupation with Moll's ambiguous sexuality and Sir Alexander's plot to thwart his son's marriage, but those considerations are subordinated to the speed and energy of Trapdoor's wit.

The sheer skill involved in such linguistic virtuosity should not be taken for granted. It drew on more commonplace linguistic connections which at other moments in *The Roaring Girl* are presented in more laboured fashion.

Sir Alexander's extended comparison between his son's unruliness and a faulty clock (2.2.101–13), or his elaborate parallels between a prison and a university (3.3.80–103), characterize his tedious moralizing, the antithesis of the spirited linguistic virtuosity of the younger generation. They also fill out the scenes, illustrating the way that the dramatists construct their plays from the raw materials of convention and set piece.

The ability to link set-piece linguistic performance to narrative and theme is by no means equally evident in all the plays. When Michael and the painter, Clarke, confront one another over Susan's love (*Arden*, 10.47–73), they too begin with a contest of wit, but their lumbering puns depend upon such laboured comparisons as to be almost incomprehensible. The scene does give a sense of their inarticulate but nonetheless powerful aggression, an expression of the seething and random violence which infests the world of the play. Exchange of language in this world is only the preliminary to physical violence; the scene ends with the alternative theatrical pleasure of a fight.

A well-managed stage fight[63] and a virtuoso display of wit mark the ends of a spectrum of theatrical pleasures offered by these four plays (and much of early modern drama). The plays could incorporate the localized pleasures of fighting, or singing or poetic recitation or clowning, and connect them to multiple plots whose stories and settings linked them to the world of their audiences. The versatility of theatrical form which the dramatists deployed was in part a result of the moment in theatre history in which they wrote. The theatre was attracting significant economic resources as it moved into the commercial market; those who worked within it were also able to draw on an enormous stock of theatrical, literary and linguistic resources. The dramatists' and the performers' skills were to transform those resources, turning comedy motifs into tragedy and back again, pushing at the boundaries of comic and tragic convention, exploiting the fluidity of language to create new forms, dramatizing—and in the process calling into question—the traditional connections between stories and their morals.

The new dynamism and change which were invigorating the theatre were also present in the life world of its audiences. Changes in the tenure of land, in the growth and organisation of cities and the attendant shifts in social relationships found an echo in the plays which in turn re-articulated them into the theatrical pleasures of suspense and laughter, emotional engagement and moral concern. Those theatrical pleasures have given the plays a place, albeit on the margins, of the modern classic repertory.[64] They are also part of the insight which the plays provide into the social world of early modern women and men.

FURTHER READING

The recognition that early modern drama is centrally concerned with the cultural and social role of women owes everything to the work of feminist scholars. The plays in this collection should be read in the context of books by Jean E. Howard, *The Stage and Social Struggle in Early Modern England* (London: Routledge, 1994); Frances E. Dolan, *Dangerous Familiars: Representations of Domestic Crime in England 1550–1700* (Ithaca and London: Cornell University Press, 1994); Lena Orlin, *Private Matters and Public Culture in Post-Reformation England* (Ithaca and London: Cornell University Press, 1994); Laura Gowing, *Domestic Dangers: Women, Words and Sex in Early Modern London* (Oxford: Clarendon Press, 1996) and Stephen Orgel, *Impersonations: The Performance of Gender in Shakespeare's England* (Cambridge: Cambridge University Press, 1996).

The plays were formed in the history of early modern London, a topic dealt with in fascinating detail by Ian W. Archer, *The Pursuit of Stability: Social Relations in Elizabethan London* (Cambridge: Cambridge University Press, 1991). They deal with relations between the city and the world beyond. Different views about those relations are dealt with in Jeremy Boulton, *Neighbourhood and Society: A London Suburb in the Seventeenth Century* (Cambridge: Cambridge University Press, 1987) and Steven Mullaney, *The Place of the Stage License: Play and Power in Renaissance England* (Chicago: University of Chicago Press, 1988).

Our sense of both that history and the version of it used for early modern drama depend on a complex interaction of material conditions and their representation in written texts. That interaction is the subject of Lawrence Manly, *Literature and Culture in Early Modern London* (Cambridge: Cambridge University Press, 1995). Essays from historians and critics on the culture of London are collected in David L. Smith, Richard Strier and David Bevington, eds, *The Theatrical City: Culture, Theatre and Politics in London 1576–1649* (Cambridge: Cambridge University Press, 1996).

The theatrical context which informed these plays is extensively analysed in the wide-ranging essays collected in John D. Cox and David Scott Kastan, eds, *A New History of Early English Drama* (New York: Columbia University Press, 1997). A magisterial overview of the drama is provided by G. K. Hunter, *English Drama 1586–1642* (Oxford: Clarendon Press, 1997).

NOTES

1 Constantia Munda, *The Worming of a Mad Dogge; or a Soppe for Cerberus the Iaylor of Hell* (London, 1617), sig. A2. Quotations from early modern texts have been silently modernized. Women's attendance at the theatre is discussed in Kathleen E. McLuskie, *Renaissance Dramatists* (Hemel Hempstead: Harvester Wheatsheaf, 1989), 87–99, and Jean Howard, *The Stage and Social Struggle in Early Modern England* (London: Routledge, 1994), 73–92.

2 More fully discussed in Kathleen E. McLuskie, 'Lawless Desires well Tempered', in *Erotic Politics: Desire on the Renaissance Stage*, ed. Susan Zimmerman (London: Routledge, 1992), 103–26.

3 *Arden of Faversham* was written some time between 1577 and the first edition in 1592. The characteristics of its text associate it with Pembroke's Men, a company which played in London and on provincial tours between 1592 and

1600. Roslyn Knutson has argued that its republication in 1599 may have been connected to a revival by the Chamberlain's Men. See E. K. Chambers, *The Elizabethan Stage* (Oxford: Clarendon Press, 1923), 128–34 and Roslyn Knutson, *The Repertory of Shakespeare's Company, 1594–1613* (Fayetteville: University of Arkansas Press, 1991), 45, 68, 115. *A Woman Killed with Kindness* was performed by Worcester's Men at the Rose in 1603; *The Roaring Girl* was performed at the Fortune Theatre by Queen Anne's Men between 1608 and 1611 and *A Chaste Maid in Cheapside* was produced by the Lady Elizabeth's Men at the Swan in 1613. For a full discussion of the dating of these plays see the original Revels editions: *Arden of Faversham*, ed. M. L. Wine (London: Methuen, 1973); Thomas Heywood, *A Woman Killed with Kindness*, ed. R. W. van Fossen (London: Methuen, 1961); Thomas Middleton and Thomas Dekker, *The Roaring Girl*, ed. Paul A. Mulholland (Manchester: Manchester University Press, 1987); Thomas Middleton, *A Chaste Maid in Cheapside*, ed. R. B. Parker (London: Methuen, 1969).

4 See Michael Shapiro, *Children of the Revels: The Boy Companies of Shakespeare's Time and Their Plays* (New York: Columbia University Press, 1977). On the competition between playing companies, see Andrew Gurr, *Playgoing in Shakespeare's London* (Cambridge: Cambridge University Press, 1987), 147–64.

5 Mulholland (1987, 262) has suggested that this refers to the appearance of Moll Cutpurse recorded in the Consistory of London Correction Book: 'being at a playe about 3 quarters of a yeare since at the ffortune in mans apparell & in her bootes & with a sword by her syde . . . And also sat there vppon the stage in the publique viewe of all the people there presente in mans apparell & playd vppon her lute and sange a songe'. See Mulholland, 'The Date of the Roaring Girl', *Review of English Studies*, n.s. 28 (1977), 19–20.

6 On the continuity of domestic narrative in the representation of women, see Laura Mulvey, 'Melodrama Inside and Outside the Home', in *Visual and Other Pleasures* (London: Macmillan, 1989), 63–77.

7 For example, Shakespeare's Lady Macbeth and Cleopatra, Marston's Sophonisba, Dorothea in Dekker's *The Virgin Martyr* or the Protestant martyr heroine of *The Duchess of Suffolk*.

8 See Elizabeth Cary, *The Tragedy of Mariam The Fair Queen of Jewry*, eds Barry Weller and Margaret W. Ferguson (Berkeley: University of California Press, 1994).

9 See *Henslowe's Diary*, eds R. A. Foakes and R. T. Rickert (Cambridge: Cambridge University Press, 1961), and the discussion of the evidence in Neil Carson, *A Companion to Henslowe's Diary* (Cambridge: Cambridge University Press, 1988); also Roslyn L. Knutson, 'The Repertory', in John D. Cox and David Scott Kastan, eds, *A New History of Early English Drama* (New York: Columbia University Press, 1997), 461–80.

10 Most notably, the so-called 'Works' of Ben Jonson and William Shakespeare were published in large Folio volumes, but this was extremely unusual. See Jeffrey Masten, 'Playwrighting: Authorship and Collaboration', in Cox and Kastan, eds, *New History*, 357–82.

11 On the controversy over the authorship, see Wine, *Arden*, Introduction, lxxxi–xcii. For a list of parallel passages connecting *Arden* to contemporary drama, see Wine, *Arden*, Appendix 1.

12 See Greg, *Henslowe's Diary*, 2.55, and Van Fossen, *Woman Killed*, Introduction, xv–xvi.

13 See Kathleen E. McLuskie, *Dekker and Heywood, Professional Dramatists* (London: Macmillan, 1994), 138–44.

14 See H. N. Hillebrand, *The Child Actors: A Chapter in Elizabethan Stage History* (Urbana: University of Illinois Press, 1926; reprint, New York: Russell and Russell, 1964) and G. K. Hunter, 'The Boy Actors and the New Dramaturgy' in *English Drama 1586–1642* (Oxford: Clarendon Press, 1997), 279–359.

15 Thomas Middleton, *The Blacke Booke* (1604) in A. H. Bullen, ed., *The Works of Thomas Middleton* (1886), 8, 35–6.

16 See Mary Edmond, 'In Search of John Webster', *Times Literary Supplement* (24 December 1976), 1621–2.

17 *The Magnificent Entertainment*, in *The Dramatic Works of Thomas Dekker*, ed. Fredson Bowers (Cambridge: Cambridge University Press, 1955), 2.230–303.

18 Thomas Dekker, *The Wonderful Year*, ed. G. B. Harrison (London: Bodley Head, 1924).

19 The theatrical implications of boys playing women are discussed in McLuskie, *Renaissance Dramatists*, chapter 5, 100–22; Peter Stallybrass, 'Transvestism and the "Body Beneath": Speculating on the Boy Actor', in Zimmerman, ed., *Erotic Politics*, 64–83, and Stephen Orgel, *Impersonations, The Performance of Gender in Shakespeare's England* (Cambridge: Cambridge University Press, 1996).

20 See Christine Eccles, *The Rose Theatre* (New York: Nick Hern Books, 1990).

21 See S. P. Ceresano, 'Raising a Playhouse from the Dust', *Shakespeare Quarterly*, 40 (1989), 483–90. Dennis Kennedy, *Looking at Shakespeare* (Cambridge: Cambridge University Press, 1993), Chapter 1, 'Shakespeare and the visual', presents a critical account of the relationship between scenography and performance.

22 See Lena Orlin, *Private Matters and Public Culture in Post-Reformation England* (Ithaca: Cornell University Press, 1994), and Diana E. Henderson, 'The Theatre and Domestic Culture', in Cox and Kastan, eds, *New History*, 153–72.

23 These images existed theatrically in the miracle plays of the Trial of Christ, the Fall of the Angels and the Woman Taken in Adultery from the York and N-Town cycles; they also had a continuing cultural impact through their representation in tapestries, painted cloths and printed images which were used as domestic decoration. See Tessa Watt, *Cheap Print and Popular Piety 1550–1640* (Cambridge: Cambridge University Press, 1991).

24 See *If You Know Not Me You Know Nobody* part 1, and *Edward IV* part 2, discussed in McLuskie, *Dekker and Heywood*, 42–3, 89–90.

25 Compare for example the emblematic use of children in Webster, *The Duchess of Malfi* (1613), the use of torture in Chapman, *Bussy D'Ambois*, 4.2, Celia's plea to be tortured in *Volpone*, 3.7.252–57, and the collapsed time-frame for adultery in *Othello* and in *The Duchess of Malfi*.

26 See especially Ian W. Archer, *The Pursuit of Stability: Social Relations in Elizabethan London* (Cambridge: Cambridge University Press, 1991), and, on Southwark, the theatre area, Jeremy Boulton, *Neighbourhood and Society: A London Suburb in the Seventeenth Century* (Cambridge: Cambridge University Press, 1987).

27 See Lawrence Manley, *Literature and Culture in Early Modern London* (Cambridge: Cambridge University Press, 1995), especially chapter 3, 'From matron to monster: London and the languages of description', 125–67.

28 On the role of women in Puritan culture see Patrick Collinson, *The Birthpangs of Protestant England: Religious and Cultural Change in the Sixteenth and Seventeenth Centuries* (London: Macmillan, 1988), 74–7. Collinson also discusses the importance of the theatre in creating the public image of the Puritan out of the complex political and theological divisions of Protestant reformers in 'The Theatre Constructs Puritanism', in David L. Smith, Richard Strier and David Bevington, eds, *The Theatrical City: Culture, Theatre and Politics in London 1576–1649* (Cambridge: Cambridge University Press, 1997), 157–69.

29 See for example Dunbar's 'The Twa Merrit Women and the Wedo'; Skelton's 'The Tunning of Eleanor Rumming', and Reynolds, ''Tis Merry When Gossips Meet'.

30 See Laura Gowing, *Domestic Dangers: Women, Words and Sex in Early Modern London* (Oxford: Clarendon Press, 1996).

31 See Archer, *The Pursuit of Stability*, 63, 130.

32 Letter from John Chamberlain to Dudley Carleton, quoted in Mulholland, 'The Date of the Roaring Girl', 25.

33 See Lesley Ferris, *Crossing the Stage: Controversies on Cross Dressing* (London: Routledge, 1993), and Jean Howard, 'Sex and Social Conflict: The Erotics of *The Roaring Girl*', in Zimmerman, ed., *Erotic Politics*, 170–90.

34 See Simon Shepherd, 'What's So Funny About Ladies' Tailors? A Survey of Some Male (Homo)sexual Types in the Renaissance', *Textual Practice*, 6.1 (1993), 17–30.

35 Compare the fights between Sir Andrew Aguecheek and first Viola and then Sebastian in *Twelfth Night*. Heywood used the same comic device in *Fair Maid of the West*, where Bess in disguise beats and humiliates the bully, Roughman.

36 See Mulholland, *Roaring Girl*, Introduction, 39.

37 On marriage law and its enforcement, see Martin Ingram, *Church Courts, Sex and Marriage in England, 1570–1640* (Cambridge: Cambridge University Press, 1987).

38 Compare Shakebag's preference for fighting 'with hands and feet', *Arden*, 14.57–65.

39 See Simon Shepherd, *Amazons and Warrior Women* (Hemel Hempstead: Harvester Wheatsheaf, 1981), 67–92, and Mulholland, *Roaring Girl*, Appendix D, 258–60.

40 Compare Shakespeare, *Cymbeline*, in which Iachimo bets Posthumous that he can seduce Posthumous's new wife Imogen. He fails to do so, but convinces Posthumous that he has been successful by showing him a bracelet which he has stolen from Imogen and describing her bedroom.

41 Christopher Hill, 'Social and Economic Consequences of the Henrician Revolution', in *Puritanism and Revolution* (London: Secker and Warburg, 1958); Christopher Kitching, 'The Disposal of Monastic and Chantry Lands', in Felicity Heal and Rosemary O'Day, eds, *Church and Society in England: Henry VIII to James I* (London: Macmillan, 1977).

42 See 13.22–5, where Arden threatens to take Reede to court for slander.

43 See Holinshed's account of this episode in Wine, *Arden*, Appendix II, 157.

44 Discussed in greater detail in Orlin, *Private Matters*.

45 N. B. Harte, 'State Control of Dress and Social Change in Pre-industrial England', in D. C. Coleman and A. H. John, eds, *Trade, Government and Economy in Pre-industrial England* (London: Weidenfeld and Nicolson, 1976), 132–65.

46 See Wine, *Arden*, Appendix II, 155, Appendix III, 161.

47 The conventions of representing assassins on stage are discussed by Martin Wiggins, *Journeymen in Murder: The Assassin in English Renaissance Drama* (Oxford: Clarendon Press, 1991). The similarities between Black Will and Shakebag and both Kyd's comic murderer in *The Spanish Tragedy* and the assassins of Clarence in Shakespeare's *Richard III* have informed discussions of the authorship of the play. See Wine, *Arden*, lxxxix–xc.

48 See J. A. Sharpe, *Defamation and Sexual Slander in Early Modern England: The Church Courts at York*, Borthwick Papers 58 (York: St Antony's Press, 1981).

49 See Susan Amussen, *An Ordered Society: Gender and Class in Early Modern England* (Oxford: Blackwell, 1988).

50 Gowing, *Domestic Dangers*, 233.

51 See Linda Austern, '"Sing againe Syren": The Female Musician and Sexual Enchantment in Elizabethan Life and Literature', *Renaissance Quarterly*, 42 (1989), 42–8.

52 Compare, for example, Celia in Jonson's *Volpone*, 3.7.252–7. See Leonard Tennenhouse, *Power on Display: The Politics of Shakespeare's Genres* (London: Methuen, 1986), and Jonathan Sawday, *The Body Emblazoned* (London: Routledge, 1995).

53 See Lorna Hutson, *The Usurer's Daughter: Male Friendship and Fictions of Women in Sixteenth-century England* (London: Routledge, 1994).

54 A production of the play at the Old Vic in 1970 had a real hawk flying round the auditorium, creating the additional pleasure of watching the hawker's skill.

55 See Hutson, *The Usurer's Daughter*, 130–4.

56 Compare Mosby in *Arden*, Iago in Shakespeare's *Othello*, and Hammon in Dekker's *The Shoemaker's Holiday*—all disruptive figures who have no social connections in the world of the plays.

57 See Joyce Oldham Appleby, *Economic Thought and Ideology in Seventeenth-century England* (Princeton: Princeton University Press, 1978), and Laura Stevenson, *Praise and Paradox: Merchants and Craftsmen in Elizabethan Popular Literature* (Cambridge: Cambridge University Press, 1984).

58 See Ingram, *Church Courts*, 27–69, and Collinson, *Birthpangs*, 28–59.

59 *Nice Wanton*, in *Specimens of the Pre-Shaksperean Drama*, ed. John M. Manly (New York: Dover Publications, 1967), I, 457–82.

60 As in the Welsh Gentlewoman's song in *Chaste Maid*, 4.1.169–74. This is a perennial problem for editors in their efforts to clarify the sexual language against misunderstanding. For different solutions see *Thomas Middleton: Five Plays*, eds Brian Loughrey and Neil Taylor (London, Penguin, 1988), which uses modern slang, giving a coarser and more direct account of the play's bawdy language.

61 See Sawday, *The Body Emblazoned*.

62 See Gail Kern Paster, *The Body Embarrassed: Drama and the Disciplines of Shame in Early Modern England* (Ithaca: Cornell University Press, 1993), 50–63.

63 Compare the fights in *The Roaring Girl*, 3.1. and *A Chaste Maid*, 4.4.

64 *A Chaste Maid* was chosen as one of the plays for the first season of the reconstructed Globe Theatre in London in 1997. *The Roaring Girl* (along with Shakespeare's *The Taming of the Shrew*) was produced in the Royal Shakespeare Company season in 1983. The Royal Shakespeare company also produced *Arden of Faversham* in 1982 and *A Woman Killed with Kindness* in 1991.

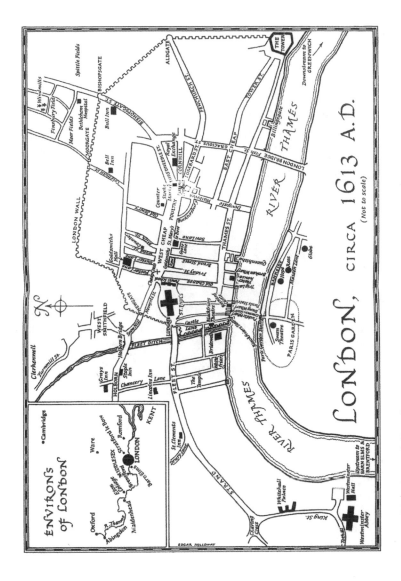

Map of London *c.* A.D. 1613

Johannes De Witt's drawing of the Swan Theatre *c.* 1596

The Roaring Girle.

OR
Moll Cut-Purse.

As it hath lately beene Acted on the Fortune-ftage by
the Prince his Players.

Written by *T. Middleton* and *T. Dekker*.

My cafe is alter'd, I muft worke for my liuing.

Printed at *London* for *Thomas Archer*, and are to be fold at his
fhop in Popes head-pallace, neere the Royall
Exchange. 1611.

Title page of the 1611 Quarto of *The Roaring Girl*

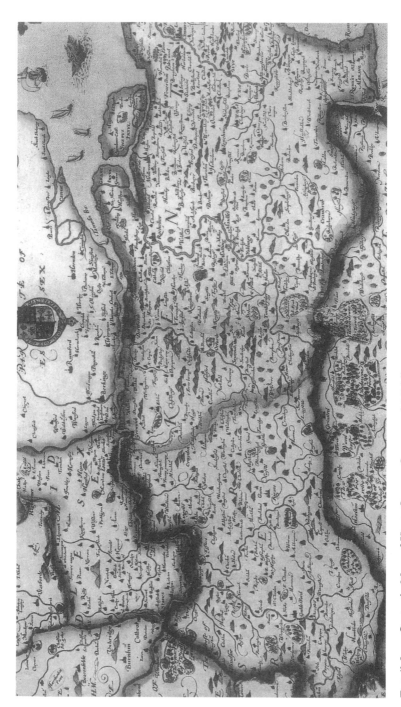

Detail from Saxton's Map of Kent, Sussex, Surrey and Middlesex, 1575

Frontispiece to the 1633 Quarto of *Arden of Faversham*, illustrating the murder of Arden at the 'game of tables'

A CHASTE MAID
IN CHEAPSIDE

THE NAMES OF THE PRINCIPAL PERSONS

MR YELLOWHAMMER, *a goldsmith.*
MAUDLIN, *his wife.*
TIM, *their son.*
MOLL, *their daughter.*
TUTOR *to Tim.*   5
SIR WALTER WHOREHOUND, *a suitor to Moll.*
SIR OLIVER KIX *and*
HIS WIFE, *kin to Sir Walter.*
MR ALLWIT *and*
HIS WIFE, *whom Sir Walter keeps.*   10
WELSH GENTLEWOMAN, *Sir Walter's whore.*
WAT *and* NICK, *his bastards.*
DAVY DAHUMMA, *his man.*
TOUCHWOOD SENIOR, *a decayed gentleman, and*
HIS WIFE.   15
TOUCHWOOD JUNIOR, *another suitor to Moll.*
Two Promoters.
Servants.
[Two] Watermen.
[A Parson.   20
A Country Wench.
A Maid to Sir Oliver *and* Lady Kix.
A Porter.
A Gentleman.
A Dry Nurse *to Mrs Allwit's baby.*   25
A Wet Nurse *to Mrs Allwit's baby.*
A Midwife.
Two Men, *with meat in their baskets.*
Two Puritan Women.
Five Gossips.   30

SCENE: LONDON.]

---

1. *YELLOWHAMMER*] (1) describing his occupation as a goldsmith; (2) a bird; (3) slang for a gold coin.

4. *MOLL*] The original name for this character may have been Mary, as she is called in one of the stage directions in the original text. 'Moll', however was a name associated with prostitutes. See *Roaring Girl*, 2.2.147–75.

7. *OLIVER KIX*] Kix (or Kex) means a dry, hollow plant stalk; figuratively 'a dried up, sapless person'.

9. *ALLWIT*] inversion of wittol, a willing cuckold.

13. *DAHUMMA*] means 'come hither' in Welsh, so, a generic name for a servant.

14. *TOUCHWOOD*] tinder; especially used for tinder to ignite the touchhole of a musket, with bawdy implication.
decayed] fallen from prosperity.

17. *Promoters*] informers.

19. *Watermen*] boatmen offering a taxi service on the Thames.

Act 1

[1.1]

Enter MAUDLIN *and* MOLL, *a shop being discovered.*

Maudlin. Have you played over all your old lessons o' the virginals?

Moll. Yes.

Maudlin. Yes? You are a dull maid o' late, methinks; you had need have somewhat to quicken your greensickness—do you   5
weep?—a husband! Had not such a piece of flesh been ordained, what had us wives been good for?—to make salads, or else cried up and down for samphire. To see the difference of these seasons! When I was of your youth, I was lightsome and quick two years before I was married. You fit for a knight's   10
bed! Drowsy-browed, dull-eyed, drossy-spirited! I hold my life you have forgot your dancing. When was the dancer with you?

Moll. The last week.

Maudlin. Last week! When I was of your bord, he missed me not a   15
night; I was kept at it; I took delight to learn, and he to teach me. Pretty brown gentleman, he took pleasure in my company.

1.1.0.1. discovered] revealed on stage.

2. *virginals*] square legless spinet (with a sexual quibble).

5. *quicken*] revive (with a suggestion of becoming pregnant).

greensickness] chlorosis, an anaemic illness in young women which made them lethargic. It was seen as caused by love sickness and cured by sexual intercourse.

6. *a piece of flesh*] i.e. a penis; a husband is reduced to his genitals.

7. *to make salads*] to become salads (because of being green).

8. *cried up and down*] shouted for sale in the street.

samphire] a kind of seaweed thought to provoke urine and menstruation by opening up the stopped entrails.

9. *lightsome*] light hearted, frivolous.

10. *quick*] (1) lively; (2) 'pregnant'. Lines 9–21 are an extended passage of *double entendre*. See Intro., p. 46.

11. *drossy-spirited*] the antithesis of *lightsome* (line 9). In alchemical discourse the *dross* was what remained after the process of refinement had removed the valuable elements from a compound.

hold] bet.

15. *bord*] (1) bore, calibre; (2) quality, condition.

15–16. *missed . . . night*] (1) taught me every evening; (2) slept with me nightly. The *double entendre* continues.

17. *brown*] dark-complexioned.

But you are dull, nothing comes nimbly from you; you dance
like a plumber's daughter, and deserve two thousand pound in
lead to your marriage, and not in goldsmith's ware.   20

Enter YELLOWHAMMER.

Yellowhammer. Now, what's the din betwixt mother and daughter,
    ha?
Maudlin. Faith, small; telling your daughter Mary of her errors.
Yellowhammer. Errors? Nay, the city cannot hold you, wife, but you
    must needs fetch words from Westminster. I ha' done, i' faith!   25
    Has no attorney's clerk been here o' late and changed his half-
    crown-piece his mother sent him, or rather cozened you with a
    gilded twopence, to bring the word in fashion for her faults or
    cracks in duty and obedience? Term 'em e'en so, sweet wife. As
    there is no woman made without a flaw,   30
    Your purest lawns have frays and cambrics bracks.
Maudlin. But 'tis a husband solders up all cracks.
Moll. What, is he come, sir?
Yellowhammer. Sir Walter's come.
    He was met at Holborn Bridge, and in his company   35
    A proper fair young gentlewoman, which I guess
    By her red hair and other rank descriptions
    To be his landed niece brought out of Wales,
    Which Tim our son, the Cambridge boy, must marry.
    'Tis a match of Sir Walter's own making,   40
    To bind us to him and our heirs for ever.
Maudlin. We are honoured, then, if this baggage would be humble

---

25. *fetch . . . Westminster*] i.e. use French expressions like the law-French used in
the courts at Westminster.

27–8. *cozened . . . twopence*] i.e. cheated you with a silver two-penny piece, gilded
to look like gold.

28. *to . . . faults*] to bring in the fashion of calling faults, or failures in duty and
obedience, 'errors'.

29. *cracks*] weaknesses, failures.

Term . . . so] i.e. Go ahead, do call Moll's faults 'errors' (sarcastically).

31. *lawns, cambrics*] fine white linens.

bracks] flaws.

32. *solders . . . cracks*] (1) makes good all faults; (2) fills up all crevices (with a
sexual meaning).

35. *Holborn Bridge*] carrying the main road from Wales across Fleet Ditch to
enter the city through Newgate.

36. *proper*] fine.

37. *rank*] (1) indicating high status; (2) coarse, unrefined.

38. *landed*] owning land.

39. *must*] is to.

42. *this baggage*] this disreputable girl (Moll).

And kiss him with devotion when he enters.
I cannot get her for my life
To instruct her hand thus, before and after,   45
Which a knight will look for, before and after.
I have told her still, 'tis the waving of a woman
Does often move a man and prevails strongly.
But, sweet, ha' you sent to Cambridge? Has Tim word on 't?
Yellowhammer. Had word just the day after, when you sent him the   50
silver spoon to eat his broth in the hall amongst the gentlemen
commoners.
Maudlin. Oh, 'twas timely.

Enter Porter.

Yellowhammer. How now?
Porter. A letter from a gentleman in Cambridge.   55
                                           [*He gives a letter.*]
Yellowhammer. Oh, one of Hobson's porters. Thou art welcome!—
I told thee, Maud, we should hear from Tim. [*He reads.*]
Amantissimis carissimisque ambobus parentibus patri et matri.
Maudlin. What's the matter?
Yellowhammer. Nay, by my troth, I know not. Ask not me. He's   60
grown too verbal; this learning is a great witch.
Maudlin. Pray, let me see it; I was wont to understand him. [*She
takes the letter and translates ignorantly.*] *Amantissimus
charissimus*: he has sent the carrier's man, he says; *ambobus
parentibus*: for a pair of boots; *patri et matri*: pay the porter or it   65
makes no matter.
Porter. Yes, by my faith, mistress. There's no true construction in
that. I have took a great deal of pains and come from the Bell
sweating. Let me come to 't, for I was a scholar forty years ago.
[*He takes the letter.*] 'Tis thus, I warrant you.   70
[*He construes.*] *Matri*: it makes no matter; *ambobus parentibus*:

45–8.] The bawdy implications of Maudlin's insistence on the importance of a
woman using her hands require some obscene gesture comically accompanying the
curtesy she is demonstrating.

49. *on 't*] i.e. of Sir Walter's arrival with his niece (whom Tim is to marry).

51–2. *gentlemen commoners*] wealthy students who paid for special privileges,
including dining together at a table separate from the poorer students.

56. *Hobson*] the famous Cambridge carrier. Milton wrote two epitaphs on his
death in 1630.

58.] To my father and mother, both my most loving and beloved parents.

65–6. *or . . . matter*] or not, as you please.

67. *There's . . . construction*] i.e. you have misconstrued the Latin. Mistakes in
Latin were a common comic trope; the Porter's vulgar adaptation of the Latin (lines
71–3) is an extension of this gag.

68. *the Bell*] an inn particularly associated with travellers from Cambridge.

for a pair of boots; *patri*: pay the porter; *amantissimis carissimis*:
he's the carrier's man, and his name is Sims.—And there
he says true, forsooth; my name is Sims indeed. I have not
forgot all my learning. A money matter; I thought I should   75
hit on 't.

Yellowhammer. Go, thou art an old fox! [*Giving money*] There's a
tester for thee.

Porter. If I see your worship at Goose Fair, I have a dish of birds for
you.   80

Yellowhammer. Why, dost dwell at Bow?

Porter. All my lifetime, sir; I could ever say boo to a goose! Farewell
to your worship.   *Exit Porter.*

Yellowhammer. A merry porter!

Maudlin. How can he choose but be so, coming with Cambridge   85
letters from our son Tim?

Yellowhammer. What's here? [*He reads.*] *Maxime diligo*? Faith, I
must to my learned counsel with this gear; 'twill ne'er be
discerned else.

Maudlin. Go to my cousin, then, at Inns of Court.   90

Yellowhammer. Fie, they are all for French; they speak no Latin.

Maudlin. The parson then will do it.

Enter a Gentleman *with a chain.*

Yellowhammer. Nay, he disclaims it, calls Latin 'papistry'; he will
not deal with it.—What is 't you lack, gentleman?

Gentleman. Pray, weigh this chain.   95
[*Yellowhammer weighs chain, and does not
see the entrance of Sir Walter and the rest.*]

Enter SIR WALTER WHOREHOUND, Welsh Gentlewoman,
and DAVY DAHUMMA.

---

72. *pay the porter*] The Porter cannily drops Maulin's translation of *matri* to mean
'or not as you please', lines 65–6.

75–6. *A money . . . on 't*] I thought I would get the money part right.

77–8. *a tester*] a sixpenny piece.

79. *your worship*] a general honorific title addressed to social superiors.

79–81. *Goose Fair . . . Bow*] A fair selling young (green) geese was held in
Whitsun week at Stratford-le-Bow, northeast of London.

87. Maxime diligo] I love most greatly. Possibly *Maxima diligo*, 'I esteem (or
choose) the greatest'.

88. *gear*] business, i.e. Tim's Latin letter.

89. *discerned*] made out.

90. *Inns of Court*] four colleges in the centre of London where students trained to
enter the legal profession.

91. *French*] Law-French; with a comic reference to French pox (syphilis).

93. *calls Latin 'papistry'*] i.e. associates all Latin with the Roman Catholic Mass,
a point of view comically associated with strict Puritans.

Sir Walter. Now, wench, thou art welcome to the heart of the city of
 London.
Welsh Gentlewoman. Dugat a whee.
Sir Walter. You can thank me in English, if you list.
Welsh Gentlewoman. I can, sir, simply.   100
Sir Walter. 'Twill serve to pass, wench. 'Twas strange that I should
 lie with thee so often to leave thee without English; that were
 unnatural. I bring thee up to turn thee into gold, wench,
 And make thy fortune shine like your bright trade;
 A goldsmith's shop sets out a city maid.   105
 Davy Dahumma, not a word!
Davy. Mum, mum, sir.
Sir Walter. Here you must pass for a pure virgin.
Davy. [*Aside*] Pure Welsh virgin! She lost her maidenhead in
 Brecknockshire.   110
Sir Walter. I hear you mumble, Davy.
Davy. I have teeth, sir; I need not mumble yet this forty years.
Sir Walter. [*Aside*] The knave bites plaguily!
Yellowhammer. [*To Gentleman*] What's your price, sir?
Gentleman. A hundred pound, sir.   115
Yellowhammer. A hundred marks the utmost; 'tis not for me else.—
 What, Sir Walter Whorehound?   [*Exit* Gentleman.]
Moll. Oh, death!   *Exit Moll.*
Maudlin. Why, daughter! Faith, the baggage!
 [*To Sir Walter*] A bashful girl, sir; these young things are
  shamefaced;   120
 Besides, you have a presence, sweet Sir Walter,
 Able to daunt a maid brought up i' the city.

     Enter MARY [MOLL].

 A brave court-spirit makes our virgins quiver
 And kiss with trembling thighs. Yet see, she comes, sir.
Sir Walter. [*To Moll*] Why, how now, pretty mistress? Now I have 125
 caught you. What, can you injure so your time to stray thus
 from your faithful servant?

---

98. *Dugat a whee*] a travesty of Welsh for 'God keep you'.
101. *'Twill . . . pass*] i.e. Your simple English is sufficient.
'Twas] it would be.
103. *up*] i.e. up to London.
104. *your bright trade*] (1) the goldsmith's trade; (2) the lucrative trade of
prostitute.
105. *sets out*] provides a suitable setting for.
110. Brecknockshire] a county in Wales (with a pun on 'nock', a slang word for
vagina).
114. *What's . . . sir*] The scene shifts back to the Yellowhammers' shop and the
transaction begun in line 94. See Intro., p. 9.
116. *marks*] A mark was worth 13 shillings and 4 pence, two-thirds of a pound.

Yellowhammer. [*To Sir Walter*] Pish! Stop your words, good
  knight—'twill make her blush else— which sound too high for
  the daughters of the freedom. 'Honour' and 'faithful servant'!   130
  They are compliments for the worthies of Whitehall or Greenwich; e'en plain, sufficient, subsidy words serves us, sir. [*Indi-*
  cating the Welsh Gentlewoman] And is this gentlewoman your
  worthy niece?
Sir Walter. You may be bold with her on these terms; 'tis she, sir,   135
  heir to some nineteen mountains.
Yellowhammer. Bless us all! You overwhelm me, sir, with love and
  riches.
Sir Walter. And all as high as Paul's.
Davy. [*Aside*] Here's work, i' faith!   140
Sir Walter. How sayest thou, Davy?
Davy. Higher, sir, by far; you cannot see the top of 'em.
Yellowhammer. What, man?—Maudlin, salute this gentlewoman—
  our daughter, if things hit right.

                    Enter TOUCHWOOD JUNIOR.

Touchwood Junior. [*Aside*] My knight, with a brace of footmen,   145
  Is come, and brought up his ewe-mutton to find
  A ram at London; I must hasten it,
  Or else peak o' famine; her blood's mine,
  And that's the surest. Well, knight, that choice spoil
  Is only kept for me.   [*He whispers to Moll from behind.*]   150
Moll. Sir?
Touchwood Junior. Turn not to me till thou mayst lawfully; it but
  whets my stomach, which is too sharp-set already. Read that
  note carefully [*Giving her a letter*]; keep me from suspicion still,
  nor know my zeal but in thy heart. Read, and send but thy liking   155

---

130. *the freedom*] those 'free', i.e. licensed, to trade within the city.
132. *Whitehall or Greenwich*] royal palaces.
subsidy] valuable enough to pay certain categories of city tax.
139. *Paul's*] St Paul's, London's largest church with the highest steeple.
140. *Here's work*] i.e. Sir Walter is working hard to impress Yellowhammer.
144. *hit right*] work out as we would like.
145. *brace*] pair, usually used of game birds. The image, along with *ewe-mutton*
and *ram* (lines 146–7) presents Sir Walter as a farmer coming to market.
146. *ewe-mutton*] *Mutton* was a slang term for a prostitute; and, as mutton is less
tender and more fatty than lamb to eat, the term suggested an old, sexually used
woman.
147–8. *I must . . . famine*] I must hurry up (with my plan to marry Moll) or lose
out and become as poor as a famine.
148–9. *her blood . . . surest*] her sexual desire matches mine and that's my strong-
est advantage.
149. *spoil*] prize.
153. *stomach*] sexual appetite.
155. *liking*] (1) consent; (2) desire.

in three words; I'll be at hand to take it.

Yellowhammer. [*To Sir Walter*] Oh, Tim, sir, Tim.
A poor plain boy, an university man;
Proceeds next Lent to a bachelor of art.
He will be called Sir Yellowhammer then   160
Over all Cambridge, and that's half a knight.

Maudlin. Please you, draw near and taste the welcome of the city,
sir?

Yellowhammer. Come, good Sir Walter, and your virtuous niece
here.   165

Sir Walter. 'Tis manners to take kindness.

Yellowhammer. Lead 'em in, wife.

Sir Walter. Your company, sir?

Yellowhammer. I'll give 't you instantly.
                                        [*Exeunt* MAUDLIN, SIR WALTER, DAVY,
                                                    and Welsh Gentlewoman.]

Touchwood Junior. [*Aside*] How strangely busy is the devil and
riches!   170
Poor soul, kept in too hard; her mother's eye
Is cruel toward her, being kind to him.
'Twere a good mirth now to set him a-work
To make her wedding ring; I must about it.
Rather than the gain should fall to a stranger,   175
'Twas honesty in me to enrich my father.

Yellowhammer. [*Aside*] The girl is wondrous peevish. I fear nothing
But that she's taken with some other love;
Then all's quite dashed. That must be narrowly looked to.
We cannot be too wary in our children.   180
[*To Touchwood Junior*] What is 't you lack?

Touchwood Junior. [*Aside to Moll*] Oh, nothing now; all that I wish
is present.
[*To Yellowhammer*] I would have a wedding ring made for a
gentlewoman with all speed that may be.

---

160. *Sir Yellowhammer*] Yellowhammer is exaggerating the elevation which
Tim's bachelor's degree will bring, though the Latin *'dominus'* (teacher) was sometimes translated as 'Sir'.

169.1–2.] This exit leaves Moll, Yellowhammer and Touchwood Junior all separately on stage, although Moll could exit here and re-enter at line 187. Or she could
be occupied writing the 'three words' which Touchwood Junior requested at line
156.

171. *Poor soul*] i.e. Moll.

172–3. *him*] This could refer to Sir Walter, especially if Maulin's exit with him
indicates some particular kindness, or it could refer to Yellowhammer, suggesting
that Maulin's cruelty to Moll is in order to enrich her husband.

176.] It would be a good deed on my part to make my father rich. Yellowhammer
will be Touchwood Junior's father(-in-law) if he succeeds in marrying Moll.

Yellowhammer. Of what weight, sir?   185
Touchwood Junior. Of some half ounce;
    Stand fair and comely, with the spark of a diamond.
    Sir; 'twere pity to lose the least grace.
Yellowhammer. Pray, let's see it.
              [He takes the stone from Touchwood Junior.]
              Indeed, sir, 'tis a pure one.
Touchwood Junior. So is the mistress.   190
Yellowhammer. Have you the wideness of her finger, sir?
Touchwood Junior. Yes, sure, I think I have her measure about me.
    Good faith, 'tis down; I cannot show 't you,
    I must pull too many things out to be certain.
    Let me see: long, and slender, and neatly jointed;   195
    Just such another gentlewoman that's your daughter, sir.
Yellowhammer. And, therefore, sir, no gentlewoman.
Touchwood Junior.   I protest
    I never saw two maids handed more alike;
    I'll ne'er seek farther, if you'll give me leave, sir.
Yellowhammer. If you dare venture by her finger, sir.   200
Touchwood Junior. Ay, and I'll 'bide all loss, sir.
Yellowhammer. Say you so, sir?— Let's see hither, girl.
                    [Moll approaches them.]
Touchwood Junior. *[To Moll]* Shall I make bold with your finger,
    gentlewoman?
Moll. Your pleasure, sir.   205
Touchwood Junior. That fits her to a hair, sir.
               [Trying the ring on Moll's finger]
Yellowhammer. What's your posy now, sir?
Touchwood Junior. Mass, that's true. Posy? I' faith, e'en thus, sir:
        'Love that's wise
        Blinds parents' eyes.'   210
Yellowhammer. How, how? If I may speak without offence, sir,
    I hold my life—
Touchwood Junior. What, sir?
Yellowhammer. Go to. You'll pardon me?

---

187. *spark*] a small stone.
193. *down*] deep down in my pocket (with a dirty joke about his penis being detumescent. The penis jokes continue for the next three lines.)
196. *that's your daughter*] as your daughter is.
197. *no gentlewoman*] Yellowhammer insists that if the lady is like his daughter she cannot be a gentlewoman (because his daughter is a citizen).
201. *I'll . . . loss*] i.e. I'll guarantee you payment, whether the ring fits or not.
207. *posy*] rhyme to go on the ring.
208. *Mass*] by the Mass (an oath).
214. *Go to*] a general expression of emphasis.
You'll pardon me?] You'll forgive what I am going to say, won't you?

Touchwood Junior. Pardon you? Ay, sir.   215
Yellowhammer. Will you, i' faith?
Touchwood Junior. Yes, faith, I will.
Yellowhammer. You'll steal away some man's daughter. Am I near
    you?
    Do you turn aside? You gentlemen are mad wags!
    I wonder things can be so warily carried,   220
    And parents blinded so; but they're served right
    That have two eyes and wear so dull a sight.
Touchwood Junior. [*Aside*] Thy doom take hold of thee!
Yellowhammer. Tomorrow noon shall show your ring well done.
Touchwood Junior. Being so, 'tis soon. Thanks, [*To Moll*] and your
    leave, sweet gentlewoman.   225
Moll. Sir, you are welcome.   *Exit* [TOUCHWOOD JUNIOR].
    [*Aside*] Oh, were I made of wishes, I went with thee!
Yellowhammer. Come now, we'll see how the rules go within.
Moll. [*Aside*] That robs my joy; there I lose all I win.   *Exeunt.*

[1.2]

        Enter DAVY *and* ALLWIT *severally.*

Davy. [*Aside*] Honesty wash my eyes! I have spied a wittol.
Allwit. What, Davy Dahumma? Welcome from North Wales, i'
    faith. And is Sir Walter come?
Davy. New come to town, sir.
Allwit. In to the maids, sweet Davy, and give order his chamber be   5
    made ready instantly. My wife's as great as she can wallow,
    Davy, and longs for nothing but pickled cucumbers and his
    coming; and now she shall ha 't, boy.
Davy. She's sure of them, sir.
Allwit. Thy very sight will hold my wife in pleasure   10

---

218. *Am . . . you?*] Have I found you out?
219. *mad wags*] an expression of coy, collusive, mock disapproval; the nearest
modern equivalent is 'young devils'.
222. *wear . . . sight*] perceive so little.
223. *Thy . . . thee*] May you be the victim of your own prophecy!
225. *Being . . . soon*] If it is well done, having it done by noon will be fast work.
228. *rules*] revels; or agreements.

1.2.0.1. severally] by separate entrances.
    1. *Honesty . . . eyes*] an unusual exclamation, suggesting that the sight of a willing
cuckold would inflict his sight, and his eyes would need washing as a result.
    wittol] a willing cuckold (a transposition of 'Allwit').
    5. *In . . . maids*] go into the maids' quarters.
    6-7. *great . . . cucumbers*] all signs of advanced pregnancy.

Till the knight come himself. Go in, in, in, Davy.
                                        Exit [DAVY].
The founder's come to town! I am like a man
Finding a table furnished to his hand,
As mine is still to me, prays for the founder:
'Bless the right worshipful the good founder's life'.   15
I thank him, h'as maintained my house this ten years;
Not only keeps my wife, but 'a keeps me
And all my family. I am at his table;
He gets me all my children, and pays the nurse
Monthly or weekly; puts me to nothing,   20
Rent, nor church-duties, not so much as the scavenger.
The happiest state that ever man was born to!
I walk out in a morning; come to breakfast,
Find excellent cheer; a good fire in winter;
Look in my coal-house about midsummer eve,   25
That's full, five or six chaldron new laid up;
Look in my back-yard, I shall find a steeple
Made up with Kentish faggots, which o'erlooks
The water-house and the windmills. I say nothing,
But smile and pin the door. When she lies in,   30
As now she's even upon the point of grunting,
A lady lies not in like her. There's her embossings,
Embroid'rings, spanglings, and I know not what,
As if she lay with all the gaudy-shops
In Gresham's Burse about her; then her restoratives,   35

---

12. *founder*] usually used of cities or institutions. Allwit speaks of Sir Walter as the founder of his family and his prosperity.

13. *to his hand*] to suit his purposes.

16. *h'as*] he (i.e. Sir Walter) has.

17. *'a*] he.

19. *gets . . . children*] maintains my family (but with the suggestion of begetting).

21. *church-duties . . . scavenger*] Church dues could be paid in cash or work. By paying cash for Allwit, Sir Walter has relieved him of the need to undertake the scavenger's job of repairing the pavements and cleaning the streets.

26. *chaldron*] cauldron, a measure of 32 bushels.

28. *faggots*] logs of firewood, here piled steeple-high.

o'erlooks] stands higher than.

30. *pin*] bolt.

lies in] prepares to give birth.

31. *grunting*] going into labour.

32. *A lady . . . her*] Even an aristocratic lady does not have so luxurious a preparation for childbirth.

embossings] embossed ornaments.

33. *spanglings*] spangles, decorative metal ornaments.

34. *gaudy-shops*] shops for finery.

35. *Gresham's Burse*] famous covered shopping centre built by Sir Thomas Gresham in 1566.

Able to set up a young pothecary,
And richly stock the foreman of a drug-shop;
Her sugar by whole loaves, her wines by runlets.
I see these things, but like a happy man
I pay for none at all; yet fools think 's mine.   40
I have the name, and in his gold I shine.
And where some merchants would in soul kiss hell
To buy a paradise for their wives, and dye
Their conscience in the bloods of prodigal heirs
To deck their night-piece, yet all this being done,   45
Eaten with jealousy to the inmost bone—
As what affliction nature more constrains
Than feed the wife plump for another's veins?—
These torments stand I freed of; I am as clear
From jealousy of a wife as from the charge.   50
Oh, two miraculous blessings! 'Tis the knight
Hath took that labour all out of my hands.
I may sit still and play; he's jealous for me,
Watches her steps, sets spies. I live at ease;
He has both the cost and torment. When the strings   55
Of his heart frets, I feed, laugh, or sing:
[Sings] La dildo, dildo la dildo, la dildo dildo de dildo.

Enter two Servants.

1 Servant. [*To his partner*] What, has he got a singing in his head
    now?
2 Servant. Now 's out of work, he falls to making dildoes.   60
Allwit. Now, sirs, Sir Walter's come.
1 Servant. Is our master come?
Allwit. Your master? What am I?
1 Servant. Do not you know, sir?
Allwit. Pray, am not I your master?   65

36.] enough to start a shop for a young pharmacist.
38. *runlets*] casks holding up to 18.5 gallons.
40. *think 's mine*] think that it's all mine.
41. *name*] reputation (for being rich).
43–4. *dye . . . heirs*] stain their consciences by extorting money from heirs to land who waste their fortunes on luxuries.
45. *To . . . night-piece*] to adorn their bed-companion.
47–8.] as, indeed, what affliction violates our true nature more grievously than to care for a wife who is then enjoyed by another man? *Veins* refers to the idea that lust comes from excess of blood. See Intro., pp. 52–3.
50. *charge*] (1) cost of keeping her; (2) imputation of being a jealous husband.
57. dildo] (1) a nonsense refrain common in ballads; (2) an artificial penis.
60. *Now 's*] now that he's.

1 Servant. Oh, you are but our mistress's husband.

Allwit. *Ergo*, knave, your master.

Enter SIR WALTER *and* DAVY.

1 Servant. *Negatur argumentum.*—Here comes Sir Walter. [*Aside to*
    2 *Servant*] Now 'a stands bare as well as we. Make the most
    of him; he's but one pip above a servingman, and so much his   70
    horns make him.

Sir Walter. [*To Allwit*] How dost, Jack?

Allwit. Proud of your worship's health, sir.

Sir Walter. How does your wife?

Allwit. E'en after your own making, sir. She's a tumbler, i' faith; the   75
    nose and belly meets.

Sir Walter. They'll part in time again.

Allwit. At the good hour they will, an 't please your worship.

Sir Walter. [*To a Servant*] Here, sirrah, pull off my boots. [*To Allwit*]
    Put on, put on, Jack.   80

Allwit. I thank your kind worship, sir.

Sir Walter. Slippers! Heart, you are sleepy!

                        [*A servant brings slippers.*]

Allwit. [*Aside*] The game begins already.

Sir Walter. Pish! Put on, Jack.

Allwit. [*Aside*] Now I must do it, or he'll be as angry now as if I had   85
    put it on at first bidding. 'Tis but observing [*Putting on his*
    hat]—'Tis but observing a man's humour once, and he may ha'
    him by the nose all his life.

---

67. *Ergo*] therefore.

68. *Negatur argumentum*] The argument is denied.

69. *'a stands bare*] he has taken off his hat. Allwit, like the servants, has removed
his hat as a mark of respect to Sir Walter.

70. *pip*] the mark of value on a die or playing card.

70-1. *and . . . him*] and the only thing that makes him a little higher than a
servant is his cuckold's horns.

75. *after your own making*] according to the way you have made her (with the
reminder that she is pregnant by Sir Walter).

75-6. *She's . . . meets*] She is so hugely pregnant that she can touch her belly with
her nose, like an acrobat.

77. *They'll . . . again*] i.e. When she has delivered her child, her belly won't be so
close to her nose.

78. *an 't*] if it.

80. *Put on*] i.e. Put on your hat. (Hats were customarily worn indoors.)

82. *Heart*] by Christ's heart (an oath).

83. *The game*] in which Allwit asserts his minimal power over Sir Walter by
refusing to put on his hat as soon as he has been asked to do so.

87. *humour*] disposition; physical constitution which had psychological effects.

87-8. *ha' . . . nose*] control him. Dangerous animals such as bulls and bears were
led by chains attached to rings pierced through the animal's nose.

Sir Walter. [*To 1 Servant*] What entertainment has lain open here?
No strangers in my absence?
1 Servant.   Sure, sir, not any.   90
Allwit. [*Aside*] His jealousy begins. Am not I happy now
That can laugh inward whilst his marrow melts?
Sir Walter. How do you satisfy me?
1 Servant. Good sir, be patient.
Sir Walter. For two months' absence I'll be satisfied.   95
1 Servant. No living creature entered—
Sir Walter. Entered? Come, swear!
1 Servant. You will not hear me out, sir.
Sir Walter. Yes, I'll hear 't out, sir.
1 Servant. Sir, he can tell, himself.   100
Sir Walter. Heart, he can tell!
Do you think I'll trust him?—as a usurer
With forfeited lordships. Him? Oh, monstrous injury!
Believe him? Can the devil speak ill of darkness?
[*To Allwit*] What can you say, sir?   105
Allwit. Of my soul and conscience, sir, she's a wife as honest of her
body to me as any lord's proud lady can be.
Sir Walter. Yet, by your leave, I heard you were once off'ring to go
to bed to her.
Allwit. No, I protest, sir!   110
Sir Walter. Heart, if you do, you shall take all. I'll marry!
Allwit. Oh, I beseech you, sir.
Sir Walter. [*Aside*] That wakes the slave, and keeps his flesh in awe.
Allwit. [*Aside*] I'll stop that gap
Where'er I find it open. I have poisoned   115
His hopes in marriage already—
Some old rich widows and some landed virgins—

Enter two Children [WAT *and* NICK].

And I'll fall to work still before I'll lose him.
He's yet too sweet to part from.
Wat. [*To Allwit*] God-den, father.   120

---

92. *marrow melts*] i.e. with jealousy. See Intro., pp. 52–3.
101. *he*] i.e. Allwit.
102–3. *as . . . lordships*] I'd trust Allwit to tell the truth as soon as I would trust a usurer with property which is forfeited for non-payment of a loan.
104.] How could I possibly believe him? Would I expect the devil to denigrate (i.e. tell the truth about) darkness?
106. *Of*] on.
111. *you . . . all*] i.e. you can have her and nothing else.
113. *slave*] wretch.
120. *God-den*] Good day.

Allwit. Ha, villain, peace!

Nick. God-den, father.

Allwit. Peace, bastard! [*Aside*] Should he hear 'em! [*Aloud*] These
    are two foolish children; they do not know the gentleman that
    sits there.   125

Sir Walter. Oh, Wat! How dost, Nick? Go to school, ply your books,
    boys, ha?

Allwit. [*Aside to boys*] Where's your legs, whoresons? [*Aside*] They
    should kneel indeed, if they could say their prayers.

Sir Walter. [*Aside*] Let me see, stay;   130
    How shall I dispose of these two brats now
    When I am married? For they must not mingle
    Amongst my children that I get in wedlock;
    'Twill make foul work, that, and raise many storms.
    I'll bind Wat prentice to a goldsmith—   135
    My father Yellowhammer, as fit as can be!
    Nick with some vintner. Good, goldsmith and vintner!
    There will be wine in bowls, i' faith.

Enter ALLWIT'S *Wife.*

Mrs Allwit.   Sweet knight,
    Welcome! I have all my longings now in town;
    Now, welcome the good hour.   [*She embraces him.*]   140

Sir Walter. How cheers my mistress?

Mrs Allwit. Made lightsome e'en by him that made me heavy.

Sir Walter. Methinks she shows gallantly, like a moon at full, sir.

Allwit. True, and if she bear a male child, there's the man in the
    moon, sir.   145

Sir Walter. 'Tis but the boy in the moon yet, goodman calf.

Allwit. There was a man; the boy had never been there else.

Sir Walter. It shall be yours, sir.

Allwit. No, by my troth, I'll swear it's none of mine. Let him that got
    it keep it!   150
    [*Aside*] Thus do I rid myself of fear,
    Lie soft, sleep hard, drink wine, and eat good cheer.

                                           [*Exeunt.*]

---

    121. *villain*] wicked child.

    128. *legs*] Allwit is urging the boys to bow to Sir Walter.

    whoresons] brats (an affectionate insult, but, like *bastard*, line 123, it could be
taken literally to mean a whore's son).

    138. *There . . . i' faith*] i.e. We can serve Nick's wine in the gold bowls made by
Wat.

    142. *Made . . . heavy*] i.e. Made cheerful by him (i.e. Sir Walter) who made me
sad (also implying 'who made me pregnant').

    146. *goodman calf*] master idiot (with a play on 'mooncalf' also meaning fool).

    147.] If there had not been a man to begin with, there would be no boy now.

Act 2

[2.1]

Enter TOUCHWOOD SENIOR *and his* Wife.

Mrs Touchwood. 'Twill be so tedious, sir, to live from you,
    But that necessity must be obeyed.
Touchwood Senior. I would it might not, wife. The tediousness
    Will be the most part mine, that understand
    The blessings I have in thee; so to part,   5
    That drives the torment to a knowing heart.
    But as thou say'st, we must give way to need
    And live awhile asunder; our desires
    Are both too fruitful for our barren fortunes.
    How adverse runs the destiny of some creatures!   10
    Some only can get riches and no children;
    We only can get children and no riches.
    Then 'tis the prudent'st part to check our wills
    And, till our state rise, make our bloods lie still.
    Life, every year a child, and some years two!   15
    Besides drinkings abroad, that's never reckoned;
    This gear will not hold out.
Mrs Touchwood.   Sir, for a time
    I'll take the courtesy of my uncle's house,
    If you be pleased to like on 't, till prosperity
    Look with a friendly eye upon our states.   20
Touchwood Senior. Honest wife, I thank thee. I ne'er knew
    The perfect treasure thou brought'st with thee more
    Than at this instant minute. A man's happy
    When he's at poorest that has matched his soul
    As rightly as his body. Had I married   25

2.1.1. *from*] away from.
4. *that*] I who.
13. *check our wills*] control our sexual desires.
14. *state*] social and financial condition.
bloods] sexual passions.
15. *Life*] abbreviation of 'by God's life' (an oath).
16. *drinkings abroad*] euphemism for having sex away from home.
17. *gear*] (1) business; (2) genitals.
19. *like on 't*] give it (the proposal) your approval.

A sensual fool now, as 'tis hard to 'scape it
'Mongst gentlewomen of our time, she would ha' hanged
About my neck and never left her hold
Till she had kissed me into wanton businesses,
Which at the waking of my better judgement   30
I should have cursed most bitterly,
And laid a thicker vengeance on my act
Than misery of the birth—which were enough
If it were born to greatness, whereas mine
Is sure of beggary, though it were got in wine.   35
Fullness of joy showeth the goodness in thee;
Thou art a matchless wife. Farewell, my joy.
Mrs Touchwood. I shall not want your sight?
Touchwood Senior.   I'll see thee often,
Talk in mirth, and play at kisses with thee—
Anything, wench, but what may beget beggars;   40
There I give o'er the set, throw down the cards,
And dare not take them up.
Mrs Touchwood.   Your will be mine, sir.   *Exit.*
Touchwood Senior. This does not only make her honesty perfect,
But her discretion, and approves her judgement.
Had her desires been wanton, they'd been blameless   45
In being lawful ever, but of all creatures
I hold that wife a most unmatchèd treasure
That can unto her fortunes fix her pleasure
And not unto her blood. This is like wedlock;
The feast of marriage is not lust, but love   50
And care of the estate. When I please blood,

26–7. *as ... time*] which is hard to avoid, given the character of gentlewomen nowadays. See Intro., pp. 46–7.

29. *wanton business*] making love.

32. *thicker vengeance*] more terrible curse.

my act] my sexual act.

33. *misery ... birth*] Pleasure in sex was thought to be a repetition of Adam and Eve's initial disobedience against God. That act was cursed by God with the pain of childbirth (see Genesis, 3.16); Touchwood Senior says his curse will be more terrible than God's.

35. *got ... wine*] begotten when I was drunk.

38. *I ... sight*] Mrs Touchwood is anxious that she will never see her husband again.

41. *There ... set*] there I abandon the game.

44. *approves*] confirms.

45–6. *they'd ... lawful*] my sexual desires would have been blameless by virtue of my being married. See Intro., pp. 46–7.

48. *fix*] set, regulate. The idea is one of appropriate proportion between, in this case, *fortune* and *pleasure*.

51–2. *When ... others*] When I give in to my desires, I merely have a good time and exploit other people.

Merely I sing and suck out others; then
'Tis many a wise man's fault, but of all men
I am the most unfortunate in that game
That ever pleased both genders: I ne'er played yet   55
Under a bastard. The poor wenches curse me
To the pit where'er I come; they were ne'er served so,
But used to have more words than one to a bargain.
I have such a fatal finger in such business
I must forth with 't, chiefly for country wenches,   60
For every harvest I shall hinder hay-making;

Enter a [Country] *Wench with a child.*

I had no less than seven lay in last progress
Within three weeks of one another's time.
Country Wench. Oh, snap-hance, have I found you?
Touchwood Senior.   How, snap-hance?
Country Wench. [*Showing him the child*] Do you see your
    workmanship? Nay, turn not from it,   65
Nor offer to escape; for if you do,
I'll cry it through the streets and follow you.
Your name may well be called Touchwood; a pox on you! You do
but touch and take. Thou hast undone me. I was a maid before;
I can bring a certificate for it from both the churchwardens.   70
Touchwood Senior. I'll have the parson's hand too, or I'll not yield
    to 't.
Country Wench. Thou shalt have more, thou villain! Nothing grieves
    me but Ellen, my poor cousin in Derbyshire; thou hast cracked
    her marriage quite; she'll have a bout with thee.   75
Touchwood Senior. Faith, when she will, I'll have a bout with her!

55–6. *I ne'er . . . bastard*] In any gambling game, I am always left with at least a
bastard. A *bastard* is a card left in the hand which scores against a player at the end
of the game.
56–7. *curse . . . pit*] damn me to hell.
58.] i.e. but used to need more than one sexual encounter before becoming
pregnant.
59. *fatal finger*] (1) unlucky effect; (2) effective penis.
60. *with 't*] i.e. with my *fatal finger* (see above).
61. *hinder hay-making*] i.e. by wasting the women harvesters' time with sexual
harassment or by making them pregnant and unable to work.
62. *lay in last progress*] who gave birth during my last 'royal tour'.
64. *snap-hance*] flintlock: the device which ignites the touchwood in the touchhole of a musket. The sexual innuendo, and extension of his name, make the
nickname particularly appropriate for Touchwood.
67. *cry*] proclaim (but also shout for sale; cf. 1.1.8).
69. *touch and take*] touch fire and burst into flame at once.
75–7. *bout*] (1) law suit; (2) sexual encounter.

Country Wench. A law bout, sir, I mean.
Touchwood Senior.   True, lawyers use
    Such bouts as other men do. And if that
    Be all thy grief, I'll tender her a husband.
    I keep of purpose two or three gulls in pickle   80
    To eat such mutton with, and she shall choose one.
    Do but in courtesy, faith, wench, excuse me
    Of this half yard of flesh, in which, I think,
    It wants a nail or two.
Country Wench. No, thou shalt find, villain,   85
    It hath right shape and all the nails it should have.
Touchwood Senior. Faith, I am poor. Do a charitable deed, wench;
    I am a younger brother and have nothing.
Country Wench. Nothing? Thou hast too much, thou lying villain,
    Unless thou wert more thankful.   90
Touchwood Senior. I have no dwelling;
    I brake up house but this morning. Pray thee, pity me;
    I am a good fellow, faith, have been too kind
    To people of your gender; if I ha 't
    Without my belly, none of your sex shall want it.   95
    [*Aside*] That word has been of force to move a woman.
    [*To her*] There's tricks enough to rid thy hand on 't, wench:
    Some rich man's porch, tomorrow before day,
    Or else anon i' the evening; twenty devices.
    [*Giving money*] Here's all I have, i' faith, take purse and all;   100
    [*Aside*] And would I were rid of all the ware i' the shop so!

---

79. *tender*] offer.
80. *gulls*] dupes.
in pickle] (1) in storage; (2) in a syphilitic state.
81. *mutton*] slang term for a whore.
83. *yard*] slang term for the penis; also referring to the child.
84, 86. *nail*] Syphilitics' children sometimes lack fingernails; hence the Country Wench's indignant reply.
88. *younger brother*] Touchwood Senior is lying, as the Country Wench apprehends.
89. *too much*] i.e. too much sperm and sexual appetite.
91–2. *I . . . morning*] Touchwood Senior explains that he cannot answer the Country Wench's paternity suit since he has no resources, having given up his house that morning.
95. *Without my belly*] 'outside my belly': i.e. not already eaten; but with a sexual innuendo.
96. *of force*] efficacious.
97. *rid . . . on 't*] take the child off your hands.
98.] For example, you could leave the child on some rich man's porch early tomorrow morning. The suggestion comes as much from folk myth as reality.
101. *rid . . . shop*] i.e. rid of my other bastards.

Country Wench. Where I find manly dealings, I am pitiful.
This shall not trouble you.
Touchwood Senior.   And I protest, wench,
The next I'll keep myself.
Country Wench.   Soft, let it be got first!
[*Aside*] This is the fifth; if e'er I venture more,   105
Where I now go for a maid, may I ride for a whore.   *Exit.*
Touchwood Senior. What shift she'll make now with this piece of
    flesh
In this strict time of Lent, I cannot imagine;
Flesh dare not peep abroad now. I have known
This city now above this seven years,   110
But, I protest, in better state of government
I never knew it yet, nor ever heard of.
There has been more religious, wholesome laws
In the half circle of a year erected
For common good than memory ever knew of,   115

            Enter SIR OLIVER KIX *and his* Lady.

Setting apart corruption of promoters
And other poisonous officers that infect
And with a venomous breath taint every goodness.
Lady Kix. Oh, that e'er I was begot, or bred, or born!
Sir Oliver. Be content, sweet wife.
Touchwood Senior. [*Aside*]   What's here to do, now?   120
I hold my life she's in deep passion
For the imprisonment of veal and mutton
Now kept in garrets; weeps for some calf's head now.
Methinks her husband's head might serve with bacon.

            Enter TOUCHWOOD JUNIOR.

Lady Kix. [*Seeing Touchwood Junior*] Hist!   125
Sir Oliver. Patience, sweet wife.   [*They walk aside.*]
Touchwood Junior.   Brother, I have sought you strangely.

---

104. *Soft*] gently, wait a minute.
got] conceived.
106. *go for*] (1) pass for; (2) walk, as opposed to ride.
107. *shift*] arrangement.
piece of flesh] i.e. the baby.
108. *strict time of Lent*] People were forbidden to eat meat during Lent, the period
between Ash Wednesday and Easter. See Intro., pp. 18–19.
110–15.] See Intro., p. 15.
116. *promoters*] informers, spies.
122–3. *imprisonment . . . garrets*] The suggestion is that people tried to evade the
Lenten restrictions by hiding meat in garrets.
123. *calf's head*] (1) delicacy for the table; (2) fool's head.

Touchwood Senior. Why, what's the business?

Touchwood Junior.   With all speed thou canst
        Procure a licence for me.

Touchwood Senior.   How, a licence?

Touchwood Junior. Cud's foot, she's lost else! I shall miss her ever.

Touchwood Senior. Nay, sure, thou shalt not miss so fair a mark   130
        For thirteen shillings fourpence.

Touchwood Junior.   Thanks by hundreds!   *Exit.*

Sir Oliver. Nay, pray thee, cease; I'll be at more cost yet.
        Thou know'st we are rich enough.

Lady Kix.   All but in blessings,
        And there the beggar goes beyond us. Oh, Oh, Oh!
        To be seven years a wife and not a child,   135
        Oh, not a child!

Sir Oliver.   Sweet wife, have patience.

Lady Kix. Can any woman have a greater cut?

Sir Oliver. I know 'tis great, but what of that, wife?
        I cannot do withal. There's things making,
        By thine own doctor's advice, at pothecaries'.   140
        I spare for nothing, wife. No, if the price
        Were forty marks a spoonfull,
        I'd give a thousand pound to purchase fruitfulness.

                                    [*Exit* TOUCHWOOD SENIOR.]

        'Tis but bating so many good works
        In the erecting of bridewells and spittlehouses,   145
        And so fetch it up again; for, having none,

---

128. *licence*] exceptional authorization from the church to marry without announcing the proposed marriage in the parish church (calling the banns) on three consecutive Sundays, as required by canon law.

129. *Cud's foot*] a corruption of the oath 'by God's foot'.

she's] Moll is.

130. *mark*] target.

131. *thirteen . . . fourpence*] the value of the coin called a mark.

131 SD.] Probably Touchwood Senior lingers long enough to hear the Kixes quarrel about fertility.

132. *I'll . . . yet*] I'll spend yet more money.

137. *cut*] (1) disappointment; (2) vagina.

138–9. *I know . . . withal*] The pun on *cut* (see line 137 above) allows Kix to acknowledge the enormity both of his wife's disappointment and her vagina and to say that he cannot do anything with either.

144. *bating*] abating, reducing. Sir Oliver can afford to spend more on getting his wife pregnant if he cuts down on charitable expenses.

145. *bridewells*] houses of correction for prostitutes.

spittlehouses] hospitals (for those with leprosy and venereal disease).

146. *fetch . . . again*] (1) bring up the level of expenditure on encouraging pregnancy; (2) have an erection.

I mean to make good deeds my children.
Lady Kix. Give me but those good deeds, and I'll find children.
Sir Oliver. Hang thee, thou hast had too many!
Lady Kix. Thou liest, brevity!   150
Sir Oliver. Oh, horrible! Dar'st thou call me 'brevity'?
  Dar'st thou be so short with me?
Lady Kix. Thou deservest worse.
  Think but upon the goodly lands and livings
  That's kept back through want on 't.   155
Sir Oliver. Talk not on 't, pray thee;
  Thou'lt make me play the woman and weep too.
Lady Kix. 'Tis our dry barrenness puffs up Sir Walter.
  None gets by your not-getting but that knight;
  He's made by th' means, and fats his fortunes shortly   160
  In a great dowry with a goldsmith's daughter.
Sir Oliver. They may be all deceived. Be but you patient, wife.
Lady Kix. I have suff'red a long time.
Sir Oliver. Suffer thy heart out. A pox suffer thee!
Lady Kix. Nay, thee, thou desertless slave!   165
Sir Oliver. Come, come, I ha' done. You'll to the gossiping
  Of Master Allwit's child?
Lady Kix. Yes, to my much joy!
  Everyone gets before me. There's my sister
  Was married but at Barthol'mew Eve last,   170
  And she can have two children at a birth.
  Oh, one of them, one of them, would ha' served my turn.
Sir Oliver. Sorrow consume thee! Thou art still crossing me,
  And know'st my nature—

                         Enter a Maid.

---

148. *good deeds*] sexual and/or charitable actions. Either sexual acts or money
with which to buy another lover will enable Lady Kix to have children.
  149. *too many*] i.e. both good deeds (financial and sexual) and possibly children
(by other men). This is said in the incoherence of a quarrel and is not necessarily
true.
  150. *brevity*] (1) stingy man; (2) sexually inadequate man. The punning continues in *short*, line 152.
  154–5. *Think . . . on 't*] Think of the property which we will lose to Sir Walter if
we fail to have children and he produces a legitimate heir.
  159. *None gets*] no one prospers.
  166. *gossiping*] christening feast.
  169. *gets*] produces children.
  170. *Barthol'mew Eve*] 23 August. Since the play's action takes place before the
middle of Lent, in late February or early March, the twins must have been conceived before marriage.
  173. *crossing*] contradicting, thwarting.

Maid. Oh, mistress! [*Aside*] Weeping or railing, that's our house   175
    harmony!
Lady Kix. What say'st, Jug?
Maid. The sweetest news!
Lady Kix. What is 't, wench?
Maid. Throw down your doctor's drugs; they're all   180
    But heretics. I bring certain remedy
    That has been taught and proved and never failed.
Sir Oliver. Oh, that, that, that, or nothing!
Maid. There's a gentleman—
    I haply have his name too—that has got   185
    Nine children by one water that he useth.
    It never misses; they come so fast upon him,
    He was fain to give it over.
Lady Kix. His name, sweet Jug?
Maid. One Master Touchwood, a fine gentleman,   190
    But run behind-hand much with getting children.
Sir Oliver. Is 't possible?
Maid. Why sir, he'll undertake,
    Using that water, within fifteen year,
    For all your wealth, to make you a poor man,   195
    You shall so swarm with children.
Sir Oliver. I'll venture that, i' faith.
Lady Kix. That shall you, husband.
Maid. But I must tell you first, he's very dear.
Sir Oliver. No matter; what serves wealth for?   200
Lady Kix. True, sweet husband.
Sir Oliver. There's land to come. Put case his water stands me in
    some five hundred pound a pint, 'twill fetch a thousand, and a
    kersten soul.
Lady Kix. And that's worth all, sweet husband.   205
Sir Oliver. I'll about it.   *Exeunt.*

175–6.] Weeping or complaining is all the harmony that is heard in our house.
177. *Jug*] a common nickname for 'Joan'.
186. *water*] medicine.
191. *run behindhand*] in debt.
195. *poor man*] i.e. because, like Touchwood Senior, you will have too many children, but also because the medicine will be ruinously expensive.
199. *dear*] expensive.
202. *There . . . come*] i.e. We are to inherit land (as a result of having this child, so it is worth the investment).
Put case] suppose.
stands me in] costs me.
203. *a thousand*] i.e. in Sir Walter's inheritance.
204. *kersten soul*] christened, Christian soul—i.e. a baby.

[2.2]

Enter ALLWIT.

Allwit. I'll go bid gossips presently myself.
That's all the work I'll do; nor need I stir,
But that it is my pleasure to walk forth
And air myself a little. I am tied
To nothing in this business; what I do   5
Is merely recreation, not constraint.
Here's running to and fro—nurse upon nurse,
Three charwomen, besides maids and neighbours' children!
Fie, what a trouble have I rid my hands on!
It makes me sweat to think on 't.   10

Enter SIR WALTER WHOREHOUND.

Sir Walter. How now, Jack?
Allwit. I am going to bid gossips for your worship's child, sir; a
goodly girl, i' faith! Give you joy on her! She looks as if she had
two thousand pound to her portion, and run away with a tailor;
a fine, plump, black-eyed slut! Under correction, sir, I take   15
delight to see her.—Nurse!

Enter Dry Nurse.

Dry Nurse. Do you call, sir?
Allwit. I call not you, I call the wet nurse hither.
                                        Exit [Dry Nurse].
Give me the wet nurse!

Enter Wet Nurse [*with child*].

Ay, 'tis thou. Come hither, come hither!   20
Let's see her once again. I cannot choose
But buss her thrice an hour.   [*He kisses the child.*]
Wet Nurse. You may be proud on 't, sir;
'Tis the best piece of work that e'er you did.
Allwit. Think'st thou so, Nurse? What sayest to Wat and Nick?   25
Wet Nurse. They're pretty children both, but here's a wench
Will be a knocker.

2.2.1. *gossips*] godparents; but extended to all women who supported a mother in
childbirth and feasted with her afterwards.

14. *run . . . tailor*] i.e. Her clothes are so fine as to suggest that she has done this.

15. *Under correction*] if you'll allow me to say so.

16.1. *Dry Nurse*] There are three nurses: a dry nurse with general responsibility
for the baby, a wet nurse to feed her and a nurse for Mrs Allwit.

22. *buss*] kiss.

27. *knocker*] (1) strikingly attractive; (2) sexually active (compare modern slang,
'a knockout').

Allwit. [*Dandling child*] Pup!—Say'st thou me so?—Pup, little
   countess!—
   Faith, sir, I thank your worship for this girl
   Ten thousand times and upward.   30
Sir Walter. I am glad I have her for you, sir.
Allwit. Here, take her in, Nurse; wipe her, and give her spoon-meat.
Wet Nurse. [*Aside*] Wipe your mouth, sir.   *Exit* [*with child*].
Allwit. And now about these gossips.
Sir Walter. Get but two; I'll stand for one myself.   35
Allwit. To your own child, sir?
Sir Walter. The better policy; it prevents suspicion.
   'Tis good to play with rumour at all weapons.
Allwit. Troth, I commend your care, sir; 'tis a thing
   That I should ne'er have thought on.
Sir Walter. [*Aside*]   The more slave!   40
   When man turns base, out goes his soul's pure flame;
   The fat of ease o'erthrows the eyes of shame.
Allwit. I am studying who to get for godmother
   Suitable to your worship. Now I ha' thought on 't.
Sir Walter. I'll ease you of that care, and please myself in 't.   45
   [*Aside*] My love, the goldsmith's daughter; if I send,
   Her father will command her.—Davy Dahumma!

Enter DAVY.

Allwit. I'll fit your worship then with a male partner.
Sir Walter. What is he?
Allwit. A kind, proper gentleman, brother to Master Touchwood.   50
Sir Walter. I know Touchwood. Has he a brother living?
Allwit. A neat bachelor.
Sir Walter. Now we know him, we'll make shift with him.
   Dispatch, the time draws near.—Come hither, Davy.
Exit [*with* DAVY].
Allwit. In troth, I pity him, he ne'er stands still;   55
   Poor knight, what pains he takes! Sends this way one,

---

28. *Pup*] kissing noise used when talking to babies.

32. *spoon-meat*] soft food eaten with a spoon for children and invalids.

36. *To . . . child*] Standing godparent to one's own children was associated with
Puritanism.

38.] It is as well to combat rumour with all available means.

48. *male partner*] fellow godparent. It was traditional to have one male and one
female godparent.

53. *we'll . . . him*] we'll make do with him.

That way another; has not an hour's leisure.
I would not have thy toil for all thy pleasure.

Enter two Promoters.

[*Aside*] Ha, how now? What are these that stand so close
At the street-corner, pricking up their ears   60
And snuffing up their noses, like rich men's dogs
When the first course goes in? By the mass, promoters!
'Tis so, I hold my life; and planted there
To arrest the dead corpse of poor calves and sheep,
Like ravenous creditors, that will not suffer   65
The bodies of their poor departed debtors
To go to th' grave, but e'en in death to vex
And stay the corpse with bills of Middlesex.
This Lent will fat the whoresons up with sweetbreads,
And lard their whores with lamb-stones; what their golls   70
Can clutch goes presently to their Molls and Dolls.
The bawds will be so fat with what they earn,
Their chins will hang like udders by Easter eve
And, being stroked, will give the milk of witches.
How did the mongrels hear my wife lies in?   75
Well, I may baffle 'em gallantly. [*To them*] By your favour,
    gentlemen,
I am a stranger both unto the city
And to her carnal strictness.
1 Promoter.   Good; your will, sir?
Allwit. Pray, tell me where one dwells that kills this Lent.

58.1. *Promoters*] informers, as at 2.1.116.
62. *When . . . in*] when the first course of a dinner is carried into the dining room.
64. *corpse*] corpses (Also in line 68); i.e. carcasses, joints of meat.
68. *bills*] writs.
Middlesex] county which included many of the London suburbs. Co-ordination in the policing of Middlesex and London became a priority for the city authorities at the turn of the century.
69. *the whoresons*] i.e. the promoters, who flourish during Lent when others are fasting.
69–70. *sweetbreads . . . lamb-stones*] the pancreas and testicles of lamb, regarded as aphrodisiac.
70. *golls*] hands (slang).
74. *stroked*] (1) as in stroking a chin; (2) as in stroking an animal's udder or a woman's breast to make the milk flow.
75. *my wife lies in*] that my wife has just been in childbirth.
76. *baffle*] cheat and disgrace.
78. *And . . . strictness*] and to the city's regulations in matters of the flesh (literally 'meat' and figuratively 'appetite').
79. *kills*] i.e. has a licence to slaughter meat in Lent; or does so illegally. (See line 96.)

1 Promoter. How, kills? [*Aside to his fellow*] Come hither, Dick; a   80
  bird, a bird!
2 Promoter. [*To Allwit*] What is 't that you would have?
Allwit. Faith, any flesh; but I long especially for veal and green-
  sauce.
1 Promoter. [*Aside*] Green-goose, you shall be sauced.   85
Allwit. I have half a scornful stomach; no fish will be admitted.
1 Promoter. Not this Lent, sir?
Allwit. Lent? What cares colon here for Lent?
1 Promoter. You say well, sir.
  Good reason that the colon of a gentleman,   90
  As you were lately pleased to term your worship, sir,
  Should be fulfilled with answerable food,
  To sharpen blood, delight health, and tickle nature.
  Were you directed hither to this street, sir?
Allwit. That I was, ay, marry.
2 Promoter.   And the butcher, belike,   95
  Should kill and sell close in some upper room?
Allwit. Some apple-loft, as I take it, or a coal-house;
  I know not which, i' faith.
2 Promoter.   Either will serve.
  [*Aside*] This butcher shall kiss Newgate 'less he turn up
  The bottom of the pocket of his apron.—   100
  You go to seek him?
Allwit.   Where you shall not find him.
  I'll buy, walk by your noses with my flesh,
  Sheep-biting mongrels, hand-basket freebooters!
  My wife lies in. A foutra for promoters!   *Exit.*

83–4. *green-sauce*] a sour sauce used with raw or underhung meat. To 'eat veal
and green sauce' was 'to be cheated'.
85. *sauced*] (1) given a sauce for the main dish; (2) given what you deserve.
90. *colon*] belly; appetite.
92. *fulfilled*] filled up, satisfied.
answerable] appropriate, fit.
93. *sharpen blood*] increase appetite.
tickle nature] please natural craving.
95. *belike*] I suppose.
96. *close*] secretly.
99. *kiss Newgate*] i.e. go to prison.
99–100. *'less . . . apron*] unless he pays a bribe.
103. *hand-basket freebooters*] pirates who ransack handbaskets; i.e small-time
thieves who attack those weaker than they are.
104. *My wife lies in*] i.e. as a woman who has recently given birth, she is allowed
to eat meat according to the exceptions of the Lenten regulations.
foutra] a term of contempt from French *foutre*: to fuck.

1 Promoter. That shall not serve your turn.—What a rogue's this!   105
    How cunningly he came over us!

                 Enter a Man *with meat in a basket.*

2 Promoter. Husht, stand close!   [*They stand aside.*]
Man. [*Aside*] I have 'scaped well thus far. They say the knaves are
    wondrous hot and busy.
1 Promoter. [*Approaching him*] By your leave, sir, we must see what   110
    you have under your cloak there.
Man. Have? I have nothing.
1 Promoter. No? Do you tell us that? What makes this lump stick out
    then? We must see, sir.
Man. What will you see, sir? A pair of sheets and two of my wife's   115
    foul smocks going to the washers?
2 Promoter. Oh, we love that sight well! You cannot please us better.
                                    [*He takes meat out of the basket.*]
    What, do you gull us? Call you these shirts and smocks?
Man. Now, a pox choke you! You have cozened me and five of my
    wife's kindred of a good dinner; we must make it up now with   120
    herrings and milk-pottage.   *Exit.*
1 Promoter. [*Examining the meat*] 'Tis all veal.
2 Promoter. All veal? Pox, the worse luck! I promised faithfully to
    send this morning a fat quarter of lamb to a kind gentlewoman
    in Turnbull Street that longs; and how I'm crossed!   125
1 Promoter. Let's share this, and see what hap comes next then.

                 Enter another [Man] *with a basket.*

2 Promoter. Agreed. Stand close again: another booty.
    What's he?
1 Promoter. [*To the Man*] Sir, by your favour.
2 Man. Meaning me, sir?   130
1 Promoter. Good Master Oliver? Cry thee mercy, i' faith!
    What hast thou there?
2 Man. A rack of mutton, sir, and half a lamb;
    You know my mistress's diet.
1 Promoter. Go, go, we see thee not; away, keep close!   135
    [*To 2 Promoter*] Heart, let him pass! Thou'lt never have the wit
    To know our benefactors.   [*Exit 2 Man.*]
2 Promoter. I have forgot him.

---

106. *came over*] outmanoeuvred.
125. *Turnbull Street*] associated with brothels. See Intro., pp. 13–14.
that longs] i.e. who has a craving associated with pregnancy.
crossed] thwarted.
135–7.] The promoters are turning a blind eye to the infractions of Lenten
regulation on the part of those (*our benefactors*, line 137) who have bribed them.

1 Promoter. 'Tis Master Beggarland's man, the wealthy merchant
  That is in fee with us.   140
2 Promoter. Now I have a feeling of him.
1 Promoter. You know he purchased the whole Lent together,
  Gave us ten groats apiece on Ash Wednesday.
2 Promoter. True, true.

> *Enter a* [Country] *Wench with a basket and a child in*
> *it under a loin of mutton.*

1 Promoter. A wench!   145
2 Promoter. Why, then, stand close indeed.
Country Wench. [*Aside*] Women had need of wit, if they'll shift here,
  And she that hath wit may shift anywhere.
1 Promoter. Look, look! Poor fool,
  She has left the rump uncovered too,   150
  More to betray her. This is like a murd'rer
  That will outface the deed with a bloody band.
2 Promoter. What time of the year is 't, sister?
Country Wench. Oh, sweet gentlemen, I am a poor servant!
  Let me go.   155
1 Promoter. You shall, wench, but this must stay with us.
                                     [*He seizes the basket.*]
Country Wench. Oh, you undo me, sir!
  'Tis for a wealthy gentlewoman that takes physic, sir;
  The doctor does allow my mistress mutton.
  Oh, as you tender the dear life of a gentlewoman!   160
  I'll bring my master to you; he shall show you
  A true authority from the higher powers,
  And I'll run every foot.
2 Promoter. Well, leave your basket then,
  And run and spare not.
Country Wench.   Will you swear then to me   165

---

139. *Master Beggarland*] a generic name for a merchant who cheats landowners.

140. *in fee*] in league; having paid a bribe covering the whole of Lent.

141. *a feeling of him*] a good sense of who you mean.

142.] You know he gave us a bribe to cover the whole of Lent.

143. *groats*] coins valued at four pence each.

Ash Wednesday] the first day of Lent.

144.1. *Wench . . . child*] the country wench from 2.1.62ff., who is now trying to get rid of her child.

147. *shift*] survive.

152.] who tries to brazen out his crime when blood stains show on his collar or cuff.

158. *takes physic*] takes medicine; another category of exception to the Lenten regulation.

To keep it till I come?
1 Promoter.   Now by this light I will.
Country Wench. What say you, gentleman?
2 Promoter.   What a strange wench 'tis!
 Would we might perish else.
Country Wench.   Nay, then I run, sir.
        [She leaves the basket and] exit.
1 Promoter. And ne'er return, I hope.
2 Promoter.   A politic baggage!
 She makes us swear to keep it.   170
 I prithee look what market she hath made.
1 Promoter. *[Inspecting the basket]* Imprimis, sir, a good fat loin of
 mutton.
 What comes next under this cloth?
 Now for a quarter of lamb.
2 Promoter. Now for a shoulder of mutton.   175
1 Promoter. Done.
2 Promoter. Why, done, sir!
1 Promoter. By the mass, I feel I have lost;
 'Tis of more weight, i' faith.
2 Promoter. Some loin of veal?   180
1 Promoter. No, faith, here's a lamb's head,
 I feel that plainly. Why, I'll yet win my wager.
        [He takes out the child.]
2 Promoter. Ha?
1 Promoter. 'Swounds, what's here?
2 Promoter. A child!   185
1 Promoter. A pox of all dissembling, cunning whores!
2 Promoter. Here's an unlucky breakfast.
1 Promoter. What shall 's do?
2 Promoter. The quean made us swear to keep it too.
1 Promoter. We might leave it else.   190
2 Promoter. Villainous strange!
 Life, had she none to gull but poor promoters
 That watch hard for a living?
1 Promoter. Half our gettings must run in sugar-sops and nurses'
 wages now, besides many a pound of soap and tallow. We have 195

---

169. *politic*] crafty.
172. Imprimis] first of all.
174–5. *Now . . . Now*] The promoters are betting what the next joint of meat will
be.
184. *'Swounds*] by God's wounds (an oath).
189. *quean*] contemptuous term for a woman.
194. *gettings*] the money that we get.
sugar-sops] moistened and sweetened bread given to babies.

need to get loins of mutton still, to save suet to change for
candles.

2 Promoter. Nothing mads me but this was a lamb's head with you;
you felt it! She has made calves' heads of us.

1 Promoter. Prithee, no more on 't.   200
There's time to get it up; it is not come
To Mid-Lent Sunday yet.

2 Promoter. I am so angry I'll watch no more today.

1 Promoter. Faith, nor I neither.

2 Promoter. Why then, I'll make a motion.   205

1 Promoter. Well, what is 't?

2 Promoter. Let's e'en go to the Checker at Queenhive and roast
the loin of mutton till young flood; then send the child to
Brentford.   [*Exeunt.*]

[2.3]

    Enter ALLWIT *in one of Sir Walter's suits and* DAVY *trussing him.*

Allwit. 'Tis a busy day at our house, Davy.

Davy. Always the kurs'ning-day, sir.

Allwit. Truss, truss me, Davy.

Davy. [*Aside*] No matter an you were hanged, sir.

Allwit. How does this suit fit me, Davy?   5

Davy. Excellent neatly; my master's things were ever fit for you, sir,
e'en to a hair, you know.

Allwit. Thou hast hit it right, Davy.
We ever jumped in one this ten years, Davy,
So, well said.

    Enter a Servant *with a box.*

    What art thou?   10

196–7. *change for candles*] turn into candles (because the baby will need attention
at night). Cheap candles were made from animal fat or tallow.

198.] Nothing makes me so angry as that you thought this was a lamb's head.

199. *calves' heads*] fools.

201. *get it up*] make good our losses.

205. *motion*] proposal.

207. *the Checker*] an inn with the sign of a chessboard.

Queenhive] the quay, west of Southwark Bridge, where most of the Lenten fish
was landed.

208. *young flood*] when the tide begins to flow up river.

209. *Brentford*] a suburb up the Thames on the north bank of the river where a
nurse might be found for the baby. See Intro., p. 19.

2.3.0.1. *trussing*] tying the laces which attached the breeches to the doublet. In
line 4, Davy plays on the secondary meaning 'hanging'.

2. *Always the kurs'ning day*] It always is on the christening day.

9. *jumped in one*] (1) agreed perfectly; (2) shared the same woman.

Servant. Your comfit-maker's man, sir.

Allwit. Oh, sweet youth, in to the nurse quick, quick!
'Tis time, i' faith. Your mistress will be here?

Servant. She was setting forth, sir.　　　　　　　　　[*Exit.*]

　　　　　　　Enter two Puritans.

Allwit. Here comes our gossips now. Oh, I shall have such kissing　15
　work today!—Sweet Mistress Underman, welcome, i' faith.

1 Puritan. Give you joy of your fine girl, sir.
　Grant that her education may be pure
　And become one of the faithful.

Allwit. Thanks to your sisterly wishes, Mistress Underman.　　　20

2 Puritan. Are any of the brethren's wives yet come?

Allwit. There are some wives within, and some at home.

1 Puritan. Verily, thanks, sir.　　　　　*Exeunt* [Puritans].

Allwit. Verily, you are an ass, forsooth.
　I must fit all these times, or there's no music.　　　　　25

　　　　　　　Enter two Gossips.

　Here comes a friendly and familiar pair.
　Now, I like these wenches well.

1 Gossip. How dost, sirrah?

Allwit. Faith, well, I thank you, neighbour, and how dost thou?

2 Gossip. Want nothing but such getting, sir, as thine.　　　30

Allwit. My gettings, wench? They are poor.

1 Gossip. Fie, that thou'lt say so! Th' hast as fine children as a man
　can get.

Davy. [*Aside*] Ay, as a man can get, and that's my master.

Allwit. They are pretty foolish things, put to making in minutes;　35
　I ne'er stand long about 'em. Will you walk in, wenches?
　　　　　　　　　　　　　　　　　[*Exeunt* Gossips.]

　　　　　　　Enter TOUCHWOOD JUNIOR *and* MOLL.

Touchwood Junior. [*To Moll*] The happiest meeting that our souls

---

11. *comfit*] crystallized fruit.

19. *become*] be fitting for.

25. *fit . . . times*] harmonize with all these times, i.e. speak to all sorts of visitors
in their own terms.

30. *getting*] offspring.

31. *gettings*] income. Allwit puns on *getting* meaning 'to earn', 'to procreate' and,
more neutrally, 'to have'. Davy picks up the joke in line 34. The Gossip is not in on
the joke.

35–6.] Allwit's conventionally modest response to the Gossip's compliment both
comically suggests that the sexual act with which the child was begotten was short
and ironically indicates that he had nothing to do with it.

could wish for! Here's the ring ready. I am beholding unto your
father's haste; h'as kept his hour.

Moll. He never kept it better.   40

                    Enter SIR WALTER WHOREHOUND.

Touchwood Junior. [*To Moll*] Back! Be silent.
Sir Walter. Mistress and partner, I will put you both
    Into one cup.   [*He drinks their health.*]
Davy. [*Aside*]   Into one cup! Most proper;
    A fitting compliment for a goldsmith's daughter.
Allwit. Yes, sir, that's he must be your worship's partner in this   45
    day's business, Master Touchwood's brother.
Sir Walter. [*To Touchwood Junior*] I embrace your acquaintance,
    sir.
Touchwood Junior. It vows your service, sir.
Sir Walter. It's near high time. Come, Master Allwit.   50
Allwit. Ready, sir.
Sir Walter. Will 't please you walk?
Touchwood Junior. Sir, I obey your time.   *Exeunt.*

[2.4]

                Enter Midwife *with the child*, [MAUDLIN,
        the two Puritans,] *and the* [*five*] Gossips *to the kurs'ning.*
                          [*Exit* Midwife *with the child.*]

1 Gossip. [*Offering precedence*] Good Mistress Yellowhammer.
Maudlin. In faith, I will not.
1 Gossip. Indeed, it shall be yours.
Maudlin. I have sworn, i' faith.
1 Gossip. I'll stand still, then.   5
Maudlin. So will you let the child go without company, and make
    me forsworn.
1 Gossip. You are such another creature.
                          [*Exeunt* 1 Gossip *and* MAUDLIN.]
2 Gossip. Before me? I pray come down a little.
3 Gossip. Not a whit; I hope I know my place.   10

---

38. *beholding*] beholden, indebted.
42–3. *Mistress . . . cup*] I drink to you both, my bride-to-be (Moll) and my fellow
godfather (Touchwood Junior).
49. *It . . . service*] i.e. My acquaintance vows to do you service.
50. *near high time*] nearly time for the christening.

2.4.3. *it*] i.e. first place in the procession.
8. *You . . . creature*] an affected expression of mock exasperation.
9. *come down*] move down the order of the procession. The Second Gossip
objects to the Third Gossip taking precedence over her by leaving the room first.

2 Gossip. Your place? Great wonder, sure! Are you any better than
    a comfit-maker's wife?

3 Gossip. And that's as good at all times as a pothecary's.

2 Gossip. Ye lie! Yet I forbear you, too.   [*Exeunt* 2 *and* 3 Gossips.]

1 Puritan. Come, sweet sister; we go in unity, and show the fruits of   15
    peace, like children of the spirit.

2 Puritan. I love lowliness.   [*Exeunt* Puritans.]

4 Gossip. True, so say I. Though they strive more,
    There comes as proud behind as goes before.

5 Gossip. Every inch, i' faith.   *Exeunt.*   20

---

12. *comfit-maker's wife*] confectioner's wife.

19.] i.e. there are as proud people at the back of a procession as at the front
(proverbial). '*Proud*' can mean 'erect' which, if emphasized, could make the exchange also refer to anal intercourse. See Intro., p. 51.

Act 3

Enter TOUCHWOOD JUNIOR *and a* Parson.

Touchwood Junior. Oh, sir, if ever you felt the force of love, pity it in
    me!
Parson. Yes. Though I ne'er was married, sir,
    I have felt the force of love from good men's daughters,
    And some that will be maids yet three years hence.   5
    Have you got a licence?
Touchwood Junior. [*Showing the licence*] Here, 'tis ready, sir
Parson. That's well.
Touchwood Junior. The ring and all things perfect, she'll steal hither.
Parson. She shall be welcome, sir. I'll not be long   10
    A-clapping you together.

Enter MOLL *and* TOUCHWOOD SENIOR.

Touchwood Junior. Oh, here she's come, sir.
Parson. What's he?
Touchwood Junior. My honest brother.
Touchwood Senior. Quick, make haste, sirs!   15
Moll. You must despatch with all the speed you can,
    For I shall be missed straight; I made hard shift
    For this small time I have.
Parson.   Then I'll not linger.
    Place that ring upon her finger.
    This the finger plays the part,   20
    Whose master-vein shoots from the heart.
            [*Touchwood Junior puts ring on Moll's finger.*]
    New join hands—

Enter YELLOWHAMMER *and* SIR WALTER.

3.1.5. *maids*] unmarried and claiming to be virgins (though the parson implies
that he had had sex with them).

17. *I . . . shift*] I had some difficulty in arranging.

19–21.] The connection between the heart and the veins of the ring finger was
both thought to be literally the case in early modern anatomy, and a metaphor for
the life-long love promised in the marriage service.

Yellowhammer. Which I will sever,
   And so ne'er again meet never!
Moll. Oh, we are betrayed!   25
Touchwood Junior. Hard fate!
Sir Walter. I am struck with wonder!
Yellowhammer. [*To Moll*] Was this the politic fetch, thou mystical
   baggage,
   Thou disobedient strumpet? [*To Sir Walter*] And were you
   So wise to send for her to such an end?   30
Sir Walter. Now I disclaim the end. You'll make me mad.
Yellowhammer. [*To Touchwood Junior*] And what are you, sir?
Touchwood Junior. An you cannot see with those two glasses, put on
   a pair more.
Yellowhammer. I dreamed of anger still!—Here, take your ring, sir.   35
               [*He takes the ring off Moll's finger.*]
   Ha, this? Life, 'tis the same! Abominable!
   Did not I sell this ring?
Touchwood Junior. I think you did; you received money for 't.
Yellowhammer. Heart, hark you, knight;
   Here's no inconscionable villainy!   40
   Set me a-work to make the wedding-ring,
   And come with an intent to steal my daughter!
   Did ever runaway match it?
Sir Walter. [*To Touchwood Senior*] 'This your brother, sir?
Touchwood Senior. He can tell that as well as I.   45
Yellowhammer. The very posy mocks me to my face:
         'Love that's wise
           Blinds parents' eyes'!
   I thank your wisdom, sir, for blinding of us;
   We have good hope to recover our sight shortly.   50
   In the meantime I will lock up this baggage
   As carefully as my gold. She shall see
   As little sun, if a close room or so
   Can keep her from the light on 't.
Moll.   Oh, sweet father,
   For love's sake, pity me!
Yellowhammer.   Away!
Moll. [*To Touchwood Junior*]   Farewell, sir.   55

---

28. *politic fetch*] cunning trick.
mystical baggage] secretive hussy.
29–30. *And . . . end*] Yellowhammer accuses Sir Walter of inviting Moll to the
Allwit christening as part of the plot for the secret marriage. Sir Walter denies any
such intention.
35. *I . . . still*] I had a premonitory dream about this.
40.] spoken sarcastically.

All content bless thee! And take this for comfort:
Though violence keep me, thou canst lose me never;
I am ever thine although we part for ever.
Yellowhammer. Ay, we shall part you, minx.   *Exit [with* MOLL].
Sir Walter. [*To Touchwood Junior*] Your acquaintance, sir,   60
    Came very lately, yet it came too soon;
    I must hereafter know you for no friend,
    But one that I must shun like pestilence
    Or the disease of lust.
Touchwood Junior. Like enough, sir. You ha' ta'en me at the worst   65
    time for words that e'er ye picked out. Faith, do not wrong me,
    sir.   *Exit [with* Parson].
Touchwood Senior. [*To Sir Walter*] Look after him, and spare not.
        There he walks
    That never yet received baffling. You're blest
    More than e'er I knew; go, take your rest.   *Exit.*   70
Sir Walter. I pardon you. You are both losers.   *Exit.*

[3.2]

    A bed thrust out upon the stage, ALLWIT's *Wife in it.*
        Enter all the Gossips[, the Puritans, MAUDLIN,
            LADY KIX, *and* Dry Nurse *with child*].

1 Gossip. How is 't, woman? We have brought you home
    A kersen soul.
Mrs Allwit.   Ay, I thank your pains.
1 Puritan. And, verily, well kursened, i' the right way,
    Without idolatry or superstition,
    After the pure manner of Amsterdam.   5
Mrs Allwit. Sit down, good neighbours.—Nurse!
Nurse.   At hand, forsooth.
Mrs Allwit. Look they have all low stools.
Nurse.   They have, forsooth.

60–1. *Your . . . lately*] You and I got to know one another recently.
68. *Look after him*] Watch out for him (i.e. Touchwood Junior). Touchwood
Senior is warning Sir Walter.
    spare not] spare no pains.
69. *baffling*] public disgrace, a jousting term for the humiliation of an unworthy
knight.
69–70. *You're . . . knew*] You're luckier than I have ever been.
71. *both*] i.e. both Touchwood brothers.

3.2.2. *kersen*] Christian.
5. *Amsterdam*] location of an English Presbyterian congregation. See Intro., p.
17.
7. *Look*] see that.

2 Gossip. Bring the child hither, Nurse.—How say you now, gossip,
　　Is 't not a chopping girl? So like the father.
3 Gossip. As if it had been spit out of his mouth!　　　　　10
　　Eyed, nosed, and browed as like a girl can be,
　　Only indeed it has the mother's mouth.
2 Gossip. The mother's mouth up and down, up and down.
3 Gossip. 'Tis a large child; she's but a little woman.
1 Puritan. No, believe me,　　　　　15
　　A very spiny creature, but all heart;
　　Well mettled, like the faithful, to endure
　　Her tribulation here and raise up seed.
2 Gossip. She had a sore labour on 't, I warrant you;
　　You can tell, neighbour.
3 Gossip.　　　　　Oh, she had great speed.　　　　　20
　　We were afraid once, but she made us all
　　Have joyful hearts again; 'tis a good soul, i' faith.
　　The midwife found her a most cheerful daughter.
1 Puritan. 'Tis the spirit. The sisters are all like her.

　　　Enter SIR WALTER *with two spoons and plate, and* ALLWIT.

2 Gossip. Oh, here comes the chief gossip, neighbours.　　　　　25
　　　　　　　　　　[*Exit* Nurse *with child.*]
Sir Walter. The fatness of your wishes to you all, ladies.
3 Gossip. O dear, sweet gentleman, what fine words he has:
　　'The fatness of our wishes'!
2 Gossip.　　　　　Calls us all 'ladies'!
4 Gossip. I promise you, a fine gentleman and a courteous.
2 Gossip. Methinks her husband shows like a clown to him.　　　　　30
3 Gossip. I would not care what clown my husband were too, so I
　　had such fine children.
2 Gossip. She's all fine children, gossip.
3 Gossip. Ay, and see how fast they come.
1 Puritan. Children are blessings, if they be got with zeal by the　　　35
　　brethren, as I have five at home.

---

9. *chopping*] vigorous, strapping.
13. *up and down*] in every way.
16. *spiny*] skinny.
17. *mettled*] (1) full of spirit; (2) half drunk.
18. *raise up seed*] breed children.
24. *The sisters*] the women of the chosen faithful.
24.1. *plate*] i.e. silver plate.
26. *The fatness*] the best part.
29. *promise*] assure.
30. *to him*] compared to him.

Sir Walter. [*To Mrs Allwit*] The worst is past, I hope now, gossip.
Mrs Allwit. So I hope too, good sir.
Allwit. [*Aside*] Why, then, so hope I too for company;
    I have nothing to do else.   40
Sir Walter. [*Giving cup and spoons*] A poor remembrance, lady,
    To the love of the babe; I pray, accept of it.
Mrs Allwit. Oh, you are at too much charge, sir!
2 Gossip. Look, look! What has he given her? What is 't, gossip?
3 Gossip. Now, by my faith, a fair high standing-cup   45
    And two great 'postle-spoons, one of them gilt.
1 Puritan. Sure that was Judas then with the red beard.
2 Puritan. I would not feed my daughter with that spoon for all the
    world, for fear of colouring her hair. Red hair the brethren like
    not, it consumes them much; 'tis not the sisters' colour.   50

              Enter Nurse *with comfits and wine.*

Allwit. Well said, Nurse.
    About, about with them amongst the gossips!
    [*Aside*] Now out comes all the tasselled handkerchers;
    They are spread abroad between their knees already.
    Now in goes the long fingers that are washed   55
    Some thrice a day in urine; my wife uses it.
    Now we shall have such pocketing!
    See how they lurch at the lower end!
1 Puritan. Come hither, Nurse.
Allwit. [*Aside*] Again? She has taken twice already.   60
1 Puritan. [*Taking comfits*] I had forgot a sisters's child that's sick.
Allwit. [*Aside*] A pox! It seems your purity loves sweet things well,
    that puts in thrice together. Had this been all my cost now,
    I had been beggared; these women have no consciences at
    sweetmeats, where'er they come. See an they have not culled 65
    out all the long plums too; they have left nothing here but short

---

39. *for company*] to do as others do.
43. *at . . . charge*] taking too much expense on yourself.
45. *standing-cup*] cup with a base or legs for standing.
46. *'postle-spoons*] silver spoons with the figure of an apostle on the handle.
47. *Judas*] Judas was the betrayer of Christ. The Gossip thinks the spoon represents Judas because the gilding has a reddish cast; a red beard was traditional in representations of Judas. Red hair was also associated with lechery.
51. *Well said*] Well done.
55–6. *washed . . . urine*] i.e. as a cosmetic.
58. *lurch*] cheat; take more sweets than their share.
lower end] far end of the room from the host.
63. *that . . . together*] you who helps yourself three times over.
66. *plums*] sugar plums.

wriggle-tail comfits, not worth mouthing! No mar'l I heard a
citizen complain once that his wife's belly only broke his back.
Mine had been all in fitters seven years since but for this worthy
knight, that with a prop upholds my wife and me and all my 70
estate buried in Bucklersbury.

Mrs Allwit. [*Pledging them*] Here, Mistress Yellowhammer and
    neighbours,
To you all that have taken pains with me,
All the good wives at once! [*The Nurse takes round wine.*]

1 Puritan. I'll answer for them. 75
They wish all health and strength, and that you may
Courageously go forward to perform
The like and many such, like a true sister,
With motherly bearing. [*She drinks.*]

Allwit. [*Aside*] Now the cups troll about to wet the gossips' whistles. 80
It pours down, i' faith; they never think of payment.

1 Puritan. Fill again, Nurse. [*She drinks.*]

Allwit. [*Aside*] Now, bless thee, two at once! I'll stay no longer; it
would kill me an if I paid for 't. [*To Sir Walter*] Will it please you
to walk down and leave the women? 85

Sir Walter. With all my heart, Jack.

Allwit. Troth, I cannot blame you.

Sir Walter. Sit you all merry, ladies.

All Gossips. Thank your worship, sir.

1 Puritan. Thank your worship, sir. 90

Allwit. [*Aside*] A pox twice tipple ye! You are last and lowest.
                    Exit [SIR WALTER *with* ALLWIT].

1 Puritan. Bring hither that same cup, Nurse; I would fain drive
away this—hup!—antichristian grief. [*She drinks.*]

3 Gossip. See, gossip, an she lies not in like a countess.
Would I had such a husband for my daughter! 95

4 Gossip. Is not she toward marriage?

3 Gossip. Oh, no, sweet gossip!

4 Gossip. Why, she's nineteen.

---

67. *No mar'l*] It is no marvel (that).
68. *his . . . back*] (1) her greed made him overwork; (2) lust exhausted him.
69. *fitters*] little bits.
71. *Bucklersbury*] a street running south from Cheapside to Walbrook with
grocers' and apothecaries' shops on it.
80. *troll*] circulate.
91. *A pox . . . ye*] May syphilis topple you over and over.
94. *she*] i.e. Mrs Allwit.
96. *she*] i.e. the Third Gossip's daughter.
toward marriage] going to be married.

3 Gossip. Ay, that she was last Lammas,
    But she has a fault, gossip, a secret fault.   100
              [*Nurse replenishes glass, then exit.*]
4 Gossip. A fault? What is 't?
3 Gossip. I'll tell you when I have drunk.   [*She drinks.*]
4 Gossip. [*Aside*] Wine can do that, I see, that friendship cannot.
3 Gossip. And now I'll tell you, gossip: she's too free.
4 Gossip. Too free?   105
3 Gossip. Oh, ay, she cannot lie dry in her bed.
4 Gossip. What, and nineteen?
3 Gossip. 'Tis as I tell you, gossip.

        [*Enter* Nurse, *and whispers to Maudlin.*]

Maudlin. Speak with me, Nurse? Who is 't?
Nurse. A gentleman from Cambridge; I think it be your son, 110
    forsooth.
Maudlin. 'Tis my son Tim, i' faith. Prithee, call him up among the
    women; 'twill embolden him well, for he wants nothing but
    audacity.   [*Exit* Nurse.]
    [*To herself*] Would the Welsh gentlewoman at home were here 115
    now!
Lady Kix. Is your son come, forsooth?
Maudlin. Yes, from the university, forsooth.
Lady Kix. 'Tis great joy on ye.
Maudlin. There's a great marriage towards for him.   120
Lady Kix. A marriage?
Maudlin. Yes, sure, a huge heir in Wales at least to nineteen moun-
    tains, besides her goods and cattle.

        Enter [Nurse *with*] TIM.

Tim. Oh, I'm betrayed!   *Exit.*
Maudlin. What, gone again?—Run after him, good Nurse.   125
              [*Exit* Nurse.]
    He's so bashful, that's the spoil of youth.
    In the university they're kept still to men,
    And ne'er trained up to women's company.
Lady Kix. 'Tis a great spoil of youth, indeed.

        Enter Nurse *and* TIM.

Nurse. [*To Tim*] Your mother will have it so.   130
Maudlin. Why, son, why, Tim! What, must I rise and fetch you? For
    shame, son!

---

  99. *Lammas*] 1 August.
  106. *lie . . . bed*] i.e. go all night without urinating.
  124. *I'm betrayed*] Tim was not expecting a room full of women.

Tim. Mother, you do entreat like a freshwoman. 'Tis against the
  laws of the university For any that has answered under bachelor
  To thrust 'mongst married wives.   135
Maudlin. Come, we'll excuse you here.
Tim. Call up my tutor, mother, and I care not.
Maudlin. What, is your tutor come? Have you brought him up?
Tim. I ha 'not brought him up; he stands at door.
  Negatur. There's logic to begin with you, mother.   140
Maudlin. Run, call the gentleman, Nurse; he's my son's tutor.
                                                          [*Exit* Nurse.]
  [*To Tim*] Here, eat some plums.
Tim. Come I from Cambridge, and offer me six plums?
Maudlin. Why, how now, Tim? Will not your old tricks yet be
  left?   145
Tim. Served like a child, when I have answered under bachelor?
Maudlin. You'll never lin till I make your tutor whip you. You know
  how I served you once at the free-school in Paul's churchyard?
Tim. Oh, monstrous absurdity!
  Ne'er was the like in Cambridge since my time.   150
  Life, whip a bachelor? You'd be laughed at soundly;
  Let not my tutor hear you! 'Twould be a jest through the whole
  university. No more words, mother.

                          Enter Tutor.

Maudlin. Is this your tutor, Tim?
Tutor. Yes, surely, lady; I am the man that brought him in league   155
  with logic and read the Dunces to him.
Tim. That did he, mother, but now I have 'em all in my own pate,
  and can as well read 'em to others.
Tutor. That can he, mistress, for they flow naturally from him.
Maudlin. I'm the more beholding to your pains, sir.   160
Tutor. Non ideo sane.

---

134. *answered . . . bachelor*] satisfied the requirements for the degree of bachelor;
also line 146.

137.] i.e. If you invite my tutor up, mother, I don't mind staying.

140. Negatur] It is denied. Tim's pedantic quibble is that he has not *brought* his
tutor *up*, since the man in still waiting downstairs. (The formal rooms for visitors are
on the upper level of the house.)

147. *lin*] stop.

148. *free-school . . . churchyard*] St Paul's school, founded by Colet in 1512.

156. *Dunces*] followers of the scholastic theologian Duns Scotus. Their ideas
were denigrated as pedantry from the mid sixteenth century, so Tim's style of
learning is fifty years or more out of date.

161. Non ideo sane] a tag in Latin disputes, meaning 'not for that reason
indeed'. Maudlin thinks 'ideo' means 'idiot'.

Maudlin. True, he was an idiot indeed, when he went out of London, but now he's well mended. Did you receive the two goose-
pies I sent you?

Tutor. And eat them heartily, thanks to your worship.   165

Maudlin. [*To Gossips*] 'Tis my son Tim; I pray, bid him welcome,
gentlewomen.

Tim. 'Tim'? Hark you: 'Timotheus', mother, 'Timotheus'.

Maudlin. How, shall I deny your name? 'Timotheus', quoth he?
Faith, there's a name! 'Tis my son Tim, forsooth.   170

Lady Kix. You're welcome, Master Tim.   *Kiss[es Tim].*

Tim. [*Aside to Tutor*] Oh, this is horrible! She wets as she kisses.
Your handkercher, sweet tutor, to wipe them off as fast as they
come on!

2 Gossip. Welcome from Cambridge.   *Kiss[es Tim].* 175

Tim. [*Aside to Tutor*] This is intolerable! This woman has a villainous sweet breath, did she not stink of comfits. Help me, sweet
tutor, or I shall rub my lips off.

Tutor. I'll go kiss the lower end the whilst.

Tim. Perhaps that's the sweeter, and we shall despatch the sooner. 180

1 Puritan. Let me come next. Welcome from the wellspring of
discipline that waters all the brethren!   *Reels and falls.*

Tim. Hoist, I beseech thee!

3 Gossip. Oh, bless the woman!—Mistress Underman!

1 Puritan. 'Tis but the common affliction of the faithful; we must   185
embrace our falls.

Tim. [*Aside to Tutor*] I'm glad I 'scaped it; it was some rotten kiss,
sure; it dropped down before it came at me.

Enter ALLWIT *and* DAVY.

Allwit. [*Aside*] Here's a noise! Not parted yet? Heyday, a looking
glass! They have drunk so hard in plate that some of them had   190
need of other vessels. [*Aloud*] Yonder's the bravest show!

All Gossips. Where, where, sir?

---

179. *the lower end*] i.e. the women at the lower end of the room; but with a
suggestion that he will kiss the women's lower ends.

180. *Perhaps . . . sweeter*] (1) perhaps the breaths of those woman are sweeter; (2)
perhaps their lower ends smell sweeter than their breaths.

181–2. *wellspring of discipline*] The University of Cambridge was associated with
Puritanism at this time.

183. *Hoist*] (1) lift her up; (2) hoist sail.

186. *embrace . . . falls*] accept our fallen nature.

188. *dropped down*] i.e. (1) like rotten fruit falling from the tree; (2) like a
drunkard.

189–90. *looking glass*] i.e. chamber pot.

191. *other vessels*] i.e. chamber pots.

bravest] finest, most spectacular.

Allwit. Come along presently by the Pissing-Conduit, with two
    brave drums and a standard-bearer.
All Gossips. Oh, brave!   195
Tim. Come, tutor!   *Exit [with* Tutor].
All Gossips. [*To Mrs Allwit*] Farewell, sweet gossip.
                                    [*Exeunt* Gossips].
Mrs Allwit. I thank you all for your pains.
1 Puritan. Feed and grow strong!
        Exeunt [MRS ALLWIT, MAUDLIN, LADY KIX, *and* Puritans.]
Allwit. You had more need to sleep than eat;   200
    Go, take a nap with some of the brethren, go,
    And rise up a well-edified, boldified sister!
    Oh, here's a day of toil well passed o'er,
    Able to make a citizen hare-mad!
    How hot they have made the rooms with their thick bums!   205
    Dost not feel it, Davy?
Davy. Monstrous strong, sir.
Allwit. What's here under the stools?
Davy. Nothing but wet, sir; some wine spilt here, belike.
Allwit. Is 't no worse, think'st thou?   210
    Fair needlework stools cost nothing with them, Davy.
Davy. [*Aside*] Nor you neither, i' faith.
Allwit. Look how they have laid them,
    E'en as they lie themselves, with their heels up!
    How they have shuffled up the rushes too, Davy,   215
    With their short figging little shittle-cork-heels!
    These women can let nothing stand as they find it.
    But what's the secret thou'st about to tell me,
    My honest Davy?
Davy. If you should disclose it, sir—   220
Allwit. Life, rip my belly up to the throat then, Davy.
Davy. My master's upon marriage.

---

193. *Pissing-Conduit*] the common name for a water fountain close to the Royal
Exchange at the junction of Threadneedle Street and Cornhill.

201–2.] Allwit, sneering at his wife and her friends, suggests that their religious
language is no more than a cover for sexual licence.

204. *hare-mad*] mad as a (March) hare.

211. *with them*] i.e. to them.

213. *them*] i.e. the stools.

214. *with . . . up*] with their legs in the air.

215. *rushes*] green rushes were used as a floor covering.

216. *figging*] worthless.

shittle-cork] the original form for 'shuttle-cock'. It refers to the fashionable cork
high heels on the gossips' shoes.

222. *upon*] on the verge of.

Allwit. Marriage, Davy? Send me to hanging rather!
Davy. [*Aside*] I have stung him.
Allwit. When, where? What is she, Davy?   225
Davy. E'en the same was gossip and gave the spoon.
Allwit. I have no time to stay, nor scarce can speak!
    I'll stop those wheels, or all the work will break.   *Exit.*
Davy. I knew 'twould prick. Thus do I fashion still
    All mine own ends by him and his rank toil.   230
    'Tis my desire to keep him still from marriage;
    Being his poor nearest kinsman, I may fare
    The better at his death. There my hopes build,
    Since my Lady Kix is dry and hath no child.   *Exit.*

[3.3]

Enter both the TOUCHWOODS.

Touchwood Junior. Y' are in the happiest way to enrich yourself
    And pleasure me, brother, as man's feet can tread in;
    For, though she be locked up, her vow is fixed
    Only to me. Then time shall never grieve me;
    For by that vow e'en absent I enjoy her,   5
    Assuredly confirmed that none else shall,
    Which will make tedious years seem gameful to me.
    In the mean space, lose you no time, sweet brother.
    You have the means to strike at this knight's fortunes
    And lay him level with his bankrupt merit.   10
    Get but his wife with child; perch at tree-top
    And shake the golden fruit into her lap.
    About it, before she weep herself to a dry ground
    And whine out all her goodness.
Touchwood Senior.   Prithee, cease.

---

223. *hanging*] Wedding and hanging were linked in proverbs.
226. *E'en . . . gossip*] i.e. Moll, who acted as godparent, 'gossip', to the Allwits'
child.
229. *I . . . prick*] i.e. I knew that my telling Allwit about Sir Walter's plan to
marry would goad him into action.
230. *him*] Allwit.
231. *him*] Sir Walter.
234. *dry*] barren.

3.3.8. *mean space*] meantime.
10.] and bring his fortunes down to the bankrupt level of his poor merits.
11–12. *perch . . . lap*] The plan for Touchwood Senior to impregnate Lady Kix is
compared with a harvester shaking fruit from a tree into the spread apron of a helper
below. The fruit is *golden* because a child will ensure the Kixes' inheritance.
13. *weep . . . ground*] Lady Kix's weeping will empty out her natural juices and
make her completely infertile, like dry ground. See Intro., p. 53.

I find a too much aptness in my blood   15
For such a business without provocation.
You might' well spared this banquet of eryngoes,
Artichokes, potatoes, and your buttered crab;
They were fitter kept for your own wedding dinner.
Touchwood Junior. Nay, an you'll follow my suit and save my
    purse too,   20
Fortune dotes on me. He's in happy case
Finds such an honest friend i' the Common place.
Touchwood Senior. Life, what makes thee so merry? Thou hast no
    cause
That I could hear of lately since thy crosses,
Unless there be news come with new additions.   25
Touchwood Junior. Why, there thou hast it right. I look for her
    This evening, brother.
Touchwood Senior.   How's that? Look for her?
Touchwood Junior. I will deliver you of the wonder straight, brother.
    By the firm secrecy and kind assistance
Of a good wench i' the house, who, made of pity,   30
Weighing the case her own, she's led through gutters,
Strange hidden ways, which none but love could find
Or ha' the heart to venture. I expect her
Where you would little think.
Touchwood Senior.   I care not where,
    So she be safe, and yours.
Touchwood Junior.   Hope tells me so;   35
But from your love and time my peace must grow.
Touchwood Senior. You know the worst then, brother.
                  Exit [TOUCHWOOD JUNIOR].
                  Now to my Kix,
The barren he and she. They're i' the next room;
But to say which of their two humours hold them

---

17. *might'*] might have. The apostrophe in the quarto text stands for the missing
'have'.

   eryngoes] candied sea-holly root, considered an aphrodisiac, like the other foods
in the list.

22. *i' the Common place*] i.e. at need. Literally, 'in the Court of Common Pleas'.
The whole sentence is proverbial as in 'a friend in need is a friend indeed'.

24. *crosses*] setbacks.

28.] either (1) I will rescue you from your wonderment at once, brother; or (2) I
will deliver the wondrous news to you, brother.

31. *Weighing*] considering.

36.] but my happiness depends upon your willingness to give me your love and
your time.

37. *You . . . brother*] You know all there is to know about me and know that you
can depend upon me.

39. *their two humours*] i.e. hating each other and devising how to have children.

Now at this instant, I cannot say truly.   40
Sir Oliver. [*To his lady within*] Thou liest, barrenness!
Touchwood Senior. Oh, is 't that time of day? Give you joy of your
    tongue!
There's nothing else good in you.—This their life
The whole day, from eyes open to eyes shut,
Kissing or scolding, and then must be made friends;   45
Then rail the second part of the first fit out,
And then be pleased again, no man knows which way;
Fall out like giants and fall in like children;
Their fruit can witness as much.

    Enter SIR OLIVER KIX *and his* Lady.

Sir Oliver.   'Tis thy fault.
Lady Kix. Mine, drought and coldness?
Sir Oliver.   Thine; 'tis thou art barren.   50
Lady Kix. I barren? O life, that I durst but speak now
In mine own justice, in mine own right! I barren?
'Twas otherways with me when I was at court;
I was ne'er called so till I was married.
Sir Oliver. I'll be divorced.
Lady Kix.   Be hanged! I need not wish it.   55
That will come too soon to thee. I may say
'Marriage and hanging goes by destiny',
For all the goodness I can find in 't yet.
Sir Oliver. I'll give up house and keep some fruitful whore,
Like an old bachelor, in a tradesman's chamber;   60
She and her children shall have all.
Lady Kix.   Where be they?
Touchwood Senior. [*Approaching them*]   Pray, cease.
When there are friendlier courses took for you
To get and multiply within your house
At your own proper costs, in spite of censure,
Methinks an honest peace might be established.   65
Sir Oliver. What, with her? Never.
Touchwood Senior.   Sweet sir—
Sir Oliver.   You work all in vain.

---

46. *fit*] part of a song. The Kixes' quarrel is compared with a refrain to which
they always return.
  48. *fall in*] (1) make up; (2) fall into each others' arms.
  49. *Their fruit*] i.e. the children they don't have.
  55. *it*] i.e. that you should be hanged.
  62. *took*] taken.
  64. *proper*] personal.

Lady Kix. [*To Sir Oliver*] Then he doth all like thee.
Touchwood Senior.   Let me entreat, sir—
Sir Oliver. Singleness confound her! I took her with one smock.
Lady Kix. But, indeed, you came not so single when
    You came from shipboard.
Sir Oliver. [*Aside*]   Heart, she bit sore there!   70
    [*To Touchwood Senior*] Prithee, make 's friends.
Touchwood Senior. [*Aside*] Is 't come to that? The peal begins to
    cease.
Sir Oliver. [*To Lady Kix*] I'll sell all at an outcry!
Lady Kix. Do thy worst, slave!
    [*To Touchwood Senior*] Good sweet sir, bring us into love
    again.   75
Touchwood Senior. [*Aside*] Some would think this impossible to
    compass.
    [*To them*] Pray, let this storm fly over.
Sir Oliver. Good sir, pardon me. I'm master of this house,
    Which I'll sell presently; I'll clap up bills this evening.
Touchwood Senior. Lady, friends, come!   80
Lady Kix. If e'er ye loved woman, talk not on 't, sir.
    What, friends with him? Good faith, do you think I'm mad?
    With one that's scarce the hinder quarter of a man?
Sir Oliver. Thou art nothing of a woman.
Lady Kix. Would I were less than nothing!   *Weeps.*   85
Sir Oliver. Nay, prithee, what dost mean?
Lady Kix. I cannot please you.
Sir Oliver. I' faith, thou art a good soul; he lies that says it. Buss,
    buss, pretty rogue.   [*He kisses her.*]
Lady Kix. You care not for me.   90
Touchwood Senior. [*Aside*] Can any man tell now which way they
    came in? By this light, I'll be hanged then!
Sir Oliver. Is the drink come?
Touchwood Senior. (*Aside* [*producing a vial*]) Here's a little vial of
    almond-milk,

---

67. *Then . . . thee*] i.e. if Touchwood Senior works 'in vain' as you say, then he's
just like you; your attempts at sexual performance are all in vain.
    68. *Singleness*] i.e. divorce.
    with one smock] i.e. with a dowry consisting of only one petticoat.
    69. *single*] unaccompanied. The implication is that he was lousy.
    72. *The peal*] i.e. the noise of quarelling.
    73. *outcry*] public auction.
    76. *compass*] encompass.
    79. *clap up bills*] stick up posters advertising the house-sale.
    80. *friends*] be friends.
    88. *it*] i.e. that you cannot please me.
    Buss] kiss.
    91-2. *which . . . in*] i.e. how they were behaving when they came in.

That stood me in some threepence.   95

Sir Oliver. I hope to see thee, wench, within these few years,
  Circled with children, pranking up a girl,
  And putting jewels in their little ears;
  Fine sport, i' faith!

Lady Kix. Ay, had you been aught, husband,   100
  It had been done ere this time.

Sir Oliver. Had I been aught? Hang thee! Hadst thou been aught!
  But a cross thing I ever found thee.

Lady Kix. Thou art a grub to say so.

Sir Oliver. A pox on thee!   105

Touchwood Senior. [*Aside*] By this light, they are out again at the
  same door, and no man can tell which way! [*To Sir Oliver*]
  Come, here's your drink, sir.

Sir Oliver. I will not take it now, sir,
  An I were sure to get three boys ere midnight.   110

Lady Kix. Why, there thou show'st now of what breed thou com'st,
  To hinder generation. O thou villain,
  That knows how crookedly the world goes with us
  For want of heirs, yet put by all good fortune!

Sir Oliver. Hang, strumpet! I will take it now in spite.   115

Touchwood Senior. Then you must ride upon 't five hours.
                    [*He gives a vial to Sir Oliver.*]

Sir Oliver. I mean so.—Within there!

                    Enter a Servant.

Servant. Sir?

Sir Oliver. Saddle the white mare.   [*Exit* Servant.]
  I'll take a whore along and ride to Ware.   120

Lady Kix. Ride to the devil!

Sir Oliver. I'll plague you every way.
  Look ye, do you see? 'Tis gone.   *Drinks.*

Lady Kix. A pox go with it!

Sir Oliver. Ay, curse and spare not now.   125

---

95. *stood . . . in*] cost me.
97. *pranking up*] prettifying.
100. *aught*] anything (i.e. sexually).
103. *But . . . thee*] I have always found you to be nothing but bad-tempered and contrary.
110. *An*] even if.
112. *hinder generation*] prevent procreation.
114. *put . . . fortune*] set aside all opportunity for good fortune.
115. *it*] i.e. the drink.
116.] Then you must go riding for five hours after you have taken the drink.
120. *Ware*] a town twenty miles north of London. It was famous for an enormous bed in the Saracen's Head Inn, and for assignations.

Touchwood Senior. Stir up and down, sir; you must not stand.

Sir Oliver. Nay, I'm not given to standing.

Touchwood Senior. So much the better, sir, for the—

Sir Oliver. I never could stand long in one place yet;
 I learned it of my father, ever figient.   130
 How if I crossed this, sir?   *Capers.*

Touchwood Senior. Oh, passing good, sir, and would show well a-
 horseback. When you come to your inn, if you leaped over a
 joint-stool or two 'twere not amiss (*Aside*) although you brake
 your neck, sir.   135

Sir Oliver. What say you to a table thus high, sir? [*He capers.*]

Touchwood Senior. Nothing better, sir [*Aside*] if it be furnished with
 good victuals. [*To him*] You remember how the bargain runs
 about this business?

Sir Oliver. Or else I had a bad head: you must receive, sir, four 140
 hundred pounds of me at four several payments; one hundred
 pound now in hand.

Touchwood Senior. Right, that I have, sir.

Sir Oliver. Another hundred when my wife is quick; the third when
 she's brought a-bed; and the last hundred when the child cries, 145
 for, if it should be still-born, it doth no good, sir.

Touchwood Senior. All this is even still. A little faster, sir.

Sir Oliver. Not a whit, sir;
 I'm in an excellent pace for any physic.

Enter a Servant.

Servant. Your white mare's ready.   150

Sir Oliver. I shall up presently.   [*Exit* Servant.]
 [*To Lady Kix*]   One kiss, and farewell. [*He kisses her.*]

Lady Kix. Thou shalt have two, love.

Sir Oliver. Expect me about three.   *Exit.*

---

126. *Stir . . . stand*] Touchwood Senior claims that the potion will not work unless Sir Oliver keeps moving. With a bawdy pun on *stand* and *standing* (127).

130. *figient*] fidgety.

131. *crossed this*] i.e. jumped over this (stool).

132. *passing*] very.

SD. Capers] He jumps up high while dancing.

137–8. *if . . . victuals*] i.e. if the table actually had some food on it, it might be worth something.

140. *Or . . . head*] If I didn't, it would show that I had a bad head for business.

141. *several*] separate.

144. *quick*] pregnant.

147. *even still*] exactly right, as we agreed.

A little faster] Dance a little faster. (Sir Oliver has been jumping up and down throughout this exchange.)

149. *physic*] medicine.

151. *up*] mount my horse (with a sexual double meaning).

Lady Kix. With all my heart, sweet.   155

Touchwood Senior. [*Aside*] By this light, they have forgot their anger
    since, and are as far in again as e'er they were. Which way the
    devil came they? Heart, I saw 'em not; their ways are beyond
    finding out. [*To Lady Kix*] Come, sweet lady.

Lady Kix. How must I take mine, sir?   160

Touchwood Senior. Clean contrary; yours must be taken lying.

Lady Kix. A-bed, sir?

Touchwood Senior. A-bed, or where you will for your own ease;
    Your coach will serve.

Lady Kix.   The physic must needs please.

                Exit [*with* TOUCHSTONE SENIOR].

158.] i.e. How the devil did they change so quickly? By God's heart, it happened
too rapidly for me to see.

161. *Clean contrary*] quite the opposite way (from Sir Oliver).

164. *coach*] Coaches were notorious locations for illicit sex.

Act 4

Enter TIM *and* Tutor.

Tim. Negatur argumentum, tutor.

Tutor. Probo tibi, pupil: *stultus non est animal rationale.*

Tim. Falleris sane.

Tutor. Quaeso ut tacea. Probo tibi—

Tim. Quomodo probas, domine?   5

Tutor. Stultus non habet rationem, ergo non est animal rationale.

Tim. Sic argumentaris, domine: stultus non habet rationem, ergo non est animal rationale. Negatur argumentum again, tutor.

Tutor. Argumentum iterum probo tibi, domine: qui non participat de ratione, nullo modo potest vocari rationalis; but *stultus non*   10
  participat de ratione, ergo stultus nullo modo potest dici rationalis.

Tim. Participat.

Tutor. Sic disputas. Qui participat, quomodo participat?

Tim. Ut homo. Probabo tibi in syllogismo.

Tutor. Hunc proba.   15

Tim. Sic probo, domine: stultus est homo sicut tu et ego sumus; homo est animal rationale, sicut stultus est animal rationale.

Enter MAUDLIN.

4.1.1–17.] *Tim.* Your proof is denied, tutor.
Tutor. I demonstrate it to you, pupil, a fool is not a rational creature.
Tim. You will certainly fail.
Tutor. I beg you to be silent. I prove it to you—
Tim. How do you prove it, sir?
Tutor. A fool has not the power of reason, therefore he is not a rational creature.
Tim. Thus you argue, sir: a fool has not the power of reason, therefore he is not a rational creature. Your argument is denied again, tutor.
Tutor. Again, I demonstrate the proof, sir: he who does not share the power of reason, in no wise can be said to be rational; but a fool does not share the power of reason, therefore a fool in no wise can be said to be rational.
Tim. He does share it.
Tutor. So you argue. Who shares it, how does he share it?
Tim. As a man. I will prove it to you by a syllogism.
Tutor. Prove this.
Tim. Thus I prove it, sir: a fool is a man just as you and I are; a man is a rational creature, just so a fool is a rational creature.
(Tim's proof is an example of the fallacy of the excluded middle, the most elementary mistake in logic.)

Maudlin. Here's nothing but disputing all the day long with 'em!

Tutor. Sic disputas: stultus est homo sicut tu et ego sumus; homo est animal rationale, sicut stultus est animal rationale.   20

Maudlin. Your reasons are both good, whate'er they be;
Pray, give them o'er. Faith, you'll tire yourselves.
What's the matter between you?

Tim. Nothing but reasoning about a fool, mother.

Maudlin. About a fool, son? Alas, what need you trouble your heads   25
about that? None of us all but knows what a fool is.

Tim. Why, what's a fool, mother? I come to you now.

Maudlin. Why, one that's married before he has wit.

Tim. 'Tis pretty, i' faith, and well guessed of a woman never
brought up at the university; but bring forth what fool you will,   30
mother, I'll prove him to be as reasonable a creature as myself
or my tutor here.

Maudlin. Fie, 'tis impossible.

Tutor. Nay, he shall do 't, forsooth.

Tim. 'Tis the easiest thing to prove a fool by logic; by logic I'll prove   35
anything.

Maudlin. What, thou wilt not!

Tim. I'll prove a whore to be an honest woman.

Maudlin. Nay, by my faith, she must prove that herself, or logic will
never do 't.   40

Tim. 'Twill do 't, I tell you.

Maudlin. Some in this street would give a thousand pounds that you
could prove their wives so.

Tim. Faith, I can, and all their daughters too, though they had three
bastards! When comes your tailor hither?   45

Maudlin. Why, what of him?

Tim. By logic I'll prove him to be a man, let him come when he
will.

Maudlin. [*To Tutor*] How hard at first was learning to him! Truly,
sir, I thought he would never ha' took the Latin tongue. How   50
many accidences do you think he wore out ere he came to his
grammar?

19–20.] So you contend: a fool is a man just as you and I are; a man is a rational
creature, just so a fool is a rational creature. (The Tutor's response simply repeats
Tim's disputation word for word.)

27. *I . . . now*] Let me take you on now, in disputation.

37. *What . . . not!*] I don't believe you can do that! (Said in astonished
admiration.)

45–7. *tailor . . . man*] Tailors were proverbially effeminate. Tim is going to use
logic to prove the opposite.

51. *accidences*] books containing the rules for the Latin endings of words; a more
elementary stage than 'grammar' (line 52) which deals with the construction of
sentences.

Tutor. Some three or four.

Maudlin. Believe me, sir, some four and thirty.

Tim. Pish, I made haberdins of 'em in church porches.   55

Maudlin. He was eight years in his grammar, and stuck horribly at
a foolish place there called *as in praesenti.*

Tim. Pox, I have it here now.   [*He taps his forehead.*]

Maudlin. He so shamed me once before an honest gentleman that
knew me when I was a maid.   60

Tim. These women must have all out!

Maudlin. '*Quid est grammatica?*' says the gentleman to him—I shall
remember by a sweet, sweet token—but nothing could he
answer.

Tutor. How now, pupil, ha? *Quid est grammatica?*   65

Tim. *Grammatica?* Ha, ha, ha!

Maudlin. Nay, do not laugh, son, but let me hear you say it now.
There was one word went so prettily off the gentleman's
tongue; I shall remember it the longest day of my life.

Tutor. Come, *quid est grammatica?*   70

Tim. Are you not ashamed, tutor? *Grammatica:* why, *recte scribendi
atque loquendi ars,* sir-reverence of my mother.

Maudlin. That was it, i' faith! Why now, son, I see you are a deep
scholar. And, Master Tutor, a word I pray: [*Aside to Tutor*] let
us withdraw a little into my husband's chamber. I'll send in the   75
North-Wales gentlewoman to him; she looks for wooing. I'll
put together both and lock the door.

Tutor. I give great approbation to your conclusion.

                                        Exit [MAUDLIN *with* Tutor].

Tim. I mar'l what this gentlewoman should be that I should have in
marriage. She's a stranger to me. I wonder what my parents   80
mean, i' faith, to match me with a stranger so, a maid that's
neither kiff nor kin to me. Life, do they think I have no more
care of my body than to lie with one that I ne'er knew, a mere
stranger, one that ne'er went to school with me neither, nor ever

---

55. *haberdins*] literally, dried pilchards. Tim may be saying that he cut books into
paper fish, but the reference is obscure.

57. *as in praesenti*] a common schoolboy joke playing on the assonance between
Latin *as* (the ending of some verbs in the present tense) and English 'ass'.

61. *must . . . out*] insist on telling everything.

62, 65, 71–2. Quid . . . ars] What is grammar . . . the art of writing and speaking
correctly. The word that Maudlin so fondly remembers is *ars.*

72. *sir-reverence . . . mother*] i.e. with an apology to my mother for saying a rude
word (*ars,* suggesting 'arse').

76. *looks for wooing*] expects to be wooed.

79. *mar'l*] wonder.

82. *kiff*] kith, friend or neighbour.

play-fellows together? They're mightily o'erseen in 't, methinks.   85
They say she has mountains to her marriage; she's full of cattle,
some two thousand runts. Now what the meaning of these runts
should be, my tutor cannot tell me. I have looked in Rider's
Dictionary for the letter R, and there I can hear no tidings of
these runts neither. Unless they should be Romford hogs, I   90
know them not.

Enter Welsh Gentlewoman.

And here she comes. If I know what to say to her now in the
way of marriage, I'm no graduate! Methinks, i' faith, 'tis boldly
done of her to come into my chamber, being but a stranger;
she shall not say I'm so proud yet but I'll speak to her. Marry,   95
as I will order it, she shall take no hold of my words, I'll warrant
her.   [*The Welsh Gentlewoman curtsies.*]
She looks and makes a cur'sey!—[*To her*] *Salve tu quoque, puella*
pulcherrima! Quid vis nescio nec sane curo—Tully's own phrase to
a hair!   100
Welsh Gentlewoman. [*Aside*] I know not what he means. A suitor,
        quoth a?
I hold my life he understands no English.
Tim. Fertur, mehercule, tu virgo,
        Wallia ut opibus abundas maximis.
Welsh Gentlewoman. [*Aside*] What's this *fertur* and *abundundis?*   105
He mocks me sure, and calls me a bundle of farts.
Tim. [*Aside*] I have no Latin word now for their runts; I'll
make some shift or other. [*To her*] *Iterum dico, opibus abundas*
maximis montibus et fontibus et, ut ita dicam, rontibus; attamen vero

---

85. *o'erseen*] mistaken.
86. *to her marriage*] as her marriage dowry.
87. *runts*] a small breed of cattle, often found in Wales.
88–9. *Rider's Dictionary*] a popular Latin–English and English–Latin dictionary of 1598, often reprinted.
90. *Romford*] Essex town, famous for its weekly hog market.
98–9.] Save thee also, lovely maiden! What you want I do not know, nor truly do I care.
99. *Tully*] Cicero, the Roman orator whose writing was commonly used to teach Latin and rhetoric.
101. *quoth a*] said he.
103–4.] It is said, by Hercules, maiden, that you abound with great wealth in Wales.
108–11.] Again, I say, you abound in great riches, in mountains and fountains and, as I may call them, in 'runts' [inventing a Latin form *rontibus*]; yet truly, I am a little man by nature and also a bachelor by training [i.e. Bachelor of Arts], actually not prepared for bed.

homunculus ego sum natura simul et arte baccalaureus, lecto profecto   110
non paratus.
Welsh Gentlewoman. [*Aside*] This is most strange. Maybe he can
  speak Welsh.—*Avedera whee comrage, der due cog foginis.*
Tim. [*Aside*] *Cog foggin?* I scorn to cog with her; I'll tell her so too,
  in a word near her own language. [*To her*] *Ego non cogo.*   115
Welsh Gentlewoman. Rhegosin a whiggin harle ron corid ambre.
Tim. [*Aside*] By my faith, she's a good scholar, I see that already.
  She has the tongues, plain; I hold my life she has travelled.
  What will folks say? There goes the learned couple! Faith, if the
  truth were known she hath proceeded!   120

Enter MAUDLIN.

Maudlin. How now, how speeds your business?
Tim. [*Aside*] I'm glad my mother's come to part us.
Maudlin. [*To Welsh Gentlewoman*] How do you agree, forsooth?
Welsh Gentlewoman. As well as e'er we did before we met.
Maudlin. How's that?   125
Welsh Gentlewoman. You put me to a man I understand not;
  Your son's no Englishman, methinks.
Maudlin. No Englishman! Bless my boy, and born i' the heart of
  London?
Welsh Gentlewoman. I ha' been long enough in the chamber with
  him,   130
  And I find neither Welsh nor English in him.
Maudlin. Why, Tim, how have you used the gentlewoman?
Tim. As well as a man might do, mother, in modest Latin.
Maudlin. Latin, fool?
Tim. And she recoiled in Hebrew.   135
Maudlin. In Hebrew, fool? 'Tis Welsh!
Tim. All comes to one, mother.
Maudlin. She can speak English too.
Tim. Who told me so much? Heart, an she can speak English, I'll
  clap to her! I thought you'd marry me to a stranger.   140

113.] Can you speak Welsh? Middleton's Welsh is a phonetic rendering of some
set Welsh phrases which make little sense together. The joke is that Tim's grasp of
learned languages is so weak that he assumes the Welsh Gentlewoman is speaking
Hebrew. See line 135.
  114. *cog*] cheat.
  115. Ego non cogo] This Latin is nonsense. Tim is echoing the Welsh word *cog*
and adding an 'o' to make it sound like the first person singular of a verb.
  116.] Some cheese and whey after taking a walk.
  120. *proceeded*] taken her degree. An impossibility, of course, for women.
  137. *All . . . one*] Welsh, Hebrew, it's all the same.
  140. *clap to her*] stick close to her (with a suggestion of catching gonorrhea).

Maudlin. [*To Welsh Gentlewoman*] You must forgive him. He's so
    inured to Latin, he and his tutor, that he hath quite forgot to
    use the Protestant tongue.
Welsh Gentlewoman. 'Tis quickly pardoned, forsooth.
Maudlin. Tim, make amends and kiss her. [*To Welsh Gentlewoman*]   145
    He makes towards you, forsooth.
                    [*Tim kisses the Welsh Gentlewoman.*]
Tim. Oh, delicious! One may discover her country by her kissing;
    'tis a true saying: 'There's nothing tastes so sweet as your Welsh
    mutton.' [*To Welsh Gentlewoman*] It was reported you could
    sing.   150
Maudlin. Oh, rarely, Tim, the sweetest British songs.
Tim. And 'tis my mind, I swear, before I marry,
    I would see all my wife's good parts at once,
    To view how rich I were.
Maudlin. Thou shalt hear sweet music, Tim.   155
    [*To Welsh Gentlewoman*] Pray, forsooth.
                    Music and Welsh Song.

The Song

Welsh Gentlewoman.   Cupid is Venus's only joy,
                    But he is a wanton boy,
                    A very, very wanton boy.
                    He shoots at ladies' naked breasts;   160
                    He is the cause of most men's crests—
                    I mean upon the forehead,
                    Invisible but horrid.
                    'Twas he first thought upon the way
                    To keep a lady's lips in play.   165

                    Why should not Venus chide her son
                    For the pranks that he hath done,
                    The wanton pranks that he hath done?
                    He shoots his fiery darts so thick,
                    They hurt poor ladies to the quick,   170

---

143. *Protestant tongue*] Latin was associated with Roman Catholics who used the
Latin liturgy. (Cf. 1.1.93.)

    149. *mutton*] (1) sheep meat; (2) whore (cf. 1.1.146).

    151. *rarely*] excellently.

    British] i.e. Welsh. Popular history associated the Celts of Wales with ancient
Britons.

    153. *good parts*] (1) good accomplishments; (2) body parts.

    156.2. *The Song*] Songs were often used to characterize the Welsh. This song also
occurs in Middleton's *More Dissemblers Besides Women*. It may be that the original
song from this part of the play had been lost before the play was printed in 1630 and
another Middleton song was susbtituted.

Ah me, with cruel wounding!
His darts are so confounding
That life and sense would soon decay
But that he keeps their lips in play.

Can there be any part of bliss   175
In a quickly fleeting kiss,
A quickly fleeting kiss?
To one's pleasure leisures are but waste;
The slowest kiss makes too much haste;
. . . .   180
And lose it ere we find it.
The pleasing sport they only know
That close above and close below.

Tim. I would not change my wife for a kingdom! I can do somewhat
too in my own lodging.   185

       Enter YELLOWHAMMER *and* ALLWIT [*disguised*].

Yellowhammer. Why, well said, Tim! The bells go merrily;
I love such peals o' life. Wife, lead them in a while;
Here's a strange gentleman desires private conference.
      [*Exeunt* MAUDLIN, Welsh Gentlewoman, *and* TIM.]
[*To Allwit*] You're welcome, sir, the more for your name's sake.
Good Master Yellowhammer, I love my name well.   190
And which o' the Yellowhammers take you descent from,
If I may be so bold with you? Which, I pray?
Allwit. The Yellowhammers in Oxfordshire near Abingdon.
Yellowhammer. And those are the best Yellowhammers, and truest
bred; I came from thence myself, though now a citizen. I'll be   195
bold with you; you are most welcome.
Allwit. I hope the zeal I bring with me shall deserve it.
Yellowhammer. I hope no less. What is your will, sir?
Allwit. I understand, by rumours, you have a daughter,
Which my bold love shall henceforth title 'cousin'.   200
Yellowhammer. I thank you for her, sir.
Allwit. I heard of her virtues and other confirmed graces.

178.] Leisure is a waste of time when one is seeking pleasure.
180.] The metrical pattern of rhymes indicates a missing line.
183.] i.e. who lock together in an embrace of lips and body.
184–5. *do somewhat too*] carry on with my usual sexual practices (homosexuality
or masturbation) in private.
185.1.] Allwit is disguised as Yellowhammer's country cousin.
188. *strange*] unknown (i.e. Allwit).
193. *Abingdon*] a town on the Thames, five miles from Oxford.
195. *citizen*] i.e. Londoner.

Yellowhammer. A plaguy girl, sir!

Allwit. Fame sets her out with richer ornaments
    Than you are pleased to boast of; 'tis done modestly.   205
    I hear she's towards marriage.

Yellowhammer. You hear truth, sir.

Allwit. And with a knight in town, Sir Walter Whorehound.

Yellowhammer. The very same, sir.

Allwit. I am the sorrier for 't.   210

Yellowhammer. The sorrier? Why, cousin?

Allwit. 'Tis not too far past, is 't? It may be yet recalled?

Yellowhammer. Recalled? Why, good sir?

Allwit. Resolve me in that point, ye shall hear from me.

Yellowhammer. There's no contract passed.   215

Allwit. I am very joyful, sir.

Yellowhammer. But he's the man must bed her.

Allwit. By no means, coz. She's quite undone then, and you'll
    curse the time that e'er you made the match; he's an arrant
    whoremaster, consumes his time and state——[*He whispers.*]   220
    whom in my knowledge he hath kept this seven years; nay, coz,
    another man's wife too.

Yellowhammer. Oh, abominable!

Allwit. Maintains the whole house, apparels the husband, pays serv-
    ants' wages, not so much but——   [*He whispers.*]   225

Yellowhammer. Worse and worse! And doth the husband know this?

Allwit. Knows? Ay, and glad he may too; 'tis his living;
    As other trades thrive, butchers by selling flesh,
    Poulters by vending conies, or the like, coz.

Yellowhammer. What an incomparable wittol 's this!   230

Allwit. Tush, what cares he for that?
    Believe me, coz, no more than I do.

Yellowhammer. What a base slave is that!

Allwit. All's one to him; he feeds and takes his ease,
    Was ne'er the man that ever broke his sleep   235
    To get a child yet, by his own confession,
    And yet his wife has seven.

Yellowhammer. What, by Sir Walter?

---

203. *plaguy*] troublesome. Yellowhammer is being affectedly modest rather than critical about his own child.

204–5. *Fame . . . of*] her reputation suggests that she is more accomplished than you are willing to make out (continuing the arch, polite flattery).

214.] If you can assure me on that point, I'll speak further.

218. *coz*] short for 'cousin'.

229. *Poulters*] poultry merchants, selling the fowl and small animals which were the responsibility of women in farming communities.

vending conies] selling rabbits. Also a slang term for dealing with a fool or a whore.

Allwit. Sir Walter's like to keep 'em and maintain 'em
   In excellent fashion; he dares do no less, sir.   240
Yellowhammer. Life, has he children too?
Allwit. Children! Boys thus high,
   In their Cato and Cordelius.
Yellowhammer. What? You jest, sir!
Allwit. Why, one can make a verse and is now at Eton College.   245
Yellowhammer. Oh, this news has cut into my heart, coz!
Allwit. It had eaten nearer, if it had not been prevented: one Allwit's
   wife.
Yellowhammer. Allwit? Foot, I have heard of him;
   He had a girl kursened lately?   250
Allwit. Ay, that work did cost the knight above a hundred mark.
Yellowhammer. I'll mark him for a knave and villain for 't; a thou-
   sand thanks and blessings! I have done with him.
Allwit. [*Aside*] Ha, ha, ha! This knight will stick by my ribs still;
   I shall not lose him yet. No wife will come;   255
   Where'er he woos, I find him still at home. Ha, ha!   *Exit.*
Yellowhammer. Well, grant all this, say now his deeds are black,
   Pray, what serves marriage but to call him back?
   I've kept a whore myself, and had a bastard
   By Mistress Anne, in *anno*——   260
   I care not who knows it. He's now a jolly fellow,
   H'as been twice warden. So may his fruit be;
   They were but base begot, and so was he.
   The knight is rich; he shall be my son-in-law.
   No matter, so the whore he keeps be wholesome;   265

---

243. *Cato and Cordelius*] common schoolbooks of the time, with a puritanical
bias.
245. *make a verse*] write Latin verse.
Eton College] a famous public school.
247. *It . . . nearer*] i.e. this news would have cut even more deeply into your
heart.
249. *Foot*] by God's foot (an oath).
251. *a hundred mark*] £66 13s 4d.
254. *stick . . . ribs*] provide me with sustenance.
255–6.] i.e. Sir Walter will get no wife out of this; wherever he goes after women,
he will always come home to me.
258. *call him back*] retrieve him i.e. from the brink of sin.
260. anno—] the year—.
261. *He's*] i.e. my bastard son is.
262. *warden*] a member of the governing body of one of the City companies; also
a kind of pear (hence the play on 'fruit').
262–3. *his fruit . . . They*] i.e. Sir Walter's children with Mrs Allwit.
263. *he*] i.e. my bastard son.
265. *wholesome*] i.e. free of veneral disease.

My daughter takes no hurt then. So, let them wed.
I'll have him sweat well ere they go to bed.

Enter MAUDLIN.

Maudlin. Oh, husband, husband!
Yellowhammer. How now, Maudlin?
Maudlin. We are all undone! She's gone, she's gone!   270
Yellowhammer. Again? Death! Which way?
Maudlin. Over the houses. Lay the waterside; she's gone for ever,
      else.
Yellowhammer. Oh, vent'rous baggage!   *Exit* [*with* MAUDLIN].

[4.2]

Enter TIM *and* Tutor.

Tim. Thieves, thieves! My sister's stol'n! Some thief hath got her.
      Oh, how miraculously did my father's plate 'scape! 'Twas all
      left out, tutor.
Tutor. Is 't possible?
Tim. Besides three chains of pearl and a box of coral.   5
      My sister's gone. Let's look at Trig-stairs for her;
      My mother's gone to lay the common stairs
      At Puddle-wharf; and at the dock below
      Stands my poor silly father. Run, sweet tutor, run!
                                    Exit [*with* Tutor].

[4.3]

Enter both the TOUCHWOODS.

Touchwood Senior. I had been taken, brother, by eight sergeants,
      But for the honest watermen; I am bound to them.
      They are the most requitefull'st people living,
      For, as they get their means by gentlemen,

---

267. *sweat*] i.e. in a steam tub, to cure him of venereal disease.
272. *Over the houses*] across the roofs.
Lay] search.

4.2.3. *plate*] silver plate.
6. *Trig-stairs*] steps down to the river Thames at the end of Trig-lane. See map,
p. 61.
7. *lay . . . stairs*] search another point of embarkation, upriver from Trig-stairs.
8. *Puddle-wharf*] a watergate on to the Thames. See map, p. 61.

4.3.1. *sergeants*] sheriff's officers, responsible for arresting debtors.
2. *watermen*] boatmen, rowing customers on the Thames. See Intro., p. 15.
3. *requitefull'st*] most willing to return favours.

They are still the forwardest to help gentlemen.   5
You heard how one 'scaped out of the Blackfriars,
But a while since, from two or three varlets
Came into the house with all their rapiers drawn,
As if they'd dance the sword-dance on the stage,
With candles in their hands, like chandlers' ghosts,   10
Whilst the poor gentleman so pursued and banded
Was by an honest pair of oars safely landed.
Touchwood Junior. I love them with my heart for 't.

Enter three or four Watermen.

1 Waterman. Your first man, sir.
2 Waterman. Shall I carry you gentlemen with a pair of oars?   15
Touchwood Senior. These be the honest fellows.
     Take one pair and leave the rest for her.
Touchwood Junior. Barn Elms.
Touchwood Senior. No more, brother.   [*Exit.*]
1 Waterman. Your first man.   20
2 Waterman. Shall I carry your worship?
Touchwood Junior. Go.   [*Exit* First Waterman.]
               And you honest watermen that stay,
     Here's a French crown for you.   [*He gives money.*]
     There comes a maid with all speed to take water;
     Row her lustily to Barn Elms after me.   25
2 Waterman. To Barn Elms, good, sir.—Make ready the boat, Sam;
     We'll wait below.   *Exit* [*with the other* Waterman].

Enter MOLL.

Touchwood Junior. What made you stay so long?
Moll. I found the way more dangerous than I looked for.
Touchwood Junior. Away, quick! There's a boat waits for you,   30
     And I'll take water at Paul's-wharf and overtake you.
Moll. Good sir, do; we cannot be too safe.   [*Exeunt.*]

---

6. *Blackfriars*] Blackfriars Theatre, the indoor house of the King's Men.
8. *Came*] who came.
9. *sword-dance*] dance usually performed in a ring of drawn swords.
10. *chandlers'*] candlemarkers'.
11. *banded*] bandied; pushed to and fro.
14. *Your first man, sir*] The boatman is calling for trade.
18. *Barn Elms*] a manor-house upriver on the Thames; another resort associated with sexual assignations. See Intro., pp. 13–16.
19. *No more*] Say no more.
23. *French crown*] coin worth five shillings.
25. *lustily*] vigorously.

[4.4]

Enter SIR WALTER, YELLOWHAMMER, TIM, *and* Tutor.

Sir Walter. Life! Call you this close keeping?
Yellowhammer. She was kept under a double lock.
Sir Walter. A double devil!
Tim. [*To Tutor*] That's a buff sergeant, tutor; he'll ne'er wear out.
Yellowhammer. How would you have women locked?   5
Tim. With padlocks, father. The Venetian uses it; my tutor reads
  it.
Sir Walter. Heart, if she were so locked up, how got she out?
Yellowhammer. There was a little hole looked into the gutter;
  But who would have dreamt of that?   10
Sir Walter. A wiser man would.
Tim. He says true, father. A wise man for love will seek every hole;
  my tutor knows it.
Tutor. Verum poeta dicit.
Tim. Dicit Virgilius, father.   15
Yellowhammer. Prithee, talk of thy jills somewhere else; she's played
  the jill with me. Where's your wise mother now?
Tim. Run mad, I think. I thought she would have drowned herself;
  she would not stay for oars, but took a smelt-boat. Sure, I think
  she be gone a-fishing for her!   20
Yellowhammer. She'll catch a goodly dish of gudgeons now
  Will serve us all to supper.

Enter MAUDLIN *drawing* MOLL *by the hair, and* Watermen.

Maudlin. I'll tug thee home by the hair.
1 Waterman. Good mistress, spare her!
Maudlin. Tend your own business.   25
2 Waterman. You are a cruel mother.

Exit [*with other* Watermen].

4.4.1. *close keeping*] careful supervision.
4. *That's ... sergeant*] i.e. a *buff sergeant* is a *double devil* in that this buff (oxhide)
jerkin (uniform) is as hard as his determined pursuit of his victims.
6. *padlocks*] i.e. on chastity belts.
6–7. *Venetian ... it*] Venetians use it (i.e. the custom of keeping women locked
into chastity belts); my tutor reads about it. The joke lies in the contrast between
Venetian sexual practice and the tutor's vicarious experience of it.
14–15.] The poet speaks the truth. Virgil says it, father. (Tim ridiculously attributes a smutty pun on 'hole' to Virgil.)
16–17. *she's ... me*] Moll has played the bad girl with me.
19. *smelt-boat*] boat used to catch and haul smelts, a kind of small fish; used
metaphorically for fools; i.e. Maudlin is embarked in a ship of fools.
21. *gudgeons*] small fish used for bait. 'To swallow gudgeons' was proverbial for
being fooled.

Moll. Oh, my heart dies!

Maudlin. I'll make thee an example for all the neighbours'
daughters.

Moll. Farewell, life!   30

Maudlin. You that have tricks can counterfeit.

Yellowhammer. Hold, hold, Maudlin!

Maudlin. [*To Yellowhammer*] I have brought your jewel by the hair.

Yellowhammer. [*To Sir Walter*] She's here, knight.

Sir Walter. Forbear, or I'll grow worse.   35

Tim. [*Aside to Tutor*] Look on her, tutor! She hath brought her from
the water like a mermaid; she's but half my sister now; as far as
the flesh goes, the rest may be sold to fishwives.

Maudlin. Dissembling, cunning baggage!

Yellowhammer. Impudent strumpet!   40

Sir Walter. Either give over, both, or I'll give over!
[*To Moll*] Why have you used me thus, unkind mistress?
Wherein have I deserved?

Yellowhammer. You talk too fondly, sir. We'll take another course
and prevent all; we might have done 't long since. We'll lose no   45
time now, nor trust to 't any longer. Tomorrow morn, as early
as sunrise, we'll have you joined.

Moll. Oh, bring me death tonight, love-pitying Fates!
Let me not see tomorrow up upon the world!

Yellowhammer. Are you content, sir, till then she shall be watched? 50

Maudlin. Baggage, you shall!   *Exit* [MAUDLIN *with* MOLL].

Tim. Why, father, my tutor and I will both watch in armour.
                                        [*Exit* YELLOWHAMMER.]

Tutor. How shall we do for weapons?

Tim. Take you no care for that. If need be I can send for conquering
metal, tutor, ne'er lost day yet; 'tis but at Westminster. I   55
am acquainted with him that keeps the monuments; I can

---

35. *grow worse*] grow angrier. Sir Walter is concerned that Moll is being handled
too roughly. See line 41.

36. *She*] Maudlin.

37. *mermaid*] (1) mythological creature, half woman, half fish; (2) whore (slang).

37–8. *she's . . . goes*] she is only half my sister because a mermaid is half fish, half
flesh.

38. *fishwives*] 'Fishmonger' was slang for 'pimp'.

41.] Either both of you stop bullying Moll, or I'll call off the marriage.

44. *fondly*] (1) indulgently; (2) foolishly.

52. *watch in armour*] stay awake on guard duty, like the London citizens' watch
which paraded in city festivities.

54–5. *conquering . . . yet*] armour which has always defeated its enemies and
never yet been used on the losing side but always won the day.

56. *keeps the monuments*] has custody over the tombs and ancient relics. The
tombs of English kings and other worthies were in Westminster Abbey and had
already become a tourist attraction with a guide who gave an account of them.

borrow Harry the Fifth's sword. 'Twill serve us both to watch
with.   *Exit* [TIM *with* Tutor].
Sir Walter. I never was so near my wish
    As this chance makes me! Ere tomorrow noon   60
    I shall receive two thousand pound in gold
    And a sweet maidenhead worth forty.

                Enter TOUCHWOOD JUNIOR *with* [First] Waterman.

Touchwood Junior. [*To the Waterman*] Oh, thy news splits me!
1 Waterman. Half drowned! She cruelly tugged her by the hair,
    Forced her disgracefully, not like a mother.   65
Touchwood Junior. Enough! Leave me, like my joys.
                                              Exit Waterman.
    [*To Sir Walter*] Sir, saw you not a wretched maid pass this way?
    [*Recognizing him*] Heart, villain, is it thou?
Sir Walter.   Yes, slave, 'tis I! *Both draw and fight.*
Touchwood Junior. I must break through thee, then. There is no stop
    That checks my tongue and all my hopeful fortunes,   70
    That breast excepted, and I must have way.
Sir Walter. Sir, I believe 'twill hold your life in play.
                              [*He wounds Touchwood Junior.*]
Touchwood Junior. [*Counterattacking*] So, you'll gain the heart in
    my breast at first?
Sir Walter. There is no dealing, then? Think on the dowry
    For two thousand pounds.   75
Touchwood Junior. Oh, now 'tis quit, sir.   [*He wounds Sir Walter.*]
Sir Walter. And being of even hand, I'll play no longer.
Touchwood Junior. No longer, slave?
Sir Walter.   I have certain things to think on
    Before I dare go further.   [*Exit.*]
Touchwood Junior.   But one bout?
    I'll follow thee to death, but ha' 't out.   *Exit.*   80

---

57. *Harry the Fifth's sword*] Henry V was the heroic king, particularly associated
with London apprentices, who re-took France in the campaign which culminated in
the battle of Agincourt. However, his sword was not especially famous. Tim is
confusing it with Edward III's seven-foot double-handed sword. The idea of using
these national treasures to stand guard over a girl is absurd.

62. *forty*] i.e. forty pounds.

69–71. *There . . . excepted*] There is no barrier that reduces me to silence and
stops my future happiness except that breast of yours, Sir Walter.

72. *'twill . . . play*] it (the action of challenging Sir Walter) will put your life at
risk.

73.] i.e. You will have to take the heart in my breast first.

74. *dealing*] (1) coming to terms, (2) play on 'dealing' in a card game.

76. *quit*] requited, accounted for.

77. *being . . . hand*] since the score is even between us.

80. *ha' 't out*] have it out, finish the duel.

Act 5

Enter ALLWIT, *his* Wife, *and* DAVY DAHUMMA.

Mrs Allwit. A misery of a house!
Allwit. What shall become of us?
Davy. I think his wound be mortal.
Allwit. Think'st thou so, Davy?
    Then am I mortal too, but a dead man, Davy;   5
    This is no world for me; whene'er he goes,
    I must e'en truss up all and after him, Davy;
    A sheet with two knots, and away!

    Enter SIR WALTER, *led in hurt* [*by two* Servants].

Davy. Oh, see, sir,
    How faint he goes! Two of my fellows lead him.   10
Mrs Allwit. Oh, me!   [*She faints.*]
Allwit. Heyday, my wife's laid down too! Here's like to be
    A good house kept, when we are all together down.
    Take pains with her, good Davy, cheer her up there.
    Let me come to his worship, let me come.   15
        [*Allwit approaches Sir Walter, who has been set down.*]
Sir Walter. Touch me not, villain! My wound aches at thee,
    Thou poison to my heart!
Allwit.   He raves already,
    His senses are quite gone, he knows me not.
    [*To him*] Look up, an 't like your worship; heave those eyes,
    Call me to mind. Is your remembrance left?   20
    Look in my face. Who am I, an 't like your worship?
Sir Walter. If anything be worse than slave or villain,
    Thou art the man!
Allwit.   Alas, his poor worship's weakness!
    He will begin to know me by little and little.

5.1.3. *his*] Sir Walter's.
5. *a dead man*] i.e. I am finished.
7. *truss up*] (1) pack up; (2) hang myself.
8. *A sheet . . . knots*] (1) a shroud; (2) an improvised rope to escape from the house or to hang oneself with.
12–13. *Here's . . . kept*] i.e. (sarcastically) We are likely to be well provided for.

Sir Walter. No devil can be like thee!
Allwit.   Ah, poor gentleman,   25
    Methinks the pain that thou endurest—
Sir Walter. Thou know'st me to be wicked, for thy baseness
    Kept the eyes open still on all my sins.
    None knew the dear account my soul stood charged with
    So well as thou, yet, like hell's flattering angel,   30
    Wouldst never tell me on 't, let'st me go on
    And join with death in sleep, that if I had not
    Waked now by chance, even by a stranger's pity,
    I had everlastingly slept out all hope
    Of grace and mercy.
Allwit.   Now he is worse and worse.   35
    Wife, to him, wife; thou wast wont to do good on him.
Mrs Allwit. [*To Sir Walter*] How is 't with you, sir?
Sir Walter.   Not as with you,
    Thou loathsome strumpet!—Some good pitying man
    Remove my sins out of my sight a little!
    I tremble to behold her; she keeps back   40
    All comfort while she stays.—Is this a time,
    Unconscionable woman, to see thee?
    Art thou so cruel to the peace of man
    Not to give liberty now? The devil himself
    Shows a far fairer reverence and respect   45
    To goodness than thyself. He dares not do this,
    But parts in time of penitence, hides his face;
    When man withdraws from him, he leaves the place.
    Hast thou less manners and more impudence
    Than thy instructor? Prithee show thy modesty,   50
    If the least grain be left, and get thee from me.
    Thou shouldst be rather locked many rooms hence
    From the poor miserable sight of me,
    If either love or grace had part in thee.
Mrs Allwit. He is lost for ever!   [*She weeps.*]
Allwit.   Run, sweet Davy, quickly,   55
    And fetch the children hither. Sight of them

---

33. *Waked*] i.e. wakened to my sinful state.
a stranger's] i.e. Touchwood Junior's. His action in wounding Sir Walter has
made the knight aware of his own mortality and sinfulness.
37. *Not . . . you*] i.e. I am not in the same spiritual peril as you.
39. *my sins*] i.e. the Allwits' presence reminds him of his sins of fornication and
fathering bastards.
44. *liberty*] freedom from sin.
50. *thy instructor*] i.e. the devil.

Will make him cheerful straight.   [*Exit* DAVY.]
Sir Walter. [*To Mrs Allwit*]   Oh, death! Is this
　　A place for you to weep? What tears are those?
　　Get you away with them! I shall fare the worse;
　　As long as they are a-weeping, they work against me.   60
　　There's nothing but thy appetite in that sorrow;
　　Thou weep'st for lust; I feel it in the slackness
　　Of comforts coming towards me. I was well
　　Till thou began'st to undo me. This shows like
　　The fruitless sorrow of a careless mother   65
　　That brings her son with dalliance to the gallows
　　And then stands by and weeps to see him suffer.

　　　　Enter DAVY *with* [NICK, WAT, *and*] *the* [*other*] Children.

Davy. There are the children, sir; an 't like your worship,
　　Your last fine girl. In troth she smiles;
　　Look, look, in faith, sir.
Sir Walter.   Oh, my vengeance!   70
　　Let me for ever hide my cursèd face
　　From sight of those that darkens all my hopes
　　And stands between me and the sight of heaven!
　　Who sees me now, her too and those so near me,
　　May rightly say I am o'ergrown with sin.   75
　　Oh, how my offences wrestle with my repentance!
　　It hath scarce breath;
　　Still my adulterous guilt hovers aloft
　　And with her black wings beats down all my prayers
　　Ere they be half way up. What's he knows now   80
　　How long I have to live? Oh, what comes then?
　　My taste grows bitter; the round world all gall now;
　　Her pleasing pleasures now hath poisoned me,
　　Which I exchanged my soul for.
　　Make way, a hundred sighs, at once for me!   85
Allwit. Speak to him, Nick.
Nick.   I dare not; I am afraid.

64–7.] These lines encapsulate a familiar moralizing narrative of the over-indulgent mother whose children fall into crime and execution. See Intro., pp. 47–8.

70. *my vengeance*] Sir Walter sees the children as the sign of God's vengeance on him.

74. *Who*] whoever.

80. *up*] up to heaven.

82. *gall*] a bitter-tasting substance; often used as a metaphor for bitterness of spirit.

85.] i.e. May the hundred sighs I now breathe clear a pathway to heaven for me.

Allwit. Tell him he hurts his wounds, Wat, with making moan.
Sir Walter. Wretched, death of seven!
Allwit. [*To the others*]   Come, let's be talking
    Somewhat to keep him alive.—Ah, sirrah Wat,
    And did my lord bestow that jewel on thee   90
    For an epistle thou mad'st in Latin?
    Thou art a good forward boy; there's great joy on thee.
Sir Walter. Oh, sorrow!
Allwit. [*To the others*]   Heart, will nothing comfort him?
                                          [*Exeunt* Children.]
    If he be so far gone, 'tis time to moan.
    [*To him*] Here's pen and ink and paper, and all things ready;   95
    Will 't please your worship for to make your will?
Sir Walter. My will? Yes, yes, what else? Who writes apace, now?
Allwit. That can your man Davy, an 't like your worship,
    A fair, fast, legible hand.
Sir Walter.   Set it down then.   [*Davy writes.*]
    Imprimis, I bequeath to yonder wittol   100
    Three times his weight in curses.
Allwit.   How!
Sir Walter.   All plagues
    Of body and of mind.
Allwit.   Write them not down, Davy.
Davy. It is his will; I must.
Sir Walter.   Together also
    With such a sickness ten days ere his death.
Allwit. There's a sweet legacy! I am almost choked with 't.   105
Sir Walter. Next I bequeath to that foul whore his wife
    All barrenness of joy, a drought of virtue,
    And dearth of all repentance; for her end,
    The common misery of an English strumpet,
    In French and Dutch; beholding ere she dies   110
    Confusion of her brats before her eyes,
    And never shed a tear for it.

Enter a Servant.

1 Servant.   Where's the knight?
    Oh, sir, the gentleman you wounded is

---

   88. *death of seven*] Sir Walter fears that his seven bastards will suffer spiritual death because of him as well as causing his own spiritual death.
   92. *forward*] promising, eager to learn.
   100. Imprimis] item one. (Technical legal language.)
  yonder wittol] i.e. that cuckold, Allwit.
   110. *French and Dutch*] i.e. venereal disease.
   111. *Confusion*] ruin.

Newly departed!
Sir Walter.   Dead? Lift, lift! Who helps me?
Allwit. Let the law lift you now, that must have all;   115
   I have done lifting on you, and my wife too.
1 Servant. [*To Sir Walter*] You were best lock yourself close.
Allwit.   Not in my house, sir!
   I'll harbour no such persons as men-slayers,
   Lock yourself where you will.
Sir Walter.   What's this?
Mrs Allwit.   Why, husband!
Allwit. I know what I do, wife.
Mrs Allwit.   You cannot tell yet;   120
   For, having killed the man in his defence,
   Neither his life nor estate will be touched, husband.
Allwit. Away, wife! Hear a fool! His lands will hang him.
Sir Walter. Am I denied a chamber? [*To Mrs Allwit*] What say
      you, forsooth?
Mrs Allwit. Alas, sir, I am one that would have all well,   125
   But must obey my husband. [*To Allwit*] Prithee, love,
   Let the poor gentleman stay, being so sore wounded.
   There's a close chamber at one end of the garret
   We never use; let him have that, I prithee.
Allwit. We never use? You forget sickness, then,   130
   And physic-times; is 't not a place of easement?

                Enter a [*second*] *Servant.*

Sir Walter. Oh, death! Do I hear this with part
   Of former life in me?—What's the news now?
2 Servant. Troth, worse and worse; you're like to lose your land,
   If the law save your life, sir, or the surgeon.   135

114–15. *Lift . . . lift*] Sir Walter asks to be lifted physically; Allwit retorts that he
will by lifted (arrested) by the law.

116. *lifting on*] (1) helping; (2) robbing. As applied to Mrs Allwit, the phrase
means 'supporting your weight in sex'.

117. *You . . . close*] The servant advises Sir Walter to hide from the law, since he
has killed Touchwood Junior.

120. *tell*] i.e. tell how the case will be decided.

123. *Hear a fool!*] Listen to the fool talk!
His . . . him] Those wishing to seize his lands will ensure that the plea of self-
defence is not accepted.

124. *Am . . . chamber*] Won't you even let me have a bedroom (in my wounded
condition)?

128. *a close chamber*] a small, hidden room.

131. *place of easement*] (1) a place of comfort in sickness; (2) a privy.

135. *If*] even if.

Allwit. Hark you there, wife.
Sir Walter.   Why, how, sir?
2 *Servant.* Sir Oliver Kix's wife is new quickened;
    That child undoes you, sir.
Sir Walter.   All ill at once!
Allwit. I wonder what he makes here with his consorts?
    Cannot our house be private to ourselves   140
    But we must have such guests?—I pray, depart, sirs,
    And take your murderer along with you;
    Good he were apprehended ere he go.
    H'as killed some honest gentleman. Send for officers!
Sir Walter. I'll soon save you that labour.
Allwit.   I must tell you, sir,   145
    You have been somewhat bolder in my house
    Than I could well like of; I suffered you
    Till it stuck here at my heart. I tell you truly
    I thought you had been familiar with my wife once.
Mrs Allwit. With me? I'll see him hanged first! I defy him,   150
    And all such gentlemen in the like extremity.
Sir Walter. If ever eyes were open, these are they.
    Gamesters, farewell, I have nothing left to play.
                                Exit [carried by Servants].
Allwit. And therefore get you gone, sir.
Davy. [*To Allwit*]   Of all wittols
    Be thou the head! [*To Mrs Allwit*] Thou, the grand whore of
        spittles!   *Exit.*   155
Allwit. So, since he's like now to be rid of all,
    I am right glad I am so well rid of him.
Mrs Allwit. I knew he durst not stay when you named officers.
Allwit. That stopped his spirits straight.
    What shall we do now, wife?   160
Mrs Allwit. As we were wont to do.
Allwit. We are richly furnished, wife, with household stuff.
Mrs Allwit. Let's let out lodgings, then,
    And take a house in the Strand.

---

136. *Hark . . . wife*] i.e. What did I tell you? (See lines 115–20.)
137. *quickened*] become pregnant.
139. *he makes*] Sir Walter is doing.
141. *sirs*] Sir Walter's servants.
143.] It were best he should be arrested before he escapes.
153. *Gamesters*] gamblers, players.
155. *spittles*] hospitals (as the place where venereal disease is treated).
156. *like . . . all*] likely to be stripped of all wealth.
164. *the Strand*] a wide street running from Charing Cross to St Paul's. In proposing to move to the west of the City, the Allwits are following a fashionable trend. See Intro., p 15.

Allwit. In troth, a match, wench.   165
    We are simply stocked with cloth-of-tissue cushions
    To furnish out bay-windows. Push, what not that's quaint
    And costly, from the top to the bottom!
    Life, for furniture, we may lodge a countess.
    There's a close-stool of tawny velvet too,   170
    Now I think on 't, wife.
Mrs Allwit. There's that should be, sir.
    Your nose must be in everything!
Allwit. I have done, wench;
    And let this stand in every gallant's chamber: 175
    'There's no gamester like a politic sinner,
    For whoe'er games, the box is sure a winner.'   *Exeunt.*

[5.2]

        Enter YELLOWHAMMER *and his* Wife.

Maudlin. Oh, husband, husband, she will die, she will die!
    There is no sign but death.
Yellowhammer.   'Twill be our shame then.
Maudlin. Oh, how she's changed in compass of an hour!
Yellowhammer. Ah, my poor girl! Good faith, thou wert too cruel
    To drag her by the hair.   5
Maudlin. You would have done as much, sir,
    To curb her of her humour.
Yellowhammer. 'Tis curbed sweetly! She catched her bane o' th'
    water.

            Enter TIM.

Maudlin. How now, Tim?   10
Tim. Faith, busy, mother, about an epitaph

---

165. *a match*] done, agreed.
166. *simply*] absolutely.
cloth-of tissue] fine silk cloth.
167. *Push*] Pooh (expression of airy dismissal).
quaint] delicate, exquisite.
169. *for furniture*] when it comes to furniture.
170. *a close-stool*] a chamber pot enclosed in a stool.
172. *There's . . . be*] There is everything that is appropriate.
173. *nose*] with a joking reference to the *close-stool*, line 170.
175. *stand*] i.e. be posted up as a motto.
176.] The best gambler is the one who knows when to be penitent, when to quit.
177. *box*] percentage taken by the gambling house.

5.2.1. *she*] Moll.
8. *'Tis curbed sweetly*] i.e. Her humour is sweetly curbed (said sarcastically).
bane] i.e. death.

Upon my sister's death.

Maudlin. Death! She is not dead, I hope?

Tim. No, but she means to be, and that's as good,
And when a thing's done, 'tis done; 15
You taught me that, mother.

Yellowhammer. What is your tutor doing?

Tim. Making one too, in principal pure Latin
Culled out of Ovid *de Tristibus.*

Yellowhammer. How does your sister look? Is she not changed? 20

Tim. Changed? Gold into white money was never so changed as is
my sister's colour into paleness.

Enter MOLL [*carried by* Servants].

Yellowhammer. Oh, here she's brought. See how she looks like
death!

Tim. Looks she like death, and ne'er a word made yet?
I must go beat my brains against a bed-post 25
And get before my tutor. [*Exit.*]

Yellowhammer. [*To Moll*] Speak, how dost thou?

Moll. I hope I shall be well, for I am as sick
At heart as I can be.

Yellowhammer. 'Las, my poor girl!
The doctor's making a most sovereign drink for thee,
The worst ingredients dissolved pearl and amber; 30
We spare no cost, girl.

Moll. Your love comes too late,
Yet timely thanks reward it. What is comfort,
When the poor patient's heart is past relief?
It is no doctor's art can cure my grief.

Yellowhammer. All is cast away then. 35
Prithee look upon me cheerfully.

Maudlin. Sing but a strain or two, thou wilt not think
How 'twill revive thy spirits. Strive with thy fit,

---

18. *principal*] choice, excellent.

19. *Ovid* de Tristibus] Ovid's *Tristia*, five books of sad poems, used as a textbook in the third form of grammar school.

21. *white money*] silver coins.

24. *ne'er . . . yet*] I haven't even begun my elegy.

26. *get . . . tutor*] i.e. see my tutor for help.

29. *sovereign*] special, efficacious.

30. *worst*] least expensive (i.e. the rest of the ingredients are even more expensive).

32. *Yet . . . it*] yet I give prompt thanks even so.

35. *All . . . away*] We have wasted all our efforts (and money).

37. *strain*] musical sequence.

38. *fit*] (1) attack of melancholy; (2) stave of music.

Prithee, sweet Moll.
Moll. You shall have my good will, mother.
Maudlin. Why, well said, wench. [*Moll sings.*] 40

The Song.

Moll. Weep eyes, break heart!
My love and I must part.
Cruel fates true love do soonest sever.
Oh, I shall see thee never, never, never!
Oh, happy is the maid whose life takes end 45
Ere it knows parent's frown or loss of friend!
Weep eyes, break heart!
My love and I must part.

Enter TOUCHWOOD SENIOR *with a letter.*

Maudlin. Oh, I could die with music! Well sung, girl.
Moll. If you call it so, it was. 50
Yellowhammer. She plays the swan and sings herself to death.
Touchwood Senior. By your leave, sir.
Yellowhammer. What are you, sir? Or what's your business, pray?
Touchwood Senior. I may be now admitted, though the brother
Of him your hate pursued. It spreads no further; 55
Your malice sets in death, does it not, sir?
Yellowhammer. In death?
Touchwood Senior. He's dead. 'Twas a dear love to him;
It cost him but his life, that was all, sir.
He paid enough, poor gentleman, for his love.
Yellowhammer. [*Aside*] There's all our ill removed, if she were well
now. 60
[*To Touchwood Senior*] Impute not, sir, his end to any hate
That sprung from us; he had a fair wound brought that.
Touchwood Senior. That helped him forward, I must needs confess;
But the restraint of love, and your unkindness,
Those were the wounds that from his heart drew blood. 65
But being past help, let words forget it too.
Scarcely three minutes ere his eyelids closed
And took eternal leave of this world's light,
He wrote this letter, which by oath he bound me

---

51. *swan . . . death*] The swan, normally mute, was widely supposed to sing at
the point of death.
56. *sets*] i.e. like the sun; subsides.
57. *dear*] (1) beloved; (2) costly.
60. *our ill*] our problem (i.e. Touchwood Junior's claim on Moll).
61–2.] Do not blame his death on any hate from us; a serious wound brought it
about.

To give to her own hands. That's all my business.   70
Yellowhammer. You may perform it then; there she sits.
Touchwood Senior. Oh, with a following look!
Yellowhammer.   Ay, trust me, sir,
　　I think she'll follow him quickly.
Touchwood Senior.   Here's some gold
　　He willed me to distribute faithfully
　　Amongst your servants.   [*He gives gold to Servants.*]
Yellowhammer.   'Las, what doth he mean, sir?   75
Touchwood Senior. [*To Moll*] How cheer you, mistress?
Moll.   I must learn of you, sir.
Touchwood Senior. Here's a letter from a friend of yours,
　　　　　　　　　　　　　　[*Giving letter to Moll*]
　　And where that fails in satisfaction
　　I have a sad tongue ready to supply.
Moll. How does he, ere I look on 't?
Touchwood Senior.   Seldom better;   80
　　'Has a contented health now.
Moll.   I am most glad on 't. [*She reads.*]
Maudlin. [*To Touchwood Senior*] Dead, sir?
Yellowhammer.   He is. [*Aside*] Now, wife, let's but get the girl
　　Upon her legs again, and to church roundly with her.
Moll. Oh, sick to death, he tells me. How does he after this?
Touchwood Senior. Faith, feels no pain at all: he's dead, sweet
　　mistress.   85
Moll. Peace close mine eyes!   [*She swoons.*]
Yellowhammer.   The girl! Look to the girl, wife!
Maudlin. Moll, daughter, sweet girl, speak! Look but once up,
　　Thou shalt have all the wishes of thy heart
　　That wealth can purchase!
Yellowhammer.   Oh, she's gone for ever!
　　That letter broke her heart.
Touchwood Senior.   As good now, then,   90
　　As let her lie in torment and then break it.

　　　　　　　　　　　Enter SUSAN.

Maudlin. Oh, Susan, she thou loved'st so dear is gone!
Susan. Oh, sweet maid!
Touchwood Senior. [*To the others*] This is she that helped her still.—
　　I've a reward here for thee.   [*He gives Susan a note.*]
Yellowhammer.   Take her in.

---

72. *a following look*] i.e. a look as though Moll were about to follow Touchwood
Junior in death.
81. *'Has . . . now*] i.e. He is past all his troubles.
83. *roundly*] promptly.
93. *her*] Moll.

Remove her from our sight, our shame and sorrow.   95
Touchwood Senior. Stay, let me help thee; 'tis the last cold kindness
    I can perform for my sweet brother's sake.

       [*Exeunt* TOUCHWOOD SENIOR, SUSAN, *and* Servants,
                          carrying MOLL.]

Yellowhammer. All the whole street will hate us, and the world
    Point me out cruel. It is our best course, wife,
    After we have given order for the funeral,   100
    To absent ourselves till she be laid in ground.
Maudlin. Where shall we spend that time?
Yellowhammer.   I'll tell thee where, wench:
    Go to some private church and marry Tim
    To the rich Brecknock gentlewoman.
Maudlin.   Mass, a match!
    We'll not lose all at once; somewhat we'll catch.   105

                  Exit [*with* YELLOWHAMMER].

[5.3]

        Enter SIR OLIVER *and* [*four*] Servants.

Sir Oliver. Ho, my wife's quickened; I am a man for ever!
    I think I have bestirred my stumps, i' faith.
    Run, get your fellows all together instantly,
    Then to the parish church and ring the bells.
1 Servant. It shall be done, sir.   [*Exit.*]
Sir Oliver.   Upon my love   5
    I charge you, villain, that you make a bonfire
    Before the door at night.
2 Servant.   A bonfire, sir?
Sir Oliver. A thwacking one, I charge you.
2 Servant. [*Aside*]   This is monstrous! [*Exit.*]
Sir Oliver. Run, tell a hundred pound out for the gentleman
    That gave my wife the drink, the first thing you do.   10
3 Servant. A hundred pounds, sir?
Sir Oliver.   A bargain! As our joy grows,
    We must remember still from whence it flows,
    Or else we prove ungrateful multipliers.   [*Exit* 3 Servant.]
    The child is coming and the land comes after;
    The news of this will make a poor Sir Walter.   15
    I have struck it home, i' faith!
4 Servant.   That you have, marry, sir.

---

104. *a match*] (1) agreed; (2) a wedding.
105. *somewhat we'll catch*] we'll save some part of our bargain.

5.3.9. *tell*] count out.
13. *multipliers*] breeders; profiteers.

But will not your worship go to the funeral
Of both these lovers?
Sir Oliver.   Both? Go both together?
4 Servant. Ay, sir, the gentleman's brother will have it so;
'Twill be the pitifullest sight. There's such running,   20
Such rumours, and such throngs, a pair of lovers
Had never more spectators, more men's pities,
Or women's wet eyes.
Sir Oliver.   My wife helps the number then?
4 Servant. There's such drawing out of handkerchers;
And those that have no handkerchers lift up aprons.   25
Sir Oliver. Her parents may have joyful hearts at this!
I would not have my cruelty so talked on
To any child of mine for a monopoly.
4 Servant. I believe you, sir.
'Tis cast so too that both their coffins meet,   30
Which will be lamentable.
Sir Oliver.   Come, we'll see 't.

> *Exit* [*with* Servants].

[5.4]

> *Recorders dolefully playing, enter at one door the coffin of the*
> *Gentleman* [TOUCHWOOD JUNIOR], *solemnly decked, his sword upon*
> *it, attended by many in black* [*among whom are* SIR OLIVER KIX,
> ALLWIT, *and a* Parson,] *his brother* [TOUCHWOOD SENIOR] *being*
> *the chief mourner; at the other door the coffin of the virgin* [MOLL],
> *with a garland of flowers, with epitaphs pinned on 't, attended by*
> *maids and women* [*among whom are* LADY KIX, MRS ALLWIT, *and*
> SUSAN]. *Then set them down one right over against the other. While*
> *all the company seem to weep and mourn, there is a sad song in the*
> *music-room.*

Touchwood Senior. Never could death boast of a richer prize
From the first parent; let the world bring forth

---

19. *the gentleman's brother*] Touchwood Senior.
23. *helps*] increases.
26. *Her parents may*] her parents will be able to (spoken sarcastically).
28. *monopoly*] exclusive right to commercial exploitation of a particular commodity. The monopolies granted by James I were notoriously profitable.
30. *cast*] arranged.

5.4.0.9. *seem . . . mourn*] make mourning gestures in dumb-show. (There is no suggestion of hypocrisy, though Touchwood Senior is pretending.)
0.10. *music-room*] a balcony above the stage. See Intro., pp 7–8.
2. *From . . . parent*] since the time of Adam.

A pair of truer hearts. To speak but truth
Of this departed gentleman, in a brother
Might, by hard censure, be called flattery,   5
Which makes me rather silent in his right
Than so to be delivered to the thoughts
Of any envious hearer, starved in virtue
And therefore pining to hear others thrive;
But for this maid, whom envy cannot hurt   10
With all her poisons, having left to ages
The true, chaste monument of her living name,
Which no time can deface, I say of her
The full truth freely, without fear of censure:
What nature could there shine that might redeem   15
Perfection home to woman, but in her
Was fully glorious, beauty set in goodness
Speaks what she was: that jewel so infixed,
There was no want of anything of life
To make these virtuous precedents man and wife.   20
Allwit. Great pity of their deaths!
All.   Ne'er more pity!
Lady Kix. It makes a hundred weeping eyes, sweet gossip.
Touchwood Senior. I cannot think there's anyone amongst you
    In this full fair assembly, maid, man, or wife,
    Whose heart would not have sprung with joy and gladness   25
    To have seen their marriage day.
All. It would have made a thousand joyful hearts.
Touchwood Senior. [*To Touchwood Junior and Moll*] Up then apace,
    and take your fortunes;
    Make these joyful hearts; here's none but friends.
              [*Touchwood Junior and Moll rise out of their coffins.*]
All.   Alive, sir? Oh sweet, dear couple!
Touchwood Senior. Nay, do not hinder 'em now; stand from about   30
    'em.

2–3. *let . . . hearts*] I challenge the world to find a pair of truer lovers.
5. *censure*] judgement.
8. *starved in*] lacking in.
9. *pining*] resenting, disliking.
15–17. *What . . . glorious*] What nature, able to restore women's fallen perfection, could shine forth, that she did not possess in all its glory.
17. *set*] set like a jewel.
20. *precedents*] exemplars, i.e. beauty and virtue, which in Touchwood Senior's rhetoric stand in for Moll and Touchwood Junior.
31. *stand . . . 'em*] stand back from them.

If she be caught again, and have this time,
I'll ne'er plot further for 'em, nor this honest chambermaid
That helped all at a push.
Touchwood Junior. [*To the Parson*] Good sir, apace!
Parson. Hands join now, but hearts for ever,   35
  Which no parents' mood shall sever.
  [*To Touchwood Junior*] You shall forsake all widows, wives,
    and maids;
  [*To Moll*] You, lords, knights, gentlemen, and men of trades;
  And if in haste any article misses,
  Go interline it with a brace of kisses.   40
Touchwood Senior. Here's a thing trolled nimbly.—Give you joy,
    brother!
  Were 't not better thou shouldst have her
  Than the maid should die?
Mrs Allwit. To you, sweet mistress bride.
All. Joy, joy to you both.   45
Touchwood Senior. Here be your wedding sheets you brought along
  with you; you may both go to bed when you please to.
Touchwood Junior. My joy wants utterance.
Touchwood Senior. Utter all at night then, brother.
Moll. I am silent with delight.   50
Touchwood Senior. Sister, delight will silence any woman,
  But you'll find your tongue again among maidservants,
  Now you keep house, sister.
All. Never was hour so filled with joy and wonder.
Touchwood Senior. To tell you the full story of this chambermaid,   55
  And of her kindness in this business to us,
  'Twould ask an hour's discourse. In brief, 'twas she
  That wrought it to this purpose cunningly.
All. We shall all love her for 't.

      Enter YELLOWHAMMER *and his* Wife [MAUDLIN].

Allwit. See who comes here now!   60
Touchwood Senior. A storm, a storm, but we are sheltered for it.
Yellowhammer. I will prevent you all and mock you thus,

---

32. *and . . . time*] The exact meaning of this phrase is obscure; the sense is 'and lose this opportunity'.
33. *this honest chambermaid*] Susan. See 3.3.30–3 and 5.2.91–3.
34. *at a push*] at a critical moment.
39. *article misses*] legal detail is missing.
40. *interline*] insert additional clauses (in a legal document).
41. *trolled*] moved along, uttered rapidly.
46. *wedding sheets*] i.e. the shrouds from which they have just emerged.
62. *prevent*] (1) 'stop'; (2) 'anticipate'. The double meaning allows a momentary dramatic excitement over how Yellowhammer will react to the marriage.

You and your expectations: I stand happy
Both in your lives and your hearts' combination!
Touchwood Senior. Here's a strange day again!   65
Yellowhammer. The knight's proved villain.
    All's come out now: his niece an arrant baggage;
    My poor boy Tim is cast away this morning,
    Even before breakfast, married a whore
    Next to his heart.
All.   A whore?
Yellowhammer.   His 'niece', forsooth!   70
Allwit. [*Aside to his Wife*] I think we rid our hands in good time of
    him.
Mrs Allwit. I knew he was past the best when I gave him over.
    [*To Yellowhammer*] What is become of him, pray, sir?
Yellowhammer. Who, the knight? He lies i' th' knights' ward.   75
    [*To Lady Kix*] Now your belly, lady, begins to blossom, there's
    no peace for him, his creditors are so greedy.
Sir Oliver. [*To Touchwood Senior*] Master Touchwood, hear'st thou
    this news?
    I am so endeared to thee for my wife's fruitfulness
    That I charge you both, your wife and thee,   80
    To live no more asunder for the world's frowns.
    I have a purse, and bed, and board for you.
    Be not afraid to go to your business roundly;
    Get children, and I'll keep them.
Touchwood Senior. Say you so, sir?   85
Sir Oliver. Prove me with three at a birth, an thou dar'st now.
Touchwood Senior. Take heed how you dare a man, while you live,
    sir,
    That has good skill at his weapon.

        Enter TIM, Welsh Gentlewoman[, *and* Tutor].

Sir Oliver. Foot, I dare you, sir!
Yellowhammer. Look, gentlemen, if ever you saw the picture   90
    Of the unfortunate marriage, yonder 'tis.
Welsh Gentlewoman. Nay, good sweet Tim—

---

66. *The knight's*] i.e. Sir Walter is.
70. *His*] Sir Walter's.
75. *th' knights' ward*] the second most comfortable section of a debtor's prison.
79. *for*] because of.
83. *go . . . roundly*] have sex energetically.
84. *keep*] support.
86. *Prove*] try, test.
88. *good . . . weapon*] (with a joke about sexual prowess).

Tim. Come from the university
   To marry a whore in London, with my tutor too!
   O tempora! O mors!   95
Tutor. Prithee, Tim, be patient.
Tim. I bought a jade at Cambridge;
   I'll let her out to execution, tutor,
   For eighteen pence a day, or Brentford horse-races;
   She'll serve to carry seven miles out of town well.   100
   Where be these mountains? I was promised mountains,
   But there's such a mist I can see none of 'em.
   What are become of those two thousand runts?
   Let's have a bout with them in the meantime.
   A vengeance runt thee!
Maudlin.   Good, sweet Tim, have patience.   105
Tim. Flectere si nequeo superos, Acheronta movebo, mother.
Maudlin. I think you have married her in logic, Tim.
   You told me once by logic you would prove
   A whore an honest woman; prove her so, Tim,
   And take her for thy labour.
Tim.   Troth, I thank you.   110
   I grant you I may prove another man's wife so,
   But not mine own.
Maudlin.   There's no remedy now, Tim;
   You must prove her so as well as you may.
Tim. Why then, my tutor and I will about her
   As well as we can.   115
   Uxor non est meretrix, ergo falleris.
Welsh Gentlewoman. Sir, if your logic cannot prove me honest,
   There's a thing called marriage, and that makes me honest.
Maudlin. Oh, there's a trick beyond your logic, Tim.
Tim. I perceive then a woman may be honest according to the   120
   English print, when she is a whore in the Latin; so much for

---

95. *O tempora! O mors!*] The more common Latin expression is 'O tempora! O mores!', 'O! the times, O! the manners!' The quarto text prints 'mors' (death), suggesting either that Tim is incapable of quoting the most familiar Latin correctly or that he is making a joke, since marrying a whore might be considered worse than death.

97. *jade*] (1) worn-out horse; (2) a whore.

98–9.] Tim's plan to make money hiring out and racing his horse implies that he will force the Welsh woman into prostitution, acting as her pimp.

106. Flectere . . . movebo] If I cannot move the gods, I will appeal to the lower world (Virgil, *Aeneid*, Book 7, line 312).

116. Uxor . . . falleris] A wife is not a whore, therefore you lie.

120–1. *honest . . . Latin*] i.e. 'meretrix' is whore in Latin but in English sounds like 'merry tricks'.

marriage and logic! I'll love her for her wit, I'll pick out my
runts there; and for my mountains, I'll mount upon—
Yellowhammer. So Fortune seldom deals two marriages
    With one hand, and both lucky; the best is,   125
    One feast will serve them both. Marry, for room,
    I'll have the dinner kept in Goldsmiths' Hall,
    To which, kind gallants, I invite you all.   [*Exeunt.*]

FINIS.

---

126. *for room*] to provide adequate room.
127. *Goldsmiths' Hall*] the hall of the Goldsmith's company, in Foster Lane,
north of Cheapside.

THE ROARING GIRL

[THE EPISTLE]

To the Comic Play-readers: Venery and Laughter.

The fashion of play-making I can properly compare to nothing so
naturally as the alteration in apparel. For in the time of the great-
crop doublet, your huge bombasted plays, quilted with mighty
words to lean purpose, was only then in fashion; and as the doublet   5
fell, neater inventions began to set up. Now in the time of spruce-
ness, our plays follow the niceness of our garments: single plots,
quaint conceits, lecherous jests, dressed up in hanging sleeves; and
those are fit for the times and the termers. Such a kind of light-
colour summer stuff, mingled with divers colours, you shall find this   10
published comedy—good to keep you in an afternoon from dice, at
home in your chambers; and for venery, you shall find enough for
sixpence, but well couched an you mark it. For Venus, being a
woman, passes through the play in doublet and breeches: a brave
disguise and a safe one, if the statute untie not her codpiece point!   15
The book I make no question but is fit for many of your companies,
as well as the person itself, and may be allowed both gallery-room at
the playhouse and chamber-room at your lodging. Worse things, I

---

1. *Venery*] good hunting, with a secondary sense of sexual hunting. Also in line
12.
3–4. *great-crop doublet*] short men's jacket.
4. *bombasted*] stuffed with raw cotton padding (as in the 'great-crop doublet')
but frequently used figuratively of overblown rhetoric.
6. *fell*] (1) grew longer; (2) fell out of fashion.
7. *niceness*] neatness, precision, fussiness.
single plots] The term does not apply to this or most other plays of the time. A
possible ironic reference to classical dramatic theory.
8. *quaint conceits*] far-fetched expressions.
hanging sleeves] long, open sleeves hanging to the knee or foot; hinting here at
lame and drooping theatrical effects.
9. *termers*] persons who came to London during the Inns of Court terms for
study, business or pleasure.
9–10. *light-colour . . . stuff*] refers to the fashion for imported lighter cloth which
was perceived as a threat to the English wool trade and was consequently denounced in writing about fashion. Glancing here at lightweight comedy.
11. *published*] announced as.
13. *sixpence*] the normal price of a printed play.
couched] (1) hidden; (2) expressed in language; (3) worked into the pattern, like
embroidery on fabric.
an] if
14. *brave*] (1) splendid, showy; (2) courageous.
15. *the statute*] Laws on precise regulation of dress according to status were
repealed in 1603. However a general sense that cross-dressing was illegal remained.
See Intro., pp. 21–2.
untie . . . codpiece point] i.e. does not discover her true sex. Codpiece points were
laces used to tie the breeches to the doublet, and were connected to the *codpiece*,
covering the male genitals.

must needs confess, the world has taxed her for than has been
written of her; but 'tis the excellency of a writer to leave things better   20
than he finds 'em. Though some obscene fellow, that cares not what
he writes against others, yet keeps a mystical bawdy-house himself
and entertains drunkards to make use of their pockets and vent his
private bottle-ale at midnight—though such a one would have
ripped up the most nasty vice that ever hell belched forth and   25
presented it to a modest assembly, yet we rather wish in such
discoveries, where reputation lies bleeding, a slackness of truth than
fullness of slander.

THOMAS MIDDLETON.

---

19. *taxed her for*] accused her of.

22. *mystical*] secret, hidden. The term is common in Middleton, frequently
linked to a sexually suggestive term.

23–4. *vent . . . midnight*] This allegation is obscure. It has to do with selling
unlicensed home-made liquor, but it could also have sexual overtones: 'vent' means
'discharge'; bottled beer was notoriously explosive, and the shape of a bottle could
suggest both a penis and a vagina.

25. *ripped up*] exposed.

DRAMATIS PERSONAE

SIR ALEXANDER WENGRAVE, and NEATFOOT *his man.*
SIR ADAM APPLETON.
SIR DAVY DAPPER.
SIR BEAUTEOUS GANYMEDE.
[SIR THOMAS LONG.]   5
LORD NOLAND.
YOUNG [SEBASTIAN] WENGRAVE.
JACK DAPPER, *and* GULL *his page.*
GOSHAWK.
GREENWIT.   10
LAXTON.
TILTYARD[, *a feather seller*]   ⎫
OPENWORK[, *a sempster*]   ⎬ *Citizens.*
[HIPPOCRATES] GALLIPOT[, *an apothecary*] ⎭
[MRS TILTYARD]   ⎫   15
[MRS ROSAMOND OPENWORK]   ⎬ [*Citizens'*] *wives.*
[MRS PRUDENCE GALLIPOT]   ⎭
MOLL [CUTPURSE], *the Roaring Girl.*
TRAPDOOR.
[TEARCAT.]   20

The first Quarto includes the Dramatis Personae after the Prologue.

1. *NEATFOOT*] an ox's foot prepared for eating: with a suggestion of one who shows a neat or tidy foot in his mannered style of dressing.

4. *BEAUTEOUS GANYMEDE*] The name of Jove's cupbearer suits this character's function in assisting the marriage at the end of the play. The name also has a homosexual resonance which does not apply in this case but may have been an in-joke about King James's notoriously homosexual court.

6. *NOLAND*] Jokes about landless aristocrats were satiric commonplaces (see 2.1.62 and note). The joke is not appropriate here since Lord Noland acts as a figure of authority in the play. See Intro., pp. 25–6.

8. *JACK DAPPER*] An inversion of 'dapper jack', used in mockery or scorn of an upstart.

GULL] a gullible target for a confidence trickster.

9. *GOSHAWK*] a large short-winged hawk, used in falconry.

10. *GREENWIT*] Green means 'immature'; so, a silly fellow.

11. *LAXTON*] a word play on 'lack-stone' meaning (1) he has sold all his land, and (2) he has no testicles.

12. *TILTYARD*] named after the feathers used by combatants in the tiltyard.

13. *OPENWORK*] The name suggests openness and ingenuousness in business dealings and in sexual relationships.

14. *HIPPOCRATES GALLIPOT*] a comic combination of the name of the founder of medicine and a small earthenware pot for medicines and ointments.

18. *MOLL*] a pet name for 'Mary' and a general name for a whore.

19. *TRAPDOOR*] a potentially dangerous opening in the floor. The name suits a character who is treacherous to all those who employ him.

20. *TEARCAT*] 'To tear a cat' means 'to give an exaggerated, overblown heroic performance'.

SIR GUY FITZALLARD.
MARY FITZALLARD, *his daughter.*
CURTALAX, *a sergeant, and*
HANGER, *his yeoman.*
Ministri.   25
[Fellow *with a long rapier.*
Porter.
Tailor.
Coachman.
Several Cutpurses.   30
Servants.

SCENE: LONDON.]

---

23. *CURTALAX*] a cutlass.
24. *HANGER*] a loop or strap from which the sword hung on a sword belt.
Curtalax and Hanger go comically together.
25. *Ministri*] attendants.

Prologue

A play expected long makes the audience look
For wonders—that each scene should be a book
Composed to all perfection. Each one comes
And brings a play in 's head with him; up he sums
What he would of a roaring girl have writ;   5
If that he finds not here, he mews at it.
Only we entreat you think our scene
Cannot speak high, the subject being but mean.
A roaring girl, whose notes till now never were,
Shall fill with laughter our vast theatre.   10
That's all which I dare promise; tragic passion,
And such grave stuff, is this day out of fashion.
I see attention sets wide ope her gates
Of hearing, and with covetous list'ning waits
To know what girl this roaring girl should be;   15
For of that tribe are many. One is she
That roars at midnight in deep tavern bowls,
That beats the watch, and constables controls;
Another roars i' th' daytime, swears, stabs, gives braves,
Yet sells her soul to the lust of fools and slaves: 20
Both these are suburb-roarers. Then there's besides
A civil, city-roaring girl, whose pride,
Feasting, and riding, shakes her husband's state,
And leaves him roaring through an iron grate.
None of these roaring girls is ours; she flies   25
With wings more lofty. Thus her character lies—

Prol.1. *long*] for a long time.
6. *mews*] makes a cat noise with which audiences registered disapproval.
8. *high*] as in 'high' tragedy.
mean] of lower estate, a proper subject for comedy.
9. *never were*] never were heard in the theatre.
10. *vast theatre*] i.e. the Fortune Theatre in Golden Lane.
14. *covetous*] eager, greedy.
19. *gives braves*] makes a show of defiance, issues challenges.
23. *state*] (1) financial status; (2) standing in the community.
24. *roaring . . . grate*] begging for food and money through the bars of a debtors' prison.
26. *character*] Summary accounts of familiar types were collected in books of 'characters'.

Yet what need characters, when to give a guess
Is better than the person to express?
But would you know who 'tis? Would you hear her name?
She is called Mad Moll; her life our acts proclaim.   30

27–8. *when . . . express?*] It is futile to suppose that the stereotypes of a written 'character' can express the truth about a person better than the enactment of her story on stage.

Act 1

Enter MARY FITZALLARD *disguised like a sempster, with a case
for bands, and* NEATFOOT, *a servingman, with her, with a napkin
on his shoulder and a trencher in his hand, as from table.*

Neatfoot. The young gentleman, our young master, Sir Alexander's
son—it is into his ears, sweet damsel, emblem of fragility, you
desire to have a message transported, or to be transcendent?

Mary. A private word or two, sir, nothing else.

Neatfoot. You shall fructify in that which you come for; your pleas-　5
ure shall be satisfied to your full contentation. I will, fairest tree
of generation, watch when our young master is erected—that is
to say, up—and deliver him to this your most white hand.

Mary. Thanks, sir.

Neatfoot. And withal certify him that I have culled out for him, now　10
his belly is replenished, a daintier bit or modicum than any lay
upon his trencher at dinner. Hath he notion of your name, I
beseech your chastity?

Mary. One, sir, of whom he bespake falling-bands.

Neatfoot. Falling-bands: it shall so be given him. If you please to　15
venture your modesty in the hall amongst a curl-pated company

---

1.1.0.1. *sempster*] someone who did sewing: could be a man or a woman.

0.1–2. *a case for bands*] a box for neck-bands or collars.

0.3. *trencher*] a wooden plate or shallow dish.

3. *transcendent*] moved across. This elaborate and repetitious way of saying simple things is typical of Neatfoot's affected speech.

5. *fructify*] be fruitful; this word and the title 'fairest tree of generation' (lines 6–
7) insist on Mary's reproductive capacities as a woman.

6. *contentation*] content.

7. *erected*] i.e. risen from table: but the word begins the undertow of bawdy
which runs throughout the play. See Intro., pp. 50–2.

8. *white hand*] (1) beautiful handwriting: (2) elegant hand, white because it is
unused to physical work.

14. *bespake falling-bands*] placed an order for bands or collars; with a pun on
'band', i.e. 'bond' (her marriage precontract to Sebastian) or 'band' i.e. marriage
banns.

15. *given him*] reported to him. (Also in line 24.)

16. *curl-pated*] curly-haired.

of rude servingmen and take such as they can set before you,
you shall be most seriously and ingenuously welcome—
Mary. I have dined indeed already, sir.
Neatfoot. Or will you vouchsafe to kiss the lip of a cup of rich   20
Orleans in the butt'ry amongst our waiting-women?
Mary. Not now, in truth, sir.
Neatfoot. Our young master shall then have a feeling of your being
here presently. It shall so be given him.
Mary. I humbly thank you, sir.   *Exit* NEATFOOT.
                     But that my bosom   25
Is full of bitter sorrows, I could smile
To see this formal ape play antic tricks;
But in my breast a poisoned arrow sticks,
And smiles cannot become me. Love woven slightly,
Such as thy false heart makes, wears out as lightly,   30
But love being truly bred i' th' soul, like mine,
Bleeds even to death at the least wound it takes.
The more we quench this fire, the less it slakes.
Oh, me!

      Enter SEBASTIAN WENGRAVE *with* NEATFOOT.

Sebastian. A sempster speak with me, say'st thou?   35
Neatfoot. Yes, sir, she's there, *viva voce*, to deliver her auricular
confession.
Sebastian. [*To Mary*] With me, sweetheart? What is 't?
Mary. I have brought home your bands, sir.
Sebastian. Bands?—Neatfoot!   40
Neatfoot. Sir?
Sebastian. Prithee look in, for all the gentlemen are upon rising.
Neatfoot. Yes, sir, a most methodical attendance shall be given.
Sebastian. And, dost hear, if my father call for me, say I am busy
with a sempster.   45

---

17. *rude*] (1) simple; (2) unmannerly.
21. *Orleans*] wine from the Loire region in France.
23. *feeling*] sense.
24. *presently*] immediately.
25. *But that*] were it not that.
27. *formal*] rigorously observant of polite forms.
29. *slightly*] loosely, slackly.
30. *thy*] Mary is mentally addressing Sebastian, who she fears has abandoned her. See lines 52–5.
33. *slakes*] weakens.
36. viva voce] a Latin tag, meaning 'with a living voice', or, 'by word of mouth'.
36–7. *auricular confession*] a term usually used for confession of sins to a priest.
42. *look in*] look into the dining room.
upon rising] about to leave the table.

Neatfoot. Yes, sir, he shall know it that you are busied with a
    needlewoman.
Sebastian. In 's ear, good Neatfoot.
Neatfoot. It shall be so given him.   *Exit* NEATFOOT.
Sebastian. Bands? You're mistaken, sweetheart, I bespake none.   50
    When, where, I prithee? What bands? Let me see them.
Mary. Yes, sir, a bond fast sealed with solemn oaths,
    Subscribed unto, as I thought, with your soul,
    Delivered as your deed in sight of heaven.
    Is this bond cancelled? Have you forgot me?   55
Sebastian. Ha! Life of my life! Sir Guy Fitzallard's daughter!
    What has transformed my love to this strange shape?
    Stay, make all sure. [*Shuts doors.*] So. Now speak and be brief,
    Because the wolf's at door that lies in wait
    To prey upon us both. Albeit mine eyes   60
    Are blessed by thine, yet this so strange disguise
    Holds me with fear and wonder.
Mary.   Mine's a loathed sight.
    Why from it are you banished else so long?
Sebastian. I must cut short my speech. In broken language,
    Thus much, sweet Moll: I must thy company shun;   65
    I court another Moll. My thoughts must run
    As a horse runs that's blind: round in a mill,
    Out every step, yet keeping one path still.
Mary. Um! Must you shun my company? In one knot
    Have both our hands by th' hands of heaven been tied   70
    Now to be broke? I thought me once your bride—
    Our fathers did agree on the time when—
    And must another bedfellow fill my room?
Sebastian. Sweet maid, let's lose no time. 'Tis in heaven's book
    Set down that I must have thee; an oath we took   75
    To keep our vows; but when the knight, your father,

---

47. *needlewoman*] Neatfoot's change from 'sempster' to 'needlewoman' could be
loaded with sexual meaning because of the possible connection between a needle
and a penis.

50–2. *Bands . . . bond*] These words were often used with a pun on the two
meanings (as in line 14 above).

60–2. *Albeit . . . wonder*] Although my eyes rejoice at seeing you, as though
blessed by your goodness, this disguise frightens and amazes me.

62. *Mine's . . . sight*] I am a loathsome sight to look at.

63. *it*] my sight.

67–8.] A horse used to turn a millstone would be blindfolded to prevent dizzi-
ness. It would walk in a constant circle and never arrive at its object.

68. *Out*] i.e. stumbling.

69–76. *In one knot . . . vows*] Sebastian and Mary have entered into a precontract
known as 'spousals de futuro', which required no witnesses but was widely regarded
as binding.

Was from mine parted, storms began to sit
Upon my covetous father's brows, which fell
From them on me. He reckoned up what gold
This marriage would draw from him—at which he swore,   80
To lose so much blood could not grieve him more.
He then dissuades me from thee, called thee not fair,
And asked, 'What is she but a beggar's heir?'
He scorned thy dowry of five thousand marks.
If such a sum of money could be found,   85
And I would match with that, he'd not undo it,
Provided his bags might add nothing to it;
But vowed, if I took thee—nay more, did swear it—
Save birth from him I nothing should inherit.
Mary. What follows then—my shipwreck?
Sebastian.   Dearest, no.   90
Though wildly in a labyrinth I go,
My end is to meet thee. With a side wind
Must I now sail, else I no haven can find,
But both must sink for ever. There's a wench
Called Moll, Mad Moll, or Merry Moll, a creature   95
So strange in quality, a whole city takes
Note of her name and person. All that affection
I owe to thee, on her, in counterfeit passion,
I spend to mad my father; he believes
I dote upon this roaring girl, and grieves   100
As it becomes a father for a son
That could be so bewitched. Yet I'll go on
This crooked way, sigh still for her, feign dreams
In which I'll talk only of her. These streams
Shall, I hope, force my father to consent   105
That here I anchor, rather than be rent
Upon a rock so dangerous. Art thou pleased,
Because thou see'st we are waylaid, that I take
A path that's safe, though it be far about?

---

84. *five thousand marks*] A mark was an amount, two thirds of a pound, not a coin. Five thousand marks was a considerable sum.

85–9.] If Mary's father was willing to pay the dowry of five thousand marks, Sebastian's father would not stop the marriage, but he would not add anything from his own wealth to the marriage portion. If Sebastian insisted on marrying Mary, all he would inherit from his father would be his family name and title.

86. *match*] marry.

87. *bags*] money-bags.

89. *birth*] family name and title.

90. *shipwreck*] ruin.

106. *here*] i.e. with you.

rent] torn apart.

Mary. My prayers with heaven guide thee!
Sebastian.   Then I will on.   110
    My father is at hand; kiss and be gone.
    Hours shall be watched for meetings. I must now,
    As men for fear, to a strange idol bow.
Mary. Farewell!
Sebastian.   I'll guide thee forth. When next we meet,
    A story of Moll shall make our mirth more sweet.   *Exeunt.*   115

[1.2]

    Enter SIR ALEXANDER WENGRAVE, SIR DAVY DAPPER, SIR
    ADAM APPLETON, GOSHAWK, LAXTON, *and* Gentlemen.

All. Thanks, good Sir Alexander, for our bounteous cheer.
Sir Alexander. Fie, fie! In giving thanks you pay too dear.
Sir Davy. When bounty spreads the table, faith, 'twere sin,
    At going off, if thanks should not step in.
Sir Alexander. No more of thanks, no more.—Ay, marry, sir,   5
    Th'inner room was too close; how do you like
    This parlour, gentlemen?
All.   Oh, passing well!
Sir Adam. What a sweet breath the air casts here—so cool!
Goshawk. I like the prospect best.
Laxton.   See how 'tis furnished.
Sir Davy. A very fair sweet room.
Sir Alexander.   Sir Davy Dapper,   10
    The furniture that doth adorn this room
    Cost many a fair grey groat ere it came here;
    But good things are most cheap when they're most dear.
    Nay, when you look into my galleries—
    How bravely they are trimmed up—you all shall swear   15
    You're highly pleased to see what's set down there:
    Stories of men and women, mixed together,

   1.2.3. *faith*] in faith (a mild oath).

   4. *going off*] leaving.

   7. *parlour*] The gentlemen who were leaving the table at 1.1.42 have now come
into the room where Sebastian and Mary were conferring. The room is extended to
the whole theatre in Sir Alexander's description at lines 14–32. See Intro., p. 12.

   passing] exceedingly.

   12. *grey groat*] an emphatic equivalent of 'groat'. A groat, worth 4 pennies, was
often used generally to express a small sum.

   13. *good . . . dear*] i.e. good things are the best value when they are most cared
for. With wordplay on *dear*: (1) cherished, valued; (2) expensive.

   14–32.] This description of Sir Alexander's galleries hung with paintings also
contains an ingenious description of faces in the audience seated in the theatre
galleries and (lines 29–32) in the pit below the level of the stage.

   15. *bravely*] handsomely.

Fair ones with foul, like sunshine in wet weather.
Within one square a thousand heads are laid
So close that all of heads the room seems made;   20
As many faces there, filled with blithe looks,
Show like the promising titles of new books
Writ merrily, the readers being their own eyes,
Which seem to move and to give plaudities;
And here and there, whilst with obsequious ears   25
Thronged heaps do listen, a cutpurse thrusts and leers
With hawk's eyes for his prey. I need not show him;
By a hanging villainous look yourselves may know him,
The face is drawn so rarely. Then, sir, below,
The very floor, as 'twere, waves to and fro,   30
And, like a floating island, seems to move
Upon a sea bound in with shores above.

Enter SEBASTIAN *and* MASTER GREENWIT.

All. These sights are excellent!
Sir Alexander.   I'll show you all;
    Since we are met, make our parting comical.
Sebastian. This gentleman—my friend—will take his leave, sir.   35
Sir Alexander. Ha? Take his leave, Sebastian? Who?
Sebastian.   This gentleman.
Sir Alexander. [*To Greenwit*] Your love, sir, has already given me
        some time,
    And if you please to trust my age with more,
    It shall pay double interest. Good sir, stay.
Greenwit. I have been too bold.
Sir Alexander.   Not so, sir. A merry day   40
    'Mongst friends being spent is better than gold saved.—
    Some wine, some wine! Where be these knaves I keep?

Enter three or four Servingmen *and* NEATFOOT.

---

19. *square*] the frame of the painting; with reference also to the square shape of
the Fortune Theatre itself.
22. *Show*] appear.
23. *the readers . . . eyes*] The spectators, described as though in a painting, view
both the action on stage and themselves.
24. *plaudities*] bursts of applause.
27. *show him*] point him out to you.
29. *rarely*] excellently.
30–1. *The very floor . . . island*] The image invokes the island of the stage surrounded on three sides by the moving mass of spectators.
34. *comical*] happy, fortunate.
35. *This gentleman*] i.e. Greenwit.
37. *love*] courtesy.
38. *trust my age*] be indulgent with an old man.
42. *knaves I keep*] servants in my household.

Neatfoot. At your worshipful elbow, sir.

Sir Alexander.   You are
      Kissing my maids, drinking, or fast asleep.

Neatfoot. Your worship has given it us right.

Sir Alexander.   You varlets, stir!   45
      Chairs, stools, and cushions.

                              [*Servants bring on wine, chairs, etc.*]
                              —Prithee, Sir Davy Dapper,
      Make that chair thine.

Sir Davy.   'Tis but an easy gift,
      And yet I thank you for it, sir; I'll take it.

Sir Alexander. [*To Servants*] A chair for old Sir Adam Appleton.

Neatfoot. [*Providing a chair*] A back-friend to your worship.

Sir Adam.   Marry, good Neatfoot,   50
      I thank thee for it. Back-friends sometimes are good.

Sir Alexander. Pray make that stool your perch, good Master
      Goshawk.

Goshawk. I stoop to your lure, sir.

Sir Alexander.   Son Sebastian,
      Take Master Greenwit to you.

Sebastian.   Sit, dear friend.

Sir Alexander. Nay, Master Laxton. [*To a Servant*] Furnish
      Master Laxton   55
      With what he wants—a stone—a stool, I would say,
      A stool.

Laxton.   I had rather stand, sir.

Sir Alexander. I know you had, good Master Laxton. So, so.

                              Exeunt [NEATFOOT *and*] Servants.
      Now here's a mess of friends; and gentlemen,
      Because time's glass shall not be running long,   60
      I'll quicken it with a pretty tale.

Sir Davy.   Good tales do well
      In these bad days, where vice does so excel.

Sir Adam. Begin, Sir Alexander.

Sir Alexander.   Last day I met

---

45. *given it us*] described us.

50. *A back-friend*] a chair with a back, but also a wordplay on (1) a false friend;
(2) a sergeant (alluding to the method of making an arrest).

53. *stoop to your lure*] a technical expression for having hawks in training come
down to take food. Goshawk responds to Sir Alexander's witticism of *perch*, line 52.

56. *a stone*] comically drawing attention to Laxton's (Lacks stone) name. Since
'stone' was a term for testicle, this could begin a strain of obscenity, taking in (line
56) *stool* (bowel movement) and extending (line 57) to *stand* (to have an erection).
See Intro., p. 23.

59. *a mess*] a company of four.

63. *Last day*] yesterday.

       An agèd man upon whose head was scored
       A debt of just so many years as these   65
       Which I owe to my grave. The man you all know.
All. His name, I pray you, sir?
Sir Alexander.   Nay, you shall pardon me.
       But when he saw me, with a sigh that brake,
       Or seemed to break, his heart-strings, thus he spake:
       'O my good knight', says he—and then his eyes   70
       Were richer even by that which made them poor,
       They had spent so many tears they had no more—
       'O sir', says he, 'you know it, for you ha' seen
       Blessings to rain upon mine house and me;
       Fortune, who slaves men, was my slave; her wheel   75
       Hath spun me golden threads, for, I thank heaven,
       I ne'er had but one cause to curse my stars.'
       I asked him then what that one cause might be.
All. So. sir.
Sir Alexander. He paused, and—as we often see
       A sea so much becalmed there can be found   80
       No wrinkle on his brow, his waves being drowned
       In their own rage, but when th' imperious winds
       Use strange invisible tyranny to shake
       Both heaven's and earth's foundation at their noise,
       The seas, swelling with wrath to part that fray,   85
       Rise up and are more wild, more mad, than they—
       Even so this good old man was by my question
       Stirred up to roughness. You might see his gall
       Flow even in 's eyes; then grew he fantastical.
Sir Davy. Fantastical? Ha, ha!
Sir Alexander.   Yes, and talked oddly.   90
Sir Adam. Pray, sir, proceed. How did this old man end?
Sir Alexander. Marry, sir, thus:
       He left his wild fit to read o'er his cards;
       Yet then, though age cast snow on all his hairs,
       He joyed, 'Because,' says he, 'the god of gold   95

64–6. *upon . . . grave*] i.e. he was the same age as Sir Alexander.

75–6. *Fortune . . . threads*] The speaker confuses Fortune's wheel, which raises men only to bring them down, with the spinning wheel on which the Fates spin out the thread of life.

81. *his*] i.e. the sea's.

85. *part that fray*] i.e. end the disturbance begun by the winds.

88. *gall*] bile; bitterness.

89. *fantastical*] bizarre in his behaviour.

93. *read . . . cards*] consider his position (?). Sometimes emended to 'cares', though *cards* meaning 'maps' would continue the maritime imagery of the earlier part of the speech.

Has been to me no niggard. That disease
Of which all old men sicken, avarice,
Never infected me—'

Laxton. [*Aside*] He means not himself, I'm sure.

Sir Alexander. 'For, like a lamp   100
    Fed with continual oil, I spend and throw
    My light to all that need it, yet have still
    Enough to serve myself. Oh but,' quoth he,
    'Though heaven's dew fall thus on this agèd tree,
    I have a son that's like a wedge doth cleave   105
    My very heart-root.'

Sir Davy.   Had he such a son?

Sebastian. [*Aside*] Now I do smell a fox strongly.

Sir Alexander. Let's see—no, Master Greenwit is not yet
    So mellow in years as he, but as like Sebastian,
    Just like my son Sebastian—such another.   110

Sebastian. [*Aside*] How finely, like a fencer, my father fetches his by-
    blows to hit me! But if I beat you not at your own weapon of
    subtlety—

Sir Alexander. 'This son', saith he, 'that should be
    The column and main arch unto my house,   115
    The crutch unto my age, becomes a whirlwind
    Shaking the firm foundation—'

Sir Adam.   'Tis some prodigal.

Sebastian. [*Aside*] Well shot, old Adam Bell!

Sir Alexander. No city monster neither, no prodigal,
    But sparing, wary, civil, and—though wifeless—   120
    An excellent husband; and such a traveller,
    He has more tongues in his head than some have teeth.

Sir Davy. I have but two in mine.

Goshawk.   So sparing and so wary.
    What then could vex his father so?

Sir Alexander.   Oh, a woman.

Sebastian. [*Aside*] A flesh-fly. That can vex any man!   125

---

101. *continual*] inexhaustible.

105. *doth*] that does.

106. *heart-root*] i.e. the seat of the deepest emotion.

107. *smell a fox*] Cf. 'smell a rat'; a fox is also a kind of sword, which would initiate the fencing imagery of line 110.

111–12. *by-blows*] side blows (with a sword).

118. *Adam Bell*] an archer and fencer, celebrated in ballads. Sebastian is sarcastically comparing Adam Bell's skill in hitting the target with Sir Adam's trite explication of the obvious moral of Sir Alexander's story.

121. *excellent husband*] thrifty householder.

122. *tongues*] languages.

125. *A flesh-fly*] a fly which lays its eggs and lives on injured flesh; a common emblem for lust.

Sir Alexander. A scurvy woman,
    On whom the passionate old man swore he doted.
    'A creature', saith he, 'nature hath brought forth
    To mock the sex of woman.' It is a thing
    One knows not how to name: her birth began   130
    Ere she was all made. 'Tis woman more than man,
    Man more than woman, and—which to none can hap—
    The sun gives her two shadows to one shape;
    Nay, more, let this strange thing walk, stand, or sit,
    No blazing star draws more eyes after it.   135
Sir Davy. A monster! 'Tis some monster!
Sir Alexander.   She's a varlet!
Sebastian. [*Aside*] Now is my cue to bristle.
Sir Alexander. A naughty pack.
Sebastian.   'Tis false!
Sir Alexander.   Ha, boy?
Sebastian.   'Tis false!
Sir Alexander. What's false? I say she's naught.
Sebastian.   I say that tongue
    That dares speak so—but yours—sticks in the throat   140
    Of a rank villain.—Set yourself aside—
Sir Alexander. So, sir, what then?
Sebastian.   Any here else had lied.
    (*Aside*) I think I shall fit you.
Sir Alexander. Lie?
Sebastian.   Yes.
Sir Davy.   Doth this concern him?
Sir Alexander.   Ah, sirrah boy,
    Is your blood heated? Boils it? Are you stung?   145
    I'll pierce you deeper yet.—O my dear friends,

---

127. *he*] i.e. the son.

130–1. *her birth . . . made*] Sir Alexander alludes to the idea that women's genitals were inverted or incomplete versions of men's. Moll, in this view, was meant to be a man but was born before the process of forming her was complete, emerging as a hermaphrodite. See Intro., pp. 53–4.

132. *hap*] happen.

133. *two shadows*] i.e. one for each sex; further evidence of her monstrosity.

135. *blazing star*] comet.

138. *naughty pack*] person of worthless character.

139. *naught*] immoral, worthless.

139–41. *that tongue . . . villain*] any person who dares speak so, excepting yourself, lies in his throat like a villain.

141–2. *Set . . . lied*] If anyone other than you had said such a thing, I'd say he lied.

143. *fit you*] measure up to your charges; pay you back as you deserve.

144. *sirrah*] a term used to address children and social inferiors.

I am that wretched father, this that son
That sees his ruin, yet headlong on doth run.
Sir Adam. [*To Sebastian*] Will you love such a poison?
Sir Davy.   Fie, fie!
Sebastian.   You're all mad!
Sir Alexander. Thou'rt sick at heart, yet feel'st it not. Of all these,   150
   What gentleman but thou, knowing his disease
   Mortal, would shun the cure?—O Master Greenwit,
   Would you to such an idol bow?
Greenwit.   Not I, sir.
Sir Alexander. Here's Master Laxton: has he mind to a woman
   As thou hast?
Laxton.   No, not I, sir.
Sir Alexander.   Sir, I know it.   155
Laxton. Their good parts are so rare, their bad so common,
   I will have naught to do with any woman.
Sir Davy. 'Tis well done, Master Laxton.
Sir Alexander. [*To Sebastian*]   O thou cruel boy,
   Thou wouldst with lust an old man's life destroy;
   Because thou seest I'm half-way in my grave,   160
   Thou shovel'st dust upon me. Would thou mightest have
   Thy wish, most wicked, most unnatural!
Sir Davy. Why, sir, 'tis thought Sir Guy Fitzallard's daughter
   Shall wed your son Sebastian.
Sir Alexander.   Sir Davy Dapper,
   I have upon my knees wooed this fond boy   165
   To take that virtuous maiden.
Sebastian.   Hark you a word, sir.
   You on your knees have cursed that virtuous maiden,
   And me for loving her; yet do you now
   Thus baffle me to my face? Wear not your knees
   In such entreats! Give me Fitzallard's daughter!   170
Sir Alexander. I'll give thee ratsbane rather!
Sebastian.   Well then, you know
   What dish I mean to feed upon.
Sir Alexander.   Hark, gentlemen,
   He swears to have this cutpurse drab to spite my gall.

---

156. *rare*] (1) seldom found; (2) excellent.
157. *naught*] Laxton slyly puns on *naught* = nothing and *naught* = immoral
behaviour, i.e. he will commit immoral acts with women or he will have nothing to
do with women. See line 139 above and Intro., p. 23.
169. *baffle*] (1) cheat; (2) challenge, disagree.
Wear] wear out.
170. *entreats*] entreaties.
171. *ratsbane*] rat poison.
173. *drab*] slut, whore.

All. Master Sebastian!

Sebastian.   I am deaf to you all!
　　I'm so bewitched, so bound to my desires,   175
　　Tears, prayers, threats, nothing can quench out those fires
　　That burn within me!   *Exit* SEBASTIAN.

Sir Alexander. [*Aside*]   Her blood shall quench it then.
　　[*To them*] Lose him not. Oh, dissuade him, gentlemen!

Sir Davy. He shall be weaned, I warrant you.

Sir Alexander.   Before his eyes
　　Lay down his shame, my grief, his miseries.   180

All. No more, no more; away!   *Exeunt all but Sir Alexander.*

Sir Alexander.   I wash a negro,
　　Losing both pains and cost. But take thy flight;
　　I'll be most near thee when I'm least in sight.
　　Wild buck, I'll hunt thee breathless; thou shalt run on,
　　But I will turn thee when I'm not thought upon.   185

　　　　　Enter RALPH TRAPDOOR [*with a letter*].

　　Now, sirrah, what are you? Leave your ape's tricks and speak.

Trapdoor. A letter from my captain to your worship.

Sir Alexander. Oh, Oh, now I remember, 'tis to prefer thee into my
　　service.

Trapdoor. To be a shifter under your worship's nose of a clean   190
　　trencher, when there's a good bit upon 't.

Sir Alexander. Troth, honest fellow. [*Aside*] Hm—ha—let me see—
　　This knave shall be the axe to hew that down
　　At which I stumble. 'Has a face that promiseth
　　Much of a villain; I will grind his wit,   195
　　And if the edge prove fine, make use of it.
　　[*To him*] Come hither, sirrah. Canst thou be secret, ha?

Trapdoor. As two crafty attorneys plotting the undoing of their
　　clients.

Sir Alexander. Didst never, as thou hast walked about this town,   200
　　Hear of a wench called Moll—Mad, Merry Moll?

---

178. *Lose him not*] Don't give up on him.

179. *weaned*] turned away from his inclination.

181–2. *I wash . . . cost*] It was proverbially impossible 'to wash the Ethiop white'.

183.] i.e. I'll be aware of all your doings when you least suspect.

185. *turn thee*] force you to turn about and confront your pursuer like a hunted deer.

187.] Trapdoor is a discharged soldier.

188. *prefer*] recommend.

190–1.] i.e. to clear the tables and eat the leftovers.

192–6.] Sir Alexander's aside reveals his plan to use Trapdoor's wicked nature (evident in his face) against his son.

194. *promiseth*] gives signs of.

Trapdoor. Moll Cutpurse, sir?

Sir Alexander. The same; dost thou know her, then?

Trapdoor. As well as I know 'twill rain upon Simon and Jude's day
   next. I will sift all the taverns i' th' city, and drink half-pots with   205
   all the watermen o' th' Bankside, but if you will, sir, I'll find her
   out.

Sir Alexander. That task is easy; do 't then. Hold thy hand up.
   [*Examines his hand.*] What's this? Is 't burnt?

Trapdoor. No, sir, no. A little singed with making fireworks.   210

Sir Alexander. [*Giving money*] There's money. Spend it; that being
   spent, fetch more.

Trapdoor. Oh, sir, that all the poor soldiers in England had such a
   leader! For fetching, no water-spaniel is like me.

Sir Alexander. This wench we speak of strays so from her kind,
   Nature repents she made her; 'tis a mermaid   215
   Has tolled my son to shipwreck.

Trapdoor. I'll cut her comb for you.

Sir Alexander. I'll tell out gold for thee then. Hunt her forth;
   Cast out a line hung full of silver hooks
   To catch her to thy company. Deep spendings   220
   May draw her that's most chaste to a man's bosom.

Trapdoor. The jingling of golden bells, and a good fool with a
   hobby-horse, will draw all the whores i' th' town to dance in a
   morris.

Sir Alexander. Or rather—for that's best—they say sometimes   225
   She goes in breeches: follow her as her man.

Trapdoor. And when her breeches are off, she shall follow me!

Sir Alexander. Beat all thy brains to serve her.

204–5. *As . . . next*] Simon and Jude's day, 28 October, was the day before the
Lord Mayor's pageant, when rain would be particularly inconvenient. Rain stopped
the pageant in 1605 and 1606.

206. *watermen o' the Bankside*] boatmen for hire on the southern shore of the
Thames. See Intro., p. 15.

209. *burnt*] i.e. branded as a felon.

215–16. *mermaid . . . shipwreck*] Mermaids were commonly associated with sirens who lured sailors to their doom. Their combination of human and fish made
them seem monstrous, like Moll, and so they were often presented as a figure for a
whore. See Intro., p. 54.

216. *Has tolled*] who has enticed, lured.

217. *cut . . . comb*] A cock's comb was cut on castration. Trapdoor will destroy
Moll's masculinity and lower her pride.

218. *tell out*] count out.

221. *her . . . chaste*] even the most chaste of women.

223. *hobby-horse*] a figure of a horse made of wicker-work fastened round the
dancer's waist.

224. *morris*] country dance.

226. *man*] servant.

Trapdoor. Zounds, sir, as country wenches beat cream till butter
    comes.   230
Sir Alexander. Play thou the subtle spider; weave fine nets
    To ensnare her very life.
Trapdoor.   Her life?
Sir Alexander.   Yes, suck
    Her heart-blood if thou canst. Twist thou but cords
    To catch her; I'll find law to hang her up.
Trapdoor. Spoke like a worshipful bencher!   235
Sir Alexander. Trace all her steps; at this she-fox's den
    Watch what lambs enter. Let me play the shepherd
    To save their throats from bleeding, and cut hers.
Trapdoor. This is the goll shall do 't.
Sir Alexander.   Be firm, and gain me
    Ever thine own. This done, I entertain thee.   240
    How is thy name?
Trapdoor. My name, sir, is Ralph Trapdoor—honest Ralph.
Sir Alexander. Trapdoor, be like thy name: a dangerous step
    For her to venture on; but unto me—
Trapdoor. As fast as your sole to your boot or shoe, sir.   245
Sir Alexander. Hence then; be little seen here as thou canst.
    I'll still be at thine elbow.
Trapdoor.   The trap-door's set.
    Moll, if you budge, you're gone. This me shall crown:
    A roaring boy the Roaring Girl puts down.
Sir Alexander. God-a-mercy, lose no time.   *Exeunt.*   250

---

229. *Zounds*] by God's wounds (an oath).

229–30. *country wenches . . . comes*] with a sexual double meaning of ejaculation.

235. *worshipful bencher*] distinguished senior member of one of the Inns of Court;
a magistrate.

239. *goll*] hand.

239–40. *gain . . . own*] win me as your friend and patron.

240. *entertain*] take into service.

249. *roaring boy*] loutish, noisy, violent young man.

250. *God-a-mercy*] a mild oath.

Act 2

[2.1]

The three shops open in a rank: the first a pothecary's shop,
the next a feather shop, the third a sempster's shop. MRS GALLIPOT
in the first, MRS TILTYARD *in the next,* MASTER OPENWORK *and his* Wife
in the third. To them enters LAXTON, GOSHAWK, *and* GREENWIT.

Mrs Openwork. Gentlemen, what is 't you lack? What is 't you buy?
See fine bands and ruffs, fine lawns, fine cambrics. What is 't
you lack, gentlemen, what is 't you buy?

Laxton. Yonder's the shop.

Goshawk. Is that she?   5

Laxton. Peace!

Greenwit. She that minces tobacco?

Laxton. Ay. She's a gentlewoman born, I can tell you, though it be
her hard fortune now to shred Indian pot-herbs.

Goshawk. Oh, sir, 'tis many a good woman's fortune, when her   10
husband turns bankrupt, to begin with pipes and set up again.

Laxton. And indeed the raising of the woman is the lifting up of the
man's head at all times: if one flourish, t' other will bud as fast,
I warrant ye.

Goshawk. Come, thou'rt familiarly acquainted there, I grope that.   15

Laxton. An you grope no better i' th' dark, you may chance lie i' th'
ditch when you're drunk.

Goshawk. Go, thou'rt a mystical lecher!

Laxton. I will not deny but my credit may take up an ounce of pure
smoke.   20

2.1.0.1–4.] See Intro., pp. 7–9, for a discussion of staging.

0.1. rank] row.

pothecary] apothecary; seller of drugs and medicines, including tobacco.

1–3. *what . . . buy*] traditional cries to attract customers.

5. *she*] Mrs Gallipot.

7. *minces*] cuts up finely.

11. *pipes*] Tobacco pipes—but with a bawdy reference to a penis. The sexual
banter continues with *raising* and *lifting up* (line 12), *man's head* (line 13), *grope* (lines
15 and 16), all of which refer to sexual intercourse or foreplay.

15. *grope*] (1) understand; (2) handle, feel.

16. *An*] if.

18. *mystical*] secret, hidden, as in the Epistle, line 22.

19. *credit*] (1) reputation; (2) financial viability.

19–21. *an ounce . . . smock*] This laboured joke depends on the assonance be-

Goshawk. May take up an ell of pure smock! Away, go! [*Aside*] 'Tis
the closest striker! Life, I think he commits venery forty foot
deep; no man's aware on 't. I, like a palpable smockster, go to
work so openly with the tricks of art that I'm as apparently seen
as a naked boy in a vial; and were it not for a gift of treachery   25
that I have in me to betray my friend when he puts most trust
in me—mass, yonder he is, too—and by his injury to make good
my access to her, I should appear as defective in courting as a
farmer's son the first day of his feather, that doth nothing at
court but woo the hangings and glass windows for a month   30
together and some broken waiting-woman for ever after. I find
those imperfections in my venery that, were 't not for flattery
and falsehood, I should want discourse and impudence; and he
that wants impudence among women is worthy to be kicked out
at bed's feet.—He shall not see me yet.   [*He stands aside.*]   35

[*At the pothecary's or tobacco shop.*]

Greenwit. Troth, this is finely shred.
Laxton. Oh, women are the best mincers!
Mrs Gallipot. 'T had been a good phrase for a cook's wife, sir.
Laxton. But 'twill serve generally, like the front of a new almanac, as
thus: calculated for the meridian of cooks' wives, but generally   40
for all Englishwomen.
Mrs Gallipot. Nay, you shall ha 't, sir; I have filled it for you.

She puts it to the fire.

---

tween 'smoke' and 'smock' (referring to the loose undergarment worn by early
modern women). An *ounce* is a small measure of dry goods while an *ell* is a large
measure of fabric, measured with a 'rod' and so associated with a penis. Behind the
exchange there lies the proverbial saying 'give an ounce and take an ell'.

22. *closest striker*] most secret lecher.

Life] upon my life (a mild oath).

venery] indulgence in sexual desire (also in line 32). Compare Prologue, line 1.

23. *smockster*] wencher; one who seduces women.

25. *naked . . . vial*] abortion preserved in a glass jar; with a possible allusion to
Cupid, often represented as a naked boy.

26. *my friend*] i.e. Openwork, whose wife Goshawk will try to seduce.

27. *mass*] by the mass (a mild oath).

29. *the first . . . feather*] the first day he enters fashionable society.

30. *woo the hangings*] practise courtly gestures in front of the tapestries which
decorated the walls at court.

31. *broken*] used, degraded.

33. *want*] lack (also in line 34).

37. *mincers*] (1) shredders of tobacco; (2) women who chop and mince words.

39. *almanac*] book giving astrological and other predictions. The advice in almanacs was so generalized as to be meaningless, so that belief in them was associated
with gullibility.

40. *calculated . . . meridian*] worked out for the astral configuration.

42. *ha 't*] have the pipe you ordered.

Laxton. The pipe's in a good hand, and I wish mine always so.

Greenwit. But not to be used o' that fashion!

Laxton. Oh, pardon me, sir, I understand no French. [*To Goshawk*]   45
I pray be covered. Jack, a pipe of rich smoke?

Goshawk. Rich smoke. That's sixpence a pipe, is 't?

Greenwit. To me, sweet lady.

Mrs Gallipot. [*Aside to Laxton*] Be not forgetful; respect my credit;
seem strange. Art and wit makes a fool of suspicion; pray be   50
wary.   [*The men smoke.*]

Laxton. [*Aside to Mrs Gallipot*] Push, I warrant you. [*To them*]
Come, how is 't, gallants?

Greenwit. Pure and excellent.

Laxton. I thought 'twas good, you were grown so silent. You are   55
like those that love not to talk at victuals, though they make a
worse noise i' the nose than a common fiddler's prentice, and
discourse a whole supper with snuffling. [*Aside to Mrs Gallipot*]
I must speak a word with you anon.

Mrs Gallipot. [*Aside to Laxton*] Make your way wisely, then.   60
[*Laxton and Mrs Gallipot stand together.*]

Goshawk. [*To Greenwit*] Oh, what else, sir? He's perfection itself:
full of manners, but not an acre of ground belonging to 'em.

Greenwit. Ay, and full of form; 'has ne'er a good stool in 's chamber.

Goshawk. But above all religious: he preyeth daily upon elder
brothers.   65

Greenwit. And valiant above measure: h'as run three streets from a
sergeant.

43.] with bawdy double entendre suggesting the man's penis in the woman's
hand.

44.] i.e. not to be put in the fire (burned with syphilis).

45. *French*] bawdy language; venereal disease.

46. *be covered*] i.e. replace your hat on your head. (Said to Goshawk, who has
just joined them.)

47. *sixpence a pipe*] a rather high price for tobacco.

48.] Greenwit asks to be served too.

49–50. *respect . . . strange*] pay attention to my good name by not being too
familiar.

52. *Push*] Pooh! (a common exclamation, indicating dismissal or lack of concern).
I . . . you] you can count on me.

58. *discourse . . . supper*] make up a whole meal's worth of conversation.

61. *He's*] i.e. Laxton is.

62. *manners*] punning on 'manors' meaning an estate. The relative social importance of manners and land was a major concern and informs the rest of the gallants'
snide coversation about Laxton. See Intro., p. 22.

63. *form*] punning on 'form', meaning a bench, a lower class of furniture even
than a stool.

64–5. *preyeth . . . brothers*] (1) sponges on heirs to fortunes; (2) prays with senior
officers of the sectarian churches. With wordplay on 'preyeth' and 'prayeth'.

67. *sergeant*] who might arrest him for debt.

Laxton. (*He blows tobacco*[*-smoke*] *in their faces.*) Pooh, pooh.
Greenwit, Goshawk. [*Coughing*] Oh, pooh, ho, ho!
[*They move away.*]
Laxton. So, so.   70
Mrs Gallipot. What's the matter now, sir?
Laxton. I protest I'm in extreme want of money. If you can supply
me now with any means, you do me the greatest pleasure, next
to the bounty of your love, as ever poor gentleman tasted.
Mrs Gallipot. What's the sum would pleasure ye, sir? Though you   75
deserve nothing less at my hands.
Laxton. Why, 'tis but for want of opportunity, thou know'st. [*Aside*]
I put her off with opportunity still! By this light, I hate her, but
for means to keep me in fashion with gallants; for what I take
from her I spend upon other wenches, bear her in hand still.   80
She has wit enough to rob her husband, and I ways enough to
consume the money. [*To Gallants*] Why, how now? What, the
chin-cough?
Goshawk. Thou hast the cowardliest trick to come before a man's
face and strangle him ere he be aware. I could find in my heart   85
to make a quarrel in earnest.
Laxton. Pox, an thou dost—thou know'st I never use to fight with
my friends—thou'll but lose thy labour in 't.

Enter JACK DAPPER *and his man* GULL.

Jack Dapper!
Greenwit. Monsieur Dapper, I dive down to your ankles.   90
Jack Dapper. Save ye, gentlemen, all three, in a peculiar salute.
Goshawk. He were ill to make a lawyer: he dispatches three at once!
Laxton. So, well said! [*Receiving purse from Mrs Gallipot*] But is this
of the same tobacco, Mistress Gallipot?

---

76. *nothing less*] i.e. than (sexual) pleasure.

77–8. *opportunity . . . opportunity*] Laxton tells Mrs Gallipot that he fails to accept
the offered sexual pleasure only because of the lack of opportunity to make love to
her. He then boasts to the audience that this is just an excuse.

80. *bear . . . still*] delude her continually with false hopes; lead her on.

83. *chin-cough*] whooping cough; Laxton has made the gallants cough by blow-
ing smoke in their faces.

87. *Pox*] an obscene oath or exclamation.
an . . . dost] if you do.
use] make it a practice.

90. *dive . . . ankles*] i.e. bow deeply, like a 'dive dapper'.

91. *Save ye*] God save you (a greeting).
peculiar] single, special.

92. *He . . . once*] He would make a poor lawyer, since he deals with three clients
at the same time (instead of making the most money out of each of them separately).

93–4. *But . . . tobacco*] Laxton pretends that the purse Mrs Gallipot gives him
contains tobacco rather than money.

Mrs Gallipot. The same you had at first, sir.   95
Laxton. I wish it no better. This will serve to drink at my chamber.
Goshawk. Shall we taste a pipe on 't?
Laxton. Not of this, by my troth, gentlemen; I have sworn before
    you.
Goshawk. What, not Jack Dapper?   100
Laxton. Pardon me, sweet Jack, I'm sorry I made such a rash oath,
    but foolish oaths must stand. [*Dapper starts to leave.*] Where art
    going, Jack?
Jack Dapper. Faith, to buy one feather.
Laxton. One feather? [*Aside*] The fool's peculiar still!   105
Jack Dapper. Gull.
Gull. Master?
Jack Dapper. Here's three halfpence for your ordinary, boy; meet
    me an hour hence in Paul's.

             [*Dapper proceeds to the feather shop.*]

Gull. [*Aside*] How? Three single halfpence? Life, this will scarce   110
    serve a man in sauce: a ha'p'orth of mustard, a ha'p'orth of oil,
    and a ha'p'orth of vinegar—what's left then for the pickle
    herring? This shows like small beer i' th' morning after a great
    surfeit of wine o'ernight. He could spend his three pound last
    night in a supper amongst girls and brave bawdy-house boys. I   115
    thought his pockets cackled not for nothing; these are the eggs
    of three pound. I'll go sup 'em up presently.   *Exit* GULL.
Laxton. [*Aside*] Eight, nine, ten angels. Good wench, i' faith, and
    one that loves darkness well: she puts out a candle with the best
    tricks of any drugster's wife in England. But that which mads   120
    her: I rail upon opportunity still, and take no notice on 't. The

---

  96. *drink*] smoke.
  100. *What . . . Dapper?*] i.e. not even Jack Dapper will be allowed to smoke
Laxton's special tobacco? Laxton was busy with Mrs Gallipot when the other
gallants were greeting Jack and did not notice he was among them.
  104. *feather*] The association of fools and feathers was proverbial.
  108. *ordinary*] an eating house which served fixed-price meals; or the meal itself.
  109. *Paul's*] Paul's walk in the middle aisle of St Paul's Cathedral.
  111. *ha'p'orth*] halfpenny worth.
  113. *small beer*] thin or weak beer.
  116. *cackled*] The chinking of small change sounded like the cackling of a hen
laying an egg; the three halfpence are the small eggs laid by (i.e. left over from) the
three pounds that Dapper spent on his supper.
  117. *presently*] at once.
  118. *angels*] valuable gold coins, stamped with the design of the archangel
Michael slaying a dragon.
  121. *rail upon opportunity*] i.e. pretend to lament the lack of opportunity to make
love to her. (See lines 77–8 above.)

other night she would needs lead me into a room with a candle
in her hand to show me a naked picture, where no sooner
entered but the candle was sent of an errand. Now I, not
intending to understand her, but like a puny at the inns of   125
venery, called for another light innocently. Thus reward I all her
cunning with simple mistaking. I know she cozens her husband
to keep me, and I'll keep her honest, as long as I can, to make
the poor man some part of amends. An honest mind of a
whoremaster! [*To the Gallants*] How think you amongst you?   130
What, a fresh pipe? Draw in a third man.
Goshawk. No, you're a hoarder. You engross by th' ounces.

At the feather shop now.

Jack Dapper. [*Examining a feather*] Pooh, I like it not.
Mrs Tiltyard.   What feather is 't you'd have, sir?
These are most worn and most in fashion
Amongst the beaver gallants, the stone-riders,   135
The private stage's audience, the twelvepenny-stool gentlemen.
I can inform you 'tis the general feather.
Jack Dapper. And therefore I mislike it. Tell me of general!
Now a continual Simon and Jude's rain
Beat all your feathers as flat down as pancakes!   140

---

123. *naked picture*] picture of a nude.
124. *sent . . . errand*] put out (so that Mrs Openwork could make a pass at
Laxton in the dark).
125–6. *puny . . . venery*] beginner in the schools of lechery.
127. *cozens*] deceives.
128. *keep*] i.e. financially.
128–9. *I'll . . . amends*] Laxton jokes that he will refrain from sleeping with her,
thus serving his own preference and incidentally doing her husband a good turn.
129–30. *An . . . whoremaster*] i.e. Fancy that, a lecher dealing honestly with a
husband!
132. *hoarder . . . engross*] terms normally used of those who hoarded grain illegally in times of shortage. Goshawk resents Laxton's refusal to share the 'tobacco'
he got from Mrs Gallipot earlier.
132.1. *At . . . now*] All three shops are displayed on the stage and the action
moves from one shop front to another. See Intro., pp. 7–9.
135. *beaver gallants*] gallants who wear fashionable and expensive beaver hats.
stone-riders] riders of stallions; with a sexual quibble from 'stone' meaning
'testicle'.
136. *private stage*] the theatres for a more exclusive audience established in halls
around the city; i.e. not the audience at the Fortune. See Intro., p. 5.
twelvepenny-stool] an exaggeration; at sixpence, a stool at the private theatre cost
only half that.
137. *the general feather*] the feather generally in fashion.
139. *Simon . . . rain*] See I.2.204 and note.

Show me—a—spangled feather.
Mrs Tiltyard.   Oh, to go a-feasting with!
You'd have it for a hench-boy; you shall.

At the sempster's shop now.

Openwork. Mass, I had quite forgot!
His honour's footman was here last night, wife.
Ha' you done with my lord's shirt?
Mrs Openwork.   What's that to you, sir?   145
I was this morning at his honour's lodging
Ere such a snail as you crept out of your shell.
Openwork. Oh, 'twas well done, good wife.
Mrs Openwork.   I hold it better, sir,
Than if you had done 't yourself.
Openwork.   Nay, so say I;
But is the countess's smock almost done, mouse?   150
Mrs Openwork. Here lies the cambric, sir, but wants, I fear me.
Openwork. I'll resolve you of that presently.
                         [*He takes the work and retires.*]
Mrs Openwork. Heyday! Oh, audacious groom,
Dare you presume to noblewomen's linen?
Keep you your yard to measure shepherd's holland?   155
I must confine you, I see that.

At the tobacco shop now.

Goshawk. What say you to this gear?
Laxton. I dare the arrant'st critic in tobacco to lay one fault upon 't.

Enter MOLL *in a frieze jerkin and a black safeguard.*

Goshawk. Life, yonder's Moll.
Laxton. Moll? Which Moll?   160
Goshawk. Honest Moll.

---

142. *hench-boy*] page. (With a suggestion of sexual favouritism.)
144–5. *His . . . lord's*] Openwork is referring to his aristocratic customers (also *countess*, line 150). The exchange with Mrs Openwork also suggests that dealing in personal linen such as shirts and smocks offers an opportunity to provide sexual services too.
150. *mouse*] a common term of endearment.
151. *wants*] is short of fabric.
152. *resolve . . . that*] check that for you.
155. *yard*] (1) tailor's measuring rod; (2) penis.
shepherd's holland] coarse linen cloth from Holland, suitable for shepherds.
157. *gear*] i.e. the tobacco.
158. *arrantest*] most audacious.
158.1. frieze jerkin] coarse cloth jacket, normally worn by men.
safeguard] an outer skirt won by women to protect their dress when riding.
Moll is *not* wearing breeches. See Intro., pp. 21–2.

Laxton. Prithee let's call her.—Moll!
All Gallants. Moll, Moll, psst, Moll!
Moll. How now, what's the matter?
Goshawk. A pipe of good tobacco, Moll?   165
Moll. I cannot stay.
Goshawk. Nay, Moll—pooh—prithee hark, but one word, i' faith.
Moll. Well, what is 't?   [*She takes tobacco and smokes.*]
Greenwit. Prithee come hither, sirrah.
Laxton. [*Aside*] Heart, I would give but too much money to be   170
    nibbling with that wench. Life, sh' has the spirit of four great
    parishes, and a voice that will drown all the city! Methinks a
    brave captain might get all his soldiers upon her, and ne'er be
    beholding to a company of Mile End milksops, if he could come
    on and come off quick enough. Such a Moll were a marrow-   175
    bone before an Italian: he would cry 'bona-roba' till his ribs
    were nothing but bone. I'll lay hard siege to her. Money is that
    aquafortis that eats into many a maidenhead: where the walls are
    flesh and blood, I'll ever pierce through with a golden auger.
Goshawk. Now thy judgement, Moll. Is 't not good?   180
Moll. Yes, faith, 'tis very good tobacco. How do you sell an ounce?
    Farewell. God buy you, Mistress Gallipot.
Goshawk. Why Moll, Moll!
Moll. I cannot stay now, i' faith; I am going to buy a shag ruff. The
    shop will be shut in presently.   [*She heads for the other shops.*] 185
Goshawk. 'Tis the maddest, fantastical'st girl! I never knew so much
    flesh and so much nimbleness put together.
Laxton. She slips from one company to another like a fat eel
    between a Dutchman's fingers. [*Aside*] I'll watch my time for her.
Mrs Gallipot. Some will not stick to say she's a man, and some, both 190
    man and woman.

---

169. *sirrah*] a form of address to social inferiors (of either sex).
170. *Heart*] i.e. by God's heart (an oath).
172-4. *Methinks . . . milksops*] Moll's vigour is imagined to extend to her capacity
as a breeder of strong men. *Get* means 'beget'.
174. *beholding*] beholden.
Mile End] the location of the training ground for London's citizen militia.
174-5. *come on . . . off*] military terms meaning 'advance' and 'retire', but with
an obvious bawdy sense.
175-6. *marrowbone*] the jelly inside a boiled beef shin bone; an aphrodisiac
delicacy.
176. *Italian*] i.e. man with a reputation for lust and perversion.
bona-roba] i.e. whore (Italian). With a play on *bona/bone*.
178. aquafortis] concentrated nitric acid.
179. *auger*] tool for boring holes (with an obvious bawdy implication).
181. *How*] at what price.
182. *God buy you*] a greeting: may God be with you.
184. *shag ruff*] ruff made of worsted or silk cloth with a velvet nap on one side.
190. *stick*] hesitate.

Laxton. That were excellent: she might first cuckold the husband
and then make him do as much for the wife!

The feather shop again.

Moll. Save you. How does Mistress Tiltyard?
Jack Dapper. Moll!   195
Moll. Jack Dapper!
Jack Dapper. How dost, Moll?
Moll. I'll tell thee by and by. I go but to th' next shop.
Jack Dapper. Thou shalt find me here this hour about a feather.
Moll. Nay, an feather hold you in play a whole hour, a goose will   200
last you all the days of your life!

The sempster['s] shop.

Let me see a good shag ruff.
Openwork. Mistress Mary, that shalt thou, i' faith, and the best in
the shop.
Mrs Openwork. How now? Greetings! Love terms, with a pox   205
between you! Have I found out one of your haunts? I send you
for hollands, and you're i' the low countries with a mischief. I'm
served with good ware by th' shift that makes it lie dead so long
upon my hands, I were as good shut up shop, for when I open
it, I take nothing.   210
Openwork. Nay, an you fall a-ringing once, the devil cannot stop
you; I'll out of the belfry as fast as I can.—Moll!
Mrs Openwork. [*To Moll*] Get you from my shop!
Moll. I come to buy.
Mrs Openwork. I'll sell ye nothing; I warn ye my house and shop.   215
Moll. You, goody Openwork, you that prick out a poor living
And sews many a bawdy skin-coat together,
Thou private pandress between shirt and smock,
I wish thee for a minute but a man;

206–10. *I send . . . nothing*] There are multiple layers of sexual meaning in this
passage. See Intro., pp. 50–2: the 'low countries' is Holland, as in the name of the
fabric (see line 155), signifying also the 'low' parts of London, the brothels and the
stews, and the physical nether regions of both Mrs Openwork and Moll. The 'good
ware' that Mrs Openwork is served is either, sarcastically, her husband's inadequate
sexual performance, or her own autoeroticism (*dead on my hands*). She must shut up
the shop where she sells her wares with Openwork or shut herself up from him
sexually.

212.] Openwork does not leave the stage but goes to join one of the other groups
in which he emerges (line 277) in conversation with Goshawk.

215. *warn ye*] warn you away from.

216. *goody*] a term applied to a housewife.

prick out] Moll's sewing image extends Mrs Openwork's bawdy reference.

217. *skin-coat*] a coat of skins, but also a person's skin: Moll is suggesting that
Mrs Openwork is a bawd.

Thou shouldst never use more shapes. But as th' art,   220
I pity my revenge. Now my spleen's up,
I would not mock it willingly.

Enter a Fellow *with a long rapier by his side.*

Ha, be thankful.
Now I forgive thee.

Mrs Openwork. Marry, hang thee! I never asked forgiveness in my
life.   225

Moll. [*To the Fellow*] You, goodman swine's face!   [*Moll draws.*]

Fellow. What, will you murder me?

Moll. You remember, slave, how you abused me t' other night in a
tavern?

Fellow. Not I, by this light.   230

Moll. No, but by candlelight you did. You have tricks to save your
oaths, reservations have you, and I have reserved somewhat for
you. [*Striking him.*] As you like that, call for more. You know
the sign again.

Fellow. Pox on 't! Had I brought any company along with me to   235
have borne witness on 't, 'twould ne'er have grieved me; but to
be struck and nobody by, 'tis my ill fortune still. Why, tread
upon a worm, they say 'twill turn tail; but indeed a gentleman
should have more manners.   *Exit* Fellow.

Laxton. Gallantly performed, i' faith, Moll, and manfully! I love   240
thee for ever for 't. Base rogue, had he offered but the least
counterbuff, by this hand, I was prepared for him.

Moll. You prepared for him? Why should you be prepared for him?
Was he any more than a man?

Laxton. No, nor so much by a yard and a handful, London measure.   245

Moll. Why do you speak this, then? Do you think I cannot ride a
stone-horse unless one lead him by th' snaffle?

---

221. *I . . . revenge*] I pity you and so withhold revenge.
spleen] temper.
222. *willingly*] i.c. if I were you.
222.1. *long rapier*] A royal proclamation of 1562 had attempted to regulate the
length of swords in the interests of public safety. The fellow is clearly violating the
statute.
224. *Marry*] i.e. by the Virgin Mary (an oath).
230. *by this light*] by the light of day (a mild oath).
231-2. *tricks . . . oaths*] i.e. tricks to avoid doing as you have sworn. Also a
reference to writers' and printers' devices to change oaths to more innocuous
formulations in order to comply with the statute against blasphemy.
236. *have borne witness*] have testified in support of a law suit against Moll for
battery (a cowardly thing to do).
242. *counterbuff*] blow in return.
245. *yard and a handful*] a generous measure; with a pun on yard = penis.
247. *stone-horse*] stallion.

Laxton. Yes, and sit him bravely, I know thou canst, Moll. 'Twas
   but an honest mistake through love, and I'll make amends for 't
   any way. Prithee, sweet plump Moll, when shall thou and I go   250
   out o' town together?
Moll. Whither? To Tyburn, prithee?
Laxton. Mass, that's out o' town indeed! Thou hang'st so many
   jests upon thy friends still. I mean honestly to Brentford,
   Staines, or Ware.   255
Moll. What to do there?
Laxton. Nothing but be merry and lie together; I'll hire a coach with
   four horses.
Moll. I thought 'twould be a beastly journey. You may leave out one
   well: three horses will serve if I play the jade myself.   260
Laxton. Nay, push, thou'rt such another kicking wench! Prithee be
   kind and let's meet.
Moll. 'Tis hard but we shall meet, sir.
Laxton. Nay, but appoint the place then. [*Offering money*] There's
   ten angels in fair gold, Moll; you see I do not trifle with you. Do   265
   but say thou wilt meet me, and I'll have a coach ready for thee.
Moll. [*Offering her hand*] Why, here's my hand I'll meet you, sir.
Laxton. [*Aside*] O good gold! [*To her*] The place, sweet Moll?
Moll. It shall be your appointment.
Laxton. Somewhat near Holborn, Moll.   270
Moll. In Gray's Inn Fields, then.
Laxton. A match.
Moll. I'll meet you there.
Laxton. The hour?
Moll. Three.   275
Laxton. That will be time enough to sup at Brentford.

Fall from them to the other.

Openwork. [*To Goshawk*] I am of such a nature, sir, I cannot endure
   the house when she scolds; sh' has a tongue will be heard further
   in a still morning than St Antholin's bell. She rails upon me for

---

252. *Tyburn*] the place to the west of the city where criminals were executed.
254–5. *Brentford, Staines, or Ware*] towns to the west and north of London,
proverbially used for out-of-town jaunts and assignations.
259. *beastly*] (1) involving animals; (2) brutish.
260. *jade*] (1) low-grade horse; (2) unruly woman.
261. *such another*] such a.
263. *hard*] with a bawdy pun on male erection.
270. *Holborn*] one of the main roads in London, running through the lawyers'
area and flanked by the Inns of Court.
271. *Gray's Inn Fields*] an open space north of Gray's Inn.
276.1.] Moll and Laxton move into the other group on stage.
279. *St Antholin's*] an ancient church in Watling Street. A morning service for
which the bell began to ring at 5 a.m. was established there in 1599.

foreign wenching, that I, being a freeman, must needs keep a   280
whore i' th' suburbs, and seek to impoverish the liberties. When
we fall out, I trouble you still to make all whole with my wife.
Goshawk. No trouble at all: 'tis a pleasure to me to join things
together.
Openwork. Go thy ways. [*Aside*] I do this but to try thy honesty,   285
Goshawk.

The feather shop.

Jack Dapper. [*Trying on feathers*] How lik'st thou this, Moll?
Moll. Oh, singularly; you're fitted now for a bunch. [*Aside*] He looks
for all the world with those spangled feathers like a nobleman's
bedpost. The purity of your wench would I fain try; she seems   290
like Kent unconquered, and I believe as many wiles are in her.
Oh, the gallants of these times are shallow lechers. They put not
their courtship home enough to a wench; 'tis impossible to
know what woman is throughly honest, because she's ne'er
thoroughly tried. I am of that certain belief there are more   295
queans in this town of their own making than of any man's
provoking. Where lies the slackness then? Many a poor soul
would down, and there's nobody will push 'em!
Women are courted but ne'er soundly tried;
As many walk in spurs that never ride.   300

The sempster's shop.

Mrs Openwork. Oh, abominable!

280-1. *foreign . . . liberties*] Mrs Openwork scolds her husband for taking a whore
in the suburbs instead of bestowing his favours at home in *the liberties* where he
enjoys the privileges of a *freeman.*

282. *fall out*] quarrel.

283-4.] Goshawk is glad to take credit for patching up the quarrels of Openwork
and his wife, while in fact seeking to *join things together* by seducing her himself.

285. *Go thy ways*] i.e. Carry on; do as you please.

289-90. *nobleman's bedpost*] Feathers were used as an ornament for beds in noble
households, where going to bed and rising were public occasions.

290. *your wench*] i.e. Mrs Tiltyard. Moll's plan is not carried through.

291. *Kent unconquered*] a common Kentish boast; here with a bawdy quibble on
'Kent'/'cunt'.

wiles] Moll makes a far-fetched quibble on the 'weald' or 'wiles', the forest area
on the Sussex border, notorious for highway robbery.

292-3. *put . . . enough*] (1) do not press their suit energetically enough; (2) are
weak thrusters in copulation.

294. *throughly*] thoroughly.

296. *queans*] loose women.

300.] i.e. Many men claim to be 'riders' of women without succeeding.

301.] Mrs Openwork's outburst shifts attention back to the sempstress's shop
and shows that Goshawk has immediately abused Openwork's confidences by
tattling to his wife.

Goshawk. Nay, more, I tell you in private, he keeps a whore i' th'
    suburbs.
Mrs Openwork. Oh, spittle dealing! I came to him a gentlewoman
    born. I'll show you mine arms when you please, sir.   305
Goshawk. [*Aside*] I had rather see your legs, and begin that way!
Mrs Openwork. 'Tis well known he took me from a lady's service
    where I was well-beloved of the steward. I had my Latin tongue
    and a spice of the French before I came to him, and now doth
    he keep a suburban whore under my nostrils.   310
Goshawk. There's ways enough to cry quit with him—hark in thine
    ear.   [*He whispers.*]
Mrs Openwork. There's a friend worth a million.

            [*Before the feather shop.*]

Moll. [*Aside*] I'll try one spear against your chastity, Mistress
    Tiltyard, though it prove too short by the burr.   315

            Enter RALPH TRAPDOOR.

Trapdoor. [*Aside*] Mass, here she is! I'm bound already to serve her,
    though it be but a sluttish trick. [*To her*] Bless my hopeful young
    mistress with long life and great limbs, send her the upper hand
    of all bailiffs and their hungry adherents!
Moll. How now, what art thou?   320
Trapdoor. A poor ebbing gentleman that would gladly wait for the
    young flood of your service.
Moll. My service! What should move you to offer your service to
    me, sir?
Trapdoor. The love I bear to your heroic spirit and masculine   325
    womanhood.

---

304. *spittle*] i.e. foul. Probably refers to St Mary's Spittle (hospital), which chiefly
treated cases of venereal disease.
    305. *arms*] i.e. coat of arms, a certificate of gentle birth, but with an obvious
double meaning of showing her physical arms.
    309. *spice of the French*] (1) smattering of the French language: (2) a venereal
infection.
    310. *suburbian*] a common form, equivalent in meaning to 'suburban'.
    311. *cry quit with him*] pay him back.
    315. *burr*] a broad ring of iron behind the handle of a tilting lance. Moll says that
she will test Mrs Tiltyard even if her weapons for doing so come short.
    316. *bound*] i.e. by agreement with Sir Alexander.
    317–18. *my . . . mistress*] the mistress I hope to serve. Bawdy double meanings
based on the sexual meaning of 'service' run throughout this dialogue. See Intro.,
pp. 50–2.
    319. *of*] over.
    321. *ebbing*] declining.
    322. *young flood*] the flow of the tide up river; continuing the metaphor begun
with *ebbing*.

Moll. So, sir, put case we should retain you to us: what parts are
there in you for a gentlewoman's service?

Trapdoor. Of two kinds right worshipful: movable and immovable—
movable to run of errands, and immovable to stand when you   330
have occasion to use me.

Moll. What strength have you?

Trapdoor. Strength, Mistress Moll? I have gone up into a steeple and
stayed the great bell as 't has been ringing, stopped a windmill
going.   335

Moll. And never struck down yourself?

Trapdoor. Stood as upright as I do at this present.

                          Moll trips up his heels; he falls.

Moll. Come, I pardon you for this. It shall be no disgrace to you; I
have struck up the heels of the high German's size ere now.
What, not stand?   340

Trapdoor. I am of that nature where I love, I'll be at my mistress'
foot to do her service.

Moll. Why, well said! But say your mistress should receive injury:
have you the spirit of fighting in you? Durst you second her?

Trapdoor. Life, I have kept a bridge myself, and drove seven at a   345
time before me.

Moll. Ay?

Trapdoor. (*Aside*) But they were all Lincolnshire bullocks, by my
troth.

Moll. Well, meet me in Gray's Inn Fields between three and four   350
this afternoon, and upon better consideration we'll retain you.

Trapdoor. I humbly thank your good mistress-ship. [*Aside*] I'll crack
your neck for this kindness.   *Exit* TRAPDOOR.

                 Moll meets Laxton.

Laxton. Remember three.

Moll. Nay, if I fail you, hang me.   355

Laxton. Good wench, i' faith.

            Then [Moll meets] Openwork.

Moll. Who's this?

Openwork. 'Tis I, Moll.

Moll. Prithee tend thy shop and prevent bastards!

---

    327. *put case*] suppose.

    339. *high German's size*] A number of dramatists refer to a very tall and strong
German fencer in London at the time.

    345. *kept*] defended, guarded.

    351. *upon . . . you*] after I've thought carefully about this, I will hire you.

    357. *Who's this*] Some motivation is required for this line. Openwork may be in
disguise, or he may have crept up behind Moll.

Openwork. We'll have a pint of the same wine, i' faith, Moll.   360
                              [*Exit* OPENWORK *with* MOLL.]
                                                The bell rings.
Goshawk. Hark, the bell rings; come, gentlemen. Jack Dapper,
     where shall 's all munch?
Jack Dapper. I am for Parker's Ordinary.
Laxton. [*To the others*] He's a good guest to 'em, he deserves his
     board: he draws all the gentlemen in a term time thither.—We'll   365
     be your followers, Jack; lead the way.—Look you, by my faith,
     the fool has feathered his nest well.   *Exeunt* Gallants.

     Enter MASTER GALLIPOT, MASTER TILTYARD, *and* Servants,
                    with water-spaniels and a duck.

Tiltyard. Come, shut up your shops. Where's Master Openwork?
Mrs Openwork. Nay, ask not me, Master Tiltyard.
Gallipot. Where's his water-dog? Pooh—psst!—hurr—hurr—psst!   370
Tiltyard. Come, wenches, come, we're going all to Hogsden.
Mrs Gallipot. To Hogsden, husband?
Gallipot. Ay, to Hogsden, pigsney.
Mrs Tiltyard. I'm not ready, husband.
Tiltyard. Faith, that's well. (*Spits in the dog's mouth.*) Hum—psst!   375
     Psst!
Gallipot. Come Mistress Openwork, you are so long.
Mrs Openwork. I have no joy of my life, Master Gallipot.
Gallipot. Push, let your boy lead his water-spaniel along, and we'll
     show you the bravest sport at Parlous Pond. Hey Trug, hey   380

---

     360. *the same wine*] punning on 'bastard', a sweet Spanish wine.
     360.2. bell] possibly the Pancake Bell that rang on Shrove Tuesday. See
Gallipot's statement (line 384) that 'this is the sportful'st day'.
     363. *Parker's Ordinary*] an eating house (see above, line 108) apparently owned
by one Parker. The reference to a named establishment creates the sense of a
shared, familiar social world. See Intro., pp. 13–15.
     364–5. *he . . . board*] he is such a good customer and attracts so many others, he
should be able to eat there free.
     365. *term time*] i.e. during the law term, when the courts met—a time when many
lawyers would be in London.
     367. *fool . . . well*] referring to the feathers that Jack is wearing. 'To feather one's
nest' is to accumulate personal wealth.
     367.2. a duck] possibly a decoy; or a duck that is let loose on a pond for dogs to
chase.
     370. *Pooh . . . psst*] sounds to call the dogs.
     371. *Hogsden*] Hoxton, a district north of London. (The spelling is preserved for
the pun; see next note.)
     373. *pigsney*] a term of endearment; playing on *Hogs*den.
     375 SD. Spits . . . mouth] a way of befriending and taming a dog.
     380. *Parlous Pond*] a pool lying behind St Luke's hospital, off the City road.
Parlous = 'perilous'.

Trug, hey Trug! Here's the best duck in England, except my
wife. Hey, hey, hey! Fetch, fetch, fetch!
Come, let's away.
Of all the year, this is the sportful'st day.   [*Exeunt.*]

[2.2]

Enter SEBASTIAN *solus.*

Sebastian. If a man have a free will, where should the use
  More perfect shine than in his will to love?
  All creatures have their liberty in that;

Enter SIR ALEXANDER *and listens to him.*

  Though else kept under servile yoke and fear,
  The very bondslave has his freedom there.   5
  Amongst a world of creatures voiced and silent,
  Must my desires wear fetters? [*Aside, seeing his father*] Yea, are
      you
  So near? Then I must break with my heart's truth,
  Meet grief at a back way. [*Aloud*] Well, why, suppose
  The two-leaved tongues of slander or of truth   10
  Pronounce Moll loathsome; if before my love
  She appear fair, what injury have I?
  I have the thing I like. In all things else
  Mine own eye guides me, and I find 'em prosper;
  Life, what should ail it now? I know that man   15
  Ne'er truly loves—if he gainsay 't, he lies—
  That winks and marries with his father's eyes;
  I'll keep mine own wide open.

Enter MOLL *and a* Porter *with a viol on his back.*

Sir Alexander. [*Aside*]   Here's brave wilfulness:
  A made match. Here she comes; they met o' purpose.

2.2.8. *break . . . truth*] i.e. stop telling the truth about my feelings.
  9. *Meet . . . way*] commune with grief in a more private place.
  10. *two-leaved*] like the two sides of a swing door which lets truth out from one
direction and slander from another.
  11. *before my love*] from the point of view of my love.
  14. *'em*] i.e. 'all things' (line 13), all my affairs.
  15. *what . . . now?*] what should it matter now?
  17. *winks*] keeps his eyes closed; i.e. does not choose his partner with his eyes
open, but trusts his father's judgement instead.
  18 SD. viol] a stringed instrument; here a bass viol, nearly the size of a double
bass.
  19. *made match*] arranged meeting.

Porter. Must I carry this great fiddle to your chamber, Mistress   20
    Mary?
Moll. Fiddle, goodman hog-rubber?—Some of these porters bear so
    much for others they have no time to carry wit for themselves.
Porter. To your own chamber, Mistress Mary?
Moll. Who'll hear an ass speak?—Whither else, goodman pageant-   25
    bearer?—They're people of the worst memories.   *Exit* Porter.
Sebastian. Why, 'twere too great a burden, love, to have them carry
    things in their minds and o' their backs together.
Moll. Pardon me, sir, I thought not you so near.
Sir Alexander. [*Aside*] So, so, so.   30
Sebastian. I would be nearer to thee, and in that fashion
    That makes the best part of all creatures honest.
    No otherwise I wish it.
Moll. Sir, I am so poor to requite you, you must look for nothing but
    thanks of me. I have no humour to marry. I love to lie o' both   35
    sides o' th' bed myself; and again, o' th' other side, a wife, you
    know, ought to be obedient, but I fear me I am too headstrong
    to obey; therefore I'll ne'er go about it. I love you so well, sir, for
    your good will, I'd be loath you should repent your bargain
    after, and therefore we'll ne'er come together at first. I have the   40
    head now of myself, and am man enough for a woman; mar-
    riage is but a chopping and changing, where a maiden loses one
    head and has a worse i' th' place.
Sir Alexander. [*Aside*] The most comfortablest answer from a
        roaring girl
    That ever mine ears drunk in.
Sebastian.   This were enough   45
    Now to affright a fool for ever from thee,
    When 'tis the music that I love thee for.

---

22. *hog-rubber*] an abusive term for a swineherd.

25. *Who'll . . . speak?*] i.e. (to the audience) Can you imagine that: an ass that
can speak? (*Ass* suggests both fool and beast of burden.)

25–6. *pageant-bearer*] comparing him with the porters who were employed to
carry the spectacular structures used in municipal shows.

26. *They're . . . memories*] Moll implies that she has already told the porter several
times where to carry the bass viol.

31–2. *in . . . honest*] i.e. in marriage. Sebastian is saying this to worry his father.

34. *I am . . . you*] I am so unworthy to respond in the terms you propose.

35. *humour*] inclination.

40–1. *I . . . myself*] I manage my own affairs, like a horse that is 'given its head',
i.e. goes unchecked by a rider. Moll plays on three meanings of head: (1) a physical
head; (2) the head of a household (usually but not always a man); (3) giving a horse
its head.

44. *most comfortablest*] Sir Alexander is relieved to hear his son's proposal
refused.

45–7. *This . . . for*] This might be enough to frighten off a fool, but it is the kind
of speech and attitude I love you for.

Sir Alexander. [*Aside*] There's a boy spoils all again!

Moll.   Believe it, sir,
  I am not of that disdainful temper
  But I could love you faithfully.

Sir Alexander. [*Aside*]   A pox   50
  On you for that word! I like you not now;
  You're a cunning roarer, I see that already.

Moll. But sleep upon this once more, sir; you may chance shift a
  mind tomorrow. Be not too hasty to wrong yourself. Never
  while you live, sir, take a wife running. Many have run out at   55
  heels that have done 't. You see, sir, I speak against myself, and
  if every woman would deal with their suitor so honestly, poor
  younger brothers would not be so often gulled with old cozening widows that turn o'er all their wealth in trust to some
  kinsman and make the poor gentleman work hard for a pension.   60
  Fare you well, sir.   [*She starts to leave.*]

Sebastian. Nay, prithee one word more!

Sir Alexander. [*Aside*] How do I wrong this girl! She puts him
  off still.

Moll. Think upon this in cold blood, sir; you make as much haste as
  if you were a-going upon a sturgeon voyage. Take deliberation,   65
  sir; never choose a wife as if you were going to Virginia.
                                [*She moves away from him.*]

Sebastian. And so we parted. My too cursèd fate!   [*He retires.*]

Sir Alexander. [*Aside*] She is but cunning, gives him longer time
  in 't.

                          Enter a Tailor.

Tailor. Mistress Moll, Mistress Moll! So ho ho, so ho!

Moll. There boy, there boy. What dost thou go a-hawking after me   70
  with a red clout on thy finger?

---

49. *that . . . temper*] such a disdainful disposition (i.e. to frighten off a fool).

55. *running*] in haste.

55–6. *out at heels*] with the heels of their stockings worn through; i.e. in poverty.

58. *younger brothers*] those with no inheritance, who marry widows in hope of
getting their fortunes.

58–9. *cozening*] deceitful.

59–60. *that . . . kinsman*] i.e. as a means of making their wealth safe from for-
tune-hunting young men.

65. *as if . . . voyage*] as if you were going on a sturgeon-fishing trip (to Russia);
i.e. you would not return for a long time.

66. *as if . . . Virginia*] as if you were going to a barbaric country where women
would be in short supply.

67.] Sebastian strikes the attitude of a rejected suitor, in order to deceive his
father.

69. *So ho*] a hunting call. Moll replies in kind.

71. *a red clout*] a blood-stained bandage; a cloth to protect a hawker's finger from
the hawk's claws. Also a cloth on a tailor's finger.

Tailor. I forgot to take measure on you for your new breeches.
                                          [*He takes measurements.*]
Sir Alexander. [*Aside*] Heyday, breeches! What, will he marry a
     monster with two trinkets? What age is this? If the wife go in
     breeches, the man must wear long coats like a fool.   75
Moll. What fiddling's here? Would not the old pattern have served
     your turn?
Tailor. You change the fashion; you say you'll have the great Dutch
     slop, Mistress Mary.
Moll. Why sir, I say so still.   80
Tailor. Your breeches then will take up a yard more.
Moll. Well, pray look it be put in, then.
Tailor. It shall stand round and full, I warrant you.
Moll. Pray make 'em easy enough.
Tailor. I know my fault now: t' other was somewhat stiff between   85
     the legs; I'll make these open enough, I warrant you.
Sir Alexander. [*Aside*] Here's good gear towards! I have brought up
     my son to marry a Dutch slop and a French doublet: a codpiece
     daughter.
Tailor. So, I have gone as far as I can go.   90
Moll. Why then, farewell.
Tailor. If you go presently to your chamber, Mistress Mary, pray
     send me the measure of your thigh by some honest body.
Moll. Well sir, I'll send it by a porter presently.   *Exit* MOLL.
Tailor. So you had need; it is a lusty one. Both of them would make   95
     any porter's back ache in England!   *Exit* Tailor.
Sebastian. [*Coming forward*] I have examined the best part of man—
     Reason and judgement—and in love, they tell me,
     They leave me uncontrolled. He that is swayed

---

74. *monster*] i.e. like a hermaphrodite. See Intro., pp. 53–4.
two trinkets] two sets of genitals; two testicles.
What . . . this?] What is this age coming to?
75. *long coats*] skirts like those worn by women and by children of both sexes.
Fools and jesters, thought of as children, would wear them too.
78–9. *Dutch slop*] wide, baggy breeches.
81. *take . . . more*] (1) require a yard more cloth; (2) have room for a penis.
82.] Moll insists the extra fabric be put in, cognizant of the common charge that
tailors stole material by cutting the cloth too short. Her line triggers another bawdy
sequence in *stand, round and full, stiff between the legs, open*, etc.
87. *Here's . . . towards!*] Here's a fine state of affairs!
95. *it*] i.e. her thigh.
95–6. *Both . . . England*] The image is of Moll astride the porter's back, either
with him carrying her or her taking up the male sexual position to enter him from
behind, the most common sexual position in contemporary representations of
intercourse.
98–9. *in love . . . uncontrolled*] Reason and judgement tell me they will not be able
to control me when I am in love.

By an unfeeling blood, past heat of love,   100
His springtime must needs err; his watch ne'er goes right
That sets his dial by a rusty clock.
Sir Alexander. [*Coming forward*] So. And which is that rusty clock,
    sir? You?
Sebastian. The clock at Ludgate, sir; it ne'er goes true.
Sir Alexander. But thou goest falser; not thy father's cares   105
Can keep thee right, when that insensible work
Obeys the workman's art, lets off the hour,
And stops again when time is satisfied;
But thou run'st on, and judgement, thy main wheel,
Beats by all stops as if the work would break,   110
Begun with long pains for a minute's ruin,
Much like a suffering man brought up with care,
At last bequeathed to shame and a short prayer.
Sebastian. I taste you bitterer than I can deserve, sir.
Sir Alexander. Who has bewitched thee, son? What devil or drug   115
Hath wrought upon the weakness of thy blood
And betrayed all her hopes to ruinous folly?
Oh, wake from drowsy and enchanted shame
Wherein thy soul sits with a golden dream
Flattered and poisoned! I am old, my son;   120
Oh, let me prevail quickly,
For I have weightier business of mine own
Than to chide thee. I must not to my grave
As a drunkard to his bed, whereon he lies
Only to sleep, and never cares to rise;   125
Let me dispatch in time. Come no more near her.
Sebastian. Not honestly? Not in the way of marriage?

99–101. *He . . . err*] He who is influenced by lack of feeling (induced by excess of reason) to wait past the point when love should be most powerful (the heat of the blood at the right temperature) mistakenly fails to take advantage of the correct moment for the spring of his life. The pun on *springtime*, meaning (1) the season of spring and (2) the spring in a watch, triggers the extended (and widely used) comparison between the workings of a watch and the well-balanced human personality. See Intro., p. 55.

107–8. *lets . . . satisfied*] strikes the right number of strokes for the hour.

109–10.] i.e. just as the malfunctioning main wheel of a clock runs free of the cogs, or *stops*, of the intersecting wheels, so your judgement slips past the restraints put on you by your father.

111.] i.e. your maimed judgement exchanging long hours of diligent training for a minute's ruinous pleasure.

113. *a short prayer*] such as criminals are allowed before execution.

117. *her*] Syntactically, this must refer to *blood*, here used metaphorically to mean 'passion', 'disposition' and so personified as female.

122. *weightier business*] i.e. the preparation for my own virtuous death.

126. *dispatch*] make my final arrangements, come to terms with my soul.

Sir Alexander. What say'st thou? Marriage? In what place? The
    sessions-house?
    And who shall give the bride, prithee? An indictment?
Sebastian. Sir, now ye take part with the world to wrong her.   130
Sir Alexander. Why, wouldst thou fain marry to be pointed at?
    Alas, the number's great; do not o'erburden 't.
    Why, as good marry a beacon on a hill,
    Which all the country fix their eyes upon,
    As her thy folly dotes on. If thou long'st   135
    To have the story of thy infamous fortunes
    Serve for discourse in ordinaries and taverns,
    Thou'rt in the way; or to confound thy name,
    Keep on, thou canst not miss it; or to strike
    Thy wretched father to untimely coldness,   140
    Keep the left hand still, it will bring thee to 't.
    Yet if no tears wrung from thy father's eyes,
    Nor sighs that fly in sparkles from his sorrows,
    Had power to alter what is wilful in thee,
    Methinks her very name should fright thee from her,   145
    And never trouble me.
Sebastian. Why is the name of Moll so fatal, sir?
Sir Alexander. Many one, sir, where suspect is entered,
    Forseek all London from one end to t' other
    More whores of that name than of any ten other.   150
Sebastian. What's that to her? Let those blush for themselves;
    Can any guilt in others condemn her?
    I've vowed to love her. Let all storms oppose me
    That ever beat against the breast of man;
    Nothing but death's black tempest shall divide us.   155
Sir Alexander. Oh, folly, that can dote on nought but shame!
Sebastian. Put case a wanton itch runs through one name

---

128. *sessions-house*] court house, suitable for a criminal trial rather than a church
wedding.
    129. *give . . . bride*] i.e. give the bride to be married (as required by the church
service).
    An indictment] An accusation in a court of law (see *sessions house* above, line 128)
will replace the form of words with which the bride is given in the marriage service.
    132. *the number's great*] the number of fools who marry only to be jeered at is too
large already.
    138. *Thou'rt . . . way*] you are going the right way about it.
    confound] bring ruin to.
    141. *left hand*] sinister way. In the myth of Heracles's choice, the right-hand path
led to virtue, the left to vice.
    143. *sparkles*] sparks.
    148–50.] When the hunt is on for a suspect, many constables look all over
London for ten times as many whores called Moll than any other name.
    157.] even supposing wanton desire is particularly associated with one name.

More than another: is that name the worse
Where honesty sits possessed in 't? It should rather
Appear more excellent and deserve more praise   160
When through foul mists a brightness it can raise.
Why, there are of the devil's, honest gentlemen,
And well descended, keep an open house;
And some o' th' good man's that are arrant knaves.
He hates unworthily that by rote contemns,   165
For the name neither saves nor yet condemns.
And for her honesty, I have made such proof on 't
In several forms, so nearly watched her ways,
I will maintain that strict against an army,
Excepting you, my father. Here's her worst: 170
Sh'has a bold spirit that mingles with mankind,
But nothing else comes near it, and oftentimes
Through her apparel somewhat shames her birth;
But she is loose in nothing but in mirth.
Would all Molls were no worse!   175

Sir Alexander. [*Aside*] This way I toil in vain and give but aim
To infamy and ruin. He will fall;
My blessing cannot stay him; all my joys
Stand at the brink of a devouring flood
And will be wilfully swallowed, wilfully!   180
But why so vain let all these tears be lost?
I'll pursue her to shame, and so all's crossed.
                                  Exit SIR ALEXANDER.

Sebastian. He is gone with some strange purpose, whose effect
Will hurt me little if he shoot so wide
To think I love so blindly. I but feed   185

---

162. *of the devil's*] i.e. of the devil's party, on the devil's side.

164. *o' th' good man's*] i.e. on the side of Jesus. The opposition in lines 162–4 between gentlemen who follow the devil and knaves who follow Jesus illustrates the commonplace contradiction.

165. *contemns*] scorns.

167. *for her honesty*] as for her chastity.

170. *Excepting . . . father*] Sebastian's sense of appropriate deference to his father makes him exclude his father from those whose opinions he will oppose. Cf. 1.2.141–2.

Here's her worst] Here is the worst that can be said about her.

171–2. *Sh'has . . . it*] her bold spirit mixes with men, but no other part does.

176. *give but aim*] only provide a target.

182. *crossed*] thwarted.

184–5. *if . . . blindly*] if he is so wide of the mark as to suppose I really am blind enough to be in love with Moll.

185. *feed*] in the sense of 'keep supplied with material' as in a mill or a machine. The whole sentence, lines 185–90, indicates that Sebastian is feeding his father's

His heart to this match to draw on th' other,
Wherein my joy sits with a full wish crowned—
Only his mood excepted, which must change
By opposite policies, courses indirect;
Plain dealing in this world takes no effect.   190
This mad girl I'll acquaint with my intent,
Get her assistance, make my fortunes known;
'Twixt lovers' hearts she's a fit instrument,
And has the art to help them to their own.
By her advice—for in that craft she's wise—   195
My love and I may meet, spite of all spies.   *Exit* SEBASTIAN.

---

suspicions about Moll so as to divert his attention while Sebastian brings about
(*draw on* means literally 'bring around') the marriage to Mary Fitzallard.
    189. *By . . . indirect*] by strategies opposed to his, carried out indirectly.
    194. *their own*] their own wishes.

Act 3

Enter LAXTON *in Gray's Inn Fields with the* Coachman.

Laxton. Coachman!

Coachman. Here, sir.

Laxton. [*Giving money*] There's a tester more. Prithee drive thy coach to the hither end of Marybone Park—a fit place for Moll to get in.   5

Coachman. Marybone Park, sir?

Laxton. Ay, it's in our way, thou know'st.

Coachman. It shall be done, sir.

Laxton. Coachman!

Coachman. Anon, sir.   10

Laxton. Are we fitted with good frampold jades?

Coachman. The best in Smithfield, I warrant you, sir.

Laxton. May we safely take the upper hand of any coached velvet cap or tuftaffety jacket? For they keep a vile swaggering in coaches nowadays; the highways are stopped with them.   15

Coachman. My life for yours, and baffle 'em too, sir! Why, they are the same jades—believe it, sir—that have drawn all your famous whores to Ware.

Laxton. Nay, then, they know their business; they need no more instructions.   20

Coachman. They're so used to such journeys, sir, I never use whip to 'em; for if they catch but the scent of a wench once, they run like devils.   *Exit* Coachman *with his whip.*

3.1.0.1. Gray's Inn Fields] an open space north of Gray's Inn.

3. *tester*] sixpence.

4. *Marybone Park*] Marylebone Park, now Regent's Park in the centre of London.

11. *frampold*] fiery, spirited.

12. *Smithfield*] a famous livestock market.

13. *take the upper hand*] go past, overtake.

13–14. *velvet . . . jacket*] richly dressed people in other coaches. Tuftaffety was a fabric woven with raised velvety stripes or spots of different colours.

16. *My life for yours*] i.e. I'll bet my life on it.

baffle] prevent (the coaches) from moving forward.

18. *Ware*] a town north of London, famous for an enormous bed in an inn, and so particularly associated with sexual assignations (cf. 2.1.255).

Laxton. Fine Cerberus! That rogue will have the start of a thousand
ones, for whilst others trot afoot he'll ride prancing to hell upon   25
a coach-horse! Stay, 'tis now about the hour of her appoint-
ment, but yet I see her not. (*The clock strikes three.*) Hark, what's
this? One, two, three: three by the clock at Savoy. This is the
hour, and Gray's Inn Fields the place, she swore she'd meet me.
Ha, yonder's two Inns o' Court men with one wench! But that's   30
not she; they walk toward Islington out of my way. I see none
yet dressed like her. I must look for a shag ruff, a frieze jerkin,
a short sword, and a safeguard, or I get none. Why, Moll,
prithee make haste or the coachman will curse us anon.

Enter MOLL *like a man.*

Moll. [*Aside*] Oh, here's my gentleman! If they would keep their   35
days as well with their mercers as their hours with their harlots,
no bankrupt would give sevenscore pound for a sergeant's
place; for, would you know a catchpole rightly derived, the
corruption of a citizen is the generation of a sergeant. How his
eye hawks for venery! [*To him*] Come, are you ready, sir?   40
Laxton. Ready? For what, sir?
Moll. Do you ask that now, sir? Why was this meeting 'pointed?
Laxton. I thought you mistook me, sir.
    You seem to be some young barrister.
    I have no suit in law; all my land's sold,   45
    I praise heaven for 't; 't has rid me of much trouble.
Moll. Then I must wake you, sir. Where stands the coach?
Laxton. Who's this? Moll? Honest Moll?
Moll. So young, and purblind? You're an old wanton in your eyes,
    I see that.   50
Laxton. Thou'rt admirably suited for the Three Pigeons at
Brentford. I'll swear I knew thee not.

---

24. *Cerberus*] mythological three-headed dog, guarding the gate of Hades.
28. *Savoy*] a hospital built by Henry VII on the north bank of the Thames.
31. *Islington*] a northern suburb of London.
32–3. *shag ruff . . . safeguard*] Moll's costume in 2.1; she has since acquired the
Dutch slop for which she was fitted in 2.2.78–9.
34.1. like a man] Moll's first appearance dressed as a man. See Intro., p. 21.
35–6. *keep . . . mercers*] pay their bills as promptly with cloth merchants.
38–9. *would . . . sergeant*] i.e. if you'd like to know the true derivation of *catchpole*,
or arresting officer, it comes about when a citizen is not paid by a gentleman, goes
into bankruptcy and is thus forced to make money by becoming an arresting
sergeant, thereby driving up the cost of fees paid by those wishing to become
sergeants. (The terms *corruption* and *generation* come from alchemy and refer to the
dissolution of one substance and its transmission into another.)
40. *hawks . . . venery*] (1) hunts game; (2) looks out for women.
49. *purblind*] partly or totally blind.
51–2. *Three Pigeons at Brentford*] name of a famous tavern.

Moll. I'll swear you did not; but you shall know me now.
Laxton. No, not here. We shall be spied, i' faith. The coach is
    better; come.   55
Moll. Stay!   *She puts off her cloak and draws [her sword].*
Laxton. What, wilt thou untruss a point, Moll?
Moll. Yes, here's the point that I untruss: 't has but one tag, 'twill
    serve though to tie up a rogue's tongue.
Laxton. How?   60
Moll. [*Showing money*] There's the gold
    With which you hired your hackney; here's her pace.
    She racks hard, and perhaps your bones will feel it.
    Ten angels of mine own I've put to thine;
    Win 'em and wear 'em!
Laxton.   Hold, Moll! Mistress Mary—   65
Moll. Draw, or I'll serve an execution on thee
    Shall lay thee up till doomsday.
Laxton. Draw upon a woman? Why, what dost mean, Moll?
Moll. To teach thy base thoughts manners. Thou'rt one of those
    That thinks each woman thy fond flexible whore.   70
    If she but cast a liberal eye upon thee,
    Turn back her head, she's thine; or, amongst company,
    By chance drink first to thee, then she's quite gone,
    There's no means to help her; nay, for a need,
    Wilt swear unto thy credulous fellow lechers   75
    That thou'rt more in favour with a lady
    At first sight than her monkey all her lifetime.
    How many of our sex by such as thou
    Have their good thoughts paid with a blasted name

---

54. *No, not here*] Laxton picks up the possible pun on 'know' (to experience sexually), perhaps reinforced by a gesture from Moll, and assumes Moll wants to have sex there and then.

57. *untruss a point*] Laxton assumes Moll is starting to undress. He refers to a codpiece point, Moll to the point of her sword.

58. *tag*] metal point at the end of a lace to be inserted into an eye-hole.

62. *hackney*] (1) hired horse; (2) prostitute.

63. *racks hard*] gallops quickly.

64. *angels*] gold coins.

65. *Win . . . 'em!*] Moll says that the money, to which she has added a considerable sum more than Laxton has spent on her, will be the prize for the winner of the duel, to be worn like a favour at a tournament.

66–7.] Draw your sword, or I'll execute a fatal arrest on you, one which will end your life.

70. *flexible*] manageable, impressionable.

71. *liberal*] free, generous.

74. *for a need*] at a pinch, in an emergency.

77. *monkey*] common as ladies' pets, and proverbially lascivious.

79. *blasted*] blighted, destroyed.

That never deserved loosely or did trip   80
In path of whoredom beyond cup and lip?
But for the stain of conscience and of soul,
Better had women fall into the hands
Of an act silent than a bragging nothing;
There's no mercy in 't. What durst move you, sir,   85
To think me whorish?—a name which I'd tear out
From the high German's throat if it lay ledger there
To dispatch privy slanders against me!
In thee I defy all men, their worst hates
And their best flatteries, all their golden witchcrafts   90
With which they entangle the poor spirits of fools.
Distressèd needlewomen and trade-fall'n wives—
Fish that must needs bite or themselves be bitten—
Such hungry things as these may soon be took
With a worm fastened on a golden hook;   95
Those are the lecher's food, his prey. He watches
For quarrelling wedlocks and poor shifting sisters;
'Tis the best fish he takes. But why, good fisherman,
Am I thought meat for you, that never yet
Had angling rod cast towards me? 'Cause you'll say   100
I'm given to sport, I'm often merry, jest.
Had mirth no kindred in the world but lust?
Oh, shame take all her friends, then! But howe'er
Thou and the baser world censure my life,
I'll send 'em word by thee, and write so much   105
Upon thy breast, 'cause thou shalt bear 't in mind.
Tell them 'twere base to yield where I have conquered.
I scorn to prostitute myself to a man,
I that can prostitute a man to me!
And so I greet thee.   [*She starts to leave.*]
Laxton. [*Drawing*]   Hear me!
Moll.   Would the spirits   110

---

81. *beyond cup and lip*] beyond drinking to or kissing a man.
82–4.] Were it not for the sin involved, women would do better to have sex, so long as it was secret, than be the object of empty male gossip.
87. *high German*] See 2.1.339 and note.
ledger] ambassador.
91. *fools*] innocents, unwary women.
92.] like Mrs Openwork and Mrs Gallipot. The whole speech recalls 2.1.
93, 98. *Fish . . . fisherman*] 'Fish' was common contemporary slang for women.
97. *wedlocks*] married couples.
shifting] trying to cope with inadequate resources.
103. *shame . . . then*] i.e. if mirth's only relations are with lust, then let all her friends be shameful.
105. *write*] i.e. carve with my sword.
110. *greet thee*] say goodbye.

Of all my slanderers were clasped in thine,
That I might vex an army at one time!   *They fight.*
                                    [*Moll wounds Laxton.*]
Laxton. I do repent me. Hold!
Moll. You'll die the better Christian, then.
Laxton. I do confess I have wronged thee, Moll.   115
Moll. Confession is but poor amends for wrong,
   Unless a rope would follow.
Laxton. I ask thee pardon.
Moll. I'm your hired whore, sir!
Laxton. I yield both purse and body.   120
Moll. Both are mine and now at my disposing.
Laxton. Spare my life!
Moll.   I scorn to strike thee basely.
Laxton. Spoke like a noble girl, i' faith. [*Aside*] Heart, I think I
   fight with a familiar, or the ghost of a fencer! Sh'has wounded
   me gallantly. Call you this a lecherous voyage? Here's blood   125
   would have served me this seven year in broken heads and cut
   fingers, and it now runs all out together! Pox o' the Three
   Pigeons! I would the coach were here now to carry me to the
   chirurgeon's.   *Exit* LAXTON.
Moll. If I could meet my enemies one by one thus,   130
   I might make pretty shift with 'em in time,
   And make 'em know, she that has wit and spirit
   May scorn to live beholding to her body for meat,
   Or for apparel, like your common dame
   That makes shame get her clothes to cover shame.   135
   Base is that mind that kneels unto her body
   As if a husband stood in awe on 's wife!
   My spirit shall be mistress of this house
   As long as I have time in 't.

                   Enter TRAPDOOR

                        Oh,
   Here comes my man that would be; 'tis his hour.   140
   Faith, a good well-set fellow, if his spirit

---

124. *a familiar*] a familiar spirit; a form taken on by the devil.
126. *broken*] with the skin cut open.
129. *chirurgeon's*] surgeon's.
131. *make pretty shift*] deal handily.
134–5. *like . . . shame*] like a woman who makes the shame of selling her body pay for the clothes to cover the shame of her nakedness.
137. *on 's*] of his.
138. *of this house*] i.e. of my body (over which, see line 136–7, Moll's mind must rule).
140. *'tis his hour*] this is the time we agreed to meet.

Be answerable to his umbles. He walks stiff,
But whether he will stand to 't stiffly, there's the point.
'Has a good calf for 't, and ye shall have many a woman
Choose him she means to make her head by his calf;   145
I do not know their tricks in 't. Faith, he seems
A man without; I'll try what he is within.

Trapdoor. [*Aside*] She told me Gray's Inn Fields 'twixt three and
      four.
I'll fit her mistress-ship with a piece of service;
I'm hired to rid the town of one mad girl.   *She jostles him.*   150
[*To her*] What a pox ails you, sir?

Moll. He begins like a gentleman.

Trapdoor. [*To Moll*] Heart, is the field so narrow, or your eye-
      sight?—
Life, he comes back again!   *She comes towards him.*

Moll. Was this spoke to me, sir?   155

Trapdoor. I cannot tell, sir.

Moll. Go, you're a coxcomb!

Trapdoor. Coxcomb?

Moll. You're a slave!

Trapdoor. I hope there's law for you, sir!   160

Moll. Yea, do you see, sir?   *Turn[s] his hat.*

Trapdoor. Heart, this is no good dealing. Pray let me know what
      house you're of.

Moll. One of the Temple, sir.   *Fillips him.*

---

142. *umbles*] the edible guts of an animal, usually a deer. Here used figuratively to refer to Trapdoor's physique.

143. *stand to 't stiffly*] stand up under pressure (with the suggestion of a sexual erection).

144. *good calf*] good legs, which showed up in hose, were an admired feature in men.

144–5. *many . . . calf*] many a woman chooses her husband, who should be her head (in the sense of having authority over her) by his good legs.

146. *I . . . in 't*] I don't know what strategies they use (*their tricks* is ambiguous; it could mean either the women's pattern of behaviour in choosing men so carelessly, or the men's devices in making themselves attractive to women).

149. *I'll . . . service*] Trapdoor is being sarcastic about the nature of the service he will give Moll. It will be both disloyal in that he is acting for Sir Alexander and potentially sexual in that she is a woman. The nearest modern slang equivalent is 'I'll give her a bit of service all right!'

157–9. *coxcomb, slave*] common insults indicating the aspiring affectation and low social status of the person insulted.

160. *law*] Trapdoor is reminding Moll of the laws against slander and assault.

162–3. *what . . . of*] in what household you serve.

164. *Temple*] i.e. Middle or Inner Temple, two Inns of Court.

164 SD. *Fillips him*] Flicks him with her nails. Moll's gestures are insulting as much as violent, and Trapdoor's failure to respond shows him to be a coward.

Trapdoor. Mass, so methinks.   165

Moll. And yet sometime I lie about Chick Lane.

Trapdoor. I like you the worse because you shift your lodging so
  often; I'll not meddle with you for that trick, sir.

Moll. A good shift, but it shall not serve your turn.

Trapdoor. You'll give me leave to pass about my business, sir?   170

Moll. Your business? I'll make you wait on me
  Before I ha' done, and glad to serve me too.

Trapdoor. How, sir, serve you? Not if there were no more men in
  England!

Moll. But if there were no more women in England,   175
  I hope you'd wait upon your mistress, then.

                                   [*Moll reveals her identity.*]

Trapdoor. Mistress!

Moll. Oh, you're a tried spirit at a push, sir.

Trapdoor. What would your worship have me do?

Moll. You a fighter?   180

Trapdoor. No, I praise heaven, I had better grace and more
  manners.

Moll. As how, I pray, sir?

Trapdoor. Life, 't had been a beastly part of me to have drawn my
  weapons upon my mistress; all the world would ha' cried shame   185
  of me for that.

Moll. Why, but you knew me not.

Trapdoor. Do not say so, mistress; I knew you by your wide straddle
  as well as if I had been in your belly.

Moll. Well, we shall try you further. I' th' meantime, we give you 190
  entertainment.

Trapdoor. Thank your good mistress-ship.

Moll. How many suits have you?

Trapdoor. No more suits than backs, mistress.

Moll. Well, if you deserve, I cast off this next week, and you may   195
  creep into 't.

Trapdoor. Thank your good worship.

---

166. *lie*] live, reside.

Chick Lane] a notoriously rough street in Smithfield.

169. *A . . . shift*] A good try (playing on *shift*, 'move' in line 167).

178. *tried spirit*] experienced fighter (referring to Trapdoor's boasts in 2.1.333–
49).

at a push] when the occasion demands it. (*Push* can also be read sexually.)

184–5. *drawn my weapons*] with a sexual meaning.

189. *as if . . . belly*] (1) as if I had been your child; (2) as if I had been your sexual
partner.

191. *entertainment*] employment.

195. *this*] i.e. the suit I am wearing.

Moll. Come, follow me to St Thomas Apostles; I'll put a livery cloak
     upon your back the first thing I do.
Trapdoor. I follow my dear mistress.   *Exeunt omnes.*   200

[3.2]

          Enter MRS GALLIPOT *as from supper, her* Husband *after her.*

Gallipot. What, Prue! Nay, sweet Prudence!
Mrs Gallipot. What a pruing keep you! I think the baby would have
     a teat, it kyes so. Pray be not so fond of me; leave your city
     humours. I'm vexed at you to see how like a calf you come
     bleating after me.   5
Gallipot. Nay, honey Prue, how does your rising up before all the
     table show? And flinging from my friends so uncivilly? Fie,
     Prue, fie! Come.
Mrs Gallipot. Then up and ride, i' faith.
Gallipot. Up and ride? Nay, my pretty Prue, that's far from my   10
     thought, duck. Why mouse, thy mind is nibbling at something.
     Whats is 't? What lies upon thy stomach?
Mrs Gallipot. Such an ass as you! Heyday, you're best turn midwife
     or physician; you're a pothecary already, but I'm none of your
     drugs.   15
Gallipot. Thou art a sweet drug, sweetest Prue, and the more thou
     art pounded, the more precious.
Mrs Gallipot. Must you be prying into a woman's secrets? Say ye?
Gallipot. Woman's secrets?
Mrs Gallipot. What? I cannot have a qualm come upon me but your   20
     teeth waters till your nose hang over it.

---

198. *St Thomas Apostles*] a church in the clothiers' district of London.
livery cloak] personal uniform showing that Trapdoor is in Moll's service.

3.2.2. *What . . . you*] i.e. Stop pestering me. *Pruing* is a nonce-word derived from
'Prudence', Mrs Gallipot's name.
3. *kyes*] cries (baby talk).
3–4. *city humours*] i.e. being uxoriously attentive, in the city fashion.
6–7. *before . . . table*] before the other dinner guests.
7. *show*] appear, look.
flinging] abruptly departing.
9. *up and ride*] 'Ride' was common slang for sexual intercourse. The line could
either be a sexual invitation or an insulting dismissal.
11. *duck, mouse*] terms of affection.
12. *What . . . stomach?*] What has upset your stomach? (with a coy reference to
the possibility of pregnancy).
15. *drugs*] playing on 'drudge'; a menial servant or an oppressed lover.
17. *pounded*] (1) pounded to mix ingredients in a drug: (2) pounded in sexual
intercourse.
20. *qualm*] nausea, stomach upset.
21. *teeth waters*] a proverbial sign of excited anticipation (as in 'mouth water').

Gallipot. It is my love, dear wife.

Mrs Gallipot. Your love? Your love is all words; give me deeds! I
　　cannot abide a man that's too fond over me—so cookish! Thou
　　dost not know how to handle a woman in her kind.　　　　25

Gallipot. No, Prue? Why, I hope I have handled—

Mrs Gallipot. Handle a fool's head of your own! Fie, fie!

Gallipot. Ha, ha, 'tis such a wasp! It does me good now to have her
　　sting me, little rogue.

Mrs Gallipot. Now, fie, how you vex me! I cannot abide these　　30
　　apron husbands. Such cotqueans! You overdo your things; they
　　become you scurvily.

Gallipot. [*Aside*] Upon my life, she breeds. Heaven knows how I
　　have strained myself to please her night and day. I wonder why
　　we citizens should get children so fretful and untoward in the　　35
　　breeding, their fathers being for the most part as gentle as milch
　　kine. [*To her*] Shall I leave thee, my Prue?

Mrs Gallipot. Fie, fie, fie!

Gallipot. Thou shalt not be vexed no more, pretty kind rogue; take
　　no cold, sweet Prue.　　　　　　　*Exit* MASTER GALLIPOT.　　40

Mrs Gallipot. As your wit has done! Now Master Laxton, show your
　　head. What news from you? [*She produces a letter.*] Would any
　　husband suspect that a woman crying 'Buy any scurvy-grass'
　　should bring love letters amongst her herbs to his wife? Pretty
　　trick! Fine conveyance! Had jealousy a thousand eyes, a silly　　45
　　woman with scurvy-grass blinds them all.
　　　Laxton, with bays
　　Crown I thy wit for this; it deserves praise.
　　This makes me affect thee more; this proves thee wise.
　　'Lack, what poor shift is love forced to devise?—　　　　　50
　　To the point.　　　　　　　　　　　*She reads the letter.*
　　　'O sweet creature'—a sweet beginning—'pardon my long
　　absence, for thou shalt shortly be possessed with my pres-

---

25. *in her kind*] according to her nature; as she desires.

31. *cotqueans*] domesticated men.

33. *Upon . . . breeds*] i.e. My wife is behaving so imperiously she must be pregnant. (Pregnancy was thought to induce demanding behaviour of this sort.)

35. *get*] beget.
untoward] difficult to manage.

36–7. *milch kine*] milking cows.

41. *As . . . done*] i.e. just as your wit has taken cold, is sluggish and feeble.

43. *scurvy-grass*] spoonwort, a herb used against scurvy and for stomach ail-
ments. It grew along the Thames.

45. *Fine conveyance*] a clever way of bringing the letters.
silly] simple, helpless, foolish.

47. *bays*] laurel leaves, traditionally awarded to warriors and poets.

48. *affect*] love; be attracted to.

50. *shift*] subterfuge, stratagem.

ence. Though Demophon was false to Phyllis, I will be to
thee as Pan-da-rus was to Cres-sida; though Aeneas made an   55
ass of Dido, I will die to thee ere I do so. O sweetest creature,
make much of me, for no man beneath the silver moon shall
make more of a woman than I do of thee. Furnish me
therefore with thirty pounds; you must do it of necessity
for me. I languish till I see some comfort come from thee.   60
Protesting not to die in thy debt, but rather to live so, as
hitherto I have and will,   Thy true Laxton ever.'
Alas, poor gentleman! Troth, I pity him.
How shall I raise this money? Thirty pound?
'Tis thirty sure: a three before an O—   65
I know his threes too well. My childbed linen?
Shall I pawn that for him? Then if my mark
Be known, I am undone! It may be thought
My husband's bankrupt. Which way shall I turn?
Laxton, what with my own fears and thy wants,   70
I'm like a needle 'twixt two adamants.

                Enter MASTER GALLIPOT *hastily.*

Gallipot. Nay, nay, wife, the women are all up. [*Aside*] Ha? How?
Reading o' letters? I smell a goose. A couple of capons and a
gammon of bacon from her mother out of the country, I hold
my life. Steal—steal—   [*He sneaks up behind her.*]   75

---

54. *Demophon . . . Phyllis*] a story of love betrayed, from Ovid's *Metamorphoses*,
the source of a number of sad love stories and the type of elegant learning. Laxton
could have got the reference from a book of sample letters or a mythological
dictionary.

55. *Pan-da-rus . . . Cres-sida*] Mrs Gallipot laboriously spells out the unfamiliar
names. The joke is that Pandarus was not Cressida's lover but the go-between in her
affair with Troilus. Nor did any of the other lovers mentioned in the letter consummate their love.

58. *make more*] deliberately ambivalent; Laxton's meaning thoughout is financial
while Mrs Gallipot interprets it amorously.

66. *childbed linen*] linen used for childbirth and confinement. It was often em-
broidered and expensive and was an important financial and symbolic component
of a woman's wealth.

67. *mark*] device or character sewn into linen as a sign of ownership.

71. *adamants*] extremely hard stones; often confused (as here) with loadstones or
magnets.

72. *Nay . . . up*] Gallipot reproaches his wife for being out of the room, neglect-
ing her guests, when the women have left the table.

73-4. *I . . . country*] Gallipot assumes the letter is bringing an offer of food from
Mrs Gallipot's family in the country.

74. *hold*] bet.

75. *Steal*] i.e. creep gently up behind her.

Mrs Gallipot. Oh, beshrew your heart!

Gallipot. What letter's that? I'll see 't.   *She tears the letter.*

Mrs Gallipot. Oh, would thou hadst no eyes to see
  The downfall of me and thyself! I'm for ever,
  For ever I'm undone.   80

Gallipot. What ails my Prue? What paper's that thou tear'st?

Mrs Gallipot. Would I could tear
  My very heart in pieces! For my soul
  Lies on the rack of shame that tortures me
  Beyond a woman's suffering.

Gallipot.   What means this?   85

Mrs Gallipot. Had you no other vengeance to throw down,
  But even in height of all my joys—

Gallipot.   Dear woman!

Mrs Gallipot. When the full sea of pleasure and content
  Seemed to flow over me?

Gallipot. As thou desirest to keep me out of Bedlam,   90
  Tell me what troubles thee! Is not thy child
  At nurse fall'n sick, or dead?

Mrs Gallipot.   Oh, no!

Gallipot. Heavens bless me! Are my barns and houses
  Yonder at Hockley Hole consumed with fire?
  I can build more, sweet Prue.

Mrs Gallipot.   'Tis worse, 'tis worse!   95

Gallipot. My factor broke? Or is the *Jonas* sunk?

Mrs Gallipot. Would all we had were swallowed in the waves,
  Rather than both should be the scorn of slaves!

Gallipot. I'm at my wit's end!

Mrs Gallipot.   Oh, my dear husband,
  Where once I thought myself a fixèd star   100
  Placed only in the heaven of thine arms,
  I fear now I shall prove a wanderer.—

---

76. *beshrew your heart*] devil take your heart. A common, not very forceful, imprecation.

86. *Had . . . vengeance*] Mrs Gallipot rails in a grand, but unspecific, tragic style at the powers who have dealt her such a blow. See Intro., p. 50.

90. *Bedlam*] the hospital of St Mary of Bethlehem outside Bishopsgate to which mad people were sent. A madhouse of any kind.

92. *at nurse*] Children, at this time, were commonly sent to wet nurses away from home.

94. *Hockley Hole*] a village on the edge of London, northwest of Clerkenwell Green. The sexual possibilities of the name might cause a snigger.

96. *My factor broke?*] Is my agent financially ruined?

98. *slaves*] contemptible and socially inferior persons.

100. *fixèd star*] i.e. Polaris, the star which always seems to occupy the same place in the heavens. A poetic metaphor for a constant person.

> O Laxton, Laxton, is it then my fate
> To be by thee o'erthrown?
> *Gallipot.*   Defend me, wisdom,
>   From falling into frenzy! On my knees,   105
>   Sweet Prue, speak! What's that Laxton who so heavy
>   Lies on thy bosom?
> *Mrs Gallipot.*   I shall sure run mad!
> *Gallipot.* I shall run mad for company, then. Speak to me;
>   I'm Gallipot, thy husband. Prue! Why, Prue!
>   Art sick in conscience for some villainous deed   110
>   Thou wert about to act? Didst mean to rob me?
>   Tush, I forgive thee. Hast thou on my bed
>   Thrust my soft pillow under another's head?
>   I'll wink at all faults, Prue; 'las, that's no more
>   Than what some neighbours near thee have done before.   115
>   Sweet honey Prue, what's that Laxton?
> *Mrs Gallipot.*   Oh!
> *Gallipot.* Out with him!
> *Mrs Gallipot.*   Oh, he's born to be my undoer!
>   This hand which thou call'st thine to him was given;
>   To him was I made sure i' th' sight of heaven.
> *Gallipot.* I never heard this thunder!
> *Mrs Gallipot.*   Yes, yes, before   120
>   I was to thee contracted, to him I swore.
>   Since last I saw him, twelve months three times told
>   The moon hath drawn through her light silver bow;
>   For o'er the seas he went, and it was said—
>   But rumour lies—that he in France was dead.   125
>   But he's alive, oh, he's alive! He sent
>   That letter to me, which in rage I rent,
>   Swearing with oaths most damnably to have me
>   Or tear me from this bosom. O heavens, save me!
> *Gallipot.* My heart will break.—Shamed and undone for ever! 130
> *Mrs Gallipot.* So black a day, poor wretch, went o'er thee never!

---

114. *wink at*] seem not to see.

119. *made . . . heaven*] betrothed. Mrs Gallipot suggests that Laxton could sue her for marrying Gallipot when she was precontracted to him. In practice, pre-contracts were more often invoked as a woman's defence against accusations of bearing a bastard. See Intro., p. 24.

120. *I . . . thunder*] I never heard such thunderous information. Gallipot is indicating that he is thunderstruck, but also, comically, that he is baffled by this unexpected news.

122-3. *twelve . . . bow*] three years have passed. On this high-flown language, see Intro., p. 50.

128. *Swearing*] i.e. he swearing.

129. *this bosom*] my husband's bosom.

Gallipot. If thou shouldst wrestle with him at the law,
　Thou'rt sure to fall; no odd sleight, no prevention.
　I'll tell him thou'rt with child.
Mrs Gallipot.　　　　　　　Um!
Gallipot.　　　　　　　　　Or give out
　One of my men was ta'en abed with thee.　　　　　　135
Mrs Gallipot. Um, um!
Gallipot.　　　　　Before I lose thee, my dear Prue,
　I'll drive it to that push.
Mrs Gallipot.　　　　　Worse, and worse still!
　You embrace a mischief to prevent an ill.
Gallipot. I'll buy thee of him, stop his mouth with gold.
　Think'st thou 'twill do?
Mrs Gallipot.　　　　Oh, me! Heavens grant it would!　　140
　Yet, now my senses are set more in tune,
　He writ, as I remember in his letter,
　That he in riding up and down had spent,
　Ere he could find me, thirty pounds. Send that;
　Stand not on thirty with him.
Gallipot.　　　　　　Forty, Prue.　　　　　　145
　Say thou the word, 'tis done. We venture lives
　For wealth, but must do more to keep our wives.
　Thirty or forty, Prue?
Mrs Gallipot.　　　　Thirty, good sweet;
　Of an ill bargain let's save what we can.
　I'll pay it him with my tears. He was a man,　　　　150
　When first I knew him, of a meek spirit;
　All goodness is not yet dried up, I hope.
Gallipot. He shall have thirty pound. Let that stop all;
　Love's sweets taste best when we have drunk down gall.

　　　Enter MASTER TILTYARD *and his* Wife, MASTER
　　　　GOSHAWK, *and* MRS OPENWORK.

　God-so, our friends! Come, come, smooth your cheek;　　155
　After a storm, the face of heaven looks sleek.
Tiltyard. Did I not tell you these turtles were together?
Mrs Tiltyard. [*To Gallipot*] How dost thou, sirrah?—Why, sister
　Gallipot!

---

　133. *no odd sleight*] there's no trick that can succeed.
　134–5.] Gallipot is prepared to slander his wife with an accusation of adultery rather than fighting the case of precontract at law.
　145. *Stand not on*] do not scruple.
　146. *venture lives*] risk our lives.
　155. *God-so*] an interjection of surprise or alarm; cf. 'By God's soul'; but also perhaps derived from *cazzo*, Italian for penis.
　157. *turtles*] turtle-doves; types of attentive lovers.

Mrs Openwork. Lord, how she's changed!   160
Goshawk. [*To Gallipot*] Is your wife ill, sir?
Gallipot. Yes indeed, la, sir, very ill, very ill, never worse.
Mrs Tiltyard. How her head burns! Feel how her pulses work.
Mrs Openwork. Sister, lie down a little. That always does me good.
Mrs Tiltyard. In good sadness, I find best ease in that too. Has she   165
     laid some hot thing to her stomach?
Mrs Gallipot. No, but I will lay something anon.
Tiltyard. Come, come, fools, you trouble her.—Shall 's go, Master
     Goshawk?
Goshawk. Yes, sweet Master Tiltyard.   170
                         [*He talks apart with Mrs Openwork.*]
     Sirrah Rosamond, I hold my life Gallipot hath vexed his wife.
Mrs Openwork. She has a horrible high colour indeed.
Goshawk. We shall have your face painted with the same red soon at
     night, when your husband comes from his rubbers in a false
     alley; thou wilt not believe me that his bowls run with a wrong   175
     bias?
Mrs Openwork. It cannot sink into me that he feeds upon stale
     mutton abroad, having better and fresher at home.
Goshawk. What if I bring thee where thou shalt see him stand at
     rack and manger?   180
Mrs Openwork. I'll saddle him in 's kind and spur him till he kick
     again.
Goshawk. Shall thou and I ride our journey, then?
Mrs Openwork. Here's my hand.
Goshawk. No more. [*To Tiltyard*] Come Master Tiltyard, shall we   185
     leap into the stirrups with our women and amble home?
Tiltyard. Yes, yes.—Come, wife.
Mrs Tiltyard. [*To Mrs Gallipot*] In troth, sister, I hope you will do
     well for all this.
Mrs Gallipot. I hope I shall. Farewell, good sister, sweet Master   190
     Goshawk.

---

164. *lie down*] with a bawdy possibility which extends throughout the women's
advice.
165. *In good sadness*] in all seriousness. A weak oath associated with women.
168. *Shall 's*] shall we.
174. *rubbers*] a set of (usually) three games; here of bowls, but with a bawdy
double entendre continued in *false alley.*
175–6. *with a wrong bias*] in the wrong direction. The bias was a weight on one
side of the bowl which made it run in a curve. The suggestion is that Openwork has
been on a sexual adventure.
177–8. *stale mutton*] slang for a prostitute.
179–80. *at rack and manger*] at his feed (with a bawdy sense). The imagery runs
from bowls to food to horsemanship, all with sexual double meanings.
181. *in 's kind*] according to his nature.
183. *ride our journey*] i.e. have an affair.

Gallipot. Welcome, brother; most kindly welcome, sir.

All Guests. Thanks, sir, for our good cheer.

Exeunt all but Gallipot and his Wife.

Gallipot. It shall be so, because a crafty knave
Shall not outreach me nor walk by my door   195
With my wife arm in arm as 'twere his whore.
I'll give him a golden coxcomb: thirty pound.
Tush, Prue, what's thirty pound? Sweet duck, look cheerly.

Mrs Gallipot. Thou art worthy of my heart; thou buy'st it dearly.

Enter LAXTON *muffled.*

Laxton. [*Aside*] Ud's light, the tide's against me! A pox of your   200
pothecaryship! Oh for some glister to set him going! 'Tis one of
Hercules' labours to tread one of these city hens, because their
cocks are still crowing over them. There's no turning tail here;
I must on.

Mrs Gallipot. Oh, husband, see, he comes!   205

Gallipot. Let me deal with him.

Laxton. Bless you, sir.

Gallipot. Be you blest too, sir, if you come in peace.

Laxton. Have you any good pudding-tobacco, sir?

Mrs Gallipot. Oh, pick no quarrels, gentle sir! My husband   210
Is not a man of weapon, as you are.
He knows all: I have opened all before him
Concerning you.

Laxton. [*Aside*] Zounds, has she shown my letters?

Mrs Gallipot. Suppose my case were yours, what would you do?   215
At such a pinch, such batteries, such assaults,
Of father, mother, kindred, to dissolve
The knot you tied, and to be bound to him?
How could you shift this storm off?

Laxton. If I know, hang me!   220

199.1. *muffled*] Laxton is described as 'muffled' in all his entrances after 3.1. He
may be hiding from creditors, or disguised in order to approach Mrs Gallipot for his
money.

200. *Ud's light*] corruption of 'by God's light'; a mild oath.

201. *glister*] suppository.

202. *Hercules' labours*] a proverbially impossible task involving hard physical
work.

tread] used of a cock copulating with a hen.

209. *pudding-tobacco*] tobacco pressed into little rolls resembling a pudding or
sausage.

211. *Is . . . weapon*] (1) is not experienced at sword fighting; (2) has a small penis.

215–20.] Mrs Gallipot has quickly to acquaint the baffled Laxton with the story
she has told her husband. She asks how she could have resisted the pressure from
her family to abandon Laxton and marry Gallipot, especially when Laxton was
reported dead.

Mrs Gallipot. Besides, a story of your death was read
     Each minute to me.
Laxton. [*Aside*] What a pox means this riddling?
Gallipot. Be wise, sir; let not you and I be tossed
     On lawyers' pens. They have sharp nibs and draw   225
     Men's very heart-blood from them. What need you, sir,
     To beat the drum of my wife's infamy,
     And call your friends together, sir, to prove
     Your precontract, when sh'has confessed it?
Laxton.   Um, sir—
     Has she confessed it?
Gallipot.   Sh' has, faith, to me, sir,   230
     Upon your letter sending.
Mrs Gallipot.   I have, I have.
Laxton. [*Aside*] If I let this iron cool, call me slave!
     [*To her*] Do you hear, you dame Prudence? Think'st thou, vile
          woman,
     I'll take these blows and wink?
Mrs Gallipot.   Upon my knees—
Laxton. Out, impudence!
Gallipot.   Good sir—
Laxton.   You goatish slaves!   235
     No wildfowl to cut up but mine?
Gallipot.   Alas, sir,
     You make her flesh to tremble. Fright her not;
     She shall do reason, and what's fit.
Laxton. [*To Mrs Gallipot*]   I'll have thee,
     Wert thou more common than an hospital
     And more diseased—
Gallipot.   But one word, good sir!
Laxton.   So, sir.   240
Gallipot. I married her, have lain with her, and got
     Two children on her body; think but on that.

---

227. *beat the drum*] i.e. make public.

234. *wink*] shut my eyes; turn a blind eye.

235–6.] Laxton pretends to be outraged by Gallipot's violation of Laxton's right
to marry Mrs Gallipot, expressing fury in obscure metaphors. Mrs Gallipot is a
wildfowl because she has been outside the home coop while Laxton was away
(*wildfowl* was also occasional slang for prostitutes because they were women who
lived outside domestic environments). Gallipot and Mrs Gallipot are described as
goatish because, it is implied, their lust (traditionally associated with goats, because
of the confusion with satyrs) had led them to ignore Laxton's rights of precontract
and to get married.

238. *I'll have thee*] (1) I'll insist on the right of precontract and marry you; (2) I
will take you sexually.

239. *more . . . hospital*] more frequented than hospitals for venereal diseases,
which were charitable foundations open to all. Laxton says he would take her even
if she were a whore.

Have you so beggarly an appetite,
When I upon a dainty dish have fed,
To dine upon my scraps, my leavings? Ha, sir?   245
Do I come near you now, sir?
Laxton.   Be lady, you touch me.
Gallipot. Would not you scorn to wear my clothes, sir?
Laxton.   Right, sir.
Gallipot. Then pray, sir, wear not her, for she's a garment
So fitting for my body I'm loath
Another should put it on; you will undo both.   250
Your letter, as she said, complained you had spent
In quest of her some thirty pound; I'll pay it.
Shall that, sir, stop this gap up 'twixt you two?
Laxton. Well, if I swallow this wrong, let her thank you.
The money being paid, sir, I am gone;   255
Farewell. Oh, women! Happy's he trusts none.
Mrs Gallipot. Dispatch him hence, sweet husband.
Gallipot.   Yes, dear wife.—
Pray, sir, come in. [*To Wife*] Ere Master Laxton part,
Thou shalt in wine drink to him.
Mrs Gallipot.   With all my heart.
                                Exit MASTER GALLIPOT.
How dost thou like my wit?
Laxton.   Rarely.
                                [*Exit*] *his* [*Gallipot's*] *Wife.*
                                That wile   260
By which the serpent did the first woman beguile
Did ever since all women's bosoms fill:
You're apple-eaters all, deceivers still!   *Exit* LAXTON.

[3.3]

>   *Enter* SIR ALEXANDER WENGRAVE, SIR DAVY DAPPER, SIR ADAM
>   APPLETON *at one door, and* TRAPDOOR *at another door.*

Sir Alexander. Out with your tale, Sir Davy, to Sir Adam.
A knave is in mine eye deep in my debt.

---

246. *Do . . . now*] Am I getting to you now?
Be lady] a corruption of 'By our lady'.
254. *swallow this wrong*] put up with this insult.
257. *Dispatch him hence*] Settle the business and get rid of him.
263. *apple-eaters*] referring to Eve eating the forbidden apple, offered by the
serpent (see line 261) in the Garden of Eden.

3.3.1–2.] The company enters in mid-conversation. Sir Alexander disentangles
himself in order to talk to Trapdoor. He pretends (see lines 41–2 below) that
Trapdoor owes him money.

Sir Davy. Nay, if he be a knave, sir, hold him fast.

                [*Sir Alexander talks apart with Trapdoor.*]

Sir Alexander. Speak softly: what egg is there hatching now?

Trapdoor. A duck's egg, sir—a duck that has eaten a frog. I have   5
    cracked the shell, and some villainy or other will peep out
    presently. The duck that sits is the bouncing ramp, that roaring
    girl, my mistress; the drake that must tread is your son, Sebas-
    tian.

Sir Alexander. Be quick.   10

Trapdoor. As the tongue of an oyster-wench.

Sir Alexander. And see thy news be true.

Trapdoor. As a barber's every Saturday night. Mad Moll—

Sir Alexander. Ah!

Trapdoor. Must be let in without knocking at your back gate.   15

Sir Alexander. So.

Trapdoor. Your chamber will be made bawdy.

Sir Alexander. Good!

Trapdoor. She comes in a shirt of mail.

Sir Alexander. How, shirt of mail?   20

Trapdoor. Yes, sir, or a male shirt, that's to say, in man's apparel.

Sir Alexander. To my son?

Trapdoor. Close to your son; your son and her moon will be in
    conjunction, if all almanacs lie not. Her black safeguard is
    turned into a deep slop, the holes of her upper body to button-   25
    holes, her waistcoat to a doublet, her placket to the ancient seat
    of a codpiece; and you shall take 'em both with standing collars.

Sir Alexander. Art sure of this?

---

5. *duck . . . frog*] Trapdoor suggests that Moll has swallowed the bait.

7. *bouncing ramp*] blustering, swaggering girl. Trapdoor is using underworld slang. See Intro., p. 26.

8. *tread*] copulate with, as at 3.2.202.

13. *barber's*] proverbially the source of unreliable news and gossip.

15. *let . . . knocking*] i.e. as if for a secret assignation.

back gate] with the suggestion of anal sex.

19. *shirt of mail*] as in armour: Trapdoor is punning on mail/male.

23–4. *in conjunction*] a term taken from astrological prophecy and often used with a sexual meaning, it refers to heavenly bodies whose orbits bring them into close proximity as seen from the Earth.

24–5. *Her black safeguard . . . deep slop*] Her skirt has been changed for breeches (referring to the costume change prepared in 2.2.78–86).

25–6. *holes . . . button-holes*] The *upper body* or bodice on a woman's dress looked similar to the doublet worn by men and was commented on in writing about cross-dressing. The eyelets used in the female garment for fastening with points and laces are bawdily contrasted with the buttons and button holes of the male doublet, all with sexual double meanings.

26. *placket*] the opening at the waist of a skirt or petticoat.

27. *standing collars*] high straight collars, fastened in the front.

Trapdoor. As every throng is sure of a pickpocket; as sure as a whore
    is of the clients all Michaelmas Term, and of the pox after the   30
    term.
Sir Alexander. The time of their tilting?
Trapdoor. Three.
Sir Alexander. The day?
Trapdoor. This.   35
Sir Alexander. Away, ply it! Watch her.
Trapdoor. As the devil doth for the death of a bawd. I'll watch her;
    do you catch her.
Sir Alexander. She's fast; here, weave thou the nets. Hark—
Trapdoor. They are made.   40
Sir Alexander. I told them thou didst owe me money. Hold it up,
    maintain 't.
Trapdoor. Stiffly, as a Puritan does contention. [*As in a quarrel*]
    Fox, I owe thee not the value of a halfpenny halter!
Sir Alexander. Thou shalt be hanged in 't ere thou 'scape so. Varlet,   45
    I'll make thee look through a grate!
Trapdoor. I'll do 't presently: through a tavern grate. Drawer!
    Pish!   *Exit* TRAPDOOR.
Sir Adam. Has the knave vexed you, sir?
Sir Alexander.   Asked him my money;
    He swears my son received it. Oh, that boy
    Will ne'er leave heaping sorrows on my heart   50
    Till he has broke it quite!
Sir Adam.   Is he still wild?
Sir Alexander. As is a Russian bear.
Sir Adam.   But he has left
    His old haunt with that baggage?
Sir Alexander.   Worse still and worse!
    He lays on me his shame, I on him my curse.
Sir Davy. My son, Jack Dapper, then shall run with him   55
    All in one pasture.
Sir Adam.   Proves your son bad too, sir?

---

30. *Michaelmas Term*] the autumn term for the law courts, when lawyers and
their clients would be in London as customers for the prostitutes.
    32. *tilting*] sexual encounter.
    39. *fast*] as good as caught fast.
    40.] i.e. the nets are ready.
    41–2. *Hold . . . maintain 't*] Back me up, carry it out.
    46. *a grate*] i.e. a grating over a prison window.
    47. *Drawer!*] Trapdoor speaks contemptuously to Sir Alexander as if he were a
waiter in a tavern.
    48. *Asked him*] I asked him for. Sir Alexander is playing out the fiction that his
conversation with Trapdoor has been about money.
    53. *baggage*] i.e. Moll.

Sir Davy. As villainy can make him. Your Sebastian
    Dotes but on one drab, mine on a thousand.
    A noise of fiddlers, tobbacco, wine, and a whore,
    A mercer that will let him take up more,   60
    Dice, and a water-spaniel with a duck—oh,
    Bring him abed with these! When his purse jingles,
    Roaring boys follow at 's tail. Fencers and ningles—
    Beasts Adam ne'er gave name to—these horse-leeches suck
    My son; he being drawn dry, they all live on smoke.   65
Sir Alexander. Tobacco?
Sir Davy.   Right; but I have in my brain
    A windmill going that shall grind to dust
    The follies of my son, and make him wise
    Or a stark fool. Pray lend me your advice.
Sir Alexander, Sir Adam. That shall you, good Sir Davy.
Sir Davy.   Here's the springe   70
    I ha' set to catch this woodcock in: an action
    In a false name—unknown to him—is entered
    I' th' Counter to arrest Jack Dapper.
Sir Alexander, Sir Adam.   Ha, ha, he!
Sir Davy. Think you the Counter cannot break him?
Sir Adam.   Break him?
    Yes, and break 's heart too, if he lie there long.   75
Sir Davy. I'll make him sing a counter-tenor, sure.
Sir Adam. No way to tame him like it; there shall he learn
    What money is indeed, and how to spend it.
Sir Davy. He's bridled there.
Sir Alexander.   Ay, yet knows not how to mend it.
    Bedlam cures not more madmen in a year   80
    Than one of the counters does; men pay more dear
    There for their wit than anywhere. A counter,

---

59. *noise*] usual word for a company of musicians.

60. *take up more*] buy more on credit.

61. *a water-spaniel . . . duck*] The exasperated culmination of Sir Davy's list of his son's frivolous pastimes; hunting duck is traditionally the sport of citizens, not gentlemen. See 2.1.368–84.

62. *Bring . . . these*] i.e. I wish he could be cured of them.

63. *ningles*] i.e. favourites, homosexual hangers-on.

64. *Adam . . . name to*] referring to Adam naming the beasts after the creation. *horse-leeches*] bloodsuckers; whores.

67. *A windmill*] i.e. a far-fetched project. Aristocratic investment in agricultural innovation was a source of contemporary gossip and scandal.

70–1. *the springe . . . woodcock in*] the snare to catch this little bird. A woodcock is a bird that is proverbially easy to catch.

73. *th' Counter*] a prison for debtors.

76. *sing a counter-tenor*] sing a new tune (with a pun on *Counter*, prison).

79. *He's*] he'll be.

Why, 'tis an university! Who not sees?
As scholars there, so here men take degrees
And follow the same studies, all alike.   85
Scholars learn first logic and rhetoric;
So does a prisoner. With fine honeyed speech
At 's first coming in he doth persuade, beseech
He may be lodged with one that is not itchy,
To lie in a clean chamber, in sheets not lousy;   90
But when he has no money, then does he try
By subtle logic and quaint sophistry
To make the keepers trust him.
Sir Adam.   Say they do?
Sir Alexander. Then he's a graduate.
Sir Davy.   Say they trust him not?
Sir Alexander. Then is he held a freshman and a sot,   95
And never shall commence; but, being still barred,
Be expulsed from the Master's Side to th' Twopenny Ward,
Or else i' th' Hole be placed.
Sir Adam.   When then, I pray,
Proceeds a prisoner?
Sir Alexander.   When, money being the theme,
He can dispute with his hard creditors' hearts   100
And get out clear, he's then a Master of Arts.
Sir Davy, send your son to Wood Street College;
A gentleman can nowhere get more knowledge.
Sir Davy. There gallants study hard.
Sir Alexander.   True: to get money.
Sir Davy. 'Lies by th' heels, i' faith. Thanks, thanks; I ha' sent for a 105
couple of bears shall paw him.

      Enter SERGEANT CURTALAX *and* YEOMAN HANGER.

Sir Adam. Who comes yonder?
Sir Davy. They look like puttocks; these should be they.
Sir Alexander. I know 'em; they are officers. Sir, we'll leave you.

---

86. *logic and rhetoric*] part of the standard curriculum for undergraduates.
92. *subtle*] cunning, crafty.
quaint] ingenious.
96. *commence*] take the full degree of Master or Doctor at a University.
97–8. *Master's Side . . . Hole*] The rooms in prisons were graded according to payment: prisoners paid higher prices to be housed on the Master's Side. The lowest and most horrible room was the Hole.
99. *Proceeds*] advances from graduation as a Bachelor of Arts to a higher degree.
102. *Wood Street College*] One of the debtors' prisons was in Wood Street.
105. *'Lies by th' heels*] he lies in jail with his legs in irons.
106. *bears*] i.e. the sergeants that Sir Davy has hired to arrest his son.
108. *puttocks*] kites, birds of prey; slang for sergeants, arresting officers.

Sir Davy. My good knights,   110
    Leave me; you see I'm haunted now with sprites.
Sir Alexander, Sir Adam. Fare you well, sir.
                        Exeunt [SIR] ALEXANDER *and* [SIR] ADAM.
Curtalax. [*To Hanger*] This old muzzle chops should be he, by the
    fellow's description. [*To Sir Davy*] Save you, sir.
Sir Davy. Come hither, you mad varlets. Did not my man tell you   115
    I watched here for you?
Curtalax. One in a blue coat, sir, told us that in this place an old
    gentleman would watch for us—a thing contrary to our oath,
    for we are to watch for every wicked member in a city.
Sir Davy. You'll watch, then, for ten thousand. What's thy name,   120
    honesty?
Curtalax. Sergeant Curtalax, I, sir.
Sir Davy. An excellent name for a sergeant, Curtalax;
    Sergeants indeed are weapons of the law.
    When prodigal ruffians far in debt are grown,   125
    Should not you cut them, citizens were o'erthrown.
    Thou dwell'st hereby in Holborn, Curtalax?
Curtalax. That's my circuit, sir; I conjure most in that circle.
Sir Davy. And what young toward whelp is this?
Hanger. Of the same litter: his yeoman, sir; my name's Hanger.   130
Sir Davy. Yeoman Hanger.
    One pair of shears, sure, cut out both your coats;
    You have two names most dangerous to men's throats.
    You two are villainous loads on gentlemen's backs;
    Dear ware, this Hanger and this Curtalax.   135

---

111. *sprites*] spirits, i.e. sergeants.
113. *muzzle chops*] with prominent nose and mouth.
116. *watched*] waited.
117. *One in a blue coat*] i.e. a servant.
118–19.] Curtalax plays on *watch* meaning both 'to wait' and 'to act as the town
watch'. Allowing someone else to *watch for us* would be against the oath taken when
they were appointed as the town watch. There was some contemporary concern
over citizens who did not want to undertake watch duties, paying others to do it for
them.
120. *for ten thousand*] i.e. the large number of *wicked members* whom Curtalax will
have either to watch out for or on whose behalf he will watch.
126.] If you didn't cut them (the debtors) out of the society, citizens would suffer
financial loss.
128. *conjure . . . circle*] operate most in that district; continuing the sense of
'sprites' from line 111 above.
129. *toward whelp*] promising puppy.
130. *Hanger*] the strap used to attach a sword to a belt; an appropriate name for
one attached to a curtleaxe, or battle-axe.
134. *villainous . . . backs*] referring to the heavy hand of a sergeant making an
arrest and to the weight of swords on the shoulders.
135. *Dear ware*] expensive equipment.

Curtalax. We are as other men are, sir; I cannot see but he who
   makes a show of honesty and religion, if his claws can fasten to
   his liking, he draws blood. All that live in the world are but great
   fish and little fish, and feed upon one another. Some eat up
   whole men; a sergeant cares but for the shoulder of a man. They   140
   call us knaves and curs, but many times he that sets us on
   worries more lambs one year than we do in seven.
Sir Davy. Spoke like a noble Cerberus! Is the action entered?
Hanger. His name is entered in the book of unbelievers.
Sir Davy. What book's that?   145
Curtalax. The book where all prisoners' names stand; and not one
   amongst forty when he comes in believes to come out in haste.
Sir Davy. Be as dogged to him as your office allows you to be.
Curtalax, Hanger. Oh, sir!
Sir Davy. You know the unthrift Jack Dapper?   150
Curtalax. Ay, ay, sir, that gull? As well as I know my yeoman.
Sir Davy. And you know his father too, Sir Davy Dapper?
Curtalax. As damned a usurer as ever was among Jews. If he were
   sure his father's skin would yield him any money, he would,
   when he dies, flay it off and sell it to cover drums for children   155
   at Barthol'mew Fair.
Sir Davy. [*Aside*] What toads are these, to spit poison on a man to
   his face? [*To them*] Do you see, my honest rascals? Yonder
   Greyhound is the dog he hunts with: out of that tavern, Jack
   Dapper will sally. Sa, sa! Give the counter! On, set upon him!   160

136–8. *I cannot ... blood*] i.e. as far as I can see, men who profess piety are quick
enough to draw blood when they fasten on their prey.

140. *shoulder*] because men are arrested by being held on the shoulder.

141. *sets us on*] hires us to arrest someone.

142. *worries more lambs*] harrasses more innocent persons.

143. *Cerberus*] the three-headed dog that kept the gates of hell; a common term
for a gaoler.

Is ... entered?] Is the suit registered?

144. *the book of unbelievers*] i.e. the official register; carrying on the image of souls
entering hell.

153–6.] Innocently insulting someone to their face was a standard clown routine.
Curtalax has been told (lines 117–18) only that *an old gentleman would watch for us.*
He does not necessarily know who Sir Davy is. In any case, continuity is often
sacrificed to comedy.

156. *Barthol'mew Fair*] London's largest annual fair, lasting a fortnight from
August 24. Originally a cloth fair, it had become a more general place for an outing
and a treat for children.

158–9. *Yonder Greyhound*] Sir Davy points to one of the upstage doors to indicate the Greyhound Tavern from which Jack will enter. A Greyhound Tavern was
known in Fleet Street, not in Holborn where this scene is set.

160. *Sa, sa!*] a noise made to encourage dogs when hunting: Sir Davy is excit-
edly and comically putting the officers through their drill.

counter] (1) parry in fencing: (2) opposite direction to that taken by hunted game.

Curtalax, Hanger. We'll charge him upo' th' back, sir.
Sir Davy. Take no bail; put mace enough into his caudle.
    Double your files! Traverse your ground!
Curtalax, Hanger. Brave, sir!
            [*They perform a comic version of the manual of arms.*]
Sir Davy. Cry arm, arm, arm!   165
Curtalax, Hanger. Thus, sir.
Sir Davy. There boy, there boy, away! Look to your prey, my true
    English wolves, and—and so I vanish.   *Exit* SIR DAVY.
Curtalax. Some warden of the sergeants begat this old fellow, upon
    my life!—Stand close.   170
Hanger. Shall the ambuscado lie in one place?
Curtalax. No, nook thou yonder.   [*They take cover.*]

                    Enter MOLL *and* TRAPDOOR.

Moll. Ralph.
Trapdoor. What says my brave captain, male and female?
Moll. This Holborn is such a wrangling street.   175
Trapdoor. That's because lawyers walks to and fro in 't.
Moll. Here's such jostling as if everyone we met were drunk and
    reeled.
Trapdoor. Stand, mistress. Do you not smell carrion?
Moll. Carrion? No, yet I spy ravens.   180
Trapdoor. Some poor wind-shaken gallant will anon fall into sore
    labour, and these men-midwives must bring him to bed i' the
    Counter; there all those that are great with child with debts lie
    in.

---

161. *upo' th' back*] from the rear.
    162. *put mace . . . caudle*] i.e. give him the full treatment; punning on *mace*, the
staff carried by a sergeant, and the spice used in a caudle or warm drink of gruel
mixed with ale or wine.
    163. *Double your files*] Double the length of your lines by marching other men
into them. A ridiculous idea with only two men.
    Traverse your ground] Move from side to side to cover the ground in fencing or
battle.
    169. *warden . . . sergeants*] official appointed in each ward to be responsible for
the arresting officers. This post would only be open to a citizen. Sir Davy is being
obscurely insulted with the suggestion that he is a citizen's bastard, not a gentleman.
    170. *close*] concealed.
    171. *Shall . . . place?*] Shall we set the ambush together?
    172. *nook*] hide.
    174. *brave*] (1) courageous; (2) dashing, handsome.
    179. *carrion*] dead flesh.
    180. *ravens*] (1) scavenging birds; (2) the sergeants.
    181. *wind-shaken*] with a cracked heart, like a wind-shaken tree.
    181-2. *fall . . . labour*] (1) give birth to sorrowful debt; (2) be incarcerated (for
debt) and subjected to hard labour.

Moll. Stand up!   185
Trapdoor. Like your new maypole!
Hanger. [*To Curtalax*] Whist, whew!
Curtalax. [*To Hanger*] Hump, no!
Moll. Peeping? It shall go hard, huntsmen, but I'll spoil your game.
   [*To Trapdoor*] They look for all the world like two infected   190
   maltmen coming muffled up in their cloaks in a frosty morning
   to London.
Trapdoor. A course, captain! A bear comes to the stake.

            Enter JACK DAPPER *and* GULL.

Moll. It should be so, for the dogs struggle to be let loose.
Hanger. [*To Curtalax*] Whew!   195
Curtalax. [*To Hanger*] Hemp!
Moll. Hark, Trapdoor, follow your leader.
Jack Dapper. Gull.
Gull. Master?
Jack Dapper. Didst ever see such an ass as I am, boy?   200
Gull. No, by my troth, sir, to lose all your money, yet have false dice
   of your own! Why, 'tis as I saw a great fellow used t'other day:
   he had a fair sword and buckler, and yet a butcher dry-beat him
   with a cudgel.
Moll, Trapdoor. Honest sergeant! [*To Jack*] Fly! Fly, Master Dap-   205
   per, you'll be arrested else!
Jack Dapper. Run, Gull, and draw!
Gull. Run, master! Gull follows you!
          Exit [JACK] DAPPER *and* GULL.
Curtalax. [*Moll holding him*] I know you well enough: you're but a
   whore to hang upon any man.   210

185.] Stand with me. Moll is urging Trapdoor to support her in the expected
fight with the sergeants.

187–8. *Whist . . . no*] Hanger (perhaps with a gesture) is asking Curtalax if Moll
and Trapdoor are their next victims.

190–1. *infected maltmen*] i.e. with the plague. Maltmen were supposed to be
particularly susceptible to plague because they carried rags, which may have been
infected, back to the country for use as manure.

193. A *course*] the animal pursued in chasing sports with hounds.

stake] post to which a bear was tethered for baiting.

194. *the dogs*] Curtalax and Hanger; see lines 129–30. Moll observes that the
sergeants are eager to arrest Dapper.

202–4. *great fellow . . . cudgel*] referring to an incident at the Fortune Theatre.
See Intro., p. 26.

203. *buckler*] small round shield.

dry-beat] beat him up without drawing blood.

205. *Honest sergeant*] Moll and Trapdoor attract the officer's attention and urge
Jack Dapper to take the opportunity to escape.

Moll. Whores then are like sergeants; so now hang you! [*To Trapdoor*] Draw, rogue, but strike not. For a broken pate they'll keep their beds and recover twenty marks damages.

Curtalax. You shall pay for this rescue! [*To Hanger*] Run down Shoe Lane and meet him!   215

Trapdoor. Shoo! Is this a rescue, gentlemen, or no?

                              [*Exeunt* CURTALAX *and* HANGER.]

Moll. Rescue? A pox on 'em! Trapdoor, let's away;
I'm glad I have done perfect one good work today.
If any gentleman be in scrivener's bands,
Send but for Moll, she'll bail him by these hands!   *Exeunt.*   220

212–13. *Draw . . . damages*] Moll warns Trapdoor not to hit the sergeants or else they will make the most of a small wound and sue.

212. *broken pate*] cut forehead.

214–15. *Shoe Lane*] a street running north from Fleet Street to Holborn.

219. *in scrivener's bands*] in debt. A scrivener was a copyist for legal and other documents, but could also act as a broker for money.

Act 4

Enter SIR ALEXANDER WENGRAVE *solus.*

Sir Alexander. Unhappy in the follies of a son,
    Led against judgement, sense, obedience,
    And all the powers of nobleness and wit—
    O wretched father!

                    Enter TRAPDOOR.

              Now, Trapdoor, will she come?
Trapdoor. In man's apparel, sir; I am in her heart now, and share in   5
    all her secrets.
Sir Alexander. Peace, peace, peace.
    Here, take my German watch, hang 't up in sight
    That I may see her hang in English for 't.
                     [He gives a watch.]
Trapdoor. I warrant you for that now, next sessions rids her,   10
    sir. This watch will bring her in better than a hundred
    constables.
Sir Alexander. Good Trapdoor, say'st thou so? Thou cheer'st my
      heart
    After a storm of sorrow. My gold chain, too:
    Here, take a hundred marks in yellow links.   15
                [He gives a chain and money.]
Trapdoor. That will do well to bring the watch to light, sir, and
    worth a thousand of your headboroughs' lanterns.
Sir Alexander. Place that o' the court-cupboard; let it lie

4.1.0.1. *solus*] alone.

5. *heart*] confidence.

8, 11. *watch*] playing on *watch* meaning 'timepiece' and 'officers who guard a
town at night'; see *constables* in line 12.

9. *hang in English*] i.e. be hanged under English law.

15–16. *links . . . light*] punning on *links* meaning a torch as well as the links in a
chain.

17. *headboroughs' lanterns*] lanterns carried at night by the watch; playing on *light*,
line 16.

18. *court-cupboard*] a moveable sideboard used to display plate and to store wine,
linen and cutlery.

Full in the view of her thief-whorish eye.

[Trapdoor places the objects on a sideboard.]

Trapdoor. She cannot miss it, sir; I see 't so plain that I could steal   20
    't myself.

Sir Alexander. Perhaps thou shalt, too—
    That or something as weighty. What she leaves,
    Thou shalt come closely in and filch away,
    And all the weight upon her back I'll lay.   25

Trapdoor. You cannot assure that, sir.

Sir Alexander. No? What lets it?

Trapdoor. Being a stout girl, perhaps she'll desire pressing; then all
    the weight must lie upon her belly.

Sir Alexander. Belly or back, I care not, so I've one.   30

Trapdoor. You're of my mind for that, sir.

Sir Alexander. Hang up my ruff band with the diamond at it;
    It may be she'll like that best.

Trapdoor. It's well for her that she must have her choice. *[Aside]* He
    thinks nothing too good for her! *[To him]* If you hold on this   35
    mind a little longer, it shall be the first work I do to turn thief
    myself: would do a man good to be hanged when he is so well
    provided for!   *[The ruff band is hung up in plain view.]*

Sir Alexander. So, well said! All hangs well; would she hung so too.
    The sight would please me more than all their glisterings.   40
    Oh, that my mysteries to such straits should run,
    That I must rob myself to bless my son!   *Exeunt.*

Enter SEBASTIAN *with* MARY FITZALLARD *like a page,*
and MOLL *[dressed as a man].*

Sebastian. Thou hast done me a kind office, without touch
    Either of sin or shame; our loves are honest.

Moll. I'd scorn to make such shift to bring you together else.   45

Sebastian. Now have I time and opportunity
    Without all fear to bid thee welcome, love.   *Kiss[es Mary].*

---

27. *lets*] hinders, prevents.

28. *stout*] (1) spirited; (2) big-bellied.

pressing] (1) pressing to death—a torture which involved loading stones on accused persons until they answered a charge or died; (2) bearing the weight of a sexual partner.

30. *so I've one*] (1) so long as we make an arrest; (2) so long as I get a share of the sexual action.

32. *ruff band*] probably a ruff collar (smaller than a full ruff) in contrast to the new fashion for falling bands. See 1.1.14n.

36–7. *it shall . . . myself*] i.e. before I do anything else, I will become a thief myself (on account of the rich things they are setting out as bait).

37. *would*] it would.

41. *mysteries*] skills, craft.

Mary. Never with more desire and harder venture!
Moll. How strange this shows, one man to kiss another!
Sebastian. I'd kiss such men to choose, Moll;   50
 Methinks a woman's lip tastes well in a doublet.
Moll. Many an old madam has the better fortune then,
 Whose breaths grew stale before the fashion came.
 If that will help 'em, as you think 'twill do,
 They'll learn in time to pluck on the hose too!   55
Sebastian. The older they wax, Moll. Troth, I speak seriously:
 As some have a conceit their drink tastes better
 In an outlandish cup than in our own,
 So methinks every kiss she gives me now
 In this strange form is worth a pair of two.   60
 Here we are safe, and furthest from the eye
 Of all suspicion: this is my father's chamber,
 Upon which floor he never steps till night.
 Here he mistrusts me not, nor I his coming;
 At mine own chamber he still pries unto me.   65
 My freedom is not there at mine own finding,
 Still checked and curbed; here he shall miss his purpose.
Moll. And what's your business, now you have your mind, sir?
 At your great suit I promised you to come.
 I pitied her for name's sake, that a Moll   70
 Should be so crossed in love, when there's so many
 That owes nine lays apiece, and not so little.
 My tailor fitted her. How like you his work?
Sebastian. So well, no art can mend it for this purpose.
 But to thy wit and help we're chief in debt,   75
 And must live still beholding.
Moll.   Any honest pity
 I'm willing to bestow upon poor ring doves.
Sebastian. I'll offer no worse play.
Moll.   Nay, an you should, sir,

---

50. *to choose*] by choice.
52–5.] Moll's joke is that if, as Sebastian says, women are more kissable when dressed in men's clothes, old bawds with stale breath would dress in men's clothes to make them more attractive too.
57. *conceit*] notion (that).
58. *outlandish*] (1) foreign; (2) unfamiliar.
64. *mistrusts*] suspects; fears.
67. *checked*] hindered.
71–2. *when . . . little*] i.e. when there are many who own nine prizes apiece, and even more than that. The meaning of *nine lays* is uncertain; the joke associating the name Moll with a prostitute suggests that some bawdy meaning is likely.
76. *still beholding*] for ever in debt.
77. *ring doves*] i.e. lovers. Doves were proverbially faithful for life.
78. *I'll . . . play*] I'm proposing no worse sport than what you suggest.

I should draw first and prove the quicker man!   [*She draws.*]

Sebastian. Hold, there shall need no weapon at this meeting;   80
    But 'cause thou shalt not loose thy fury idle,
             [*Taking down and giving her a viol*]
    Here, take this viol; run upon the guts
    And end thy quarrel singing.

Moll.   Like a swan above bridge;
    For, look you, here's the bridge and here am I.

Sebastian. Hold on, sweet Moll.   85

Mary. I've heard her much commended, sir, for one that was ne'er
    taught.

Moll. I'm much beholding to 'em. Well, since you'll needs put us
    together, sir, I'll play my part as well as I can. It shall ne'er be
    said I came into a gentleman's chamber and let his instrument   90
    hang by the walls!

Sebastian. Why, well said, Moll, i' faith; it had been a shame for that
    gentleman, then, that would have let it hang still and ne'er
    offered thee it.

Moll. There it should have been still then, for Moll, for, though the   95
    world judge impudently of me, I ne'er came into that chamber
    yet where I took down the instrument myself.

Sebastian. Pish, let 'em prate abroad! Thou'rt here where thou art
    known and loved. There be a thousand close dames that will
    call the viol an unmannerly instrument for a woman, and there-   100
    fore talk broadly of thee, when you shall have them sit wider to
    a worse quality.

Moll. Push, I ever fall asleep and think not of 'em, sir; and thus I
    dream.

Sebastian. Prithee let's hear thy dream, Moll.   105

---

    82. *run . . . guts*] draw a bow across the gut strings of the viol, instead of running
through a man's guts with a weapon.

    83. *swan*] supposed to sing sweetly before death.

    83, 84. *bridge*] with a pun on the bridge of the viol.

    85.] i.e. Hold forth, Moll; let's hear you sing.

    90–7.] an extended bawdy exchange in which *instrument* refers to a man's penis.
Moll insists that she has never initiated a sexual affair.

    95. *for Moll*] as far as I, Moll, am concerned.

    98. *prate abroad*] gossip around the town.

    99. *close*] prudish, severe. Literally, women who remain inside the domestic
environments.

    100. *unmannerly instrument*] because, like the modern cello, it was played holding
the instrument between the player's legs.

    101. *broadly*] rudely, coarsely.

    101–2. *when . . . quality*] i.e. when they have opened their legs wider for things of
worse quality than a viol.

The Song.

Moll. [Sings]   I dream there is a mistress,
                             And she lays out the money;
                           She goes unto her sisters;
                             She never comes at any.

Enter SIR ALEXANDER behind them [and remains concealed from them].

                  She says she went to th' Burse for patterns;   110
                    You shall find her at Saint Kathern's,
                      And comes home with never a penny.
Sebastian. That's a free mistress, faith.
Sir Alexander. [Aside] Ay, ay, ay, like her that sings it; one of thine
    own choosing.   115
Moll. But shall I dream again?
    [She sings.]   Here comes a wench will brave ye,
                            Her courage was so great;
                          She lay with one o' the navy,
                            Her husband lying i' the Fleet.   120
                          Yet oft with him she cavilled.
                            I wonder what she ails.
                          Her husband's ship lay gravelled
                            When hers could hoise up sails;
                          Yet she began, like all my foes,   125
                          To call whore first; for so do those.
                            A pox of all false tails!
Sebastian. Marry, amen, say I!
Sir Alexander. [Aside] So say I, too.
Moll. Hang up the viol now, sir; all this while I was in a dream.   130
    One shall lie rudely then; but being awake, I keep my legs
    together.—A watch: what's o'clock here?

---

108. *sisters*] (1) neighbours; (2) fellow prostitutes.

109. *any*] (1) any income; (2) any sexual partners or sexual fulfilment.

110. *Burse*] the original name for the Royal Exchange, an area surrounded by small shops selling fancy goods.

111. *Saint Kathern's*] a dockside district in the east end of London.

117. *will brave ye*] who will challenge you.

120. *Fleet*] (1) navy; (2) Fleet prison.

121. *cavilled*] found fault.

123. *gravelled*] beached, stranded.

124. *hoise up sails*] (1) hoist sail; (2) solicit as a prostitute.

126. *for . . . those*] for that's the way such people (including my enemies) behave.

127. *false tails*] (1) unreliable women; (2) diseased female genitals; (3) untrue stories.

131. *rudely*] i.e. with legs apart, like Moll when playing the viol.

Sir Alexander. [*Aside*] Now, now, she's trapped!

Moll. Between one and two; nay then I care not. A watch and a
musician are cousin-germans in one thing: they must both keep   135
time well or there's no goodness in 'em. The one else deserves
to be dashed against a wall, and t' other to have his brains
knocked out with a fiddle-case.   [*She sees the displayed objects.*]
What? A loose chain and a dangling diamond!
Here were a brave booty for an evening thief, now.   140
There's many a younger brother would be glad
To look twice in at a window for 't,
And wriggle in and out like an eel in a sandbag.
Oh, if men's secret youthful faults should judge 'em,
'Twould be the general'st execution   145
That e'er was seen in England!
There would be but few left to sing the ballads. There would be
so much work, most of our brokers would be chosen for hang-
men—a good day for them! They might renew their wardrobes
of free cost then.   150

Sebastian. [*To Mary*] This is the roaring wench must do us good.

Mary. [*To Sebastian*] No poison, sir, but serves us for some use,
Which is confirmed in her.

Sebastian.   Peace, peace!—
Foot, I did hear him sure, where'er he be.

Moll. Who did you hear?

Sebastian.   My father;   155
'Twas like a sigh of his. I must be wary.

Sir Alexander. [*Aside*] No? Will 't not be? Am I alone so wretched
That nothing takes? I'll put him to his plunge for 't.

Sebastian. [*Seeing Sir Alexander*] Life, here he comes!
                    [*Aloud to Moll*] Sir, I beseech you take it.
Your way of teaching does so much content me   160
I'll make it four pound; here's forty shillings, sir.

---

135. *cousin-germans*] first cousins, with a punning reference to the German watch
(see line 8).

141. *younger brother*] i.e. one not destined to inherit his father's land, and so in
need of cash.

145. *general'st*] involving everyone.

147. *ballads*] i.e. telling the stories of the crime and punishment of the hanged
people.

148. *brokers*] pimps.

149. *renew their wardrobes*] Hangmen traditionally received the hanged person's
clothes.

150. *of free cost*] free of charge.

154. *Foot*] i.e. by God's foot (an oath).

158. *takes*] takes effect, works, is successful.

plunge] crisis, dilemma.

I think I name it right. [*Aside to Moll*] Help me, good Moll.
[*Aloud*] Forty in hand.   [*Offering money*]
Moll.   Sir, you shall pardon me;
I have more of the meanest scholar I can teach.
This pays me more than you have offered yet.   165
Sebastian. At the next quarter,
When I receive the means my father 'lows me,
You shall have t' other forty.
Sir Alexander. [*Aside*]   This were well now,
Were 't to a man whose sorrows had blind eyes;
But mine behold his follies and untruths   170
With two clear glasses.   [*He comes forward.*]
                    [*To Sebastian*] How now?
Sebastian.   Sir?
Sir Alexander.   What's he there?
Sebastian. You're come in good time, sir. I've a suit to you;
I'd crave your present kindness.
Sir Alexander.   What is he there?
Sebastian. A gentleman, a musician, sir: one of excellent
      fing'ring—
Sir Alexander. Ay, I think so. [*Aside*] I wonder how they 'scaped her?   175
Sebastian. 'Has the most delicate stroke, sir—
Sir Alexander. [*Aside*] A stroke indeed. I feel it at my heart!
Sebastian. Puts down all your famous musicians.
Sir Alexander. [*Aside*] Ay. A whore may put down a hundred of
      'em!   180
Sebastian. Forty shillings is the agreement, sir, between us. Now,
      sir, my present means mounts but to half on 't.
Sir Alexander. And he stands upon the whole.
Sebastian. Ay indeed does he, sir.
Sir Alexander. And will do still; he'll ne'er be in other tale.   185
Sebastian. Therefore I'd stop his mouth, sir, an I could.

164.] I receive more than this from the poorest scholars I teach.

171, 173. *he*] i.e. Moll.

174. *fingering*] (1) musical fingering; (2) deftness in stealing; (3) sexual foreplay.

175. *I wonder . . . her*] Sir Alexander assumes Moll has not noticed the jewels set out to tempt her.

176–7. *stroke . . . stroke indeed*] There are multiple puns here: (1) on the bow stroke when playing a viol; (2) on heart stroke; (3) on sexual thrust. These double entendres trigger a sequence of bawdy puns, in *puts down, mounts, do, stands, tale* (*tail*), etc.

181. *Forty shillings*] Sebastian has originally offered Moll four pounds (see line 161) and said that he could only pay forty shillings (two pounds). He now says that the total sum is forty shillings. The confusion must be a mistake.

183. *stands . . . whole*] insists on the full payment.

185. *he'll . . . tale*] he (Moll) will never change his story (or forget the debt).

Sir Alexander. H'm, true. There is no other way indeed.
   [*Aside*] His folly hardens; shame must needs succeed.
   [*To Moll*] Now sir, I understand you profess music.
Moll. I am a poor servant to that liberal science, sir.   190
Sir Alexander. Where is it you teach?
Moll. Right against Clifford's Inn.
Sir Alexander. H'm, that's a fit place for it. You have many scholars?
Moll. And some of worth, whom I may call my masters.
Sir Alexander. [*Aside*] Ay, true, a company of whoremasters!   195
   [*To Moll*] You teach to sing, too?
Moll. Marry, do I, sir.
Sir Alexander. I think you'll find an apt scholar of my son, especially
   for prick-song.
Moll. I have much hope of him.   200
Sir Alexander. [*Aside*] I am sorry for 't; I have the less for that.
   [*To Moll*] You can play any lesson?
Moll. At first sight, sir.
Sir Alexander. There's a thing called 'The Witch'. Can you play
   that?   205
Moll. I would be sorry anyone should mend me in 't.
Sir Alexander. Ay, I believe thee. [*Aside*] Thou hast so bewitched
   my son,
   No care will mend the work that thou hast done.
   I have bethought myself, since my art fails,
   I'll make her policy the art to trap her.   210
   Here are four angels marked with holes in them,
   Fit for his cracked companions. Gold he will give her;
   These will I make induction to her ruin,
   And rid shame from my house, grief from my heart.
   [*To Sebastian*] Here, son, in what you take content and
   pleasure,   215

---

188. *succeed*] follow.
189. *profess*] claim expertise in.
190. *liberal science*] Music was one of the so-called liberal arts.
192. *against Clifford's Inn*] next to the oldest of the Inns of Chancery; on the north side of Fleet Street, between Chancery Lane and Fetter Lane.
199. *prick-song*] song with the music written (or 'pricked') down. The bawdy pun is standard.
206. *mend*] (1) improve on; (2) set right.
210.] I will use her own stratagem (of posing as a musician) as the means to entrap her.
211. *angels . . . them*] This plot is never fully carried through. It might have involved an accusation of theft with the marked coins used as evidence, or of possessing false coinage, which was a criminal offence.
212. *his*] Sebastian's.
cracked] morally blemished.

Want shall not curb you. [*He gives money.*] Pay the gentleman
His latter half in gold.
Sebastian.   I thank you, sir.
Sir Alexander. [*Aside*] Oh, may the operation on 't end three:
In her, life; shame in him; and grief in me! *Exit* ALEXANDER.
Sebastian. [*Giving Moll the money*] Faith, thou shalt have 'em; 'tis
my father's gift.   220
Never was man beguiled with better shift.
Moll. He that can take me for a male musician,
I cannot choose but make him my instrument
And play upon him.   *Exeunt omnes.*

[4.2]

Enter MRS GALLIPOT *and* MRS OPENWORK.

Mrs Gallipot. Is then that bird of yours, Master Goshawk, so wild?
Mrs Openwork. A goshawk, a puttock, all for prey! He angles for
fish, but he loves flesh better.
Mrs Gallipot. Is 't possible his smooth face should have wrinkles in
't, and we not see them?   5
Mrs Openwork. Possible? Why, have not many handsome legs in silk
stockings villainous splay feet for all their great roses?
Mrs Gallipot. Troth, sirrah, thou sayst true.
Mrs Openwork. Didst never see an archer, as thou'st walked by
Bunhill, look asquint when he drew his bow?   10
Mrs Gallipot. Yes; when his arrows have fline toward Islington, his
eyes have shot clean contrary towards Pimlico.
Mrs Openwork. For all the world, so does Master Goshawk double
with me.
Mrs Gallipot. Oh, fie upon him! If he double once, he's not for me. 15
Mrs Openwork. Because Goshawk goes in a shag-ruff band, with a

---

217. *His . . . gold*] The remaining forty shillings Sebastian owes (see lines 161–3).
221. *beguiled . . . shift*] tricked by a more clever stratagem.

4.2.2. *puttock*] kite hawk.
7. *great roses*] ornamental knots of ribbon in the shape of a rose, tied at the front
of a shoe. The idea that the devil would hide his cloven hoof with great roses was
commonplace.
8. *sirrah*] sometimes used to address women. (Also in lines 31, 41, and 62.)
10. *Bunhill*] a street on the west side of the Artillery Ground near Moorfields.
11. *fline*] flown.
11–12. *Islington . . . Pimlico*] districts of London, Islington to the north-east and
Pimlico to the south-west. The point is that the archer's eyes seem to go in the
opposite direction to his arrows.
15. *double*] act deceitfully.
16–17. *in a shag-ruff . . . in 't*] with his small head sticking out of an enormous
ruff.

face sticking up in 't which shows like an agate set in a cramp-
ring, he thinks I'm in love with him.

Mrs Gallipot. 'Las, I think he takes his mark amiss in thee.

Mrs Openwork. He has, by often beating into me, made me believe   20
that my husband kept a whore.

Mrs Gallipot. Very good.

Mrs Openwork. Swore to me that my husband this very morning
went in a boat with a tilt over it to the Three Pigeons at
Brentford, and his punk with him under his tilt.   25

Mrs Gallipot. That were wholesome!

Mrs Openwork. I believed it; fell a-swearing at him, cursing of harlots, made me ready to hoise up sail and be there as soon as he.

Mrs Gallipot. So, so.

Mrs Openwork. And for that voyage, Goshawk comes hither   30
incontinently. But, sirrah, this water-spaniel dives after no duck
but me; his hope is having me at Brentford to make me cry
quack.

Mrs Gallipot. Art sure of it?

Mrs Openwork. Sure of it? My poor innocent Openwork came in as   35
I was poking my ruff; presently hit I him i' the teeth with the
Three Pigeons. He forswore all. I up and opened all, and now
stands he, in a shop hard by, like a musket on a rest, to hit
Goshawk i' the eye when he comes to fetch me to the boat.

Mrs Gallipot. Such another lame gelding offered to carry me   40
through thick and thin—Laxton, sirrah—but I am rid of him
now.

Mrs Openwork. Happy is the woman can be rid of 'em all! 'Las, what
are your whisking gallants to our husbands, weigh 'em rightly,
man for man?   45

17–18. *cramp-ring*] ring worn as a protection against the cramp.

19. *takes . . . thee*] aims in the wrong direction in pursuing you.

20. *often . . . me*] i.e. repeatedly telling me.

24, 25. *tilt*] boat awning.

31. *incontinently*] immediately.

32–3. *cry quack*] continuing the image of Mrs Openwork as the duck pursued by
the water-spaniel Goshawk (see lines 31–2). As a duck she will *cry quack* in orgasm.

36. *poking my ruff*] stiffening the pleats on my ruff by laying each one over a stick
and leaving them to dry while the ruff was wet with starch. (The process was a
continual source of bawdy jokes.)

hit . . . with] confronted him with.

37. *opened all*] revealed all I knew.

38. *a musket . . . rest*] a gun at the ready. Heavy muskets had to be supported by
a forked wooden pole.

40. *gelding*] castrated horse. Mrs Gallipot plays on Laxton's (Lacks stones)
name, in a comic culmination of the play on horsemanship and sex which has
characterized the Laxton plot.

44. *whisking*] brisk, lively.

to] compared to.

Mrs Gallipot. Troth, mere shallow things.

Mrs Openwork. Idle, simple things, running heads. And yet—let 'em run over us never so fast—we shopkeepers, when all's done, are sure to have 'em in our purse-nets at length, and when they are in, Lord, what simple animals they are! Then they hang the 50 head—

Mrs Gallipot. Then they droop—

Mrs Openwork. Then they write letters—

Mrs Gallipot. Then they cog—

Mrs Openwork. Then deal they underhand with us, and we must 55 ingle with our husbands abed; and we must swear they are our cousins, and able to do us a pleasure at court.

Mrs Gallipot. And yet when we have done our best, all's but put into a riven dish; we are but frumped at and libelled upon.

Mrs Openwork. Oh, if it were the good Lord's will there were a law 60 made, no citizen should trust any of 'em all!

Enter GOSHAWK.

Mrs Gallipot. Hush, sirrah! Goshawk flutters.

Goshawk. How now, are you ready?

Mrs Openwork. Nay, are you ready? A little thing, you see, makes us ready. 65

Goshawk. Us? [*To Mrs Openwork*] Why, must she make one i' the voyage?

Mrs Openwork. Oh, by any means. Do I know how my husband will handle me?

Goshawk. [*Aside*] Foot, how shall I find water to keep these two 70 mills going? [*To them*] Well, since you'll needs be clapped under

---

47. *running heads*] footmen, lackeys; with the suggestion of a diseased, dripping penis

49. *purse-nets*] nets which could be pulled into a drawstring bag, used for catching rabbits; slang for vagina.

49–50. *when . . . in*] with a suggestion of male inadequacy at sexual intercourse. The image is continued in *droop* line 52.

54. *cog*] cheat, fawn; wheedle.

56. *ingle*] fondle, caress (as compensation or to allay suspicion).

swear] i.e. to our husbands.

they] i.e. the gallants.

58–9. *all's . . . riven dish*] all our effort is wasted. *Riven* means broken.

59. *frumped at*] mocked.

64. *A little thing*] Mrs Openwork quips that women are ready sooner than men—with a bawdy hint of being ready for sex, and perhaps with a disparaging putdown of men and their supposed sexual prowess.

68–9. *Do . . . me?*] Mrs Openwork suggests that having Mrs Gallipot along will protect her from Openwork's suspicions.

70. *water*] energy (with a suggestion of semen).

71. *mills*] References to grinding mills often carried sexual meaning. Goshawk is wondering how to keep two women satisfied at once.

71–2. *clapped under hatches*] (1) stowed safely on board; (2) fornicated with.

hatches, if I sail not with you both till all split, hang me up at the
main-yard and duck me. [*Aside*] It's but liquoring them both
soundly, and then you shall see their cork heels fly up high, like
two swans when their tails are above water and their long necks   75
under water, diving to catch gudgeons. [*To them*] Come, come!
Oars stand ready; the tide's with us. On with those false faces.
Blow winds, and thou shalt take thy husband casting out his net
to catch fresh salmon at Brentford.

Mrs Gallipot. I believe you'll eat of a cod's-head of your own dress-   80
ing before you reach half way thither.

Goshawk. So, so, follow close. Pin as you go.

                        [*The women put on masks.*]

            Enter LAXTON *muffled.*

Laxton. Do you hear?   [*He talks apart with Mrs Gallipot.*]

Mrs Gallipot. Yes, I thank my ears.

Laxton. I must have a bout with your pothecary-ship.   85

Mrs Gallipot. At what weapon?

Laxton. I must speak with you.

Mrs Gallipot. No!

Laxton. No? You shall!

Mrs Gallipot. Shall? Away, soused sturgeon, half fish, half flesh!   90

Laxton. Faith, gib, are you spitting? I'll cut your tail, puss-cat, for
this.

Mrs Gallipot. 'Las, poor Laxton, I think thy tail's cut already. Your
worst!

---

72. *till all split*] until we are shipwrecked. The phrase was also commonly used to
mean 'to the utmost'.

72–3. *hang . . . duck me*] suspend me from the boom of the main-sail and drop
me into the water. Goshawk is affecting seafaring language, comical when they are
only going on a short trip up river.

73–4. *liquoring . . . soundly*] getting them thoroughly drunk.

74. *cork heels*] high heels made of cork.

76. *gudgeons*] small fish used for bait.

77. *false faces*] masks, commonly worn by women.

79–80. *salmon . . . cod's head*] contrasting the most expensive with the cheapest
fish in the familiar connection between fishing, eating and sex. Gallipot will be
caught hunting for new prostitutes; Goshawk will be foiled by his own foolish
pleasures.

82. *Pin*] i.e. pin your mask.

85. *a bout*] an encounter (with a sexual suggestion).

90. *soused sturgeon*] pickled fish; a low insult.

half fish, half flesh] neither one thing nor another; possibly refers to Laxton's
ambiguous sexuality.

91. *gib*] cat.

93. *tail's cut*] suggesting that Laxton is impotent.

93–4. *Your worst*] i.e. Do your worst. An aggressive response to a gesture from
Laxton.

Laxton. If I do not—   *Exit* LAXTON.   95
Goshawk. Come, ha' you done?

Enter MASTER OPENWORK.

    [*To Mrs Openwork*] 'Sfoot, Rosamond, your husband!
Openwork. How now? Sweet Master Goshawk! None more
    welcome!
    I have wanted your embracements. When friends meet,
    The music of the spheres sounds not more sweet
    Than does their conference. Who is this? Rosamond?   100
    Wife? [*To Mrs Gallipot*] How now, sister?
Goshawk. [*To Mrs Openwork*] Silence, if you love me!
Openwork. Why masked?
Mrs Openwork. Does a mask grieve you, sir?
Openwork. It does.   105
Mrs Openwork. Then you're best get you a-mumming.
Goshawk. [*Aside to Mrs Openwork*] 'Sfoot, you'll spoil all!
Mrs Gallipot. May not we cover our bare faces with masks
    As well as you cover your bald heads with hats?
Openwork. No masks. Why, they're thieves to beauty, that rob eyes   110
    Of admiration in which true love lies.
    Why are masks worn? Why good? Or why desired?
    Unless by their gay covers wits are fired
    To read the vil'st looks. Many bad faces—
    Because rich gems are treasured up in cases—   115
    Pass by their privilege current; but as caves
    Damn misers' gold, so masks are beauties' graves.
    Men ne'er meet women with such muffled eyes
    But they curse her that first did masks devise,
    And swear it was some beldame. Come, off with 't.   120
Mrs Openwork. I will not.
Openwork. Good faces, masked, are jewels kept by sprites.
    Hide none but bad ones, for they poison men's sights;
    Show them as shopkeepers do their broidered stuff,

---

98. *wanted*] missed; desired.

99. *music of the spheres*] The heavenly spheres holding the planets in the Ptolemaic system were thought to make perfect music as they spun round. Perfect love made them audible.

106. *you're . . . a-mumming*] you'd best go round with the mummers' plays. (An impudent response.)

114-16. *Many . . . current*] Just as gems are hidden in cases, people imagine that the face behind a mask must also be good, and so a bad (old, out of date) face can pass as a good (young, genuine, currently acceptable) one.

116-17. *as caves . . . gold*] Hoarding money or goods, keeping them out of the markct, was considered morally reprehensible.

120. *beldame*] hag.

By owl-light; fine wares cannot be open enough.   125
Prithee, sweet Rose, come strike this sail.
Mrs Openwork.   Sail?
Openwork.   Ha?
   Yes, wife, strike sail, for storms are in thine eyes.
Mrs Openwork. They're here, sir, in my brows, if any rise.
Openwork. Ha, brows? [*To Mrs Gallipot*] What says she, friend?
   [*To them both*] Pray tell me why
   Your two flags were advanced. The comedy?   130
   Come, what's the comedy?
Mrs Gallipot.   *Westward Ho.*
Openwork.   How?
Mrs Openwork. 'Tis *Westward Ho*, she says.
Goshawk.   Are you both mad?
Mrs Openwork. Is 't market day at Brentford, and your ware
   Not sent up yet?
Openwork.   What market day? What ware?
Mrs Openwork. A pie with three pigeons in 't; 'tis drawn and stays   135
   your cutting up.
Goshawk. [*Aside to Mrs Openwork*] As you regard my credit—
Openwork. [*To Mrs Openwork*] Art mad?
Mrs Openwork. Yes, lecherous goat! Baboon!
Openwork. Baboon? Then toss me in a blanket.   140
Mrs Openwork. [*Aside to Mrs Gallipot*] Do I it well?
Mrs Gallipot. [*To Mrs Openwork*] Rarely!
Goshawk. [*To Openwork*] Belike, sir, she's not well; best leave her.
Openwork.   No,

---

125. *owl-light*] twilight, half light. The bad lighting in drapers' shops, suggesting that they were trying to sell shoddy goods, was a frequent source of jokes.

126. *strike this sail*] i.e. pull down this mask.

128. *in my brows*] This requires a gesture to her forehead, indicating that her anger (the storms in her eyes) is a result of her being affronted by Openwork's supposed infidelity.

130. *flags*] i.e. masks.

flags . . . comedy] Playhouses flew flags when they were open for performances.

131. Westward Ho] the cry of the Thames boatmen, indicating the direction in which they would take customers; also the title of a comedy by Dekker and Webster in which citizens' wives are taken westward to Brentford by gallants but do not allow themselves to be seduced.

135. *three pigeons*] playing on the name of the inn at Brentford.

drawn] taken from the oven. Mrs Openwork is making sly references to Goshawk's allegations against her husband.

stays] awaits.

137. *regard my credit*] care about my reputation.

140. *toss . . . blanket*] a rough, humiliating punishment. Openwork is denying his wife's accusation.

143. *Belike*] perhaps.

I'll stand the storm now, how fierce soe'er it blow.
Mrs Openwork. Did I for this lose all my friends? Refuse   145
    Rich hopes and golden fortunes to be made
    A stale to a common whore?
Openwork.   This does amaze me!
Mrs Openwork. Oh, God, oh, God! Feed at reversion now?
    A strumpet's leaving?
Openwork. Rosamond!   150
Goshawk. [*Aside*] I sweat! Would I lay in Cold Harbour.
Mrs Openwork. [*To Openwork*] Thou hast struck ten thousand
    daggers through my heart.
Openwork. Not I, by heaven, sweet wife.
Mrs Openwork. Go, devil, go! That which thou swear'st by damns
    thee!
Goshawk. [*Aside to Mrs Openwork*] 'S heart, will you undo me?   155
Mrs Openwork. [*To Openwork*] Why stay you here? The star by
    which you sail
    Shines yonder above Chelsea; you lose your shore.
    If this moon light you, seek out your light whore.
Openwork. Ha?
Mrs Gallipot. Push! Your western pug!   160
Goshawk. [*Aside*] Zounds, now hell roars!
Mrs Openwork. With whom you tilted in a pair of oars
    This very morning.
Openwork.   Oars?
Mrs Openwork.   At Brentford, sir!
Openwork. Rack not my patience.—Master Goshawk,
    Some slave has buzzed this into her, has he not?—   165
    I run a-tilt in Brentford with a woman?
    'Tis a lie!
    What old bawd tells thee this? 'Sdeath, 'tis a lie!
Mrs Openwork. 'Tis one to thy face shall justify all that I speak.
Openwork. Ud' soul, do but name that rascal!   170

---

147. *A stale*] a former lover or mistress whose devotion is turned into ridicule.
148. *reversion*] remains or leftovers from a meal.
151. *Cold Harbour*] a slum area near London Bridge. Goshawk plays on the name, wishing for a cold place which would relieve his sweating.
154. *That . . . thee*] i.e. heaven itself, to which you appeal, damns you.
156. *The star . . . sail*] i.e. the whore that you follow.
157. *above Chelsea*] in the direction of Chelsea. Chelsea was a village on the river, west of London on the way to Brentford.
158. *light . . . light*] provide illumination like the moon's light . . . frivolous, wanton.
162. *pair of oars*] boat rowed by two men.
165. *buzzed*] whispered.
169. *'Tis one*] the *old bawd* you talk about is one who.
170. *Ud' soul*] God bless my soul.

Mrs Openwork. No, sir, I will not.

Goshawk. [*Aside*] Keep thee there, girl. [*To them*] Then!

Openwork. [*To Mrs Gallipot*] Sister, know you this varlet?

Mrs Gallipot. Yes.

Openwork. Swear true;   175
    Is there a rogue so low damned? A second Judas?
    A common hangman? Cutting a man's throat?
    Does it to his face? Bite me behind my back?
    A cur-dog? Swear if you know this hell-hound.

Mrs Gallipot. In truth I do.

Openwork.   His name?

Mrs Gallipot.   Not for the world,   180
    To have you to stab him.

Goshawk. [*Aside*]   O brave girls! Worth gold!

Openwork. A word, honest Master Goshawk.
                                      Draw[*s*] *out his sword.*

Goshawk. What do you mean, sir?

Openwork. Keep off, and if the devil can give a name
    To this new fury, holla it through my ear,   185
    Or wrap it up in some hid character.
    I'll ride to Oxford and watch out mine eyes,
    But I'll hear the Brazen Head speak; or else
    Show me but one hair of his head or beard,
    That I may sample it. If the fiend I meet   190
    In mine own house, I'll kill him—the street,
    Or at the church door. There, 'cause he seeks to untie
    The knot God fastens, he deserves most to die!

Mrs Openwork. [*Aside to Mrs Gallipot*] My husband titles him!

Openwork.   Master Goshawk, pray, sir,
    Swear to me that you know him or know him not,   195
    Who makes me at Brentford to take up a petticoat
    Besides my wife's.

Goshawk.   By heaven, that man I know not.

---

172. *Then!*] That's enough!

173. *this varlet*] Goshawk.

186. *hid character*] secret code.

187. *watch . . . eyes*] i.e. keep awake until my eyes drop out.

188. *Brazen Head*] referring to the legend of the Brazen Head of Brasenose
College, Oxford which reputedly prophesied and told secrets.

189. *his*] i.e. the seducer's. Openwork will do anything to find out the seducer's
name.

193. *The knot God fastens*] holy matrimony.

194. *My . . . him*] Openwork is addressing the very seducer he rages against!

196. *makes . . . petticoat*] reports me as taking up with a whore at Brentford.

Mrs Openwork. Come, come, you lie!
Goshawk.   Will you not have all out?
    [*To Openwork*] By heaven, I know no man beneath the moon
    Should do you wrong, but, if I had his name,   200
    I'd print it in text letters.
Mrs Openwork. [*To Goshawk*] Print thine own, then.
    Didst not thou swear to me he kept his whore?
Mrs Gallipot. And that in sinful Brentford they would commit
    That which our lips did water at, sir? Ha?
Mrs Openwork. Thou spider, that hast woven thy cunning web   205
    In mine own house t' ensnare me, hast not thou
    Sucked nourishment even underneath this roof
    And turned it all to poison, spitting it
    On thy friend's face, my husband—he as 'twere, sleeping—
    Only to leave him ugly to mine eyes,   210
    That they might glance on thee?
Mrs Gallipot.   Speak, are these lies?
Goshawk. Mine own shame me confounds.
Openwork.   No more, he's stung.
    Who'd think that in one body there could dwell
    Deformity and beauty, heaven and hell?
    Goodness, I see, is but outside; we all set,   215
    In rings of gold, stones that he counterfeit.
    I thought you none.
Goshawk.   Pardon me.
Openwork.   Truth, I do.
    This blemish grows in nature, not in you;
    For man's creation stick even moles in scorn
    On fairest cheeks.—Wife, nothing is perfect born.   220
Mrs Openwork. I thought you had been born perfect.
Openwork. What's this whole world but a gilt rotten pill?
    For at the heart lies the old core still.
    I'll tell you, Master Goshawk, ay, in your eye
    I have seen wanton fire; and then to try   225

---

198. *Will . . . out?*] either an aside to Mrs Openwork bidding her be quiet, or a bold show of innocence.
    200. *Should do*] who allegedly did.
    201. *text letters*] large or capital letters.
    202. *he*] Openwork.
    204. *did water at*] i.e. in erotic anticipation.
    218. *nature*] human nature generally.
    219–20. *For . . . checks*] referring to the practice of putting artificial moles on the face to set off unblemished cheeks.
    222–3.] The opposition between a golden outside and a rotten core was proverbial.

The soundness of my judgement, I told you
I kept a whore, made you believe 'twas true,
Only to feel how your pulse beat, but find
The world can hardly yield a perfect friend.
Come, come, a trick of youth, and 'tis forgiven;   230
This rub put by, our love shall run more even.
Mrs Openwork. You'll deal upon men's wives no more?
Goshawk.   No. You teach me
A trick for that!
Mrs Openwork.   Troth, do not; they'll o'erreach thee.
Openwork. Make my house yours, sir, still.
Goshawk.   No.
Openwork.   I say you shall.
Seeing, thus besieged, it holds out, 'twill never fall!   235

Enter MASTER GALLIPOT, *and* GREENWIT *like a sumner*
[*wearing a wig*]; LAXTON *muffled, aloof off.*

All. How now?
Gallipot. [*To Greenwit*] With me, sir?
Greenwit. [*To Gallipot*] You, sir. I have gone snuffling up and down
by your door this hour to watch for you.
Mrs Gallipot. What's the matter, husband?   240
Greenwit. I have caught a cold in my head, sir, by sitting up late in
the Rose Tavern, but I hope you understand my speech.
Gallipot. So, sir.
Greenwit. I cite you by the name of Hippocrates Gallipot, and you
by the name of Prudence Gallipot, to appear upon *Crastino*—do   245
you see—*Crastino Sancti Dunstani*, this Easter Term, in Bow
Church.
Gallipot. Where, sir?—What says he?
Greenwit. Bow—Bow Church, to answer to a libel of precontract on

---

231. *rub*] obstacle, difficulty. (A technical term in the game of bowls.)
232. *deal upon*] proceed against, set to work upon.
235.] Since our household has withstood this assault, it can never fall.
235.1. a sumner] a summoner; an officer in an ecclesiastical court who summoned persons to appear there.
235.2. aloof off] at a distance.
242. *understand . . . speech*] Greenwit is talking through his nose.
244-9. *I cite . . . libel*] In ecclesiastical court procedure, the offender was summoned to court by a writ of citation and was charged on his appearance there.
244. *Hippocrates*] Gallipot is comically given the name of the founder of medicine.
246. Crastino . . . Dunstani] i.e. the morrow after St Dunstan's day.
246-7. *Bow Church*] situated at the upper end of Hosier (Bow) Lane.
248.] Gallipot has difficulty in understanding Greenwit through his snuffling.
249. *precontract*] the charge that Prudence was betrothed to someone else when she married Gallipot. Laxton is using Mrs Gallipot's own device to extract yet more money from the Gallipots.

the part and behalf of the said Prudence and another. You're   250
best, sir, take a copy of the citation; 'tis but twelvepence.
                                        [*He offers a citation.*]
All. A citation?
Gallipot. You pocky-nosed rascal, what slave fees you to this?
Laxton. Slave? [*Comes forward; aside to Goshawk*] I ha' nothing to do
   with you, do you hear, sir?   255
Goshawk. [*Aside to Laxton*] Laxton, is 't not? What vagary is this?
Gallipot. [*To Laxton*] Trust me, I thought, sir, this storm long ago
   Had been full laid, when—if you be remembered—
   I paid you the last fifteen pound, besides
   The thirty you had first; for then you swore—   260
Laxton. Tush, tush, sir, oaths—
   Truth, yet I'm loath to vex you. Tell you what:
   Make up the money I had an hundred pound,
   And take your bellyful of her.
Gallipot.   An hundred pound?
Mrs Gallipot. What, a hundred pound? He gets none!   265
   What, a hundred pound?
Gallipot. Sweet Prue, be calm; the gentleman offers thus:
   If I will make the moneys that are past
   A hundred pound, he will discharge all courts
   And give his bond never to vex us more.   270
Mrs Gallipot. A hundred pound? 'Las, take, sir, but threescore.
   [*Aside to Laxton*] Do you seek my undoing?
Laxton.   I'll not bate one sixpence.
   [*Aside to Mrs Gallipot*] I'll maul you, puss, for spitting.
Mrs Gallipot. [*Aside to Laxton*]   Do thy worst!
   [*Aloud*] Will fourscore stop thy mouth?
Laxton.   No.
Mrs Gallipot.   You're a slave!
   Thou cheat! I'll now tear money from thy throat.—   275
   Husband, lay hold on yonder tawny-coat.

---

250. *another*] i.e. Laxton.
253. *pocky-nosed*] Gallipot insinuates that Greenwit's snuffling is a sign of syphilis, not a cold.
256. *vagary*] detour, new twist to the story.
259. *last fifteen pound*] a transaction not shown on stage.
263.] Make up the money already given to a hundred pounds.
269–70. *discharge . . . bond*] Gallipot recognizes the need to get a written agreement in order to forestall future litigation.
271. *take . . . threescore*] settle for sixty pounds.
272. *bate*] deduct.
273. *maul*] beat, with a pun on 'maule', to cry like a cat.
276. *tawny-coat*] Greenwit is disguised in the tawny-coloured livery of a summoner.

Greenwit. Nay, gentlemen, seeing your women are so hot,
I must lose my hair in their company, I see.
                                        [*He removes his wig.*]
Mrs Openwork. His hair sheds off, and yet he speaks not so much in
the nose as he did before.   280
Goshawk. He has had the better chirurgeon.—Master Greenwit, is
your wit so raw as to play no better a part than a sumner's?
Gallipot. I pray, who plays *A Knack to Know an Honest Man* in this
company?
Mrs Gallipot. Dear husband, pardon me! I did dissemble,   285
Told thee I was his precontracted wife.
When letters came from him for thirty pound,
I had no shift but that.
Gallipot. [*To Mrs Gallipot*] A very clean shift, but able to make me
lousy. On.   290
Mrs Gallipot. Husband, I plucked—when he had tempted me to
think well of him—gilt feathers from thy wings, to make him fly
more lofty.
Gallipot. O' the top of you, wife. On.
Mrs Gallipot. He, having wasted them, comes now for more,   295
Using me as a ruffian doth his whore,
Whose sin keeps him in breath. By heaven, I vow,
Thy bed he never wronged more than he does now.
Gallipot. My bed? Ha, ha, like enough! A shop-board will serve to
have a cuckold's coat cut out upon; of that we'll talk hereafter.   300
[*To Laxton*] You're a villain!
Laxton. Hear me but speak, sir! You shall find me none.
All. Pray, sir, be patient and hear him.
Gallipot. I am muzzled for biting, sir; use me how you will.

---

277. *so hot*] so sexually eager.

278. *lose my hair*] playing on the loss of hair from venereal disease and the action
of removing his disguising wig.

279–80.] Mrs Openwork extends the joke by her surprise that the syphilis which
has caused his loss of hair has reduced its effect on his nose.

282. *wit so raw*] skill so under-developed; playing on Greenwit's name.

283. A Knack to Know an Honest Man] alluding to an anonymous comedy
played by the Admiral's Men in 1594. Gallipot's point is that it would take quite a
knack to know an honest man in the present company.

288–9. *shift . . . shift*] device . . . undershirt.

290. *On*] Go on, continue with your explanation.

292. *gilt*] golden. The Quarto text reads 'Get'.

294. *O' the . . . wife*] Gallipot jibes that Laxton's high flying allowed him to 'top'
Mrs Gallipot sexually.

297. *in breath*] alive.

299–300. *A shop-board . . . upon*] suggesting that Laxton and Prudence did not
need to wrong Gallipot's bed; they could have had sex on the shop counter where
cloth is usually cut.

304. *for*] to prevent.

Laxton. The first hour that your wife was in my eye,   305
　　Myself with other gentlemen sitting by
　　In your shop tasting smoke, and speech being used
　　That men who have fairest wives are most abused
　　And hardly scaped the horn, your wife maintained
　　That only such spots in city dames were stained   310
　　Justly but by men's slanders; for her own part,
　　She vowed that you had so much of her heart,
　　No man by all his wit, by any wile
　　Never so fine spun, should yourself beguile
　　Of what in her was yours.
Gallipot.　　　　　　　　　Yet, Prue, 'tis well.—   315
　　Play out your game at Irish, sir. Who wins?
Mrs Openwork. The trial is when she comes to bearing.
Laxton. I scorned one woman, thus, should brave all men,
　　And—which more vexed me—a she-citizen;
　　Therefore I laid siege to her. Out she held,   320
　　Gave many a brave repulse, and me compelled
　　With shame to sound retreat to my hot lust.
　　Then, seeing all base desires raked up in dust,
　　And that to tempt her modest ears I swore
　　Ne'er to presume again, she said her eye   325
　　Would ever give me welcome honestly;
　　And—since I was a gentleman—if it run low,
　　She would my state relieve, not to o'erthrow
　　Your own and hers; did so. Then, seeing I wrought
　　Upon her meekness, me she set at naught;   330
　　And yet to try if I could turn that tide,
　　You see what stream I strove with. But, sir, I swear
　　By heaven and by those hopes men lay up there,

305–37.] Laxton tells a story in which he suggests that he was only testing Mrs
Gallipot's assertions of fidelity to her husband; a familiar romance plot. See Intro.,
pp. 23–4.

309. *scaped the horn*] avoided being cuckolded.

310–11. *That . . . slanders*] that accusations of infidelity made against city wives
were just only when they were not the result of men's slanders.

314. *should . . . beguile*] would be able to cheat you.

316. *Irish*] a board game, similar to backgammon. It took a long time to complete a game.

317. *bearing*] the term for removing a piece at the end of a game of Irish or
backgammon; with a pun on 'child bearing'.

318.] I was contemptuous of the idea that one woman should stand out against
all men like that.

323. *raked up in dust*] smothered (as in putting out a fire by throwing earth on it,
with a reminder of the biblical notion that all human life is dust).

330. *meekness*] compassion.
me . . . naught] she despised me.

I neither have nor had a base intent
To wrong your bed. What's done is merriment;   335
Your gold I pay back with this interest:
When I had most power to do 't, I wronged you least.

Gallipot. If this no gullery be, sir—

All.   No, no, on my life!

Gallipot. Then, sir, I am beholden—not to you, wife—
But Master Laxton, to your want of doing ill,   340
Which it seems you have not.—Gentlemen,
Tarry and dine here all.

Openwork.   Brother, we have a jest
As good as yours to furnish out a feast.

Gallipot. We'll crown our table with it.—Wife, brag no more
Of holding out. Who most brags is most whore.   345

                                                    Exeunt omnes.

---

343. *furnish out*] supply the entertainment for.
345. *Who*] whoever.

Act 5

Enter JACK DAPPER, MOLL [*dressed as a man*], SIR BEAUTEOUS
GANYMEDE, *and* SIR THOMAS LONG.

Jack Dapper. But prithee, Master Captain Jack, be plain and per-
spicuous with me: was it your Meg of Westminster's courage
that rescued me from the Poultry puttocks, indeed?

Moll. The valour of my wit, I ensure you, sir, fetched you off bravely
when you were i' the forlorn hope among those desperates. Sir 5
Beauteous Ganymede here and Sir Thomas Long heard that
cuckoo—my man Trapdoor—sing the note of your ransom
from captivity.

Sir Beauteous. Uds-so, Moll, where's that Trapdoor?

Moll. Hanged, I think, by this time; a justice in this town, that 10
speaks nothing but 'Make a mittimus, away with him to
Newgate', used that rogue like a firework to run upon a line
betwixt him and me.

All. How, how?

Moll. Marry, to lay trains of villainy to blow up my life. I smelt the 15
powder, spied what linstock gave fire to shoot against the poor
captain of the galley-foist, and away slid I my man like a shovel-

---

5.1.1. *Master Captain Jack*] Not knowing what to call Moll when she is disguised
as a man, Jack Dapper gives her a generalized title.

2. *Meg of Westminster*] a legendary powerful woman. See Intro., p. 27.

3. *Poultry puttocks*] i.e. officers of the Poultry Counter Prison.

7. *cuckoo*] (1) fool; (2) ungrateful intruder (referring to the cuckoo laying its eggs
in another bird's nest).

11–12. *Make . . . Newgate*] send him to prison; apparently a proverbial expression to characterize a stupidly severe magistrate.

12–13. *used . . . me*] i.e. used Trapdoor like a long trail of gunpowder to lead
from him to me. Moll has discovered the plot between Trapdoor and Sir Alexander.
For special effects fireworks could be made to run along a fuse before exploding at
some distance away.

15. *trains*] stratagems, tricks; also, lines of gunpowder laid as a fuse to an explosive charge. (Moll speaks metaphorically.)

16–17. *spied . . . galley-foist*] i.e. saw how the trail of gunpowder was being lit to
fire against poor me. A *linstock* is a forked staff to hold the gunner's match. A *galley-
foist* is a state barge used for celebrations like the Lord Mayor's show (at which
fireworks would also have been used).

17. *away . . . man*] i.e. I quickly got rid of my man (Trapdoor).

board shilling. He struts up and down the suburbs, I think, and
eats up whores, feeds upon a bawd's garbage.

Sir Thomas. Sirrah Jack Dapper—   20

Jack Dapper. What say'st, Tom Long?

Sir Thomas. Thou hadst a sweet-faced boy, hail-fellow with thee to
your little Gull: how is he spent?

Jack Dapper. Troth, I whistled the poor little buzzard off o' my fist
because when he waited upon me at the ordinaries the gallants   25
hit me i' the teeth still and said I looked like a painted alderman's tomb, and the boy at my elbow like a death's head.—
Sirrah Jack, Moll.

Moll. What says my little Dapper?

Sir Beauteous. Come, come, walk and talk, walk and talk.   30

Jack Dapper. Moll and I'll be i' the midst.

Moll. These knights shall have squires' places, belike then.—Well,
Dapper, what say you?

Jack Dapper. Sirrah Captain Mad Mary, the gull, my own father—
Dapper, Sir Davy—laid these London boot-halers, the catch-   35
poles, in ambush to set upon me.

All. Your father? Away, Jack!

Jack Dapper. By the tassels of this handkercher, 'tis true; and what
was his warlike stratagem, think you? He thought, because a

17–18. *shovel-board shilling*] a coin used in the game of shovel-board in which the
coin was shoved along a polished board to land on numbered compartments.

19. *eats up whores*] pimps for whores and takes the bulk of their earnings, besides
sleeping with them.

feeds . . . garbage] i.e. lives parasitically off prostitution.

22–3. *hail-fellow . . . Gull*] a close partner to your regular servant, Gull.

23. *how . . . spent?*] what has become of him? (*spent* means 'used up', 'employed').

24. *whistled . . . off*] sent off, released from (in falconry).

buzzard] inferior kind of hawk, useless for falconry.

25. *ordinaries*] eating houses.

26. *hit . . . still*] teased me continually.

26–7. *painted alderman's tomb*] coloured effigy placed on the sumptuous tomb of
a city father.

27. *death's head*] skull, placed as a *memento mori* on a tomb.

28. *Sirrah Jack, Moll*] Dapper addresses Moll both with her own name and a
generic name for a man (see 5.1.1), drawing attention to her ambiguous gender.

32. *These knights . . . places*] Jack arranges the characters on stage in a line with
himself and Moll in the middle and the knights at either end where squires would
normally stand in ceremonies.

35. *boot-halers*] highwaymen.

35–6. *catchpoles*] petty officers of justice, originally used neutrally for those who
collected taxes but always contemptuous and pejorative in early modern drama.

37. *Away, Jack!*] expression of surprise and disbelief, as in 'Get away!' or 'You
don't say!'

38. *tassels*] Small handkerchiefs with tassels or buttons at the corners were worn
in hats as decorations.

wicker cage tames a nightingale, a lousy prison could make an   40
ass of me.

All. A nasty plot!

Jack Dapper. Ay—as though a counter, which is a park in which all
the wild beasts of the city run head by head, could tame me!

Enter the LORD NOLAND.

Moll. Yonder comes my Lord Noland.   45

All. Save you, my lord.

Lord Noland. Well met, gentlemen all: good Sir Beauteous
Ganymede, Sir Thomas Long—and how does Master Dapper?

Jack Dapper. Thanks, my lord.

Moll. No tobacco, my lord?   50

Lord Noland. No, faith, Jack.

Jack Dapper. My Lord Noland, will you go to Pimlico with us? We
are making a boon voyage to that nappy land of spice cakes.

Lord Noland. Here's such a merry ging, I could find in my heart to
sail to the world's end with such company. Come, gentlemen,   55
let's on.

Jack Dapper. Here's most amorous weather, my lord.

All. Amorous weather?   *They walk.*

Jack Dapper. Is not 'amorous' a good word?

Enter TRAPDOOR *like a poor soldier with a patch o'er one eye,*
and TEARCAT *with him, all tatters.*

Trapdoor. [*To Tearcat*] Shall we set upon the infantry, these troops   60
of foot?—Zounds, yonder comes Moll, my whorish master and
mistress; would I had her kidneys between my teeth!

Tearcat. I had rather have a cow-heel.

Trapdoor. Zounds, I am so patched up she cannot discover me.
We'll on.   65

---

43. *a counter*] a prison or holding area attached to a law court. Hence the name
of the London prison and the potential for the analogy which Dapper draws with a
park for wild beasts.

52. *Pimlico*] the Pimlico Inn at Hoxton.

53. *boon voyage*] a prosperous journey; an anglicization of 'bon voyage'.
nappy] heady, intoxicating.

54. *ging*] gang.

55. *the world's end*] the end of the world. A number of taverns called 'The
World's End' were to be found on the outer edges of London, which may have
triggered a joke, playing on the contrast between accompanying good friends to the
very end of the world and going to a tavern with them.

60.] Trapdoor speaks metaphorically, as though the potential victims he sees
were enemy soldiers.

63. *cow-heel*] the foot of a cow stewed to form a jelly; like *kidneys* (line 62, above)
this was food for the poor.

64. *I . . . me*] I am so covered in patches (e.g. over my eye, on my clothes) that
she cannot uncover, or identify, me.

Tearcat. Alla corago, then.

Trapdoor. [*To the group*] Good your honours and worships, enlarge
the ears of commiseration, and let the sound of a hoarse military
organ-pipe penetrate your pitiful bowels to extract out of them
so many small drops of silver as may give a hard straw-bed   70
lodging to a couple of maimed soldiers.

Jack Dapper. Where are you maimed?

Tearcat. In both our nether limbs.

Moll. Come, come, Dapper, let's give 'em something.—'Las, poor
men, what money have you? By my troth, I love a soldier with   75
my soul.

Sir Beauteous. Stay, stay, where have you served?

Sir Thomas. In any part of the Low Countries?

Trapdoor. Not in the Low Countries, if it please your manhood, but
in Hungary against the Turk at the siege of Belgrade.   80

Lord Noland. Who served there with you, sirrah?

Trapdoor. Many Hungarians, Moldavians, Valachians, and Tran-
sylvanians, with some Sclavonians; and retiring home, sir, the
Venetian galleys took us prisoners, yet freed us, and suffered us
to beg up and down the country.   85

Jack Dapper. You have ambled all over Italy, then?

Trapdoor. Oh, sir, from Venice to Roma, Vecchio, Bononia, Roma-
nia, Bolonia, Modena, Piacenza, and Tuscana with all her
cities, as Pistoia, Valteria, Mountepulchena, Arrezzo, with the
Siennois and divers others.   90

Moll. Mere rogues. Put spurs to 'em once more.

Jack Dapper. [*To Tearcat*] Thou look'st like a strange creature—a fat
butter-box—yet speak'st English. What are thou?

*Tearcat. Ick, mine here? Ick bin den ruffling Tearcat, den brave soldado.
Ick bin dorick all Dutchlant gueresen. Der shellum das meere ine*   95
beasa, ine woert gaeb; Ick slaag um stroakes on tom cop, dastick den
hundred touzun divel halle; frollick, mine here.

Sir Beauteous. Here, here. [*About to give money*] Let's be rid of their
jabbering.

---

66. Alla corago] Take courage (popular slang).

69. *bowels*] thought to be the seat of emotion.

70. *drops of silver*] i.e. coins.

73. *nether limbs*] lower limbs; with a bawdy suggestion, continued in 'Low countries' (line 78).

80. *Hungary . . . Belgrade*] Belgrade, the capital of Serbia, was taken from the
Hungarians by the Turkish Sultan a hundred years earlier. Trapdoor's claim is
comically impossible.

82–3. *Hungarians . . . Sclavonians*] i.e. soldiers from the general areas under
Hungarian rule. But the list (like that in lines 87–90) sounds comically implausible.

92–3. *butter-box*] contemptuous term for a Dutchman.

94–7.] 'I, my lord? I am the ruffling Tearcat, the brave soldier. I have travelled

Moll. Not a cross, Sir Beauteous.—You base rogues, I have taken   100
measure of you better than a tailor can, and I'll fit you as you—
monster with one eye—have fitted me.

Trapdoor. Your worship will not abuse a soldier!

Moll. Soldier? Thou deserv'st to be hanged up by that tongue
which dishonours so noble a profession. Soldier, you skeldering   105
varlet? Hold, stand, there should be a trap-door hereabouts.
                                            Pull[s] off his patch.

Trapdoor. The balls of these glaziers of mine—mine eyes—shall be
shot up and down in any hot piece of service for my invincible
mistress.

Jack Dapper. I did not think there had been such knavery in black   110
patches as now I see.

Moll. Oh, sir, he hath been brought up in the Isle of Dogs, and can
both fawn like a spaniel and bite like a mastiff, as he finds
occasion.

Lord Noland. [*To Tearcat*] What are you, sirrah? A bird of this   115
feather too?

Tearcat. A man beaten from the wars, sir.

Sir Thomas. I think so, for you never stood to fight.

Jack Dapper. What's thy name, fellow soldier?

Tearcat. I am called by those that have seen my valour, Tearcat.   120

All. Tearcat?

Moll. A mere whip-jack, and that is, in the commonwealth of
rogues, a slave that can talk of sea-fight, name all your chief
pirates, discover more countries to you than either the Dutch,

---

through all Germany. [He is] the greater scoundrel who gives an angry word. I beat
him directly on the head, that you take out a hundred thousand devils. [Be] merry,
sir.' Tearcat takes the cue from Jack Dapper and lapses into Dutch-sounding
nonsense, a common ploy for escaping arrest.

100. *cross*] a low-value coin with a cross stamped on one side.

101. *I'll fit you*] (1) I'll sort you out; (2) I'll take your measurements (like a
tailor).

105. *skeldering*] begging, sponging, swindling.

107-9.] Trapdoor, exposed as a fraud, makes a desperate attempt to represent
himself as a loyal servant to Moll.

107. *glaziers*] eyes. (A low-life slang term.)

108. *shot . . . service*] Trapdoor compares his eyeballs to cannon-balls which will
be shot in all directions, suggesting he will be on a constant look-out on Moll's
behalf. There is also a bawdy undertone, since *hot piece of service* can mean both a
fierce battle and energetic sexual activity.

112. *Isle of Dogs*] peninsula on the southern reaches of the Thames between
Limehouse and Blackwell—a place to seek refuge from the law. Also, like *Westward
Ho* and *A Knack to Know a Knave* (4.2.131 and 283-4), the name of a play.

122. *whip-jack*] one who talks of great sea adventures which he never took part
in.

124. *discover*] present.

Spanish, French, or English ever found out; yet indeed all his   125
service is by land, and that is to rob a fair, or some such
venturous exploit. Tearcat! Foot, sirrah, I have your name, now
I remember me, in my book of horners: horns for the thumb,
you know how.

Tearcat. No indeed, Captain Moll—for I know you by sight—I am   130
no such nipping Christian, but a maunderer upon the pad, I
confess; and meeting with honest Trapdoor here, whom you
had cashiered from bearing arms, out at elbows under your
colours, I instructed him in the rudiments of roguery, and by
my map made him sail over any country you can name, so that   135
now he can maunder better than myself.

Jack Dapper. So then, Trapdoor, thou art turned soldier now.

Trapdoor. Alas, sir, now there's no wars, 'tis the safest course of life
I could take.

Moll. I hope then you can cant, for by your cudgels, you, sirrah, are   140
an upright man.

Trapdoor. As any walks the highway, I assure you.

Moll. And Tearcat, what are you? A wild rogue, an angler, or a
ruffler?

Tearcat. Brother to this upright man, flesh and blood; ruffling   145
Tearcat is my name, and a ruffler is my style, my title, my
profession.

Moll. Sirrah, where's your doxy? Halt not with me.

All. Doxy, Moll? What's that?

Moll. His wench.   150

Trapdoor. My doxy? I have, by the solomon, a doxy that carries a

---

128. *horners*] (1) workers in horn; (2) cuckolders.
horns for the thumb] horn thimbles to protect a purse cutter's thumb from the knife blade.
131. *nipping*] purse-cutting (slang).
maunderer upon the pad] professional beggar on the road.
132. *honest*] worthy (but with an ironic suggestion of 'trustworthy').
133. *cashiered*] dismissed, paid off (military).
133–4. *out . . . colours*] with the ragged remains of your livery on.
136. *maunder*] beg.
140. *cant*] speak underworld slang. See Intro., p. 26.
140–1. *cudgels . . . upright man*] The 'upright man', the second-in-command in the supposed hierarchy of criminals, was depicted in canting literature with a cudgel.
143. *A wild rogue*] a thief and vagrant who is not part of a regular organized gang.
an angler] someone who steals household goods and washing left out to dry with the help of a pole with a hook on the end.
143–4. *a ruffler*] a vagrant, formerly a soldier or a servant, like an 'upright man'. Rufflers supposedly lived by begging, and robbing country people.
148. *doxy*] a sexually experienced woman.
Halt] (1) limp; (2) pretend to be lame; (3) play false more generally.
151. *solomon*] mass.

kinchin mort in her slate at her back, besides my dell and my
dainty wild dell, with all whom I'll tumble this next darkmans
in the strommel, and drink ben booze, and eat a fat gruntling-
cheat, a cackling-cheat, and a quacking-cheat.   155

Jack Dapper. Here's old cheating!

Trapdoor. My doxy stays for me in a boozing ken, brave captain.

Moll. He says his wench stays for him in an alehouse. [*To Trapdoor
and Tearcat*] You are no pure rogues.

Tearcat. Pure rogues? No, we scorn to be pure rogues; but if you   160
come to our libken, or our stalling-ken, you shall find neither
him nor me a queer cuffin.

Moll. So, sir, no churl of you.

Tearcat. No, but a ben cove, a brave cove, a gentry cuffin.

Lord Noland. Call you this canting?   165

Jack Dapper. Zounds, I'll give a schoolmaster half a crown a week
and teach me this pedlar's French.

Trapdoor. Do but stroll, sir, half a harvest with us, sir, and you shall
gabble your bellyful.

Moll. [*To Trapdoor*] Come, you rogue, cant with me.   170

Sir Thomas. Well said, Moll. [*To Trapdoor*] Cant with her, sirrah,
and you shall have money; else not a penny.

Trapdoor. I'll have a bout, if she please.

Moll. Come on, sirrah.

Trapdoor. Ben mort, shall you and I heave a booth, mill a ken, or nip 175

151–2. *a kinchin mort*] a little girl of a year or two old, carried in a sheet on her
mother's back.

152. *slate*] sheet. Trapdoor is demonstrating his ability at canting.

152–3. *dell . . . wild dell*] young girl at puberty but still a virgin.

153. *wild*] born out of doors.

darkmans] night.

154. *strommel*] straw.

ben booze] good drink.

154–5. *a fat . . . quacking-cheat*] a fat pig, a cockerel and a duck. (*Cheat* is the cant
term for 'thief'.)

156. *old*] great, abundant.

157. *boozing ken*] alehouse.

159. *You . . . rogues*] i.e. You're not merely great beggars. As Tearcat indicates in
his response, they are thieves who receive stolen goods.

161. *libken*] place to sleep.

stalling-ken] house for receiving stolen goods.

162. *a queer cuffin*] a worthless man.

163.] So, you're not a low, worthless character.

164. *a brave cove*] a good man. (Both *cove* and *cuffin* mean 'person'.)

a gentry cuffin] a gentleman.

167. *pedlar's French*] underworld slang.

168. *half a harvest*] half a season of begging and stealing.

175–7.] See 182ff. where Moll translates these cant terms.

a bung? And then we'll couch a hogshead under the ruffmans,
and there you shall wap with me, and I'll niggle with you.

Moll. Out, you damned impudent rascal! [*She hits and kicks him.*]

Trapdoor. Cut benar whids, and hold your fambles and your stamps!

Lord Noland. Nay, nay, Moll, why art thou angry? What was his   180
gibberish?

Moll. Marry, this, my lord, says he: 'Ben mort'—good wench—
'shall you and I heave a booth, mill a ken, or nip a bung?'—shall
you and I rob a house, or cut a purse?

All. Very good!   185

Moll. 'And then we'll couch a hogshead under the ruffmans'—and
then we'll lie under a hedge.

Trapdoor. That was my desire, captain, as 'tis fit a soldier should lie.

Moll. 'And there you shall wap with me, and I'll niggle with you'—
and that's all.   190

Sir Beauteous. Nay, nay, Moll, what's that 'wap'?

Jack Dapper. Nay, teach me what 'niggling' is; I'd fain be niggling.

Moll. Wapping and niggling is all one. The rogue my man can tell
you.

Trapdoor. 'Tis fadoodling, if it please you.   195

Sir Beauteous. This is excellent. One fit more, good Moll.

Moll. [*To Tearcat*] Come, you rogue, sing with me.

The Song.

	A gage of ben Rome-booze	
	In a boozing ken of Rome-ville	
Tearcat.	Is benar than a caster,	200
	Peck, pannam, lap, or popler	
	Which we mill in Deuce-a-ville.	
Moll, Tearcat.	Oh, I would lib all the lightmans,	
	Oh, I would lib all the darkmans,	
	By the solomon, under the ruffmans,	205
	By the solomon, in the harmans,	
Tearcat.	And scour the queer cramp-ring,	

---

179. *Cut . . . stamps*] Speak better words and control your hands and feet.

187. *lie*] (1) tell untruths; (2) have sex.

195. *fadoodling*] Trapdoor makes up a euphemism for copulating.

196. *fit*] strain of music; a section of a poem or song. Sir Beauteous asks for one
more demonstration of canting.

198–210.] The song means:
A quart pot of good wine in a London alehouse is better than a cloak, meat, bread,
butter, milk or porridge which we steal in the country. Oh, I would lie all day, oh,
I would lie all night, by the mass, under the woods, by the mass, in the stocks and
wear fetters and lie till a beggar slept with my girl, so long as my drunken head could
drink wine well. Avast to the highway, let us hence etc. (Compare Moll's version at
lines 238–48.)

And couch till a palliard docked my dell,
So my boozy nab might skew Rome-booze well.

Moll, Tearcat. Avast to the pad, let us bing,   210
Avast to the pad, let us bing.

All. Fine knaves, i' faith.

Jack Dapper. The grating of ten new cart-wheels and the gruntling
of five hundred hogs coming from Romford market cannot
make a worse noise than this canting language does in my ears.   215
Pray, my Lord Noland, let's give these soldiers their pay.

Sir Beauteous. Agreed, and let them march.

Lord Noland. [*Giving money*] Here, Moll.

Moll. [*To Trapdoor, Tearcat*] Now I see that you are stalled to the
rogue and are not ashamed of your profession. Look you, my   220
Lord Noland here, and these gentlemen, bestows upon you
two, two bords and a half: that's two shillings sixpence.

                              [*She gives them the money.*]

Trapdoor. Thanks to your lordship.

Tearcat. Thanks, heroical captain.

Moll. Away!   225

Trapdoor. We shall cut ben whids of your masters and mistress-ship
wheresoever we come.

Moll. [*To Trapdoor*] You'll maintain, sirrah, the old justice's plot to
his face?

Trapdoor. Else trine me on the cheats; hang me!   230

Moll. Be sure you meet me there.

Trapdoor. Without any more maundering, I'll do 't.—Follow, brave
Tearcat.

Tearcat. *I prae, sequor*; let us go, mouse.

                              Exeunt they two, manet the rest.

Lord Noland. Moll, what was in that canting song?   235

Moll. Troth, my lord, only a praise of good drink, the only milk
which these wild beasts love to suck; and thus it was:

---

208. *a palliard*] a ragged beggar usually accompanied by a woman and carrying
a certificate to show that they are married.

214. *Romford*] a town in Essex, twelve miles north-east of London, where a hog
market was held every Tuesday.

219–20. *stalled to the rogue*] installed or ordained as a rogue.

222. *bords*] shillings.

226. *cut ben whids*] speak good words.

228. *the old justice's*] i.e. Sir Alexander Wengrave's.

230. *trine . . . cheats*] hang me on the gallows.

232. *maundering*] begging.

234. I prae, sequor] Go first, I will follow.

mouse] term of endearment usually associated with women, here comically addressed to Trapdoor.

234.1. *manet the rest*] the rest remain.

A rich cup of wine,
Oh, it is juice divine!
More wholesome for the head   240
Than meat, drink, or bread.
To fill my drunken pate
With that, I'd sit up late;
By the heels would I lie,
Under a lousy hedge die,   245
Let a slave have a pull
At my whore, so I be full
Of that precious liquor—
and a parcel of such stuff, my lord, not worth the opening.

Enter a Cutpurse *very gallant, with four or five* Men
after him, one with a wand.

Lord Noland. What gallant comes yonder?   250
Sir Thomas. Mass, I think I know him: 'tis one of Cumberland.
1 Cutpurse. [*To his companions*] Shall we venture to shuffle in
amongst yon heap of gallants, and strike?
2 Cutpurse. 'Tis a question whether there be any silver shells
amongst them, for all their satin outsides.   255
All Cutpurses. Let's try!
Moll. [*To the gentlemen*] Pox on him, a gallant? Shadow me, I know
him: 'tis one that cumbers the land indeed. If he swim near to
the shore of any of your pockets, look to your purses!
All [*the gentlemen*]. Is 't possible?   260
Moll. This brave fellow is no better than a foist.
All [*the gentlemen*]. Foist? What's that?
Moll. A diver with two fingers: a pickpocket. All his train study the
figging law, that's to say, cutting of purses and foisting. One of
them is a nip; I took him once i' the twopenny gallery at the   265
Fortune. Then there's a cloyer, or snap, that dogs any new
brother in that trade, and snaps will have half in any booty. He

---

249.1. *wand*] light walking stick.
251. *Cumberland*] a county in northwest England.
253. *strike*] pick a pocket or purse.
254. *shells*] money. Also at 269.
258. *cumbers*] harrasses, troubles. With a play on *Cumberland*, line 251.
261. *brave*] dressed up as a gallant.
foist] pickpocket (slang).
263. *train*] followers.
264. *figging law*] code of the cutpurse.
265. *nip*] cutpurse.
265–6. *the Fortune*] the theatre where *The Roaring Girl* was being performed. See
Intro., pp. 12, 26.
266. *cloyer, snap*] one who receives the cut purse.

with the wand is both a stale, whose office is to face a man i' the
streets whilst shells are drawn by another; and then, with his
black conjuring rod in his hand, he, by the nimbleness of his eye   270
and juggling stick, will, in cheaping a piece of plate at a goldsmith's stall, make four or five rings mount from the top of his
caduceus, and, as if it were at leap-frog, they skip into his hand
presently.

2 Cutpurse. Zounds, we are smoked!   275

All Cutpurses. Ha?

2 Cutpurse. We are boiled. Pox on her! See Moll, the roaring drab!

1 Cutpurse. All the diseases of sixteen hospitals boil her! Away!

Moll. Bless you, sir.

1 Cutpurse. And you, good sir.   280

Moll. Dost not ken me, man?

1 Cutpurse. No, trust me, sir.

Moll. Heart, there's a knight, to whom I'm bound for many favours,
lost his purse at the last new play i' the Swan—seven angels in
't. Make it good, you're best; do you see? No more.   285

1 Cutpurse. A synagogue shall be called, Mistress Mary. Disgrace
me not. *Pacus palabros*, I will conjure for you. Farewell.

[*Exeunt* Cutpurses.]

Moll. Did not I tell you, my lord?

Lord Noland. I wonder how thou cam'st to the knowledge of these
nasty villains.   290

Sir Thomas. And why do the foul mouths of the world call thee Moll
Cutpurse? A name, methinks, damned and odious.

---

268. *stale*] decoy.

268-9. *face . . . another*] engage the victim in conversation while his pocket is
being picked.

271. *cheaping*] bargaining for.

272-4. *make . . . presently*] refers to the trickster's ruse of putting the end of his
walking-stick surreptitiously through some rings on the goldsmith's stall and sliding
them down into his hand while the stall-holder's attention is distracted by the
business of selling the plate.

272-3. *his caduceus*] i.e. his wand (like the wand carried by Mercury).

275-7. *smoked, boiled*] discovered.

277. *drab*] whore.

281. *ken*] know.

284. *i' the Swan*] at the Swan Theatre on the south bank of the Thames, where
Middleton's *A Chaste Maid* was performed. See Intro., p. 26.

285. *Make . . . best*] You had better recompense this gentleman. Moll implies
that the Cutpurse was responsible, and threatens him.

286. *A synagogue*] a meeting of the cutpurses to inquire about the stolen purse.

286-7. *Disgrace me not*] Don't expose me as a cutpurse when I am dressed as a
gallant.

287. Pacus palabros] an approximation of the Spanish *pocas palabros*: 'few
words', i.e. 'say no more'.

conjure] i.e. perform wonders (see lines 270-4).

Moll. Dare any step forth to my face and say,
    'I have ta'en thee doing so, Moll'? I must confess,
    In younger days, when I was apt to stray,   295
    I have sat amongst such adders, seen their stings—
    As any here might—and in full playhouses
    Watched their quick-diving hands, to bring to shame
    Such rogues, and in that stream met an ill name.
    When next, my lord, you spy any one of those—   300
    So he be in his art a scholar—question him,
    Tempt him with gold to open the large book
    Of his close villainies; and you yourself shall cant
    Better than poor Moll can, and know more laws
    Of cheaters, lifters, nips, foists, puggards, curbers,   305
    Withal the devil's blackguard, than it is fit
    Should be discovered to a noble wit.
    I know they have their orders, offices,
    Circuits, and circles, unto which they are bound,
    To raise their own damnation in.
Jack Dapper.   How dost thou know it?   310
Moll. As you do: I show it you, they to me show it.
    Suppose, my lord, you were in Venice.
Lord Noland.   Well.
Moll. If some Italian pander there would tell
    All the close tricks of courtesans, would not you
    Hearken to such a fellow?
Lord Noland.   Yes.
Moll.   And here,   315
    Being come from Venice, to a friend most dear
    That were to travel thither, you would proclaim
    Your knowledge in those villainies, to save
    Your friend from their quick danger: must you have
    A black ill name because ill things you know?   320
    Good troth, my lord, I am made Moll Cutpurse so.
    How many are whores in small ruffs and still looks?
    How many chaste whose names fill slander's books?

---

    299. *and . . . name*] and in that ambiance, I acquired a bad reputation.
    301. *So . . . scholar*] provided he is accomplished in the skill he has studied.
    303. *close*] secret. (Also in line 314.)
    305.] of pickpockets and thieves of various sorts.
    306. *blackguard*] a guard of attendants, so called from their black liveries. The phrase was extended to indicate villains or the devil's attendants.
    309. *Circuits, and circles*] in which they conjured; the analogy is between thieves and magicians who can make things disappear and reappear by sleight of hand.
    310. *raise*] make to appear (as in raising spirits by conjuring).
    322. *small ruffs*] associated with Puritans.
    still looks] demure appearance.

Were all men cuckolds whom gallants in their scorns
Call so, we should not walk for goring horns.   325
Perhaps for my mad going some reprove me;
I please myself, and care not else who loves me.
All. A brave mind, Moll, i' faith.
Sir Thomas. Come, my lord, shall 's to the ordinary?
Lord Noland. Ay, 'tis noon sure.   330
Moll. Good my lord, let not my name condemn me to you or to the
    world. A fencer, I hope, may be called a coward; is he so for
    that? If all that have ill names in London were to be whipped
    and to pay but twelvepence apiece to the beadle, I would rather
    have his office than a constable's.   335
Jack Dapper. So would I, Captain Moll. 'Twere a sweet tickling
    office, i' faith.   *Exeunt.*

[5.2]

      Enter SIR ALEXANDER WENGRAVE, GOSHAWK *and*
            GREENWIT, *and others.*

Sir Alexander. My son marry a thief! That impudent girl
Whom all the world stick their worst eyes upon!
Greenwit. How will your care prevent it?
Goshawk.   'Tis impossible!
They marry close; they're gone, but none knows whither.
Sir Alexander. Oh, gentlemen, when has a father's heart-strings   5
Held out so long from breaking?

            Enter a Servant.

                Now, what news, sir?
Servant. They were met upo' th' water an hour since, sir,
Putting in towards the Sluice.
Sir Alexander.   The Sluice? Come, gentlemen,
'Tis Lambeth works against us.   [*Exit* Servant.]
Greenwit.   And that Lambeth

---

325. *for goring horns*] for fear of being wounded by the horns on the cuckolds'
heads.

326. *going*] goings-on, way I conduct myself in public.

334–5. *I . . . constable's*] i.e. I would make even more money as a beadle than as
a constable, though that is the higher office.

336. *tickling*] gratifying.

5.2.2. *stick . . . upon*] view with special distaste.

4. *close*] secretly.

8–9. *the Sluice . . . Lambeth*] The embankment on the Thames which protected
the low-lying areas of Lambeth Marsh from flooding. Lambeth Marsh was on the
south side of the Thames between Battersea and Southwark.

9. *Lambeth . . . us*] The borough of Lambeth lay outside the City's jurisdiction.

      Joins more mad matches than your six wet towns   10
      'Twixt that and Windsor Bridge, where fares lie soaking.
Sir Alexander. Delay no time, sweet gentlemen: to Blackfriars!
      We'll take a pair of oars and make after 'em.

Enter TRAPDOOR.

Trapdoor. Your son and that bold masculine ramp, my mistress,
      Are landed now at Tower.
Sir Alexander.   Heyday, at Tower?   15
Trapdoor. I heard it now reported.   [*Exit.*]
Sir Alexander.   Which way, gentlemen,
      Shall I bestow my care? I'm drawn in pieces
      Betwixt deceit and shame.

Enter SIR [GUY] FITZALLARD

Sir Guy.   Sir Alexander,
      You're well met, and most rightly served;
      My daughter was a scorn to you.
Sir Alexander.   Say not so, sir.   20
Sir Guy. A very abject she, poor gentlewoman!
      Your house has been dishonoured. Give you joy, sir,
      Of your son's gaskin-bride. You'll be a grandfather shortly
      To a fine crew of roaring sons and daughters;
      'Twill help to stock the suburbs passing well, sir.   25
Sir Alexander. Oh, play not with the miseries of my heart!
      Wounds should be dressed and healed, not vexed or left
      Wide open to the anguish of the patient,
      And scornful air let in; rather let pity
      And advice charitably help to refresh 'em.   30
Sir Guy. Who'd place his charity so unworthily,

   10–11. *Joins . . . Bridge*] Weddings could be conducted outside the City's jurisdiction. The towns which lay along the river (*wet towns*) were the most easily
accessible and so became proverbially associated with unregulated marriage and
sexual misdemeanour. Windsor Bridge connects Windsor to Eton, on either side of
the Thames.
   11. *fares*] customers for the river taxis.
   soaking] because in a *wet town*; but also because their sexual exploits might give
them venereal disease which would require soaking in hot tubs as a cure.
   12. *Blackfriars*] Blackfriars Stairs was a landing stage on the north side of the
Thames. From Blackfriars, the Tower (line 15) and Lambeth are in opposite
directions.
   14. *ramp*] bold, vulgar woman.
   20. *scorn*] object of contempt.
   23. *gaskin-bride*] i.e. a bride who wears gaskins, wide knee-breeches.
   25. *passing*] exceedingly. (Said ironically.)
   30. *refresh 'em*] restore, heal them (i.e. wounds).

Like one that gives alms to a cursing beggar?
Had I but found one spark of goodness in you
Toward my deserving child, which then grew fond
Of your son's virtues, I had eased you now;   35
But I perceive both fire of youth and goodness
Are raked up in the ashes of your age,
Else no such shame should have come near your house,
Nor such ignoble sorrow touch your heart.

Sir Alexander. If not for worth, for pity's sake assist me!   40

Greenwit. You urge a thing past sense. How can he help you?
All his assistance is as frail as ours,
Full as uncertain where's the place that holds 'em.
One brings us water-news, then comes another
With a full-charged mouth like a culverin's voice,   45
And he reports the Tower. Whose sounds are truest?

Goshawk. [*To Sir Guy*] In vain you flatter him.—Sir Alexander—

Sir Guy. I flatter him? Gentlemen, you wrong me grossly.

Greenwit. [*Aside to Goshawk*] He does it well, i' faith.

Sir Guy.   Both news are false,
Of Tower or water. They took no such way yet.   50

Sir Alexander. Oh, strange! Hear you this, gentlemen? Yet more
   plunges!

Sir Guy. They're nearer than you think for, yet more close
Than if they were further off.

Sir Alexander.   How am I lost
In these distractions!

Sir Guy.   For your speeches, gentlemen,
In taxing me for rashness, 'fore you all,   55
I will engage my state to half his wealth,
Nay, to his son's revenues, which are less,
And yet nothing at all till they come from him,
That I could, if my will stuck to my power,
Prevent this marriage yet, nay, banish her   60
For ever from his thoughts, much more his arms.

Sir Alexander. Slack not this goodness, though you heap upon me

---

37.] i.e. are stifled by your aged churlishness.

40. *worth*] my deserving.

45.] like the sound of a fully loaded cannon (*culverin*).

47. *flatter*] encourage. (Goshawk says that it is too late to be warning Sir Alexander how he might have behaved.)

51. *plunges*] crises.

54. *distractions*] confusions pulling me in different directions.

56.] I will pawn all my estate to the value of half the value of Sir Alexander's wealth.

58.] and of no value at all until he actually inherits.

60. *her*] i.e. Moll.

Mountains of malice and revenge hereafter!
I'd willingly resign up half my state to him,
So he would marry the meanest drudge I hire.   65
Greenwit. [*To Sir Alexander*] He talks impossibilities, and you
    believe 'em!
Sir Guy. I talk no more than I know how to finish;
My fortunes else are his that dares stake with me.
The poor young gentleman I love and pity;
And to keep shame from him—because the spring   70
Of his affection was my daughter's first,
Till his frown blasted all—do but estate him
In those possessions which your love and care
Once pointed out for him, that he may have room
To entertain fortunes of noble birth,   75
Where now his desperate wants casts him upon her;
And if I do not, for his own sake chiefly,
Rid him of this disease that now grows on him,
I'll forfeit my whole state, before these gentlemen.
Greenwit. [*To Sir Alexander*] Troth, but you shall not undertake
    such matches;   80
We'll persuade so much with you.
Sir Alexander. [*To Sir Guy*]   Here's my ring; [*Giving ring*]
He will believe this token. 'Fore these gentlemen
I will confirm it fully: all those lands
My first love 'lotted him, he shall straight possess
In that refusal.
Sir Guy.   If I change it not,   85
Change me into a beggar!
Greenwit.   Are you mad, sir?
Sir Guy. 'Tis done!
Goshawk. [*To Sir Alexander*] Will you undo yourself by doing,
And show a prodigal trick in your old days?
Sir Alexander. 'Tis a match, gentlemen.
Sir Guy.   Ay, ay, sir, ay!
I ask no favour, trust to you for none;   90

---

65. *So*] provided.
68.] If what I say isn't true, all my wealth goes to anyone who dares bet with me.
71. *first*] first spring, first love.
72. *Till . . . all*] until Sir Alexander's disapproval destroyed everything.
estate him] grant him legal title.
76. *casts . . . her*] throws him at her (Moll); makes him dependent on her.
78. *this disease*] i.e. Moll (see Intro., pp. 53–4); also, Sebastian's financial need.
85. *In that refusal*] if he refuses to marry Moll.
change it not] do not undo the marriage (between Sebastian and Moll).
87. *'Tis done*] It's a deal.

My hope rests in the goodness of your son.

                                       Exit FITZALLARD.

Greenwit. [*Aside to Goshawk*] He holds it up well yet.

Goshawk. [*Aside to Greenwit*]   Of an old knight, i' faith.

Sir Alexander. Cursed be the time I laid his first love barren,

    Wilfully barren, that before this hour

    Had sprung forth fruits of comfort and of honour!   95

    He loved a virtuous gentlewoman.

               Enter MOLL [*dressed as a man*].

Goshawk. Life, here's Moll!

Greenwit. Jack!

Goshawk.   How dost thou, Jack?

Moll.   How dost thou, gallant?

Sir Alexander. Impudence, where's my son?

Moll.   Weakness, go look him!

Sir Alexander. Is this your wedding gown?

Moll.   The man talks monthly.   100

    Hot broth and a dark chamber for the knight;

    I see he'll be stark mad at our next meeting.   *Exit* MOLL.

Goshawk. Why, sir, take comfort now, there's no such matter;

    No priest will marry her, sir, for a woman

    Whiles that shape's on. And it was never known,   105

    Two men were married and conjoined in one!

    Your son hath made some shift to love another.

Sir Alexander. Whate'er she be, she has my blessing with her:

    May they be rich and fruitful, and receive

    Like comfort to their issue as I take   110

    In them! 'Has pleased me now, marrying not this;

    Through a whole world he could not choose amiss.

Greenwit. Glad you're so penitent for your former sin, sir.

Goshawk. Say he should take a wench with her smock dowry,

    No portion with her but her lips and arms?   115

Sir Alexander. Why, who thrive better, sir? They have most blessing,

---

92.] Greenwit and Goshawk comment on Sir Guy's performance; with an inevitable analogy with a sexual performance.

93. *laid . . . barren*] thwarted the fruitfulness of his first love.

99. *go look him*] go and look for him.

100. *monthly*] i.e. under the influence of the moon; lunatic.

101. *Hot broth . . . dark chamber*] traditional treatments for the insane.

107. *shift*] (1) arrangement; (2) change of partner.

110. *to their issue*] in their children.

111. *this*] i.e. Moll. The absence of a noun (e.g. woman, thing etc.) suggests that Sir Alexander is still at a loss to know what to call Moll.

114. *smock dowry*] i.e. a dowry consisting only of her clothes.

115. *portion*] dowry.

Though other have more wealth and least repent.
Many that want most know the most content.
Greenwit. Say he should marry a kind youthful sinner?
Sir Alexander. Age will quench that. Any offence but theft   120
And drunkenness, nothing but death can wipe away;
Their sins are green even when their heads are grey.
Nay, I despair not now; my heart's cheered, gentlemen.
No face can come unfortunately to me.

Enter a Servant.

Now, sir, your news?
Servant.   Your son with his fair bride   125
Is near at hand.
Sir Alexander.   Fair may their fortunes be!
Greenwit. Now you're resolved, sir, it was never she?
Sir Alexander. I find it in the music of my heart.

Enter MOLL [*in female dress,*] *masked, in* SEBASTIAN'*s hand,
and [SIR GUY] FITZALLARD.

See where they come.
Goshawk.   A proper lusty presence, sir.
Sir Alexander. Now has he pleased me right. I always counselled
him   130
To choose a goodly personable creature.
Just of her pitch was my first wife, his mother.
Sebastian. Before I dare discover my offence,   [*He kneels.*]
I kneel for pardon.
Sir Alexander.   My heart gave it thee
Before thy tongue could ask it.   135
Rise; thou hast raised my joy to greater height
Than to that seat where grief dejected it.   [*Sebastian rises.*]
Both welcome to my love and care for ever!
Hide not my happiness too long. All's pardoned;

---

117. *repent*] regret the marriage.
119. *kind . . . sinner*] *Sinner* when applied to women usually means 'unchaste',
but Greenwit is not defining any precise person. The gallants are both teasing Sir
Alexander by testing his contention (line 112) that anyone in the world would be a
better match than Moll.
120–1.] The sense is confused here by the double 'but'. It reads as if Sir Alexander is saying that only death can wipe away all sins except for theft and drunkenness.
His reply to Greenwit suggests the opposite: i.e. that age will quench all sins except
theft and drunkenness, which can be overcome only by death.
127. *she*] Moll.
132. *pitch*] height.
137. *dejected it*] cast it down.

Here are our friends.—Salute her, gentlemen.   140
They unmask her.

All. Heart, who's this? Moll!

Sir Alexander. Oh, my reviving shame! Is 't I must live
   To be struck blind? Be it the work of sorrow
   Before age take 't in hand!

Sir Guy.   Darkness and death!
   Have you deceived me thus? Did I engage   145
   My whole estate for this?

Sir Alexander.   You asked no favour,
   And you shall find as little. Since my comforts
   Play false with me, I'll be as cruel to thee
   As grief to fathers' hearts.

Moll.   Why, what's the matter with you,
   'Less too much joy should make your age forgetful?   150
   Are you too well, too happy?

Sir Alexander.   With a vengeance!

Moll. Methinks you should be proud of such a daughter—
   As good a man as your son!

Sir Alexander.   Oh, monstrous impudence!

Moll. You had no note before: an unmarked knight.
   Now all the town will take regard on you,   155
   And all your enemies fear you for my sake.
   You may pass where you list, through crowds most thick,
   And come off bravely with your purse unpicked.
   You do not know the benefits I bring with me:
   No cheat dares work upon you with thumb or knife,   160
   While you've a roaring girl to your son's wife.

Sir Alexander. A devil rampant!

Sir Guy. [*To Sir Alexander*]   Have you so much charity
   Yet to release me of my last rash bargain,
   An I'll give in your pledge?

Sir Alexander.   No, sir, I stand to 't:
   I'll work upon advantage as all mischiefs   165
   Do upon me.

Sir Guy.   Content.—Bear witness all, then,

143–4. *Be . . . hand*] Let sorrow blind with tears before age does so.

144–6.] addressed to Sir Alexander or Moll.

154. *note*] distinction, fame.

unmarked] unnoticed.

162. *rampant*] rearing on hind legs and looking fierce as in heraldic emblems.

164. *An . . . pledge*] if I release you of your pledge? (Sir Guy may offer to return the ring at this point.)

165–6. *I'll . . . me*] I'll take any advantage I can, seeing that all mischiefs conspire against me.

His are the lands, and so contention ends.
Here comes your son's bride 'twixt two noble friends.

Enter the LORD NOLAND *and* SIR BEAUTEOUS GANYMEDE,
with MARY FITZALLARD *between them, the* Citizens *and*
their Wives *with them.*

Moll. [*To Sir Alexander*] Now are you gulled as you would be.
　　Thank me for 't;
　　I'd a forefinger in 't.
Sebastian. [*Kneeling to Sir Alexander*] Forgive me, father;　　170
　　Though there before your eyes my sorrow feigned,
　　This still was she for whom true love complained.
Sir Alexander. Blessings eternal and the joys of angels
　　Begin your peace here to be signed in heaven!
　　How short my sleep of sorrow seems now to me　　175
　　To this eternity of boundless comforts
　　That finds no want but utterance and expression!
　　[*To Lord Noland*] My lord, your office here appears so
　　　　honourably,
　　So full of ancient goodness, grace, and worthiness,
　　I never took more joy in sight of man　　180
　　Than in your comfortable presence now.
Lord Noland. Nor I more delight in doing grace to virtue
　　Than in this worthy gentlewoman, your son's bride,
　　Noble Fitzallard's daughter, to whose honour
　　And modest fame I am a servant vowed;　　185
　　So is this knight.
Sir Alexander.　　　　Your loves make my joys proud.
　　[*To a Servant*] Bring forth those deeds of land my care laid
　　　　ready—　　　　　　　　[*A Servant fetches the deeds.*]
　　And which, old knight, thy nobleness may challenge,
　　Joined with thy daughter's virtues, whom I prize now
　　As dearly as that flesh I call mine own.　　190
　　[*To Mary*] Forgive me, worthy gentlewoman; 'twas my
　　　　blindness.
　　When I rejected thee, I saw thee not;
　　Sorrow and wilful rashness grew like films
　　Over the eyes of judgement, now so clear

---

167. *His*] Sebastian's. See lines 82–4.
169. *would be*] would wish to be.
179. *ancient*] venerable.
181. *comfortable*] comforting, supporting.
185. *fame*] reputation.
I . . . vowed] I vow my service.
188. *challenge*] lay claim to.

I see the brightness of thy worth appear.   195
Mary. Duty and love may I deserve in those,
    And all my wishes have a perfect close.
Sir Alexander. That tongue can never err, the sound's so sweet.
                         [He gives Sebastian the deeds.]
    Here, honest son, receive into thy hands
    The keys of wealth, possession of those lands   200
    Which my first care provided; they're thine own.
    Heaven give thee a blessing with 'em! The best joys
    That can in worldly shapes to man betide
    Are fertile lands and a fair fruitful bride,
    Of which I hope thou'rt sped.
Sebastian.   I hope so too, sir.   205
Moll. Father and son, I ha' done you simple service here.
Sebastian. For which thou shalt not part, Moll, unrequited.
Sir Alexander. Thou art a mad girl, and yet I cannot now
    Condemn thee.
Moll.   Condemn me? Troth, an you should, sir,
    I'd make you seek out one to hang in my room: 210
    I'd give you the slip at gallows and cozen the people.
    [To Lord Noland] Heard you this jest, my lord?
Lord Noland.   What is it, Jack?
Moll. He was in fear his son would marry me,
    But never dreamt that I would ne'er agree!
Lord Noland. Why? Thou hadst a suitor once, Jack; when wilt
    marry?   215
Moll. Who, I, my lord? I'll tell you when, i' faith:
    When you shall hear
    Gallants void from sergeants' fear,
    Honesty and truth unslandered,
    Woman manned but never pandered,   220
    Cheaters booted but not coached,
    Vessels older ere they're broached;
    If my mind be then not varied,

---

196. *in those*] in your eyes.
205. *sped*] provided.
210. *in my room*] instead of me.
212, 214.] Lord Noland continues to call Moll Jack, even though she is now in women's clothes. Cf 5.1.1, 5.1.28 and notes.
218.] gallants not in fear of being arrested for debt. (Moll has no desire to marry a gentleman who might be in debt.)
220. *manned*] provided with a man; escorted.
221.] thieves who can afford boots, but not to ride in luxurious coaches.
222. *broached*] broken. Possibly refers to the wish that women be older before they are deflowered or married off.

Next day following, I'll be married.
Lord Noland. This sounds like doomsday.
Moll.   Then were marriage best,   225
For if I should repent, I were soon at rest.
Sir Alexander. In troth, thou'rt a good wench; I'm sorry now
The opinion was so hard I conceived of thee.

Enter TRAPDOOR.

Some wrongs I've done thee.
Trapdoor. [*Aside*]   Is the wind there now?
'Tis time for me to kneel and confess first,   230
For fear it come too late and my brains feel it.   [*He kneels.*]
[*To Moll*] Upon my paws I ask you pardon, mistress.
Moll. Pardon? For what, sir? What has your rogueship done now?
Trapdoor. I have been from time to time hired to confound you by
this old gentleman.   235
Moll. How?
Trapdoor. Pray forgive him;
But may I counsel you, you should never do 't.
Many a snare to entrap your worship's life
Have I laid privily—chains, watches, jewels—   240
And when he saw nothing could mount you up,
Four hollow-hearted angels he then gave you,
By which he meant to trap you, I to save you.
Sir Alexander. To all which, shame and grief in me cry guilty.
[*To Moll*] Forgive me! Now I cast the world's eyes from me,   245
And look upon thee freely with mine own.
I see the most of many wrongs before thee
Cast from the jaws of Envy and her people,
And nothing foul but that. I'll never more
Condemn by common voice, for that's the whore   250
That deceives man's opinion, mocks his trust,
Cozens his love, and makes his heart unjust.
Moll. [*Showing money*] Here be the angels, gentlemen; they were
given me

226.] for if I changed my mind, I would not have to live long with the decision.
229. *Is . . . now?*] i.e. Is that how things are now? (proverbial).
231. *my brains feel it*] i.e. I get beaten about the head.
235. *this old gentleman*] Sir Alexander.
238.] Unless I counsel you, you should never forgive him (because I will tell you
all the things he did to trap you).
241. *mount you up*] i.e. bring you up onto the gallows.
245. *Now . . . me*] now that I cast the world's view of you aside.
247. *before thee*] displayed before you.
248. *people*] followers.
252. *Cozens*] deceives.

As a musician. I pursue no pity.—
Follow the law; an you can cuck me, spare not;   255
Hang up my viol by me, and I care not!
Sir Alexander. So far I'm sorry, I'll thrice double 'em
To make thy wrongs amends.—
Come, worthy friends, my honourable lord,
Sir Beauteous Ganymede, and noble Fitzallard,   260
And you, kind gentlewomen, whose sparkling presence
Are glories set in marriage, beams of society,
For all your loves give lustre to my joys.
The happiness of this day shall be remembered
At the return of every smiling spring;   265
In my time now 'tis born, and may no sadness
Sit on the brows of men upon that day,
But as I am, so all go pleased away!   [*Exeunt.*]

---

255. *cuck me*] set me in the cucking stool (used to punish scolding women by
ducking).
261. *gentlewomen*] i.e. the citizens' wives who came on stage at line 168.1–3.
268.] Let everyone go away as pleased as I am.

Epilogue

A painter, having drawn with curious art
The picture of a woman—every part
Limned to the life—hung out the piece to sell.
People who passed along, viewing it well,
Gave several verdicts on it. Some dispraised   5
The hair; some said the brows too high were raised;
Some hit her o'er the lips, misliked their colour;
Some wished her nose were shorter, some the eyes fuller;
Others said roses on her cheeks should grow,
Swearing they looked too pale; others cried no.   10
The workman, still as fault was found, did mend it,
In hope to please all; but, this work being ended,
And hung open at stall, it was so vile,
So monstrous, and so ugly, all men did smile
At the poor painter's folly. Such we doubt   15
Is this our comedy. Some perhaps do flout
The plot, saying, 'tis too thin, too weak, too mean;
Some for the person will revile the scene,
And wonder that a creature of her being
Should be the subject of a poet, seeing,   20
In the world's eye, none weighs so light; others look
For all those base tricks published in a book—
Foul as his brains they flowed from—of cutpurses,
Of nips and foists, nasty, obscene discourses,
As full of lies, as empty of worth or wit,   25
For any honest ear or eye unfit.
And thus,
If we to every brain that's humorous
Should fashion scenes, we, with the painter, shall,

---

1. *curious*] skilful.
3. *Limned*] drawn.
15. *doubt*] fear.
16. *flout*] denounce.
17. *too mean*] too concerned with low-life people.
19. *a creature . . . being*] a creation made as she is (referring to Moll's alleged hermaphroditism).
21. *none . . . light*] no one seems so trivial a subject.
22–6. *base . . . unfit*] refers to the vogue for publishing pamphlet accounts of underworld life.
28. *humorous*] fanciful, capricious.

In striving to please all, please none at all.   30
Yet for such faults as either the writers' wit
Or negligence of the actors do commit,
Both crave your pardons. If what both have done
Cannot full pay your expectation,
The Roaring Girl herself, some few days hence,   35
Shall on this stage give larger recompense;
Which mirth that you may share in, herself does woo you,
And craves this sign: your hands to beckon her to you.

FINIS.

---

36. *on this stage*] suggesting that Moll Cutpurse would herself appear on the stage
of the Fortune Theatre. See Intro., p. 2.

38. *your hands*] your applause.

ARDEN
OF FAVERSHA

[*LIST OF CHARACTERS*

in order of appearance

THOMAS ARDEN, *a Gentleman of Faversham.*
FRANKLIN, *his friend.*
ALICE, *Arden's wife.*
ADAM FOWLE, *landlord of the Flower-de-Luce.*
MICHAEL, *Arden's servant.*
MOSBY, *lover of Arden's wife.*
CLARKE, *a painter.*
GREENE, *a tenant.*
SUSAN, *Mosby's sister and Alice's servingmaid.*
BRADSHAW, *a goldsmith.*
BLACK WILL } *hired murderers.*
SHAKEBAG }
A Prentice.
LORD CHEYNE *and his* Men.
A Ferryman.
DICK REEDE, *sailor and inhabitant of Faversham.*
A Sailor, *his friend.*
Mayor of Faversham *and the* Watch.

SCENE: FAVERSHAM IN KENT,
LONDON, AND ENVIRONS.]

The Tragedy of
Master Arden of Faversham

[I]

Enter ARDEN *and* FRANKLIN.

Franklin. Arden, cheer up thy spirits and droop no more.
My gracious Lord the Duke of Somerset
Hath freely given to thee and to thy heirs,
By letters patents from his majesty,
All the lands of the Abbey of Faversham. 5
Here are the deeds,   [*He hands over the papers.*]
Sealed and subscribed with his name and the king's.
Read them, and leave this melancholy mood.
Arden. Franklin, thy love prolongs my weary life;
And, but for thee, how odious were this life, 10
That shows me nothing but torments my soul,
And those foul objects that offend mine eyes,
Which makes me wish that for this veil of heaven
The earth hung over my head and covered me.
Love letters passed 'twixt Mosby and my wife, 15
And they have privy meetings in the town.
Nay, on his finger did I spy the ring
Which at our marriage day the priest put on.
Can any grief be half so great as this?
Franklin. Comfort thyself, sweet friend; it is not strange 20
That women will be false and wavering.
Arden. Ay, but to dote on such a one as he
Is monstrous, Franklin, and intolerable.
Franklin. Why, what is he?

1.0.1. *FRANKLIN*] A 'franklin' was the general name for a small landowner.

2. *Duke of Somerset*] Edward Seymour, Duke of Somerset and Lord Protector to Edward VI, made a considerable profit out of the sale and exploitation of land made available by the dissolution of the monasteries.

4. *letters patents*] open letters, usually from the monarch, which record and confer a title or right. See Intro., p. 28.

13. *for*] in place of.

16. *privy*] secret.

271

Arden. A botcher, and no better at the first,   25
    Who, by base brokage getting some small stock,
    Crept into service of a nobleman,
    And by his servile flattery and fawning
    Is now become the steward of his house,
    And bravely jets it in his silken gown.   30
Franklin. No nobleman will count'nance such a peasant.
Arden. Yes, the Lord Clifford, he that loves not me.
    But through his favour let not him grow proud;
    For, were he by the Lord Protector backed,
    He should not make me to be pointed at.   35
    I am by birth a gentleman of blood,
    And that injurious ribald that attempts
    To violate my dear wife's chastity
    (For dear I hold her love, as dear as heaven)
    Shall, on the bed which he thinks to defile,   40
    See his dissevered joints and sinews torn,
    Whilst on the planchers pants his weary body,
    Smeared in the channels of his lustful blood.
Franklin. Be patient, gentle friend, and learn of me
    To ease thy grief and save her chastity.   45
    Entreat her fair; sweet words are fittest engines
    To raze the flint walls of a woman's breast.
    In any case be not too jealous,
    Nor make no question of her love to thee;
    But, as securely, presently take horse,   50
    And lie with me at London all this term;

---

25. *botcher*] tailor who does repairs.
at the first] from his birth.
26. *base brokage*] low-level trading on the edge of the legitimate market. See Intro., p. 30.
29. *steward*] official in charge of household affairs and finances.
30. *bravely jets it*] stylishly struts about.
32. *Lord Clifford*] Mosby was actually servant to Lord North. The name was probably changed to prevent scandal in the North family.
35. *pointed at*] The public humiliation of being a cuckold was as important as the sense of personal betrayal. See Intro., p. 32.
36. *a gentleman of blood*] well born; i.e. not someone who has acquired gentry status for the first time by his own efforts.
37. *injurious ribald*] insulting dissolute person.
41. *dissevered*] torn apart.
42. *planchers*] floor planks.
46. *engines*] devices used in war.
47. *raze*] knock to the ground. A woman is being compared to a city under seige. See Intro., p. 33.
50. *as securely*] confidently.
presently] at once.
51. *lie*] stay, lodge.
term] session of the law courts.

For women, when they may, will not,
But being kept back straight grow outrageous.
Arden. Though this abhors from reason, yet I'll try it,
And call her forth, and presently take leave.—   55
How, Alice!

Here enters ALICE.

Alice. Husband, what mean you to get up so early?
Summer nights are short, and yet you rise ere day.
Had I been wake, you had not rise so soon.
Arden. Sweet love, thou know'st that we two, Ovid-like,   60
Have often chid the morning when it 'gan to peep,
And often wished that dark Night's purblind steeds
Would pull her by the purple mantle back
And cast her in the ocean to her love.
But this night, sweet Alice, thou hast killed my heart: 65
I heard thee call on Mosby in thy sleep.
Alice. 'Tis like I was asleep when I named him,
For being awake he comes not in my thoughts.
Arden. Ay, but you started up, and suddenly,
Instead of him, caught me about the neck.   70
Alice. Instead of him? Why, who was there but you?
And where but one is how can I mistake?
Franklin. Arden, leave to urge her overfar.
Arden. Nay, love, there is no credit in a dream.
Let it suffice I know thou lovest me well.   75
Alice. Now I remember whereupon it came:
Had we no talk of Mosby yesternight?
Franklin. Mistress Alice, I heard you name him once or twice.
Alice. And thereof came it, and therefore blame not me.
Arden. I know it did, and therefore let it pass.   80
I must to London, sweet Alice, presently.

52–3.] an echo of commonplaces about women's wilfulness. See Intro., p. 33.
54. *abhors from*] is repugnant to.
59. *wake; rise*] obsolete variants of the past participles 'awake' and 'risen'.
60–4.] The Classical Roman poet Ovid wrote about love in his *Amores*. His thirteenth elegy, which urges the sun not to bring on the morning and end the night of love, was often adapted and quoted and translated by Elizabethan and Jacobean poets. See Intro., pp. 32–3 and 49–50.
62. *purblind*] totally or partially blind.
67. *like*] likely.
72.] i.e. And how could I be mistaken, with only one person there?
73. *leave*] leave off, cease.
74. *no credit*] nothing that can be believed.
76. *whereupon it came*] how it came about.
77. The idea that dreams drew on the events and preoccupations of the previous day was current in contemporary dream theory.

Alice. But tell me, do you mean to stay there long?
Arden. No longer than till my affairs be done.
Franklin. He will not stay above a month at most.
Alice. A month? Ay me! Sweet Arden, come again   85
　　Within a day or two, or else I die.
Arden. I cannot long be from thee, gentle Alice.
　　Whilst Michael fetch our horses from the field,
　　Franklin and I will down unto the quay,
　　For I have certain goods there to unload.   90
　　Meanwhile prepare our breakfast, gentle Alice,
　　For yet ere noon we'll take horse and away.
　　　　　　　　　　　　Exeunt ARDEN *and* FRANKLIN.
Alice. Ere noon he means to take horse and away!
　　Sweet news is this. Oh, that some airy spirit
　　Would in the shape and likeness of a horse   95
　　Gallop with Arden 'cross the ocean
　　And throw him from his back into the waves!
　　Sweet Mosby is the man that hath my heart;
　　And he usurps it, having nought but this,
　　That I am tied to him by marriage.   100
　　Love is a god, and marriage is but words;
　　And therefore Mosby's title is the best.
　　Tush! Whether it be or no, he shall be mine
　　In spite of him, of Hymen, and of rites.

　　　　　Here enters ADAM *of the Flower-de-Luce.*

　　And here comes Adam of the Flower-de-Luce.   105
　　I hope he brings me tidings of my love.—
　　How now, Adam, what is the news with you?
　　Be not afraid; my husband is now from home.
Adam. He whom you wot of, Mosby, Mistress Alice,
　　Is come to town and sends you word by me   110
　　In any case you may not visit him.
Alice. Not visit him?
Adam. No, nor take no knowledge of his being here.
Alice. But tell me, is he angry or displeased?
Adam. Should seem so, for he is wondrous sad.   115

　　89–90. *quay . . . unload*] Faversham was a port on the River Medway at this time.
The historical Arden had been made a controller of the customs for the port through
the patronage of his wife's father. See Intro., p. 28.
　　99. *he*] Arden.
　　104. *Hymen*] god of marriage.
　　104.1. Flower-de-Luce] an inn, formerly situated in Abbey Street nearly opposite Arden's house.
　　109. *wot*] know.
　　115. *Should seem so*] it seems so.

Alice. Were he as mad as raving Hercules,
   I'll see him. Ay, and were thy house of force,
   These hands of mine should raze it to the ground
   Unless that thou wouldst bring me to my love.
Adam. Nay, an you be so impatient, I'll be gone.   120
                                   [*He starts to leave.*]
Alice. Stay, Adam, stay! Thou wert wont to be my friend.
   Ask Mosby how I have incurred his wrath;
   Bear him from me these pair of silver dice   [*Offering dice*]
   With which we played for kisses many a time,
   And when I lost I won, and so did he—   125
   Such winning and such losing Jove send me!
   And bid him, if his love do not decline,
   To come this morning but along my door
   And as a stranger but salute me there.
   This may he do without suspect or fear.   130
Adam. I'll tell him what you say, and so farewell.
Alice. Do, and one day I'll make amends for all.   *Exit* ADAM.
   I know he loves me well, but dares not come
   Because my husband is so jealous,
   And these my narrow-prying neighbours blab,   135
   Hinder our meetings when we would confer.
   But, if I live, that block shall be removed;
   And Mosby, thou that comes to me by stealth
   Shalt neither fear the biting speech of men
   Nor Arden's looks. As surely shall he die   140
   As I abhor him and love only thee.

             Here enters MICHAEL.

   How now, Michael, whither are you going?
Michael. To fetch my master's nag. I hope you'll think on me.
Alice. Ay, but Michael, see you keep your oath
   And be as secret as you are resolute.   145
Michael. I'll see he shall not live above a week.

---

116. *Hercules*] The classical hero was driven mad by the torments inflicted by a
poisoned shirt, innocently sent to him by his wronged wife Deianira, who had been
persuaded by the centaur Nessus that it would have the magic power to bring him
back. Hercules had also gone mad in another adventure when his madness took the
form of allowing himself to be dressed as a woman.
  117. *thy house*] the inn where Mosby is staying.
  of force] fortified.
  120. *an*] if.
  128. *along*] past.
  130. *suspect*] suspicion.
  137. *that block*] that obstacle to my love.
  143. *think on me*] remember me, regard me with favour. See line 148.

Alice. On that condition, Michael, here is my hand;
   None shall have Mosby's sister but thyself.
Michael. I understand the painter here hard by
   Hath made report that he and Sue is sure.   150
Alice. There's no such matter, Michael; believe it not.
Michael. But he hath sent a dagger sticking in a heart,
   With a verse or two stolen from a painted cloth,
   The which I hear the wench keeps in her chest.
   Well, let her keep it! I shall find a fellow   155
   That can both write and read and make rhyme too;
   And, if I do—well, I say no more.
   I'll send from London such a taunting letter
   As she shall eat the heart he sent with salt
   And fling the dagger at the painter's head.   160
Alice. What needs all this? I say that Susan's thine.
Michael. Why, then I say that I will kill my master
   Or anything that you will have me do.
Alice. But, Michael, see you do it cunningly.
Michael. Why, say I should be took, I'll ne'er confess   165
   That you know anything; and Susan, being a maid,
   May beg me from the gallows of the shrieve.
Alice. Trust not to that, Michael.
Michael. You cannot tell me; I have seen it, I.
   But mistress, tell her whether I live or die   170
   I'll make her more worth than twenty painters can;
   For I will rid mine elder brother away,
   And then the farm of Bolton is mine own.
   Who would not venture upon house and land
   When he may have it for a right-down blow?   175

Here enters MOSBY.

---

150. *is sure*] are engaged.

152.] The painter has sent Susan an emblem depicting his wounded heart, accompanied by a verse, in the traditional style of emblems. See Intro., p. 34.

153. *stolen*] borrowed, plagiarized.

painted cloth] hangings painted to look like tapestry, often with classical or biblical stories. They were a common part of household furniture.

159–60.] Michael pictorializes the painter's emblem (see line 152 and n.) as though the heart and dagger were real.

165. *took*] taken, arrested.

166–7. *Susan . . . shrieve*] referring to the popular belief that a virgin might save a condemned man from the gallows by offering to marry him.

167. *shrieve*] sheriff.

171. *worth*] wealthy, prosperous.

173. *Bolton*] Boughton-under-Blean, a village on the Pilgrims' Way between Faversham and Canterbury.

175. *right-down*] downright.

Alice. Yonder comes Mosby. Michael, get thee gone,
And let not him nor any know thy drifts.   *Exit* MICHAEL.
Mosby, my love!
Mosby. Away, I say, and talk not to me now.
Alice. A word or two, sweetheart, and then I will.   180
'Tis yet but early days; thou needest not fear.
Mosby. Where is your husband?
Alice. 'Tis now high water, and he is at the quay.
Mosby. There let him be; henceforward know me not.
Alice. Is this the end of all thy solemn oaths?   185
Is this the fruit thy reconcilement buds?
Have I for this given thee so many favours,
Incurred my husband's hate, and—out, alas!—
Made shipwreck of mine honour for thy sake?
And dost thou say, 'Henceforward know me not'?   190
Remember, when I locked thee in my closet,
What were thy words and mine? Did we not both
Decree to murder Arden in the night?
The heavens can witness, and the world can tell,
Before I saw that falsehood look of thine,   195
'Fore I was tangled with thy 'ticing speech,
Arden to me was dearer than my soul—
And shall be still. Base peasant, get thee gone,
And boast not of thy conquest over me,
Gotten by witchcraft and mere sorcery.   200
For what hast thou to countenance my love,
Being descended of a noble house
And matched already with a gentleman
Whose servant thou mayst be? And so farewell.
Mosby. Ungentle and unkind Alice, now I see   205
That which I ever feared and find too true:
A woman's love is as the lightning flame
Which even in bursting forth consumes itself.
To try thy constancy have I been strange.

---

177. *drifts*] plans, schemes.
181. *early days*] early in the day.
186.] i.e. Is this all that your promise of reconciliation comes to? *Buds* means
'causes to bud'.
188. *out, alas!*] an exclamation of dismay.
191. *closet*] private room.
196. *'ticing*] enticing.
200. *witchcraft*] Men could be accused of witchcraft as well as women.
201. *countenance*] be in keeping with.
202. *Being*] I being.
204. *mayst be*] deserve to be.
209. *strange*] distant, unfriendly.

Would I had never tried, but lived in hope!   210
Alice. What needs thou try me whom thou never found false?
Mosby. Yet pardon me, for love is jealous.
Alice. So lists the sailor to the mermaids' song;
          So looks the traveller to the basilisk.
          I am content for to be reconciled,   215
          And that I know will be mine overthrow.
Mosby. Thine overthrow? First let the world dissolve!
Alice. Nay, Mosby, let me still enjoy thy love;
          And, happen what will, I am resolute.
          My saving husband hoards up bags of gold   220
          To make our children rich, and now is he
          Gone to unload the goods that shall be thine,
          And he and Franklin will to London straight.
Mosby. To London, Alice? If thou'lt be ruled by me,
          We'll make him sure enough for coming there.   225
Alice. Ah, would we could!
Mosby. I happened on a painter yesternight,
          The only cunning man of Christendom,
          For he can temper poison with his oil
          That whoso looks upon the work he draws   230
          Shall, with the beams that issue from his sight,
          Suck venom to his breast and slay himself.
          Sweet Alice, he shall draw thy counterfeit,
          That Arden may, by gazing on it, perish.
Alice. Ay, but Mosby, that is dangerous;   235
          For thou or I or any other else,
          Coming into the chamber where it hangs, may die.
Mosby. Ay, but we'll have it covered with a cloth
          And hung up in the study for himself.
Alice. It may not be; for, when the picture's drawn,   240

210.] Would that I had never tested your constancy, but had been content to live
in hope!

213. *mermaids' song*] Mermaids were often associated with the classical Sirens,
whose song was supposed to lure sailors to their deaths. A commonplace image for
a deceptive woman. See Intro., p. 54.

214. *basilisk*] a fabled serpent whose look was supposed to be fatal.

215. *reconciled*] i.e. to Mosby.

221. *children*] No children appear in the play, but the historical Arden had a
daughter.

225. *for*] to prevent (him) from.

228. *only*] most.

229. *temper*] mix.

230–2.] Contemporary optical theory held that sight was produced by physical
beams going from the eye to the object seen.

233. *counterfeit*] image.

Arden, I know, will come and show it me.

Mosby. Fear not; we'll have that shall serve the turn.

　　　　　　　　　　　　　　　　[*They cross the stage.*]

　　This is the painter's house; I'll call him forth.

Alice. But, Mosby, I'll have no such picture, I.

Mosby. I pray thee leave it to my discretion.—　　　　245

　　How, Clarke!

Here enters CLARKE.

Oh, you are an honest man of your word; you served me well.

Clarke. Why, sir, I'll do it for you at any time,

　　Provided, as you have given your word,

　　I may have Susan Mosby to my wife.　　　　　　250

　　For, as sharp-witted poets, whose sweet verse

　　Make heavenly gods break off their nectar draughts

　　And lay their ears down to the lowly earth,

　　Use humble promise to their sacred Muse,

　　So we that are the poets' favourites　　　　　　255

　　Must have a love. Ay, Love is the painter's Muse,

　　That makes him frame a speaking countenance,

　　A weeping eye that witnesses heart's grief.

　　Then tell me, Master Mosby, shall I have her?

Alice. 'Tis pity but he should; he'll use her well.　　260

Mosby. Clarke, here's my hand; my sister shall be thine.

Clarke. Then, brother, to requite this courtesy,

　　You shall command my life, my skill, and all.

Alice. Ah, that thou couldst be secret!

Mosby. Fear him not. Leave; I have talked sufficient.　　265

Clarke. You know not me that ask such questions.

　　Let it suffice I know you love him well

　　And fain would have your husband made away,

　　Wherein, trust me, you show a noble mind,

　　That, rather than you'll live with him you hate,　　270

---

242. *that . . . turn*] that which will meet the situation.

242.1.] A door at the back of the stage serves as the painter's door.

246. *Clarke*] a name invented by the playwright: the historical painter was called William Blackborne.

250. *to*] as, for.

255. *favourites*] intimates, closest acquaintances. Poetry and painting are closely allied.

257. *frame . . . countenance*] The Renaissance and earlier commonplace that poetry was a speaking picture goes back to classical times. Simonides of Ceos is the usual classical citation. *Frame* means 'fashion'.

260. *but*] but that, unless.

265. *Leave*] cease.

268. *fain*] willingly, gladly.

You'll venture life and die with him you love.
      The like will I do for my Susan's sake.
Alice. Yet nothing could enforce me to the deed
      But Mosby's love. Might I without control
      Enjoy thee still, then Arden should not die;   275
      But seeing I cannot, therefore let him die.
Mosby. Enough, sweet Alice; thy kind words makes me melt.
      [*To Clarke*] Your trick of poisoned pictures we dislike;
      Some other poison would do better far.
Alice. Ay, such as might be put into his broth,   280
      And yet in taste not to be found at all.
Clarke. I know your mind, and here I have it for you.
                              [*He offers a vial of poison.*]
      Put but a dram of this into his drink
      Or any kind of broth that he shall eat,
      And he shall die within an hour after.   285
Alice. As I am a gentlewoman, Clarke, next day
      Thou and Susan shall be marrièd.
Mosby. And I'll make her dowry more than I'll talk of, Clarke.
Clarke. Yonder's your husband. Mosby, I'll be gone.

      Here enters ARDEN *and* FRANKLIN [*and* MICHAEL].

Alice. In good time, see where my husband comes.—   290
      Master Mosby, ask him the question yourself.   *Exit* CLARKE.
Mosby. Master Arden, being at London yesternight,
      The Abbey lands whereof you are now possessed
      Were offered me on some occasion
      By Greene, one of Sir Antony Ager's men.   295
      I pray you, sir, tell me, are not the lands yours?
      Hath any other interest herein?
Arden. Mosby, that question we'll decide anon.—
      Alice, make ready my breakfast; I must hence.   *Exit* ALICE.
      As for the lands, Mosby, they are mine   300
      By letters patents from his majesty.
      But I must have a mandate for my wife;
      They say you seek to rob me of her love.
      Villain, what makes thou in her company?
      She's no companion for so base a groom.   305

---

274. *control*] hindrance.
290–1.] Alice suddenly switches the conversation to make it seem as if Mosby
had come to talk to her husband on business.
302. *mandate*] order, injunction. Arden is saying that he needs to have some
authority similar to the letters patent to ensure his claim to his wife.
304. *makes thou*] are you doing.
305. *groom*] fellow, man of inferior position.

Mosby. Arden, I thought not on her; I came to thee,
   But rather than I pocket up this wrong—
Franklin. What will you do, sir?
Mosby. Revenge it on the proudest of you both.
             Then Arden draws forth Mosby's sword.
Arden. So, sirrah, you may not wear a sword!   310
   The statute makes against artificers.
   I warrant that I do. Now use your bodkin,
   Your Spanish needle, and your pressing iron,
   For this shall go with me. And mark my words—
   You, goodman botcher, 'tis to you I speak—   315
   The next time that I take thee near my house,
   Instead of legs I'll make thee crawl on stumps.
Mosby. Ah, Master Arden, you have injured me.
   I do appeal to God and to the world.
Franklin. Why, canst thou deny thou wert a botcher once?   320
Mosby. Measure me what I am, not what I was.
Arden. Why, what art thou now but a velvet drudge,
   A cheating steward, and base-minded peasant?
Mosby. Arden, now thou hast belched and vomited
   The rancorous venom of thy misswoll'n heart,   325
   Hear me but speak. As I intend to live
   With God and His elected saints in heaven,
   I never meant more to solicit her;
   And that she knows, and all the world shall see.
   I loved her once—sweet Arden, pardon me.   330
   I could not choose; her beauty fired my heart.
   But time hath quenched these overraging coals;
   And Arden, though I now frequent thy house,
   'Tis for my sister's sake, her waiting-maid,
   And not for hers. Mayest thou enjoy her long!   335
   Hellfire and wrathful vengeance light on me

---

307. *pocket up*] meekly submit to.

310. *sirrah*] a form of address used contemptuously or to social inferiors or children.

311.] The law on wearing swords forbids working men to carry them.

312. *I . . . do*] I have authorization for what I do (i.e. taking away Mosby's sword).

   bodkin] any pointed instrument, here a large tailoring needle. Arden speaks contemptuously.

313. *Spanish needle*] a rare and particularly fine kind of imported needle.

   pressing iron] continues the insult in line 310; an iron can be a sword or a tailor's instrument for pressing clothes.

315. *goodman*] a prefix indicating rank below that of a gentleman; here used insultingly.

322. *velvet drudge*] menial in a velvet livery.

If I dishonour her or injure thee!
Arden. Mosby, with these thy protestations
    The deadly hatred of my heart is appeased,
    And thou and I'll be friends if this prove true.   340
    As for the base terms I gave thee late,
    Forget them, Mosby; I had cause to speak,
    When all the knights and gentlemen of Kent
    Make common table-talk of her and thee.
Mosby. Who lives that is not touched with slanderous tongues?   345
Franklin. Then, Mosby, to eschew the speech of men,
    Upon whose general bruit all honour hangs,
    Forbear his house.
Arden. Forbear it? Nay, rather frequent it more.
    The world shall see that I distrust her not.   350
    To warn him on the sudden from my house
    Were to confirm the rumour that is grown.
Mosby. By my faith, sir, you say true.
    And therefore will I sojourn here awhile
    Until our enemies have talked their fill;   355
    And then, I hope, they'll cease and at last confess
    How causeless they have injured her and me.
Arden. And I will lie at London all this term
    To let them see how light I weigh their words.

    Here enters ALICE. [*Table, chairs, and breakfast are brought on.*]

Alice. Husband, sit down; your breakfast will be cold.   360
Arden. Come, Master Mosby, will you sit with us?
Mosby. I cannot eat, but I'll sit for company.
Arden. Sirrah Michael, see our horse be ready.
                  [*Exit* MICHAEL *but returns soon after.*]
Alice. Husband, why pause ye? Why eat you not?
Arden. I am not well. There's something in this broth   365
    That is not wholesome. Didst thou make it, Alice?
Alice. I did, and that's the cause it likes not you.
        Then she throws down the broth on the ground.
    There's nothing that I do can please your taste.
    You were best to say I would have poisoned you.—

---

341. *late*] lately; just now.
347. *bruit*] report.
359.1.] There is no break in the action here. The continuous staging of these plays allows the exterior scene of the meeting with Mosby and Arden to move straight into the breakfast scene with tables and chairs brought on to the stage.
    367. *likes not you*] (1) does not please you; (2) disagrees with your system (as a poison would do).

I cannot speak or cast aside my eye   370
But he imagines I have stepped awry.—
Here's he that you cast in my teeth so oft;
Now will I be convinced or purge myself.
[*To Mosby*] I charge thee speak to this mistrustful man,
Thou that wouldst see me hang, thou, Mosby, thou.   375
What favour hast thou had more than a kiss
At coming or departing from the town?
Mosby. You wrong yourself and me to cast these doubts;
    Your loving husband is not jealous.
Arden. Why, gentle Mistress Alice, cannot I be ill   380
But you'll accuse yourself?—
Franklin, thou hast a box of mithridate;
I'll take a little to prevent the worst.
Franklin. Do so, and let us presently take horse.
    My life for yours, ye shall do well enough.   385
Alice. Give me a spoon; I'll eat of it myself.
Would it were full of poison to the brim!
Then should my cares and troubles have an end.
Was ever silly woman so tormented?
Arden. Be patient, sweet love; I mistrust not thee.   390
Alice. God will revenge it, Arden, if thou dost;
For never woman loved her husband better
Than I do thee.
Arden. I know it, sweet Alice. Cease to complain,
Lest that in tears I answer thee again.   395
Franklin. Come, leave this dallying, and let us away.
Alice. Forbear to wound me with that bitter word;
Arden shall go to London in my arms.
Arden. Loath am I to depart, yet I must go.
Alice. Wilt thou to London then, and leave me here?   400
    Ah, if thou love me, gentle Arden, stay.
Yet, if thy business be of great import,
Go if thou wilt; I'll bear it as I may.
But write from London to me every week,
Nay, every day, and stay no longer there   405
Than thou must needs, lest that I die for sorrow.

---

373. *convinced*] convicted.
purge myself] purge myself of guilt. (But with a suggestion of 'perjure myself'.)
374. *mistrustful*] suspicious, distrustful.
382. *mithridate*] a chemical compound regarded as a universal antidote against poison.
389. *silly*] helpless, defenceless.
397. *that bitter word*] i.e. 'dallying' (line 396). Alice is offended by the suggestion that her desire for Arden to stay is mere 'dallying'. See Intro., p. 37–8.

Arden. I'll write unto thee every other tide,
     And so farewell, sweet Alice, till we meet next.
Alice. Farewell, husband, seeing you'll have it so.—
     And, Master Franklin, seeing you take him hence,   410
     In hope you'll hasten him home I'll give you this.
                              And then she kisseth him.
Franklin. And, if he stay, the fault shall not be mine.—
     Mosby, farewell, and see you keep your oath.
Mosby. I hope he is not jealous of me now.
Arden. No, Mosby, no. Hereafter think of me   415
     As of your dearest friend, and so farewell.
                    Exeunt ARDEN, FRANKLIN, *and* MICHAEL.
Alice. I am glad he is gone. He was about to stay,
     But did you mark me then how I brake off?
Mosby. Ay, Alice, and it was cunningly performed.
     But what a villain is this painter Clarke!   420
Alice. Was it not a goodly poison that he gave!
     Why, he's as well now as he was before.
     It should have been some fine confection
     That might have given the broth some dainty taste.
     This powder was too gross and populous.   425
Mosby. But, had he eaten but three spoonfuls more,
     Then had he died and our love continued.
Alice. Why, so it shall, Mosby, albeit he live.
Mosby. It is unpossible, for I have sworn
     Never hereafter to solicit thee   430
     Or, whilst he lives, once more importune thee.
Alice. Thou shalt not need; I will importune thee.
     What? Shall an oath make thee forsake my love?
     As if I have not sworn as much myself
     And given my hand unto him in the church!   435
     Tush, Mosby! Oaths are words, and words is wind,
     And wind is mutable. Then I conclude:
     'Tis childishness to stand upon an oath.
Mosby. Well proved, Mistress Alice. Yet, by your leave,
     I'll keep mine unbroken whilst he lives.   440
Alice. Ay, do, and spare not. His time is but short;
     For, if thou beest as resolute as I,

---

407. *tide*] The journey from Faversham to London was by road to Gravesend
and from there by boat up the Thames.
423. *confection*] mixture, compound.
425. *gross*] disgusting.
populous] obvious, perceptible.
441.] i.e. Go right ahead and keep your oath; Arden hasn't long to live anyway.

We'll have him murdered as he walks the streets.
In London many alehouse ruffians keep,
Which, as I hear, will murder men for gold.   445
They shall be soundly fee'd to pay him home.

Here enters GREENE.

Mosby. Alice, what's he that comes yonder? Knowest thou him?
Alice. Mosby, begone! I hope 'tis one that comes
    To put in practice our intended drifts.   *Exit* MOSBY.
Greene. Mistress Arden, you are well met.   450
    I am sorry that your husband is from home
    Whenas my purposed journey was to him.
    Yet all my labour is not spent in vain,
    For I suppose that you can full discourse
    And flat resolve me of the thing I seek.   455
Alice. What is it, Master Greene? If that I may
    Or can with safety, I will answer you.
Greene. I heard your husband hath the grant of late,
    Confirmed by letters patents from the king,
    Of all the lands of the Abbey of Faversham,   460
    Generally intitled, so that all former grants
    Are cut off, whereof I myself had one;
    But now my interest by that is void.
    This is all, Mistress Arden; is it true nor no?
Alice. True, Master Greene; the lands are his in state,   465
    And whatsoever leases were before
    Are void for term of Master Arden's life.
    He hath the grant under the Chancery seal.
Greene. Pardon me, Mistress Arden; I must speak,
    For I am touched. Your husband doth me wrong   470

---

444. *keep*] exist, live.
446. *fee'd*] paid with a fee.
to pay him home] to pay him fully, i.e. with his death.
449.] to carry out our intentions.
454. *full discourse*] fully explain.
455. *flat resolve*] completely satisfy.
461. *Generally intitled*] given a title without any exceptions; i.e. Arden had complete ownership which superseded all earlier arrangements and allowances. See Intro., pp. 28–9.
463. *my interest . . . void*] my claim to the land has been superseded by the letters patent granting the land to Arden.
465. *in state*] by right of legal ownership or possession.
468. *under . . . seal*] i.e. with the Lord Chancellor's authority, representing the highest court of judicature in the land next to the House of Lords.
470. *touched*] affected.

To wring me from the little land I have.
My living is my life; only that
Resteth remainder of my portion.
Desire of wealth is endless in his mind,
And he is greedy-gaping still for gain;   475
Nor cares he though young gentlemen do beg,
So he may scrape and hoard up in his pouch.
But, seeing he hath taken my lands, I'll value life
As careless as he is careful for to get;
And tell him this from me: I'll be revenged,   480
And so as he shall wish the Abbey lands
Had rested still within their former state.
Alice. Alas, poor gentleman, I pity you,
And woe is me that any man should want.
God knows, 'tis not my fault. But wonder not   485
Though he be hard to others when to me—
Ah, Master Greene, God knows how I am used!
Greene. Why, Mistress Arden, can the crabbèd churl
Use you unkindly? Respects he not your birth,
Your honourable friends, nor what you brought?   490
Why, all Kent knows your parentage and what you are.
Alice. Ah, Master Greene, be it spoken in secret here,
I never live good day with him alone.
When he is at home, then have I froward looks,
Hard words, and blows to mend the match withal.   495
And, though I might content as good a man,
Yet doth he keep in every corner trulls;
And, weary with his trugs at home,
Then rides he straight to London. There, forsooth,
He revels it among such filthy ones   500
As counsels him to make away his wife.
Thus live I daily in continual fear,
In sorrow, so despairing of redress
As every day I wish with hearty prayer
That he or I were taken forth the world.   505
Greene. Now trust me, Mistress Alice, it grieveth me

---

472. *living*] land.
472-3. *only . . . portion*] that land is all that remains of my inheritance.
478-9. *I'll . . . get*] I'll value my life as little as he is anxious to gain possession of
my land.
488. *crabbèd*] bad-tempered.
490. *what you brought*] i.e. what you brought to your marriage as your dowry.
494. *froward*] ill-humoured.
496. *content*] give satisfaction to.
497-8. *trulls, trugs*] women, prostitutes.

So fair a creature should be so abused.
Why, who would have thought the civil sir so sullen?
He looks so smoothly. Now, fie upon him, churl!
And if he live a day he lives too long.   510
But frolic, woman! I shall be the man
Shall set you free from all this discontent.
And if the churl deny my interest
And will not yield my lease into my hand,
I'll pay him home, whatever hap to me.   515
Alice. But speak you as you think?
Greene. Ay, God's my witness, I mean plain dealing,
For I had rather die than lose my land.
Alice. Then, Master Greene, be counsellèd by me:
Endanger not yourself for such a churl,   520
But hire some cutter for to cut him short;
And here's ten pound to wager them withal.
                                        [*She offers money.*]
When he is dead, you shall have twenty more;
And the lands whereof my husband is possessed
Shall be intitled as they were before.   525
Greene. Will you keep promise with me?
Alice. Or count me false and perjured whilst I live.
Greene. Then here's my hand; I'll have him so dispatched.
I'll up to London straight; I'll thither post
And never rest till I have compassed it.   530
Till then, farewell.
Alice. Good fortune follow all your forward thoughts!
And whosoever doth attempt the deed,
A happy hand I wish; and so farewell.   *Exit* GREENE.
All this goes well. Mosby, I long for thee   535
To let thee know all that I have contrived.

                Here enters MOSBY *and* CLARKE.

Mosby. How now, Alice, what's the news?
Alice. Such as will content thee well, sweetheart.

---

509. *churl*] low-born peasant.
511. *frolic*] cheer up.
515. *home*] all the way, to the heart.
521. *cutter*] cutthroat.
522. *to . . . withal*] with which to hire them.
525. *intitled . . . before*] have their ownership deeds set up to allow for pre-
existing tenancies.
528. *dispatched*] killed.
530. *compassed*] encompassed, achieved.
532. *forward*] eager, zealous.

Mosby. Well, let them pass awhile, and tell me, Alice,
　　　How have you dealt and tempered with my sister?   540
　　　What, will she have my neighbour Clarke or no?
Alice. What, Master Mosby! Let him woo himself.
　　　Think you that maids look not for fair words?—
　　　Go to her, Clarke; she's all alone within.
　　　Michael, my man, is clean out of her books.   545
Clarke. I thank you, Mistress Arden. I will in;
　　　And, if fair Susan and I can make a gree,
　　　You shall command me to the uttermost
　　　As far as either goods or life may stretch.   *Exit* CLARKE.
Mosby. Now, Alice, let's hear thy news.   550
Alice. They be so good that I must laugh for joy
　　　Before I can begin to tell my tale.
Mosby. Let's hear them, that I may laugh for company.
Alice. This morning, Master Greene—Dick Greene, I mean,
　　　From whom my husband had the Abbey land—   555
　　　Came hither, railing, for to know the truth
　　　Whether my husband had the lands by grant.
　　　I told him all, whereat he stormed amain
　　　And swore he would cry quittance with the churl
　　　And, if he did deny his interest,   560
　　　Stab him, whatsoever did befall himself.
　　　Whenas I saw his choler thus to rise,
　　　I whetted on the gentleman with words;
　　　And, to conclude, Mosby, at last we grew
　　　To composition for my husband's death.   565
　　　I give him ten pound to hire knaves
　　　By some device to make away the churl.
　　　When he is dead, he should have twenty more
　　　And repossess his former lands again.
　　　On this we 'greed, and he is ridden straight   570
　　　To London to bring his death about.

---

539. *them*] the news.
540. *tempered with*] worked on (as with metal).
545. *clean . . . books*] completely out of her favour.
547. *make a gree*] come to terms.
556. *for*] in order.
558. *amain*] with might and main.
559. *cry quittance*] be even.
560.] and, if Arden did deny Greene's claim to the land. (See line 463.)
562. *Whenas*] when.
choler] anger.
563. *whetted on*] stirred up.
565. *composition*] agreement.

Mosby. But call you this good news?
Alice. Ay, sweetheart, be they not?
Mosby. 'Twere cheerful news to hear the churl were dead;
     But trust me, Alice, I take it passing ill   575
     You would be so forgetful of our state
     To make recount of it to every groom.
     What? To acquaint each stranger with our drifts,
     Chiefly in case of murder? Why, 'tis the way
     To make it open unto Arden's self   580
     And bring thyself and me to ruin both.
     Forewarned, forearmed; who threats his enemy
     Lends him a sword to guard himself withal.
Alice. I did it for the best.
Mosby. Well, seeing 'tis done, cheerly let it pass.   585
     You know this Greene; is he not religious?
     A man, I guess, of great devotion?
Alice. He is.
Mosby. Then, sweet Alice, let it pass. I have a drift
     Will quiet all, whatever is amiss.   590

                Here enters CLARKE *and* SUSAN.

Alice. How now, Clarke? Have you found me false?
     Did I not plead the matter hard for you?
Clarke. You did.
Mosby. And what? Will 't be a match?
Clarke. A match, i' faith, sir. Ay, the day is mine.   595
     The painter lays his colours to the life;
     His pencil draws no shadows in his love.
     Susan is mine.
Alice. You make her blush.
Mosby. What, sister? Is it Clark must be the man?   600
Susan. It resteth in your grant. Some words are passed,
     And haply we be grown unto a match
     If you be willing that it shall be so.
Mosby. Ah, Master Clarke, it resteth at my grant;

---

575. *passing*] exceedingly.
577. *every groom*] every low fellow (who might not be trustworthy).
582. *who*] whoever.
585. *cheerly*] blithely.
589. *drift*] plan (that).
595. *the day is mine*] I have carried the day, won her consent.
596. *to the life*] as they are in real life.
601. *in your grant*] in your authority.
602. *haply*] (1) perchance; (2) happily.

You see my sister's yet at my dispose;   605
But, so you'll grant me one thing I shall ask,
I am content my sister shall be yours.
Clarke. What is it, Master Mosby?
Mosby. I do remember once in secret talk
You told me how you could compound by art   610
A crucifix impoisonèd,
That whoso look upon it should wax blind
And with the scent be stifled, that ere long
He should die poisoned that did view it well.
I would have you make me such a crucifix,   615
And then I'll grant my sister shall be yours.
Clarke. Though I am loath, because it toucheth life,
Yet, rather or I'll leave sweet Susan's love,
I'll do it, and with all the haste I may.
But for whom is it?   620
Alice. Leave that to us. Why, Clarke, is it possible
That you should paint and draw it out yourself,
The colours being baleful and impoisoned,
And no ways prejudice yourself withal?
Mosby. Well questioned, Alice.—Clarke, how answer you that?   625
Clarke. Very easily. I'll tell you straight
How I do work of these impoisoned drugs:
I fasten on my spectacles so close
As nothing can any way offend my sight;
Then, as I put a leaf within my nose,   630
So put I rhubarb to avoid the smell,
And softly as another work I paint.
Mosby. 'Tis very well, but against when shall I have it?
Clarke. Within this ten days.
Mosby. 'Twill serve the turn.—   635
Now, Alice, let's in and see what cheer you keep.
I hope, now Master Arden is from home,
You'll give me leave to play your husband's part.
Alice. Mosby, you know who's master of my heart,
He well may be the master of the house.   *Exeunt.*   640

---

605. *dispose*] disposal.
612. *wax*] grow.
617. *toucheth life*] i.e. involves murder.
618. *or*] than, ere.
631. *rhubarb*] used in medicine as a purgative, so here it would be thought
effective in repelling the harmful effects of the poison.
636. *cheer*] hospitality.
639. *who's*] that whoever is.

[2]

Here enters GREENE *and* BRADSHAW.

Bradshaw. See you them that comes yonder, Master Greene?
Greene. Ay, very well. Do you know them?

Here enters BLACK WILL *and* SHAKEBAG.

Bradshaw. The one I know not, but he seems a knave,
    Chiefly for bearing the other company;
    For such a slave, so vile a rogue as he,   5
    Lives not again upon the earth.
    Black Will is his name. I tell you, Master Greene,
    At Boulogne he and I were fellow soldiers,
    Where he played such pranks
    As all the camp feared him for his villainy.   10
    I warrant you he bears so bad a mind
    That for a crown he'll murder any man.
Greene. [Aside] The fitter is he for my purpose, marry!
Will. How now, fellow Bradshaw? Whither away so early?
Bradshaw. Oh, Will, times are changed. No fellows now,   15
    Though we were once together in the field;
    Yet thy friend to do thee any good I can.
Will. Why, Bradshaw, was not thou and I fellow soldiers at
Boulogne, where I was a corporal and thou but a base merce-
nary groom? 'No fellows now' because you are a goldsmith and   20
have a little plate in your shop? You were glad to call me 'fellow
Will' and, with a cursy to the earth, 'One snatch, good corporal'
when I stole the half ox from John the victualler and domi-
neered with it amongst good fellows in one night.
Bradshaw. Ay, Will, those days are past with me.   25
Will. Ay, but they be not past with me, for I keep that same honourable mind still. Good neighbour Bradshaw, you are too proud
to be my fellow; but, were it not that I see more company
coming down the hill, I would be fellows with you once more,

2.0.] The scene is located between Faversham and London.
    8. *Boulogne*] seaport on the English channel; captured by Henry VIII in 1544 but
surrendered back to the French in 1550.
    12. *crown*] gold coin worth five shillings.
    13. *marry*] an oath based on a corruption of 'Mary' referring to the Virgin Mary.
    19–20. *mercenary groom*] hired footsoldier.
    21. *plate*] gold or silver cups and dishes.
    22. *cursy*] curtsy.
    snatch] small piece (of meat).
    23–4. *domineered*] revelled.

and share crowns with you too. But let that pass, and tell me   30
whither you go.

Bradshaw. To London, Will, about a piece of service
Wherein haply thou mayst pleasure me.

Will. What is it?

Bradshaw. Of late Lord Cheyne lost some plate,   35
Which one did bring and sold it at my shop,
Saying he served Sir Anthony Cooke.
A search was made, the plate was found with me,
And I am bound to answer at the 'size.
Now Lord Cheyne solemnly vows,   40
If law will serve him, he'll hang me for his plate.
Now I am going to London upon hope
To find the fellow. Now, Will, I know
Thou art acquainted with such companions.

Will. What manner of man was he?   45

Bradshaw. A lean-faced, writhen knave,
Hawk-nosed and very hollow-eyed,
With mighty furrows in his stormy brows;
Long hair down his shoulders curled;
His chin was bare, but on his upper lip   50
A mutchado, which he wound about his ear.

Will. What apparel had he?

Bradshaw. A watchet satin doublet all to-torn
(The inner side did bear the greater show),
A pair of threadbare velvet hose, seam rent,   55
A worsted stocking rent above the shoe,
A livery cloak, but all the lace was off;
'Twas bad, but yet it served to hide the plate.

Will. Sirrah Shakebag, canst thou remember since we trolled the
bowl at Sittingburgh, where I broke the tapster's head of the   60
Lion with a cudgel-stick?

---

30. *share . . . you*] (1) share our money; (2) relieve you of some crowns by robbing you; (3) beat you about the head (crown).

35. *Lord Cheyne*] Sir Thomas Cheyne, Warden of the Cinque Ports and Lord Lieutenant of Kent.

39. *'size*] assize; courts held periodically in each county.

43. *the fellow*] the one who sold the stolen goods to Bradshaw.

46. *writhen*] twisted.

51. *mutchado*] moustache.

53. *watchet*] pale blue.

all to-torn] completely torn apart.

54.] i.e. more lining showed than outer garment.

55. *seam rent*] torn at the seams.

57. *livery cloak*] part of the uniform of a servant.

59–60. *since . . . bowl*] when we handed round the drinking cup.

60. *Sittingburgh*] Sittingbourne, a town in Kent, nine miles east of Faversham on the Pilgrims' Way.

60–1. *broke . . . Lion*] gave the barman at the Lion Inn a bleeding head.

Shakebag. Ay, very well, Will.

Will. Why, it was with the money that the plate was sold for.—
    Sirrah Bradshaw, what wilt thou give him that can tell thee who
    sold thy plate?   65

Bradshaw. Who, I pray thee, good Will?

Will. Why, 'twas one Jack Fitten. He's now in Newgate for stealing
    a horse, and shall be arraigned the next 'size.

Bradshaw. Why then, let Lord Cheyne seek Jack Fitten forth,
    For I'll back and tell him who robbed him of his plate.   70
    This cheers my heart.—Master Greene, I'll leave you,
    For I must to the Isle of Sheppey with speed.

Greene. Before you go, let me entreat you
    To carry this letter to Mistress Arden of Faversham
    And humbly recommend me to herself.   75
                                    [*He hands over a letter.*]

Bradshaw. That will I, Master Greene, and so farewell.—
    Here, Will, there's a crown for thy good news.
                                    [*He gives money.*]

Will. Farewell, Bradshaw; I'll drink no water for thy sake whilst this
    lasts.   *Exit* BRADSHAW.
    Now, gentleman, shall we have your company to London?   80

Greene. Nay, stay, sirs.
    A little more I needs must use your help,
    And in a matter of great consequence,
    Wherein, if you'll be secret and profound,
    I'll give you twenty angels for your pains.   85

Will. How? Twenty angels? Give my fellow George Shakebag and
    me twenty angels, and, if thou'lt have thy own father slain that
    thou mayst inherit his land, we'll kill him.

Shakebag. Ay, thy mother, thy sister, thy brother, or all thy kin.

Greene. Well, this it is: Arden of Faversham   90
    Hath highly wronged me about the Abbey land,
    That no revenge but death will serve the turn.
    Will you two kill him? Here's the angels down,
    And I will lay the platform of his death.
                                    [*He offers the money.*]

Will. Plat me no platforms! Give me the money, and I'll stab him as   95
    he stands pissing against a wall, but I'll kill him.

---

67. *Newgate*] a London prison.

68. *arraigned*] charged, tried.

72. *the Isle of Sheppey*] an island at the mouth of the River Medway, across the
River Swale from Faversham.

78. *I'll . . . water*] i.e. I will drink wine instead.

84. *profound*] cunning.

85. *angels*] gold coins stamped with the image of the archangel Michael killing
the dragon; worth 10s during the reign of Edward VI.

94. *platform*] plan, scheme.

Shakebag. Where is he?

Greene. He is now at London, in Aldersgate Street.

Shakebag. He's dead as if he had been condemned by an Act of
Parliament, if once Black Will and I swear his death.   100

Greene. Here is ten pound; and, when he is dead,
Ye shall have twenty more.   [*He gives the money.*]

Will. My fingers itches to be at the peasant. Ah, that I might be set
a-work thus through the year and that murder would grow to an
occupation, that a man might without danger of law—Zounds,   105
I warrant I should be warden of the company! Come, let us be
going, and we'll bait at Rochester, where I'll give thee a gallon
of sack to handsel the match withal.   *Exeunt.*

[3]

Here enters MICHAEL.

Michael. I have gotten such a letter as will touch the painter, and
thus it is:

Here enters ARDEN *and* FRANKLIN *and hears*
MICHAEL *read this letter.*

'My duty remembered, Mistress Susan, hoping in God you
be in good health as I, Michael, was at the making hereof. This
is to certify you that, as the turtle true, when she hath lost her   5
mate, sitteth alone, so I, mourning for your absence, do walk up
and down Paul's till one day I fell asleep and lost my master's
pantofles. Ah, Mistress Susan, abolish that paltry painter, cut

---

98. *is now at*] is currently living in.

Aldersgate Street] running south from Aldersgate into the West End of Cheapside.

105. *Zounds*] by God's wounds.

106. *warden of the company*] i.e. in charge of the association. Will imagines an
association of murderers along the lines of the livery companies which governed
other trades in the city. See Intro., p. 31.

107. *bait*] stop for food and rest.

Rochester] town overlooking the River Medway, halfway between Faversham and
London.

108. *sack*] Spanish white wine.

handsel] bless, inaugurate with omens of good luck.

3.1. *gotten*] begotten, composed.

touch] affect, put out. (See 1.470.)

5. *certify*] notify, inform. (In its lurches of tone, from formal to informal, from
Latinate to English language, this letter is a parody of elaborate writing on love. See
Intro., p. 34.)

turtle] turtle-dove; proverbially true to a single mate until death.

7. *Paul's*] the central aisle of St Paul's Cathedral; a principal meeting place in
London. Scenes 3–7 are set in London.

8. *pantofles*] slippers or galoshes.

him off by the shins with a frowning look of your crabbed
countenance, and think upon Michael, who, drunk with the   10
dregs of your favour, will cleave as fast to your love as a plaster
of pitch to a galled horseback. Thus, hoping you will let my
passions penetrate, or rather impetrate mercy of your meek
hands, I end.

        Yours,   15

        Michael, or else not Michael.'

Arden. [*Coming forward*] Why, you paltry knave,
    Stand you here loitering, knowing my affairs,
    What haste my business craves to send to Kent?
Franklin. Faith, friend Michael, this is very ill,   20
    Knowing your master hath no more but you;
    And do ye slack his business for your own?
Arden. Where is the letter, sirrah? Let me see it.

                 Then he [MICHAEL] *gives him the letter.*

    See, Master Franklin, here's proper stuff:
    Susan my maid, the painter, and my man,   25
    A crew of harlots, all in love, forsooth.—
    Sirrah, let me hear no more of this,
    Now, for thy life, once write to her a word!

        Here enter GREENE, WILL, *and* SHAKEBAG,
            [*unseen by Arden and Franklin*].

    Wilt thou be married to so base a trull?
    'Tis Mosby's sister. Come I once at home,   30
    I'll rouse her from remaining in my house.—
    Now, Master Franklin, let us go walk in Paul's.
    Come, but a turn or two, and then away.

        Exeunt [ARDEN, FRANKLIN, *and* MICHAEL].

Greene. The first is Arden, and that's his man;
    The other is Franklin, Arden's dearest friend.   35
Will. Zounds, I'll kill them all three.
Greene. Nay, sirs, touch not his man in any case;

11–12. *cleave . . . horseback*] stick as firmly to your love as a dressing made of
softened tar sticks to the chafed sore on a horse's back.

13. *impetrate*] beseech. (An inflated Latinate way of saying something simple.)

16.] i.e. I am not myself unless you love me.

19.] i.e. and knowing in what haste my business affairs require me to dispatch
you to Faversham?

21. *no . . . you*] no other servant with him but you.

26. *harlots*] whores and rascals of either sex.

27–8.] i.e. Write her one word more, and it's all your life is worth.

30–1. *Come . . . house*] As soon as I get home, I'll dismiss her as a household
servant.

But stand close, and take you fittest standing,
And, at his coming forth, speed him.
To the Nag's Head; there is this coward's haunt.   40
But now I'll leave you till the deed be done.   *Exit* GREENE.
Shakebag. If he be not paid his own, ne'er trust Shakebag.
Will. Sirrah Shakebag, at his coming forth I'll run him through, and
then to the Blackfriars and there take water and away.
Shakebag. Why, that's the best; but see thou miss him not.   45
Will. How can I miss him when I think on the forty angels I must
have more?

Here enters a Prentice.

Prentice. 'Tis very late; I were best shut up my stall, for here will be
old filching when the press comes forth of Paul's.
                    Then lets he down his window, and
                    it breaks Black Will's head.
Will. Zounds, draw, Shakebag, draw! I am almost killed.   50
Prentice. We'll tame you, I warrant.
Will. Zounds, I am tame enough already.

Here enters ARDEN, FRANKLIN, *and* MICHAEL.

Arden. What troublesome fray or mutiny is this?
Franklin. 'Tis nothing but some brabbling, paltry fray,
Devised to pick men's pockets in the throng.   55
Arden. Is 't nothing else? Come, Franklin, let us away.
                    Exeunt [ARDEN, FRANKLIN, *and* MICHAEL].
Will. What 'mends shall I have for my broken head?

---

38. *fittest standing*] the best standing place (from which to spring the ambush).
39. *speed him*] i.e. to his death.
40. *the Nag's Head*] a tavern in Cheapside (where Arden is taking his meals and
meeting his business associates).
42. *paid his own*] given what's coming to him.
44. *Blackfriars*] a fashionable residential district, the ground of a former Domini-
can monastery.
take water] travel on the Thames by boat.
48. *stall*] bookstall. Paul's churchyard was the centre of the London book trade.
49. *old filching*] plenty of stealing.
press] crowd.
49.1. *his window*] his shutter. The stall could be enclosed by a removable
shutter. On the stage it could be set up against the tiring-house wall on a portable
structure. See Intro., p. 7.
49.2. *breaks*] hits so as to break the skin and draw blood. (Also in lines 57 and
73–6; cf. 2.60–1 and note.)
51–2. *tame . . . tame*] cut or pierce . . . domesticated; quiet.
54. *brabbling*] noisy, wrangling.
57. *'mends*] amends, compensation.

Prentice. Marry, this 'mends, that, if you get you not away all the
    sooner, you shall be well beaten and sent to the Counter.

                                                    Exit Prentice.

Will. [*Calling after him*] Well, I'll be gone; but look to your signs, for   60
    I'll pull them down all.—Shakebag, my broken head grieves me
    not so much as by this means Arden hath escaped.

                        Here enters GREENE.

    I had a glimpse of him and his companion.
Greene. Why, sirs, Arden's as well as I. I met him and Franklin
    going merrily to the ordinary. What, dare you not do it?   65
Will. Yes, sir, we dare do it; but, were my consent to give again, we
    would not do it under ten pound more. I value every drop of my
    blood at a French crown. I have had ten pound to steal a dog,
    and we have no more here to kill a man. But that a bargain is a
    bargain and so forth, you should do it yourself.   70
Greene. I pray thee, how came thy head broke?
Will. Why, thou seest it is broke, dost thou not?
Shakebag. Standing against a stall, watching Arden's coming, a boy
    let down his shop window and broke his head; whereupon arose
    a brawl, and in the tumult Arden escaped us and passed by   75
    unthought on. But forbearance is no acquittance; another time
    we'll do it, I warrant thee.
Greene. I pray thee, Will, make clean thy bloody brow,
    And let us bethink us on some other place
    Where Arden may be met with handsomely.   80
    Remember how devoutly thou hast sworn
    To kill the villain; think upon thine oath.
Will. Tush, I have broken five hundred oaths!
    But wouldst thou charm me to effect this deed,
    Tell me of gold, my resolution's fee;   85
    Say thou seest Mosby kneeling at my knees,

---

59. *Counter*] a London prison, usually for debtors.
60. *signs*] shop signs.
65. *ordinary*] tavern dining room selling meals. Ordinaries were graded according to the prices they could charge. See line 123.
68. *French crown*] joke punning on *crown* meaning (1) head and (2) coin worth 5s.
The crown is *French* here because Frenchmen's heads were mocked as bald from the
effects of syphilis.
69–70. *But . . . yourself*] Were it not for the fact that I have given my word to
undertake this, you should do it without me.
76. *forbearance . . . acquittance*] being spared for a time is not the same as being
let off entirely.
84. *charm me*] betwitch me.
85. *my . . . fee*] the payment for my commitment.

Off'ring me service for my high attempt;
And sweet Alice Arden, with a lap of crowns,
Comes with a lowly cursy to the earth,
Saying, 'Take this but for thy quarterage;   90
Such yearly tribute will I answer thee.'
Why, this would steel soft-mettled cowardice,
With which Black Will was never tainted with.
I tell thee, Greene, the forlorn traveller
Whose lips are glued with summer's parching heat   95
Ne'er longed so much to see a running brook
As I to finish Arden's tragedy.
Seest thou this gore that cleaveth to my face?
From hence ne'er will I wash this bloody stain
Till Arden's heart be panting in my hand.   100
Greene. Why, that's well said; but what saith Shakebag?
Shakebag. I cannot paint my valour out with words;
But, give me place and opportunity,
Such mercy as the starven lioness,
When she is dry-sucked of her eager young,   105
Shows to the prey that next encounters her,
On Arden so much pity would I take.
Greene. So should it fare with men of firm resolve.
And now, sirs, seeing this accident
Of meeting him in Paul's hath no success,   110
Let us bethink us on some other place
Whose earth may swallow up this Arden's blood.

Here enters MICHAEL.

See, yonder comes his man. And wot you what?
The foolish knave is in love with Mosby's sister;
And for her sake, whose love he cannot get   115
Unless Mosby solicit his suit,
The villain hath sworn the slaughter of his master.
We'll question him, for he may stead us much.—
How now, Michael, whither are you going?
Michael. My master hath new supped,   120
And I am going to prepare his chamber.
Greene. Where supped Master Arden?

---

87. *service*] homage. Black Will fantasizes about the status as well as the money which will be his reward for murdering Arden.
88. *with . . . crowns*] with the lap of her skirt filled with gold coins.
90. *quarterage*] quarterly payment.
91. *answer*] guarantee.
94. *forlorn*] lost.
118. *stead*] profit.

Michael. At the Nag's Head, at the eighteenpence ordinary.—
　　How now, Master Shakebag?—What, Black Will! God's
　　dear Lady, how chance your face is so bloody?　　　　　125
Will. Go to, sirrah; there is a chance in it. This sauciness in you will
　　make you be knocked.
Michael. Nay, an you be offended, I'll be gone.
Greene. Stay, Michael. You may not 'scape us so.
　　Michael, I know you love your master well.　　　　　130
Michael. Why, so I do. But wherefore urge you that?
Greene. Because I think you love your mistress better.
Michael. So think not I. But say, i' faith, what if I should?
Shakebag. Come to the purpose, Michael. We hear
　　You have a pretty love in Faversham.　　　　　135
Michael. Why, have I two or three, what's that to thee?
Will. [*To Shakebag*] You deal too mildly with the peasant.—Thus
　　　　it is:
　　'Tis known to us you love Mosby's sister;
　　We know besides that you have ta'en your oath
　　To further Mosby to your mistress' bed　　　　　140
　　And kill your master for his sister's sake.
　　Now, sir, a poorer coward than yourself
　　Was never fostered in the coast of Kent.
　　How comes it then that such a knave as you
　　Dare swear a matter of such consequence?　　　　　145
Greene. Ah, Will—
Will. [*To Greene*] Tush, give me leave.—There's no more but this:
　　Sith thou hast sworn, we dare discover all;
　　And, hadst thou or shouldst thou utter it,
　　We have devised a complot under hand,　　　　　150
　　Whatever shall betide to any of us,
　　To send thee roundly to the devil of hell.

---

123. *eighteenpence ordinary*] Arden has eaten in one of the more expensive dining rooms at the Nag's head. See lines 40 and 65.

124. *How . . . Will*] Michael seems to know Black Will and Shakebag, though Greene had to point him out to them. At lines 113–17, Greene seems to know all about Michael and Susan, though how he knows this is not clear.

126. *Go to*] an expression of impatience.

there . . . in it] Black Will plays sardonically on Michael's '*how chance*' (line 125), i.e. how did it happen, by saying 'There's an element of chance in lots of things'.

140. *further*] assist.

141. *for . . . sake*] for the love of Mosby's sister.

147. *give me leave*] allow me to continue, don't interrupt.

148.] i.e. Since you have sworn to murder your master (see line 117), we can safely disclose our intentions.

Sith] since.

150. *complot*] conspiracy, plot.

152. *roundly*] swiftly.

And therefore thus: I am the very man,
Marked in my birth-hour by the Destinies,
To give an end to Arden's life on earth;   155
Thou but a member but to whet the knife
Whose edge must search the closet of his breast.
Thy office is but to appoint the place
And train thy master to his tragedy;
Mine to perform it when occasion serves.   160
Then be not nice, but here devise with us
How and what way we may conclude his death.
Shakebag. So shalt thou purchase Mosby for thy friend,
And by his friendship gain his sister's love.
Greene. So shall thy mistress be thy favourer,   165
And thou disburdened of the oath thou made.
Michael. Well, gentlemen, I cannot but confess,
Sith you have urged me so apparently,
That I have vowed my Master Arden's death;
And he whose kindly love and liberal hand   170
Doth challenge nought but good deserts of me
I will deliver over to your hands.
This night come to his house at Aldersgate;
The doors I'll leave unlocked against you come.
No sooner shall ye enter through the latch,   175
Over the threshold to the inner court,
But on your left hand shall you see the stairs
That leads directly to my master's chamber.
There take him and dispose him as ye please.
Now it were good we parted company.   180
What I have promisèd I will perform.
Will. Should you deceive us, 'twould go wrong with you.
Michael. I will accomplish all I have revealed.
Will. Come, let's go drink. Choler makes me as dry as a dog.
            Exeunt WILL, GREENE, *and* SHAKEBAG. *Manet* MICHAEL.
Michael. Thus feeds the lamb securely on the down   185

---

154. *the Destinies*] the three Fates who determined the length of a person's life.
156. *member*] assistant.
159. *train*] lure.
161. *nice*] squeamish, scrupulous.
168. *apparently*] openly.
171. *challenge*] demand, deserve.
174. *against you come*] in anticipation of your coming.
184. *Choler*] An excess of choler or bile among the four 'humours' in the body was thought to produce a hot and dry temperament, resulting in anger and impatience.
184.1. Manet] he remains.

Whilst through the thicket of an arbour brake
The hunger-bitten wolf o'erpries his haunt
And takes advantage to eat him up.
Ah, harmless Arden, how, how hast thou misdone
That thus thy gentle life is levelled at?   190
The many good turns that thou hast done to me
Now must I quittance with betraying thee.
I, that should take the weapon in my hand
And buckler thee from ill-intending foes,
Do lead thee with a wicked, fraudful smile,   195
As unsuspected, to the slaughterhouse.
So have I sworn to Mosby and my mistress;
So have I promised to the slaughtermen;
And, should I not deal currently with them,
Their lawless rage would take revenge on me.   200
Tush, I will spurn at mercy for this once.
Let pity lodge where feeble women lie;
I am resolved, and Arden needs must die.   *Exit* MICHAEL.

[4]

Here enters ARDEN *and* FRANKLIN.

Arden. No, Franklin, no. If fear or stormy threats,
If love of me or care of womanhood,
If fear of God or common speech of men,
Who mangle credit with their wounding words
And couch dishonour as dishonour buds,   5
Might 'join repentance in her wanton thoughts,
No question then but she would turn the leaf

---

186. *arbour brake*] clump of bushes or briers.
187. *o'erpries*] surveys, looks over.
189. *harmless*] guiltless.
how . . . misdone] what wrong have you done.
190. *levelled*] aimed.
192. *quittance*] repay.
194. *buckler*] shield.
199. *currently*] according to the agreement.
201. *spurn at*] kick away, reject. (Michael rejects mercy for Arden and also for his own soul.)
202. *feeble women*] i.e. women, who are by their nature yielding.

4.4. *credit*] good name, worthiness.
5. *couch . . . buds*] Editors have found this line obscure; A 'couch' in brewing is 'the bed or layer in which the grain is left to germinate after steeping'. The line could mean that the 'common speech of men' provides a bed for the buds of dishonour to sprout.
6. *'join*] enjoin, encourage.

And sorrow for her dissolution.
But she is rooted in her wickedness,
Perverse and stubborn, not to be reclaimed;   10
Good counsel is to her as rain to weeds,
And reprehension makes her vice to grow
As Hydra's head that plenished by decay.
Her faults, methink, are painted in my face
For every searching eye to overread;   15
And Mosby's name, a scandal unto mine,
Is deeply trenchèd in my blushing brow.
Ah, Franklin, Franklin, when I think on this,
My heart's grief rends my other powers
Worse than the conflict at the hour of death.   20
Franklin. Gentle Arden, leave this sad lament.
She will amend, and so your griefs will cease;
Or else she'll die, and so your sorrows end.
If neither of these two do haply fall,
Yet let your comfort be that others bear   25
Your woes twice doubled all with patience.
Arden. My house is irksome; there I cannot rest.
Franklin. Then stay with me in London; go not home.
Arden. Then that base Mosby doth usurp my room
And makes his triumph of my being thence.   30
At home or not at home, where'er I be,
Here, here it lies [*pointing to his heart*], ah,
    Franklin, here it lies
That will not out till wretched Arden dies.

Here enters MICHAEL.

Franklin. Forget your griefs awhile. Here comes your man.
Arden. What o'clock is't, sirrah?
Michael.   Almost ten.   35
Arden. See, see, how runs away the weary time!
    Come, Master Franklin, shall we go to bed?
Franklin. I pray you, go before; I'll follow you.
        Exeunt ARDEN *and* MICHAEL. *Manet* FRANKLIN.
    Ah, what a hell is fretful jealousy!

---

8. *dissolution*] dissoluteness.
12. *reprehension*] scolding; censure.
13. *Hydra*] a monster, slain by Hercules, who had snakes instead of hair.
decay] decapitation. As fast as the snakes' heads were cut off they grew again.
15. *overread*] read intently.
17. *trenchèd*] gashed, cut.
19. *rends*] breaks up, destroys.
24. *haply fall*] come about conveniently, or as you would wish.

What pity-moving words, what deep-fetched sighs,   40
What grievous groans and overlading woes
Accompanies this gentle gentleman!
Now will he shake his care-oppressèd head,
Then fix his sad eyes on the sullen earth,
Ashamed to gaze upon the open world;   45
Now will he cast his eyes up towards the heavens,
Looking that ways for redress of wrong.
Sometimes he seeketh to beguile his grief
And tells a story with his careful tongue;
Then comes his wife's dishonour in his thoughts   50
And in the middle cutteth off his tale,
Pouring fresh sorrow on his weary limbs.
So woe-begone, so inly charged with woe,
Was never any lived and bare it so.

Here enters MICHAEL.

Michael. My master would desire you come to bed.   55
Franklin. Is he himself already in his bed?
Michael. He is, and fain would have the light away.
Exit FRANKLIN. *Manet* MICHAEL.
Conflicting thoughts encampèd in my breast
Awake me with the echo of their strokes;
And I, a judge to censure either side,   60
Can give to neither wishèd victory.
My master's kindness pleads to me for life
With just demand, and I must grant it him;
My mistress she hath forced me with an oath
For Susan's sake, the which I may not break,   65
For that is nearer than a master's love;
That grim-faced fellow, pitiless Black Will,
And Shakebag, stern in bloody stratagem—
Two rougher ruffians never lived in Kent—
Have sworn my death if I infringe my vow,   70
A dreadful thing to be considered of.
Methinks I see them with their bolstered hair,
Staring and grinning in thy gentle face,

---

41. *overlading*] overloading (as in a ship).
48. *beguile*] cheer up.
49. *careful*] full of care.
58–9.] Michael represents his conflicting loyalties as combatants in a tournament at which he is judge.
60. *censure*] pass judgement on.
72. *bolstered*] stiff, rigid, bristly.
73. *thy*] i.e. Arden's. (Also in line 75.)

And in their ruthless hands their daggers drawn,
Insulting o'er thee with a peck of oaths   75
Whilst thou, submissive, pleading for relief,
Art mangled by their ireful instruments.
Methinks I hear them ask where Michael is,
And pitiless Black Will cries, 'Stab the slave!
The peasant will detect the tragedy.'   80
The wrinkles in his foul, death-threat'ning face
Gapes open wide, like graves to swallow men.
My death to him is but a merriment,
And he will murder me to make him sport.
He comes, he comes! Ah, Master Franklin, help!   85
Call up the neighbours, or we are but dead!

Here enters FRANKLIN *and* ARDEN.

Franklin. What dismal outcry calls me from my rest?
Arden. What hath occasioned such a fearful cry?
   Speak, Michael! Hath any injured thee?
Michael. Nothing, sir; but, as I fell asleep   90
   Upon the threshold, leaning to the stairs,
   I had a fearful dream that troubled me,
   And in my slumber thought I was beset
   With murderer thieves that came to rifle me.
   My trembling joints witness my inward fear.   95
   I crave your pardons for disturbing you.
Arden. So great a cry for nothing I ne'er heard.
   What, are the doors fast locked and all things safe?
Michael. I cannot tell; I think I locked the doors.
Arden. I like not this, but I'll go see myself.   [*He tries the doors.*]   100
   Ne'er trust me but the doors were all unlocked.
   This negligence not half contenteth me.
   Get you to bed; and, if you love my favour,
   Let me have no more such pranks as these.—
   Come, Master Franklin, let us go to bed.   105
Franklin. Ay, by my faith; the air is very cold.—
   Michael, farewell; I pray thee dream no more.   *Exeunt.*

---

75. *Insulting*] exulting. *thee*
peck] large measure.
77. *ireful*] angry.
80. *detect*] disclose.
85. *He comes*] Michael sees Black Will in his fantasy or nightmare.
94. *rifle*] rob.
100 SD. *doors*] The doors at the back of the stage could represent the outer
doors of the house. There is no need for Arden to leave the stage.
   101. *Ne'er trust me*] i.e. Never believe me again if I'm not telling the truth.
   102. *not half contenteth*] i.e. displeases.

[5]

Here enters WILL, GREENE, *and* SHAKEBAG.

Shakebag. Black night hath hid the pleasures of the day,
   And sheeting darkness overhangs the earth
   And with the black fold of her cloudy robe
   Obscures us from the eyesight of the world,
   In which sweet silence such as we triumph.   5
   The lazy minutes linger on their time,
   Loath to give due audit to the hour,
   Till in the watch our purpose be complete
   And Arden sent to everlasting night.
   Greene, get you gone and linger here about,   10
   And at some hour hence come to us again,
   Where we will give you instance of his death.
Greene. Speed to my wish, whose will soe'er says no!
   And so I'll leave you for an hour or two.   *Exit* GREENE.
Will. I tell thee, Shakebag, would this thing were done.   15
   I am so heavy that I can scarce go.
   This drowsiness in me bodes little good.
Shakebag. How now, Will, become a Precisian?
   Nay, then, let's go sleep, when bugs and fears
   Shall kill our courages with their fancy's work.   20
Will. Why, Shakebag, thou mistakes me much
   And wrongs me too in telling me of fear.
   Were 't not a serious thing we go about,
   It should be slipped till I had fought with thee
   To let thee know I am no coward, I.   25
   I tell thee, Shakebag, thou abusest me.
Shakebag. Why, thy speech bewrayed an inly kind of fear
   And savoured of a weak, relenting spirit.
   Go forward now in that we have begun,
   And afterwards attempt me when thou darest.   30

5.2. *sheeting*] covering (like a sheet).
7.] reluctant to make up the total for the hour.
8. *watch*] (1) time division of the night; (2) the act of watching for Arden.
12. *instance*] evidence, proof.
13.] Success to my wish, no matter who tries to stop you!
18. *Precisian*] Puritan (thought to be excessively precise and literal-minded in their interpretation of the Bible). Shakebag accuses Will of making his drowsiness an omen as Puritans read prophecy into the scriptures.
19. *bugs*] bugbears, terrors.
20. *fancy's work*] work upon the imagination.
24. *slipped*] postponed.
27. *bewrayed*] betrayed.
30. *attempt*] engage with, attack.

Will. And if I do not, heaven cut me off!
    But let that pass, and show me to this house,
    Where thou shalt see I'll do as much as Shakebag.
Shakebag. This is the door. [*He tries it.*] But soft, methinks 'tis shut.
    The villain Michael hath deceivèd us.   35
Will. Soft, let me see. [*He tries it.*] Shakebag, 'tis shut indeed.
    Knock with thy sword; perhaps the slave will hear.
Shakebag. [*Knocking*] It will not be; the white-livered peasant
    Is gone to bed and laughs us both to scorn.
Will. And he shall buy his merriment as dear   40
    As ever coistrel bought so little sport.
    Ne'er let this sword assist me when I need,
    But rust and canker after I have sworn,
    If I, the next time that I meet the hind,
    Lop not away his leg, his arm, or both.   45
Shakebag. And let me never draw a sword again,
    Nor prosper in the twilight, cockshut light,
    When I would fleece the wealthy passenger,
    But lie and languish in a loathsome den,
    Hated and spit at by the goers-by,   50
    And in that death may die unpitièd
    If I, the next time that I meet the slave,
    Cut not the nose from off the coward's face
    And trample on it for this villainy.
Will. Come, let's go seek out Greene; I know he'll swear.   55
Shakebag. He were a villain an he would not swear.
    'Twould make a peasant swear amongst his boys,
    That ne'er durst say before but 'yea' and 'no',
    To be thus flouted of a coisterel.
Will. Shakebag, let's seek out Greene, and in the morning   60
    At the alehouse 'butting Arden's house
    Watch the outcoming of that prick-eared cur,
    And then let me alone to handle him.   *Exeunt.*

---

31. *And if*] This could be *an if*, if.
34. *soft*] i.e. wait a minute.
38. *white-livered*] cowardly (thought to be a result of a deficiency of black bile in the liver). See Intro., pp. 52–3.
41. *coistrel*] horse-groom; hence a low person.
43. *canker*] be ulcerated with rust.
44. *hind*] rural servant; hence sneered at by urban Black Will. Compare *peasant*, line 38, and *coistrel*, lines 41 and 59.
47. *cockshut light*] evening, twilight.
48. *passenger*] traveller.
59. *coisterel*] lowbred person, as in line 41 above (*coistrel*), with varied spelling suited to the metre.
61. *'butting*] next to, abutting on.
62. *prick-eared*] with pointed ears.
63. *let me alone*] leave it to me.

[6]

    Here enters ARDEN, FRANKLIN, *and* MICHAEL.

Arden. [*To Michael*] Sirrah, get you back to Billingsgate
  And learn what time the tide will serve our turn.
  Come to us in Paul's. First go make the bed,
  And afterwards go hearken for the flood.   *Exit* MICHAEL.
  Come, Master Franklin, you shall go with me.   5
  This night I dreamed that, being in a park,
  A toil was pitched to overthrow the deer,
  And I upon a little rising hill
  Stood whistly watching for the herd's approach.
  Even there, methoughts, a gentle slumber took me   10
  And summoned all my parts to sweet repose.
  But in the pleasure of this golden rest
  An ill-thewed foster had removed the toil
  And rounded me with that beguiling home
  Which late, methought, was pitched to cast the deer.   15
  With that he blew an evil-sounding horn;
  And at the noise another herdman came
  With falchion drawn, and bent it at my breast,
  Crying aloud, 'Thou art the game we seek.'
  With this I waked and trembled every joint,   20
  Like one obscurèd in a little bush
  That sees a lion foraging about,
  And, when the dreadful forest king is gone,
  He pries about with timorous suspect
  Throughout the thorny casements of the brake,   25
  And will not think his person dangerless
  But quakes and shivers though the cause be gone.
  So, trust me, Franklin, when I did awake,
  I stood in doubt whether I waked or no,

6.1. *Billingsgate*] a gate of the city near the famous fish market and a landing place for travellers from the lower Thames.
  4. *flood*] flood tide.
  7. *A toil was pitched*] a trap was set.
  9. *whistly*] silently.
  13. *ill-thewed foster*] evil-natured forester.
  14. *rounded*] surrounded.
  beguiling home] i.e. the net.
  15. *late*] only a moment ago.
  cast] pull down.
  18. *falchion*] a curved broad-sword.
  bent] aimed.
  21. *obscurèd*] hidden.
  24. *suspect*] suspicion, fear.
  25.] out from the thorny gaps in the bush.

Such great impression took this fond surprise.   30
God grant this vision bedeem me any good!
Franklin. This fantasy doth rise from Michael's fear,
Who, being awakèd with the noise he made,
His troubled senses yet could take no rest;
And this, I warrant you, procured your dream.   35
Arden. It may be so; God frame it to the best!
But oftentimes my dreams presage too true.
Franklin. To such as note their nightly fantasies,
Some one in twenty may incur belief.
But use it not; 'tis but a mockery.   40
Arden. Come, Master Franklin, we'll now walk in Paul's,
And dine together at the ordinary,
And by my man's direction draw to the quay,
And with the tide go down to Faversham.
Say, Master Franklin, shall it not be so?   45
Franklin. At your good pleasure, sir; I'll bear you company.
                                        Exeunt.

[7]

    Here enters MICHAEL *at one door. Here enters* GREENE,
        WILL, *and* SHAKEBAG *at another door.*

Will. Draw, Shakebag, for here's that villain Michael.
Greene. First, Will, let's hear what he can say.
Will. [*To Michael*] Speak, milksop slave, and never after speak!
                                        [*They accost Michael.*]
Michael. For God's sake, sirs, let me excuse myself;
For here I swear, by heaven and earth and all,   5
I did perform the outmost of my task
And left the doors unbolted and unlocked.
But see the chance: Franklin and my master
Were very late conferring in the porch,
And Franklin left his napkin where he sat,   10
With certain gold knit in it, as he said.

30.] so great was the impression that this foolish terror gave me.
31. *bedeem . . . good*] forbodes no evil for me.
36. *frame*] construct, bring about.
40. *use it not*] i.e. do not continue to attach significance to dreams.
43. *draw to*] head towards.

7.6. *outmost*] utmost.
8. *chance*] mischance.
10. *napkin*] handkerchief.
11. *knit*] tied up.

Being in bed, he did bethink himself,
And coming down he found the doors unshut.
He locked the gates and brought away the keys,
For which offence my master rated me.   15
But now I am going to see what flood it is;
For with the tide my master will away,
Where you may front him well on Rainham Down,
A place well fitting such a stratagem.

Will. Your excuse hath somewhat mollified my choler.—   20
Why now, Greene, 'tis better now nor e'er it was.

Greene. But, Michael, is this true?

Michael. As true as I report it to be true.

Shakebag. Then, Michael, this shall be your penance:
To feast us all at the Salutation,   25
Where we will plot our purpose throughly.

Greene. And Michael, you shall bear no news of this tide
Because they two may be in Rainham Down
Before your master.

Michael. Why, I'll agree to anything you'll have me,   30
So you will except of my company.   *Exeunt.*

[8]

Here enters MOSBY.

Mosby. Disturbèd thoughts drives me from company
And dries my marrow with their watchfulness.
Continual trouble of my moody brain
Feebles my body by excess of drink

---

15. *rated*] berated, scolded.

18. *front*] confront.

Rainham Down] the country around Rainham, a village between Rochester and Faversham.

21. *nor*] than.

25. *Salutation*] a Billingsgate tavern.

27. *this tide*] i.e. the river tide which Michael has been sent to Billingsgate to find out about. See 6.1–4.

28. *they two*] i.e. Black Will and Shakebag.

31. *except . . . company*] excuse me from accompanying you. (Later versions of the text read 'accept', confusing the issue of whether Michael agrees to join the agreed feast with the conspirators.)

8.] The scene shifts to Faversham.

2. *dries my marrow*] This phrase reflects a view of the connection between psychological and physical states based on the theory of humours. see Intro., pp. 52–3.

4.] i.e. (1) Mosby's grief is leading to excessive drinking, which enfeebles his body; (2) he is metaphorically drinking in grief which enfeebles his body. See Intro., p. 53.

And nips me as the bitter northeast wind   5
Doth check the tender blossoms in the spring.
Well fares the man, howe'er his cates do taste,
That tables not with foul suspicion;
And he but pines amongst his delicates
Whose troubled mind is stuffed with discontent.   10
My golden time was when I had no gold;
Though then I wanted, yet I slept secure;
My daily toil begat me night's repose;
My night's repose made daylight fresh to me.
But, since I climbed the top bough of the tree   15
And sought to build my nest among the clouds,
Each gentle starry gale doth shake my bed
And makes me dread my downfall to the earth.
But whither doth contemplation carry me?
The way I seek to find where pleasure dwells   20
Is hedged behind me that I cannot back
But needs must on although to danger's gate.
Then, Arden, perish thou by that decree,
For Greene doth ear the land and weed thee up
To make my harvest nothing but pure corn.   25
And for his pains I'll heave him up awhile
And, after, smother him to have his wax;
Such bees as Greene must never live to sting.
Then is there Michael and the painter too,
Chief actors to Arden's overthrow,   30
Who, when they shall see me sit in Arden's seat,
They will insult upon me for my meed
Or fright me by detecting of his end.
I'll none of that, for I can cast a bone
To make these curs pluck out each other's throat;   35
And then am I sole ruler of mine own.

---

7. *cates*] luxury foods.
8. *tables*] dines.
9. *delicates*] delicacies.
17. *starry*] high up, as among the stars.
21. *back*] go back.
24. *ear*] plough.
25. *nothing . . . corn*] i.e. a full harvest, uncontaminated by the existence of Arden.
26. *heave him*] raise him, make him feel important.
27. *smother . . . wax*] referring to the practice of smoking bees from the hive in order to reach the honey and wax safely.
32. *insult . . . meed*] reward me by exulting over me.
33. *detecting . . . end*] revealing how he died.
34. *a bone*] i.e. Susan, Mosby's sister. The image is of throwing a bone to a pack of dogs to make them fight with one another.

Yet Mistress Arden lives; but she's myself,
And holy church rites makes us two but one.
But what for that I may not trust you, Alice?
You have supplanted Arden for my sake   40
And will extirpen me to plant another.
'Tis fearful sleeping in a serpent's bed,
And I will cleanly rid my hands of her.

Here enters ALICE [*holding a prayerbook*].

But here she comes, and I must flatter her.—
How now, Alice! What, sad and passionate?   45
Make me partaker of thy pensiveness;
Fire divided burns with lesser force.
Alice. But I will dam that fire in my breast
Till by the force thereof my part consume.
[*Sighing*] Ah, Mosby!   50
Mosby. Such deep pathaires, like to a cannon's burst
Discharged against a ruinated wall,
Breaks my relenting heart in thousand pieces.
Ungentle Alice, thy sorrow is my sore;
Thou know'st it well, and 'tis thy policy   55
To forge distressful looks to wound a breast
Where lies a heart that dies when thou art sad.
It is not love that loves to anger love.
Alice. It is not love that loves to murder love.
Mosby. How mean you that?   60
Alice. Thou knowest how dearly Arden lovèd me.
Mosby. And then?
Alice. And then—conceal the rest, for 'tis too bad,
Lest that my words be carried with the wind
And published in the world to both our shames.   65
I pray thee, Mosby, let our springtime wither;
Our harvest else will yield but loathsome weeds.
Forget, I pray thee, what hath passed betwixt us,

---

39. *what for that*] what about the fact that.
41. *extirpen*] root out.
43. *cleanly*] completely.
43.1. holding a prayerbook] Alice needs the prayerbook for her vow in line 116.
See Intro., pp. 35–6.
44. *flatter*] deceive.
49.] until the force of my suppressed sorrow consumes me. (*Part* could be read
as 'heart'.)
51. *pathaires*] sighs or passionate outbursts (a very unusual word).
55. *policy*] deceitfulness.
56. *forge*] contrive.
65. *published*] proclaimed.

For now I blush and tremble at the thoughts.
Mosby. What, are you changed?   70
Alice. Ay, to my former happy life again,
    From title of an odious strumpet's name
    To honest Arden's wife, not Arden's honest wife.
    Ha, Mosby, 'tis thou hast rifled me of that
    And made me sland'rous to all my kin.   75
    Even in my forehead is thy name engraven,
    A mean artificer, that low-born name.
    I was bewitched. Woe worth the hapless hour
    And all the causes that enchanted me!
Mosby. Nay, if thou ban, let me breathe curses forth;   80
    And, if you stand so nicely at your fame,
    Let me repent the credit I have lost.
    I have neglected matters of import
    That would have stated me above thy state,
    Forslowed advantages, and spurned at time.   85
    Ay, Fortune's right hand Mosby hath forsook
    To take a wanton giglot by the left.
    I left the marriage of an honest maid
    Whose dowry would have weighed down all thy wealth,
    Whose beauty and demeanour far exceeded thee.   90
    This certain good I lost for changing bad,
    And wrapped my credit in thy company.
    I was bewitched—that is no theme of thine!—
    And thou unhallowed hast enchanted me.

---

73. *honest . . . honest*] (1) worthy (in men); (2) chaste (in women).
not] even if no longer.
77. *mean artificer*] lowborn artisan. (See 1.311 and Intro., p. 30.)
78. *Woe worth*] a curse upon.
hapless] unhappy.
80. *ban*] curse.
81. *nicely*] particularly, fastidiously.
at your fame] on your reputation.
82. *credit*] reputation. (Also in line 92.)
84.] that would have placed me above you in rank.
85. *Forslowed*] put off; wasted.
spurned at time] rejected opportunities when they came up.
87. *giglot*] whore.
89. *weighed down*] outweighed.
91. *for changing bad*] in exchange for bad.
92. *wrapped*] covered over, compromised.
93. *that . . . thine*] you do not have the exclusive right to the claim you made (in
line 78) of being bewitched.
94. *unhallowed*] accursed (like a witch).

But I will break thy spells and exorcisms   95
And put another sight upon these eyes
That showed my heart a raven for a dove.
Thou art not fair—I viewed thee not till now;
Thou art not kind—till now I knew thee not.
And now the rain hath beaten off thy gilt   100
Thy worthless copper shows thee counterfeit.
It grieves me not to see how foul thou art
But mads me that ever I thought thee fair.
Go, get thee gone, a copesmate for thy hinds!
I am too good to be thy favourite.   105

Alice. Ay, now I see, and too soon find it true,
  Which often hath been told me by my friends,
  That Mosby loves me not but for my wealth,
  Which, too incredulous, I ne'er believed.
  Nay, hear me speak, Mosby, a word or two;   110
  I'll bite my tongue if it speak bitterly.
  Look on me, Mosby, or I'll kill myself;
  Nothing shall hide me from thy stormy look.
  If thou cry war, there is no peace for me;
  I will do penance for offending thee   115
  And burn this prayerbook, where I here use
  The holy word that had converted me.
  See, Mosby, I will tear away the leaves,
  And all the leaves, and in this golden cover
  Shall thy sweet phrases and thy letters dwell;   120
  And thereon will I chiefly meditate
  And hold no other sect but such devotion.
  Wilt thou not look? Is all thy love overwhelmed?
  Wilt thou not hear? What malice stops thine ears?
  Why speaks thou not? What silence ties thy tongue?   125
  Thou hast been sighted as the eagle is,
  And heard as quickly as the fearful hare,

96–7.] i.e. and attempt to see more clearly with eyes that once deluded my heart
into thinking you a gentle dove instead of the foul raven that you really are.

100. *gilt*] thin golden veneer.

104. *copesmate . . . hinds*] companion for your servants.

116–17.] Some editors have changed *where . . . use* to 'wherein I use'. The sense
of the whole phrase is that Alice will burn the prayerbook from which she had taken
the holy word which converted her away from Mosby's love.

122. *hold . . . sect*] keep no other religion.

126. *sighted*] able to see; i.e. keen-eyed.

127. *heard as quickly*] had as live hearing.

And spoke as smoothly as an orator,
When I have bid thee hear or see or speak.
And art thou sensible in none of these?　　　　130
Weigh all thy good turns with this little fault
And I deserve not Mosby's muddy looks.
A fount once troubled is not thickened still;
Be clear again, I'll ne'er more trouble thee.
Mosby. Oh, no, I am a base artificer;　　　　135
My wings are feathered for a lowly flight.
Mosby? Fie, no! Not for a thousand pound.
Make love to you? Why, 'tis unpardonable;
We beggars must not breathe where gentles are.
Alice. Sweet Mosby is as gentle as a king,　　　　140
And I too blind to judge him otherwise.
Flowers do sometimes spring in fallow lands,
Weeds in gardens, roses grow on thorns;
So, whatsoe'er my Mosby's father was,
Himself is valued gentle by his worth.　　　　145
Mosby. Ah, how you women can insinuate
And clear a trespass with your sweet-set tongue!
I will forget this quarrel, gentle Alice,
Provided I'll be tempted so no more.

　　　　Here enters BRADSHAW.

Alice. Then with thy lips seal up this new-made match.　　　　150
　　　　　　　　　　　　　　　　[*They kiss.*]
Mosby. Soft, Alice, for here comes somebody.
Alice. How now, Bradshaw, what's the news with you?
Bradshaw. I have little news, but here's a letter
That Master Greene importuned me to give you.
　　　　　　　　　　　　　　　　[*He gives a letter.*]
Alice. Go in, Bradshaw; call for a cup of beer.　　　　155
'Tis almost suppertime; thou shalt stay with us.
　　　　　　　　　　　　　　　Exit [BRADSHAW].
　　　　　　　　　　　　　　　Then she reads the letter.

---

130. *sensible . . . these*] aware in none of these senses.
133. *A fount once troubled*] The original quartos read 'A fence of trouble'. The proposed emendation allows the line to mean 'a fountain clouded by stirred-up mud does not remain so for long'.
135–9.] said sarcastically.
139. *gentles*] gentlefolk.
145.] his personal worth gives him high status. See Intro., pp. 35–6.
147. *clear a trespass*] clear away an offence.
sweet-set] sweetly composed, sweet-talking.
149. *I'll be tempted*] that I be provoked, challenged.

'We have missed of our purpose at London, but shall perform
it by the way. We thank our neighbour Bradshaw.
                    Yours,
                        Richard Greene.'   160
How likes my love the tenor of this letter?
Mosby. Well, were his date complete and expired!
Alice. Ah, would it were! Then comes my happy hour.
    Till then my bliss is mixed with bitter gall.
    Come, let us in to shun suspicion.   165
Mosby. Ay, to the gates of death to follow thee.   *Exeunt.*

[9]

Here enters GREENE, WILL, *and* SHAKEBAG.

Shakebag. Come, Will, see thy tools be in a readiness.
    Is not thy powder dank, or will thy flint strike fire?
Will. Then ask me if my nose be on my face,
    Or whether my tongue be frozen in my mouth.
    Zounds, here's a coil!   5
    You were best swear me on the inter'gatories
    How many pistols I have took in hand,
    Or whether I love the smell of gunpowder,
    Or dare abide the noise the dag will make,
    Or will not wink at flashing of the fire.   10
    I pray thee, Shakebag, let this answer thee,
    That I have took more purses in this down
    Than e'er thou handledst pistols in thy life.
Shakebag. Ay, haply thou hast picked more in a throng;
    But, should I brag what booties I have took,   15
    I think the overplus that's more than thine
    Would mount to a greater sum of money
    Than either thou or all thy kin are worth.

157–60.] The letter has obviously been sent *after* the events of scenes 3–7. It is
unconnected to the letter which Greene gave Bradshaw for Alice in 2.73–5 and
further confuses Bradshaw's role in the action.
    158. *thank*] i.e. for delivering the letter.
    162. *his*] Arden's.

    9.5. *coil*] fuss.
    6. *inter'gatories*] interrogatories; questions answered under oath.
    9. *dag*] pistol.
    10. *wink*] wince, blink.
    12. *this down*] Rainham Down, between Faversham and Rochester, where the
present ambush attempt takes place. See 7.28 and note.
    14. *picked*] pickpocketed, stolen.
    16. *overplus . . . thine*] amount in excess of what you have stolen.

Zounds, I hate them as I hate a toad
That carry a muscado in their tongue   20
And scarce a hurting weapon in their hand.
Will. Oh Greene, intolerable!
    It is not for mine honour to bear this.—
    Why, Shakebag, I did serve the king at Boulogne,
    And thou canst brag of nothing that thou hast done.   25
Shakebag. Why, so can Jack of Faversham,
    That swounded for a fillip on the nose,
    When he that gave it him holloed in his ear,
    And he supposed a cannon-bullet hit him.   *Then they fight.*
Greene. [*Separating them*] I pray you, sirs, list to Aesop's talk: 30
    Whilst two stout dogs were striving for a bone,
    There comes a cur and stole it from them both;
    So, while you stand striving on these terms of manhood,
    Arden escapes us and deceives us all.
Shakebag. Why, he begun.
Will.   And thou shalt find I'll end.   35
    I do but slip it until better time.
    But, if I do forget—   *Then he kneels down and holds*
                    up his hands to heaven.
Greene. Well, take your fittest standings, and once more
    Lime your twigs to catch this weary bird.
    I'll leave you, and at your dag's discharge   40
    Make towards, like the longing water-dog
    That coucheth till the fowling-piece be off,
    Then seizeth on the prey with eager mood.
    Ah, might I see him stretching forth his limbs
    As I have seen them beat their wings ere now!   45

---

20. *a muscado*] a sting, like that of a mosquito or a gadfly.
22. *Greene*] Will expresses to Greene his fury at what Shakebag has just said.
24. *Boulogne*] See 2.8 and note.
27. *swounded*] swooned.
fillip] punch.
29. *he*] Jack.
30. *Aesop's talk*] fable by the legendary author of animal fables. On that of the
dogs and the bone, compare 8.34–6.
31. *stout*] fierce.
36. *slip*] postpone.
38. *fittest standings*] best positions for an ambush. Cf. 3.38.
39. *Lime your twigs*] refers to the practice of covering twigs with a sticky substance known as bird-lime to catch birds. A common image for a trap.
41. *Make towards*] I will come towards you.
water-dog] dog trained to retrieve waterfowl.
42. *coucheth*] crouches, lies low.
fowling-piece] light gun for shooting wild-fowl.
45. *them*] i.e. the waterfowl.

Shakebag. Why, that thou shalt see if he come this way.
Greene. Yes, that he doth, Shakebag, I warrant thee.
    But brawl not when I am gone in any case,
    But, sirs, be sure to speed him when he comes;
    And in that hope I'll leave you for an hour.   *Exit* GREENE.   50
         [BLACK WILL *and* SHAKEBAG *conceal themselves.*]

     Here enters ARDEN, FRANKLIN, *and* MICHAEL.

Michael. 'Twere best that I went back to Rochester.
    The horse halts downright; it were not good
    He travelled in such pain to Faversham.
    Removing of a shoe may haply help it.
Arden. Well, get you back to Rochester; but, sirrah, see   55
    Ye overtake us ere we come to Rainham Down,
    For it will be very late ere we get home.
Michael. [*Aside*] Ay, God he knows, and so doth Will and
       Shakebag,
    That thou shalt never go further than that Down;
    And therefore have I pricked the horse on purpose   60
    Because I would not view the massacre.   *Exit* MICHAEL.
Arden. Come, Master Franklin, onwards with your tale.
Franklin. I assure you, sir, you task me much.
    A heavy blood is gathered at my heart,
    And on the sudden is my wind so short   65
    As hindereth the passage of my speech.
    So fierce a qualm yet ne'er assailèd me.
Arden. Come, Master Franklin, let us go on softly.
    The annoyance of the dust or else some meat
    You ate at dinner cannot brook you.   70
    I have been often so and soon amended.
Franklin. Do you remember where my tale did leave?
Arden. Ay, where the gentleman did check his wife.
Franklin. She being reprehended for the fact,
    Witness produced that took her with the deed,   75
    Her glove brought in which there she left behind,
    And many other assurèd arguments,

---

47. *that he doth*] indeed he does so; i.e. Arden is coming this way.
50.1.] Black Will and Shakebag may use a stage pillar to hide behind.
52. *halts downright*] limps badly.
60. *pricked the horse*] wounded the horse's foot.
67. *qualm*] fit of illness; figuratively, 'misgiving'.
70. *brook*] sit well with.
73. *check*] reprove.
75. *with the deed*] in the act.
77. *arguments*] proofs.

Her husband asked her whether it were not so.

Arden. Her answer then? I wonder how she looked,
 Having forsworn it with such vehement oaths,   80
 And at the instant so approved upon her.

Franklin. First did she cast her eyes down to the earth,
 Watching the drops that fell amain from thence;
 Then softly draws she forth her handkercher,
 And modestly she wipes her tear-stained face;   85
 Then hemmed she out, to clear her voice should seem,
 And with a majesty addressed herself
 To encounter all their accusations.—
 Pardon me, Master Arden, I can no more;
 This fighting at my heart makes short my wind.   90

Arden. Come, we are almost now at Rainham Down.
 Your pretty tale beguiles the weary way;
 I would you were in state to tell it out.

Shakebag. [*Aside*] Stand close, Will; I hear them coming.

    Here enters LORD CHEYNE *with his* Men
    [*just as Shakebag and Black Will are about to attack*].

Will. [*Aside*] Stand to it, Shakebag, and be resolute.   95

Lord Cheyne. Is it so near night as it seems,
 Or will this black-faced evening have a shower?—
 What, Master Arden? You are well met.
 I have longed this fortnight's day to speak with you.
 You are a stranger, man, in the Isle of Sheppey.   100

Arden. Your honour's always, bound to do you service!

Lord Cheyne. Come you from London and ne'er a man with you?

Arden. My man's coming after,
 But here's my honest friend that came along with me.

Lord Cheyne. [*To Franklin*] My Lord Protector's man, I take you
 to be.   105

Franklin. Ay, my good lord, and highly bound to you.

Lord Cheyne. You and your friend come home and sup with me.

Arden. I beseech your honour pardon me;
 I have made a promise to a gentleman,
 My honest friend, to meet him at my house.   110
 The occasion is great, or else would I wait on you.

---

81. *approved upon*] proved against.

86. *hemmed*] i.e. made throat-clearing noises, as 'ahem'.
 should] it should.

94.1. LORD CHEYNE] Sir Thomas Cheyne. He is referred to elsewhere in the play:
see 2.35.

100. *Isle of Sheppey*] an island at the mouth of the River Medway, across the river
Swale from Faversham.

111. *wait upon you*] keep you company.

Lord Cheyne. Will you come tomorrow and dine with me,
    And bring your honest friend with you?
    I have divers matters to talk with you about.
Arden. Tomorrow we'll wait upon your honour.   115
Lord Cheyne. [*To a Servant*] One of you stay my horse at the top of
    the hill.
    [*Seeing Black Will*] What, Black Will! For whose purse wait
    you?
    Thou wilt be hanged in Kent when all is done.
Will. Not hanged, God save your honour.
    I am your beadsman, bound to pray for you.   120
Lord Cheyne. I think thou ne'er saidest prayer in all thy life.
    [*To a Servant*] One of you give him a crown.—
    And, sirrah, leave this kind of life.
    If thou beest 'tainted for a penny matter
    And come in question, surely thou wilt truss.—   125
    Come, Master Arden, let us be going;
    Your way and mine lies four mile together.   *Exeunt.*
                    Manet BLACK WILL *and* SHAKEBAG.
Will. The devil break all your necks at four miles' end!
    Zounds, I could kill myself for very anger!
    His lordship chops me in even when   130
    My dag was levelled at his heart.
    I would his crown were molten down his throat!
Shakebag. Arden, thou hast wondrous holy luck.
    Did ever man escape as thou hast done?
    Well, I'll discharge my pistol at the sky,   135
    For by this bullet Arden might not die.   [*He fires.*]

                    Here enters GREENE.

Greene. What, is he down? Is he dispatched?
Shakebag. Ay, in health towards Faversham to shame us all.
Greene. The devil he is! Why, sirs, how escaped he?
Shakebag. When we were ready to shoot,   140
    Comes my Lord Cheyne to prevent his death.
Greene. The Lord of Heaven hath preservèd him.

---

120. *beadsman*] one paid to pray for others. Black Will means that he hopes Lord
Cheyne will protect him from the law.
    122. *crown*] gold coin.
    124. *'tainted*] brought before the court.
penny matter] trivial offence.
    125. *truss*] hang.
    130. *chops me in*] suddenly interrupts.
    131. *his*] Arden's.
    137. *dispatched*] dealt with, killed. But Shakebag (line 138) grimly puns on the
sense of 'sent on', or hurried home.

Will. Preserved, a fig! The Lord Cheyne hath preserved him
 And bids him to a feast to his house at Shorlow.
 But by the way once more I'll meet with him;   145
 And if all the Cheynes in the world say no,
 I'll have a bullet in his breast tomorrow.
 Therefore come, Greene, and let us to Faversham.
Greene. Ay, and excuse ourselves to Mistress Arden.
 Oh, how she'll chafe when she hears of this!   150
Shakebag. Why, I'll warrant you she'll think we dare not do it.
Will. Why, then let us go, and tell her all the matter,
 And plot the news to cut him off tomorrow. *Exeunt.*

[10]

  Here enters ARDEN *and his* Wife, FRANKLIN, *and* MICHAEL.

Arden. See how the Hours, the guardant of heaven's gate,
 Have by their toil removed the darksome clouds,
 That Sol may well discern the trampled pace
 Wherein he wont to guide his golden car.
 The season fits. Come, Franklin, let's away.   5
Alice. I thought you did pretend some special hunt
 That made you thus cut short the time of rest.
Arden. It was no chase that made me rise so early,
 But, as I told thee yesternight, to go
 To the Isle of Sheppey, there to dine   10
 With my Lord Cheyne;
 For so his honour late commanded me.
Alice. Ay, such kind husbands seldom want excuses;
 Home is a wild cat to a wand'ring wit.
 The time hath been—would God it were not past!—   15
 That honour's title nor a lord's command
 Could once have drawn you from these arms of mine.

---

144. *Shorlow*] Shurland, Lord Cheyne's residence on the Isle of Sheppey.
146. *And if*] and even if.
153.] and plot a new means to kill Arden tomorrow.

10.1. *Hours*] daughters of Jupiter and Themis who presided over the change of seasons.
3. *Sol*] the sun (personified). Arden is saying that it is morning. See Intro., p. 48.
 pace] path.
5. *The season fits*] The weather is suitable for our journey.
6. *pretend*] intend.
12. *late*] recently.
13. *want*] lack.
14.] i.e. home is insufferable to a restless mind.

But my deserts or your desires decay,
Or both; yet if true love may seem desert,
I merit still to have thy company.   20
Franklin. Why, I pray you, sir, let her go along with us.
I am sure his honour will welcome her
And us the more for bringing her along.
Arden. Content. [*To Michael*] Sirrah, saddle your mistress' nag.
Alice. No, begged favour merits little thanks.   25
If I should go, our house would run away
Or else be stol'n; therefore I'll stay behind.
Arden. Nay, see how mistaking you are.
I pray thee, go.
Alice.   No, no, not now.
Arden. Then let me leave thee satisfied in this: 30
That time nor place nor persons alter me
But that I hold thee dearer than my life.
Alice. That will be seen by your quick return.
Arden. And that shall be ere night, an if I live.
Farewell, sweet Alice; we mind to sup with thee.   *Exit* ALICE.   35
Franklin. Come, Michael, are our horses ready?
Michael. Ay, your horse are ready, but I am not ready, for I have lost
my purse with six-and-thirty shillings in it, with taking up of my
master's nag.
Franklin. Why, I pray you, let us go before   40
Whilst he stays behind to seek his purse.
Arden. Go to, sirrah! See you follow us to the Isle of Sheppey,
To my Lord Cheyne's, where we mean to dine.
            Exeunt ARDEN *and* FRANKLIN. *Manet* MICHAEL.
Michael. So, fair weather after you! For before you lies Black Will
and Shakebag in the broom close, too close for you. They'll be   45
your ferrymen to long home.

        Here enters the Painter [CLARKE, *with a poisoned crucifix*].

But who is this? The painter, my corrival, that would needs win
Mistress Susan.
Clarke. How now, Michael? How doth my mistress and all at home?

---

25. *begged favour*] a favour that has to be asked for.
35. *mind*] intend.
38. *taking up of*] ? catching.
45. *broom close*] enclosed field of gorse bushes. With a pun on *close*, near by.
46. *ferryman*] an allusion to Charon, who ferried dead souls across the river Styx
in the classical underworld.
    to long home] i.e. to the grave.
48–50. *Mistress*] Michael and Clarke play on two meanings: (1) general title for
a woman; (2) woman in a sexual relationship with a man.

Michael. Who? Susan Mosby? She is your mistress, too?   50
Clarke. Ay, how doth she and all the rest?
Michael. All's well but Susan; she is sick.
Clarke. Sick? Of what disease?
Michael. Of a great fear.
Clarke. A fear of what?   55
Michael. A great fever.
Clarke. A fever? God forbid!
Michael. Yes, faith, and of a lurdan, too, as big as yourself.
Clarke. Oh, Michael, the spleen prickles you. Go to; you carry an
     eye over Mistress Susan.   60
Michael. Ay, faith, to keep her from the painter.
Clarke. Why more from a painter than from a serving-creature like
     yourself?
Michael. Because you painters make but a painting-table of a pretty
     wench and spoil her beauty with blotting.   65
Clarke. What mean you by that?
Michael. Why, that you painters paint lambs in the lining of
     wenches' petticoats, and we servingmen put horns to them to
     make them become sheep.
Clarke. Such another word will cost you a cuff or a knock.   70
Michael. What, with a dagger made of a pencil? Faith, 'tis too weak,
     and therefore thou too weak to win Susan.
Clarke. Would Susan's love lay upon this stroke!
                              Then he breaks Michael's head.

               Here enters MOSBY, GREENE, *and* ALICE.

Alice. I'll lay my life, this is for Susan's love.
     [*To Michael*] Stayed you behind your master to this end?   75
     Have you no other time to brabble in
     But now when serious matters are in hand?—
     Say, Clarke, hast thou done the thing thou promised?
Clarke. Ay, here it is; the very touch is death.
                              [*He shows his poisoned crucifix.*]

---

58. *lurdan*] lazy person; 'fever-lurdan' was a mock-medical term for the disease
of laziness.
59. *spleen prickles*] peevish temper goads.
59–60. *carry . . . over*] have an eye on, have designs on.
64. *painting-table*] a board or other flat surface on which a picture is painted.
67–8. *lambs . . . petticoats*] obscure.
68. *horns*] i.e. cuckolds horns.
71–2.] playing on the bawdy connection between a dagger, a pencil and a penis
to suggest that the painter is not virile enough to satisfy Susan sexually.
73.1. breaks . . . head] hits Michael's head hard enough to draw blood; cf. 3.49.2.
74. *lay*] bet.
76. *brabble*] brawl.

Alice. Then this, I hope, if all the rest do fail,   80
    Will catch Master Arden
    And make him wise in death that lived a fool.
    Why should he thrust his sickle in our corn,
    Or what hath he to do with thee, my love,
    Or govern me that am to rule myself?   85
    Forsooth, for credit sake, I must leave thee!
    Nay, he must leave to live that we may love,
    May live, may love; for what is life but love?
    And love shall last as long as life remains,
    And life shall end before my love depart.   90
Mosby. Why, what's love without true constancy?
    Like to a pillar built of many stones,
    Yet neither with good mortar well compact
    Nor cement to fasten it in the joints
    But that it shakes with every blast of wind   95
    And, being touched, straight falls unto the earth
    And buries all his haughty pride in dust.
    No, let our love be rocks of adamant,
    Which time nor place nor tempest can asunder.
Greene. Mosby, leave protestations now,   100
    And let us bethink us what we have to do.
    Black Will and Shakebag I have placed
    In the broom close, watching Arden's coming.
    Let's to them and see what they have done.   *Exeunt.*

[11]

                Here enters ARDEN *and* FRANKLIN.

Arden. Oh, ferryman, where art thou?

                Here enters the Ferryman.

Ferryman. Here, here! Go before to the boat, and I will follow
    you.

---

83. *thrust . . . corn*] interfere in our affairs (proverbial).
  86.] Alice scornfully mimics the idea that she must leave Mosby for the sake of
her reputation. *Forsooth*, 'indeed', catches the tone of scorn.
    credit] reputation's.
  87. *Nay*] on the contrary. Arden is the one who must do the leaving, not Alice.
  93. *compact*] held together.
  98. *adamant*] supposedly the hardest of rocks.
  99. *asunder*] put asunder.

  11.] The scene is set at the ferry crossing between the mainland and the Isle of
Sheppey.

Arden. We have great haste; I pray thee come away.
Ferryman. Fie, what a mist is here!   5
Arden. This mist, my friend, is mystical,
     Like to a good companion's smoky brain,
     That was half-drowned with new ale overnight.
Ferryman. 'Twere pity but his skull were opened to make more
     chimney room.   10
Franklin. Friend, what's thy opinion of this mist?
Ferryman. I think 'tis like to a curst wife in a little house, that never
     leaves her husband till she have driven him out at doors with a
     wet pair of eyes. Then looks he as if his house were afire, or
     some of his friends dead.   15
Arden. Speaks thou this of thine own experience?
Ferryman. Perhaps ay, perhaps no; for my wife is as other women
     are, that is to say, governed by the moon.
Franklin. By the moon? How, I pray thee?
Ferryman. Nay, thereby lies a bargain, and you shall not have it   20
     fresh and fasting.
Arden. Yes, I pray thee, good ferryman.
Ferryman. Then for this once: let it be midsummer moon, but yet
     my wife has another moon.
Franklin. Another moon?   25
Ferryman. Ay, and it hath influences and eclipses.
Arden. Why, then, by this reckoning you sometimes play the man in
     the moon.
Ferryman. Ay, but you had not best to meddle with that moon lest
     I scratch you by the face with my bramble-bush.   30
Arden. I am almost stifled with this fog. Come, let's away.
Franklin. And, sirrah, as we go, let us have some more of your bold
     yeomanry.
Ferryman. Nay, by my troth, sir, but flat knavery.   *Exeunt.*

---

12. *curst*] shrewish, bad-tempered.
18. *governed by the moon*] i.e. changeable; a commonplace idea about women.
21. *fresh and fasting*] i.e. too soon, or too cheap. The Ferryman is tantalizing
them by delaying his answers.
24. *another moon*] i.e. monthly menstruation.
27–8. *play . . . moon*] with the bawdy suggestion that the man enters the place of
the woman's monthly menstruation.
30. *bramble-bush*] The man in the moon was supposed to have a lantern, a thorn-
bush and a dog.
33. *yeomanry*] plain speaking.
34. *flat*] out and out (punningly opposed to *bold*, i.e. standing up, *yeomanry*).

[12]

Here enters WILL *at one door and* SHAKEBAG *at another.*

Shakebag. Oh, Will, where art thou?

Will. Here, Shakebag, almost in hell's mouth, where I cannot see
my way for smoke.

Shakebag. I pray thee speak still that we may meet by the sound, for
I shall fall into some ditch or other unless my feet see better   5
than my eyes.

Will. Didst thou ever see better weather to run away with another
man's wife or play with a wench at potfinger?

Shakebag. No; this were a fine world for chandlers if this weather
would last, for then a man should never dine nor sup without   10
candlelight. But, sirrah Will, what horses are those that passed?

Will. Why, didst thou hear any?

Shakebag. Ay, that I did.

Will. My life for thine, 'twas Arden and his companion, and then all
our labour's lost.   15

Shakebag. Nay, say not so; for, if it be they, they may haply lose
their way as we have done, and then we may chance meet with
them.

Will. Come, let us go on like a couple of blind pilgrims.
> *Then* SHAKEBAG *falls into a ditch.*

Shakebag. Help, Will, help! I am almost drowned.   20

Here enters the Ferryman.

Ferryman. Who's that that calls for help?

Will. 'Twas none here; 'twas thou thyself.

Ferryman. I came to help him that called for help. Why, how now?
Who is this that's in the ditch? [*He helps Shakebag out.*] You are
well enough served to go without a guide such weather as this!   25

Will. Sirrah, what companies hath passed your ferry this morning?

Ferryman. None but a couple of gentlemen that went to dine at my
Lord Cheyne's.

Will. Shakebag, did not I tell thee as much?

Ferryman. Why, sir, will you have any letters carried to them?   30

Will. No, sir. Get you gone.

12.] Still at the ferry.

3. *smoke*] fog, mist.

8. *potfinger*] sexual foreplay.

9. *chandlers*] candlemakers.

19.1. a ditch] through the trap-door of the stage. See Intro., pp. 7–8.

22.] Will, in a panic, tries to pretend that Shakebag is not there, and responds
rudely and comically to the Ferryman.

Ferryman. Did you ever see such a mist as this?

Will. No, nor such a fool as will rather be houghed than get his way.

Ferryman. Why, sir, this is no Hough Monday; you are deceived.—

    What's his name, I pray you, sir?   35

Shakebag. His name is Black Will.

Ferryman. I hope to see him one day hanged upon a hill.

                                     Exit Ferryman.

Shakebag. See how the sun hath cleared the foggy mist,

    Now we have missed the mark of our intent.

          Here enters GREENE, MOSBY, *and* ALICE.

Mosby. Black Will and Shakebag, what make you here?   40

    What, is the deed done? Is Arden dead?

Will. What could a blinded man perform in arms?

    Saw you not how till now the sky was dark,

    That neither horse nor man could be discerned?

    Yet did we hear their horses as they passed.   45

Greene. Have they escaped you, then, and passed the ferry?

Shakebag. Ay, for a while; but here we two will stay

    And at their coming back meet with them once more.

    Zounds, I was ne'er so toiled in all my life

    In following so slight a task as this.   50

Mosby. [*To Shakebag*] How cam'st thou so berayed?

Will. With making false footing in the dark.

    He needs would follow them without a guide.

Alice. [*Giving money*] Here's to pay for a fire and good cheer.

    Get you to Faversham to the Flower-de-Luce,   55

    And rest yourselves until some other time.

Greene. Let me alone; it most concerns my state.

Will. Ay, Mistress Arden, this will serve the turn

    In case we fall into a second fog.

                  Exeunt GREENE, WILL, *and* SHAKEBAG.

Mosby. These knaves will never do it; let us give it over.   60

---

33. *houghed*] hamstrung; i.e. lamed or disabled.

get . . . way] go on his way.

34. *Hough Monday*] Hock Monday; a holiday on the second Monday after Easter when women customarily tied men up and compelled them to pay a ransom for release. (With wordplay on *houghed* in line 33.)

40. *make you*] are you doing.

42. *in arms*] using weapons.

49. *toiled*] wearied.

51. *berayed*] dirtied, spattered with mud.

53. *He*] Shakebag.

57. *Let me alone*] leave it to me, i.e. let me take care of everything. (Greene may also be offering to pay the men.)

Alice. First tell me how you like my new device:
   Soon, when my husband is returning back,
   You and I both marching arm in arm,
   Like loving friends, we'll meet him on the way
   And boldly beard and brave him to his teeth.   65
   When words grow hot and blows begin to rise,
   I'll call those cutters forth your tenement,
   Who, in a manner to take up the fray,
   Shall wound my husband Hornsby to the death.
Mosby. Ah, fine device! Why, this deserves a kiss. *[He kisses her.]*   70
                                                      Exeunt.

[13]

Here enters DICK REEDE *and a* Sailor.

Sailor. Faith, Dick Reede, it is to little end.
   His conscience is too liberal and he too niggardly
   To part from anything may do thee good.
Reede. He is coming from Shorlow, as I understand.
   Here I'll intercept him, for at his house   5
   He never will vouchsafe to speak with me.
   If prayers and fair entreaties will not serve
   Or make no batt'ry in his flinty breast,

Here enters FRANKLIN, ARDEN, *and* MICHAEL.

   I'll curse the carl and see what that will do.
   See where he comes to further my intent.—   10
   Master Arden, I am now bound to the sea.
   My coming to you was about the plot of ground
   Which wrongfully you detain from me.
   Although the rent of it be very small,
   Yet will it help my wife and children,   15
   Which here I leave in Faversham, God knows,
   Needy and bare. For Christ's sake, let them have it!
Arden. Franklin, hearest thou this fellow speak?
   That which he craves I dearly bought of him

---

61. *device*] plan.
65. *beard*] defy, challenge.
67. *cutters*] cut-throats; i.e. Black Will and Shakebag.
forth your tenement] from out of your dwelling place.
69. *Hornsby*] i.e. the cuckold.

13.2. *liberal*] easy, indifferent.
niggardly] mean.
9. *carl*] villain; churlish, miserly person of low social status.

Although the rent of it was ever mine.—   20
Sirrah, you that ask these questions,
If with thy clamorous impeaching tongue
Thou rail on me, as I have heard thou dost,
I'll lay thee up so close a twelvemonth's day
As thou shalt neither see the sun nor moon.   25
Look to it; for, as surely as I live,
I'll banish pity if thou use me thus.
Reede. What, wilt thou do me wrong and threat me too?
  Nay, then, I'll tempt thee, Arden: do thy worst.
  God, I beseech thee, show some miracle   30
  On thee or thine in plaguing thee for this!
  That plot of ground which thou detains from me—
  I speak it in an agony of spirit—
  Be ruinous and fatal unto thee!
  Either there be butchered by thy dearest friends,   35
  Or else be brought for men to wonder at,
  Or thou or thine miscarry in that place,
  Or there run mad and end thy cursèd days.
Franklin. Fie, bitter knave, bridle thine envious tongue!
  For curses are like arrows shot upright,   40
  Which, falling down, light on the shooter's head.
Reede. Light where they will! Were I upon the sea,
  As oft I have in many a bitter storm,
  And saw a dreadful southern flaw at hand,
  The pilot quaking at the doubtful storm,   45
  And all the sailors praying on their knees,
  Even in that fearful time would I fall down
  And ask of God, whate'er betide of me,
  Vengeance on Arden or some misevent
  To show the world what wrong the carl hath done.   50
  This charge I'll leave with my distressful wife;

20.] Arden indicates that Reede held the land leasehold and was bound to pay dues to Arden for it. Arden bought the lease from Reed. See Intro., pp. 28–9.
  22. *impeaching*] accusing.
  24. *lay . . . close*] lock you up so tightly (i.e. for slander).
  a twelvemonth's day] an entire year from today.
  29. *tempt*] provoke.
  32. *thou detains*] you withhold.
  36.] or else be put on public display.
  37. *miscarry*] come to harm.
  39. *envious*] spiteful, malicious.
  44. *flaw*] squall; sudden gust of wind.
  45. *doubtful*] dreaded.
  49. *misevent*] disastrous happening.

My children shall be taught such prayers as these.
And thus I go, but leave my curse with thee.

Exeunt REEDE *and* Sailor.

Arden. It is the railingest knave in Christendom,
And oftentimes the villain will be mad.   55
It greatly matters not what he says,
But I assure you I ne'er did him wrong.

Franklin. I think so, Master Arden.

Arden. Now that our horses are gone home before,
My wife may haply meet me on the way;   60
For God knows she is grown passing kind of late
And greatly changèd from the old humour
Of her wonted frowardness,
And seeks by fair means to redeem old faults.

Franklin. Happy the change that alters for the best!   65
But see in any case you make no speech
Of the cheer we had at my Lord Cheyne's,
Although most bounteous and liberal,
For that will make her think herself more wronged
In that we did not carry her along;   70
For sure she grieved that she was left behind.

Arden. Come, Franklin, let us strain to mend our pace
And take her unawares playing the cook;

Here enters ALICE *and* MOSBY [*arm in arm*].

For I believe she'll strive to mend our cheer.

Franklin. Why, there's no better creatures in the world   75
Than women are when they are in good humours.

Arden. Who is that? Mosby? What, so familiar?
Injurious strumpet and thou ribald knave,
Untwine those arms!

Alice. Ay, with a sugared kiss let them untwine.   80

[*She kisses Mosby.*]

Arden. Ah, Mosby! Perjured beast! Bear this and all!

---

61. *passing*] very.
62. *humour*] disposition.
63. *wonted frowardness*] usual perversity.
67. *cheer*] entertainment, hospitality.
72. *strain . . . pace*] make an effort to speed up.
74. *mend our cheer*] make us especially welcome.
78. *Injurious*] insulting.
ribald] scurrilous, offensive.
81. *Perjured*] because of Mosby's oath that he would sever relations with Alice.
See 1.326–9.
Bear . . . all!] Oh, that I must bear this and all the rest!

Mosby. And yet no hornèd beast; the horns are thine.
Franklin. Oh, monstrous! Nay, then, 'tis time to draw.
[ARDEN, FRANKLIN, and MOSBY draw.]

Alice. Help! help! They murder my husband.

Here enters WILL and SHAKEBAG.

Shakebag. Zounds, who injures Master Mosby?   85
[They fight. FRANKLIN wounds Shakebag;
ARDEN wounds Mosby.]

Help, Will! I am hurt.
Mosby. I may thank you, Mistress Arden, for this wound.
Exeunt MOSBY, WILL, and SHAKEBAG.

Alice. Ah, Arden, what folly blinded thee?
Ah, jealous harebrain man, what hast thou done?
When we, to welcome thy intended sport,   90
Came lovingly to meet thee on thy way,
Thou drew'st thy sword, enraged with jealousy,
And hurt thy friend, whose thoughts were free from harm—
All for a worthless kiss and joining arms,
Both done but merrily to try thy patience;   95
And me unhappy that devised the jest,
Which, though begun in sport, yet ends in blood!
Franklin. Marry, God defend me from such a jest!
Alice. Couldst thou not see us friendly smile on thee
When we joined arms and when I kissed his cheek?   100
Hast thou not lately found me overkind?
Didst thou not hear me cry they murder thee?
Called I not help to set my husband free?
No, ears and all were witched. Ah me accursed,
To link in liking with a frantic man!   105
Henceforth I'll be thy slave, no more thy wife;
For with that name I never shall content thee.
If I be merry, thou straightways thinks me light;
If sad, thou sayest the sullens trouble me;
If well attired, thou thinks I will be gadding;   110
If homely, I seem sluttish in thine eye.
Thus am I still, and shall be while I die,
Poor wench, abused by thy misgovernment.

82.] Mosby quibbles on Arden's insult, *beast*, saying at least he is not a horned beast like the cuckold Arden.
90. *to welcome . . . sport*] to give you festive welcome.
104. *witched*] bewitched.
105. *frantic*] insane.
109. *sullens*] sulks.
113. *misgovernment*] misuse of authority in the household. See Intro., pp. 36–7.

Arden. But is it for truth that neither thou nor he
    Intended'st malice in your misdemeanour?   115
Alice. The heavens can witness of our harmless thoughts.
Arden. Then pardon me, sweet Alice, and forgive this fault.
    Forget but this and never see the like.
    Impose me penance, and I will perform it,
    For in thy discontent I find a death—   120
    A death tormenting more than death itself.
Alice. Nay, hadst thou loved me as thou dost pretend,
    Thou wouldst have marked the speeches of thy friend,
    Who, going wounded from the place, he said
    His skin was pierced only through my device.   125
    And if sad sorrow taint thee for this fault,
    Thou wouldst have followed him, and seen him dressed,
    And cried him mercy whom thou hast misdone.
    Ne'er shall my heart be eased till this be done.
Arden. Content thee, sweet Alice; thou shalt have thy will,   130
    Whate'er it be. For that I injured thee
    And wronged my friend, shame scourgeth my offence.
    Come thou thyself and go along with me,
    And be a mediator twixt us two.
Franklin. Why, Master Arden, know you what you do?   135
    Will you follow him that hath dishonoured you?
Alice. Why, canst thou prove I have been disloyal?
Franklin. Why, Mosby taunts your husband with the horn.
Alice. Ay, after he had reviled him
    By the injurious name of perjured beast.   140
    He knew no wrong could spite a jealous man
    More than the hateful naming of the horn.
Franklin. Suppose 'tis true, yet is it dangerous
    To follow him whom he hath lately hurt.
Alice. A fault confessed is more than half amends,   145
    But men of such ill spirit as yourself
    Work crosses and debates 'twixt man and wife.
Arden. I pray thee, gentle Franklin, hold thy peace;
    I know my wife counsels me for the best.

---

123. *thy friend*] Mosby.
126. *taint*] accuse.
127. *dressed*] i.e. his wounds.
128. *cried . . . whom*] begged mercy of the person whom.
misdone] harmed.
131. *For that*] in that, because.
139. *he . . . him*] i.e. Arden had reviled Mosby. See line 81.
141. *He*] i.e. Mosby.
147. *crosses*] conflicts.

I'll seek out Mosby where his wound is dressed   150
And salve this hapless quarrel if I may.

Exeunt ARDEN *and* ALICE.

Franklin. He whom the devil drives must go perforce.
Poor gentleman, how soon he is bewitched!
And yet, because his wife is the instrument,
His friends must not be lavish in their speech.   155

Exit FRANKLIN.

[14]

Here enters WILL, SHAKEBAG, *and* GREENE.

Will. Sirrah Greene, when was I so long in killing a man?
Greene. I think we shall never do it. Let us give it over.
Shakebag. Nay, zounds! We'll kill him though we be hanged at his
   door for our labour.
Will. Thou knowest, Greene, that I have lived in London this twelve   5
   years, where I have made some go upon wooden legs for taking
   the wall on me; divers with silver noses for saying, 'There goes
   Black Will.' I have cracked as many blades as thou hast done
   nuts.
Greene. Oh, monstrous lie!   10
Will. Faith, in a manner I have. The bawdy-houses have paid me
   tribute; there durst not a whore set up unless she have agreed
   with me first for op'ning her shop windows. For a cross word of
   a tapster I have pierced one barrel after another with my dagger
   and held him by the ears till all his beer hath run out. In   15
   Thames Street a brewer's cart was like to have run over me; I
   made no more ado but went to the clerk and cut all the notches
   off his tallies and beat them about his head. I and my company
   have taken the constable from his watch and carried him about
   the fields on a coltstaff. I have broken a sergeant's head with his   20
   own mace, and bailed whom I list with my sword and buckler.
   All the tenpenny alehouses would stand every morning with a

---

151. *salve*] soothe.
hapless] unfortunate.

14.6–7. *taking the wall*] pushing over to the side next to the wall, i.e. away from
the dirt of the street.
7. *silver noses*] false noses made of silver.
18. *tallies*] sticks marked with notches for recording accounts.
20. *coltstaff*] a pole used to carry burdens on the shoulders of two men.
broken . . . head] injured, so as to draw blood, the head of the arresting officer.
22. *mace*] staff of office.
bailed . . . list] freed from jail whomever I wanted.
22–5. *All . . . night*] Black Will boasts that he is offered free drink by tavern
owners to protect them from his violence. See Intro., p. 31.
22. *tenpenny alehouses*] keepers of alehouses where ale cost 10*d* a quart.

quart pot in his hand, saying, 'Will it please your worship
drink?' He that had not done so had been sure to have had his
sign pulled down and his lattice borne away the next night. To   25
conclude, what have I not done? Yet cannot do this. Doubtless,
he is preserved by miracle.

Here enters ALICE *and* MICHAEL,
[*not seeing Will, Shakebag, and Greene at first*].

Greene. Hence, Will! Here comes Mistress Arden.
Alice. Ah, gentle Michael, art thou sure they're friends?
Michael. Why, I saw them when they both shook hands.   30
     When Mosby bled, he even wept for sorrow
     And railed on Franklin that was cause of all.
     No sooner came the surgeon in at doors
     But my master took to his purse and gave him money,
     And, to conclude, sent me to bring you word   35
     That Mosby, Franklin, Bradshaw, Adam Fowle,
     With divers of his neighbours and his friends,
     Will come and sup with you at our house this night.
Alice. Ah, gentle Michael, run thou back again;
     And, when my husband walks into the fair,   40
     Bid Mosby steal from him and come to me;
     And this night shall thou and Susan be made sure.
Michael. I'll go tell him.
Alice. And, as thou goest, tell John cook of our guests,
     And bid him lay it on; spare for no cost.   *Exit* MICHAEL.   45
Will. Nay, an there be such cheer, we will bid ourselves.—
     Mistress Arden, Dick Greene and I do mean to sup with you.
Alice. And welcome shall you be. Ah, gentlemen,
     How missed you of your purpose yesternight?
Greene. 'Twas long of Shakebag, that unlucky villain.   50
Shakebag. Thou dost me wrong; I did as much as any.
Will. Nay then, Mistress Alice, I'll tell you how it was. When he
     should have locked with both his hilts, he in a bravery flourished
     over his head. With that comes Franklin at him lustily and hurts

---

29. *they're*] Mosby and Arden are.
31. *he*] Arden.
36. *Adam Fowle*] the host of the Flower-de-Luce Inn in Faversham.
40. *the fair*] the fair of St Valentine. See Intro., p. 29.
44. *John cook*] John the cook.
49. *missed . . . purpose*] did you fail in your intention.
50. *long of*] because of.
53. *locked . . . hilts*] crossed swords with his opponent up to the hilts.
in a bravery] with show of bravado.
flourished] brandished his sword.
54. *lustily*] vigorously.

the slave; with that he slinks away. Now his way had been to   55
have come in hand and feet, one and two round at his costard.
He like a fool bears his sword-point half a yard out of danger. I
lie here for my life. [*He takes a position of defence.*] If the devil
come and he have no more strength than fence, he shall never
beat me from this ward. I'll stand to it, a buckler in a skilful   60
hand is as good as a castle; nay, 'tis better than a sconce, for I
have tried it. Mosby, perceiving this, began to faint. With that
comes Arden with his arming-sword and thrust him through the
shoulder in a trice.

Alice. Ay, but I wonder why you both stood still.   65
Will. Faith, I was so amazed I could not strike.
Alice. Ah, sirs, had he yesternight been slain,
      For every drop of his detested blood
      I would have crammed in angels in thy fist,
      And kissed thee, too, and hugged thee in my arms.   70
Will. Patient yourself; we cannot help it now.
      Greene and we two will dog him through the fair,
      And stab him in the crowd, and steal away.

            Here enters MOSBY[, *his arm bandaged*].

Alice. It is unpossible. But here comes he
      That will, I hope, invent some surer means.—   75
      Sweet Mosby, hide thy arm; it kills my heart.
Mosby. Ay, Mistress Arden, this is your favour.
Alice. Ah, say not so; for, when I saw thee hurt,
      I could have took the weapon thou lett'st fall
      And run at Arden, for I have sworn   80
      That these mine eyes, offended with his sight,
      Shall never close till Arden's be shut up.
      This night I rose and walked about the chamber,

---

55. *the slave*] Shakebag.
    55–6. *Now . . . feet*] Shakebag should have fought closer in to his opponent, using his fists and feet. See Intro., pp. 25 and 59 n. 38.
    56. *round . . . costard*] roundly at his head. (A *costard* is literally a large apple.)
    57–8. *I . . . life*] This is the fencing position I adopted to defend myself.
    59. *fence*] fencing skill.
    60. *ward*] defensive posture.
    I'll . . . it] I'll take the position that.
    61. *sconce*] small fort.
    62. *this*] i.e. that Shakebag was getting the worst of it.
    faint] lose courage.
    63. *arming-sword*] sword with which he is armed.
    67. *he*] Arden.
    71. *Patient yourself*] be patient.
    77. *favour*] gift (e.g. a scarf or glove) given to a lover to be worn conspicuously. Mosby is referring sarcastically to his bandage.
    83. *This night*] last night.

And twice or thrice I thought to have murdered him.
Mosby. What, in the night? Then had we been undone!   85
Alice. Why, how long shall he live?
Mosby. Faith, Alice, no longer than this night.—
　　Black Will and Shakebag, will you two
　　Perform the complot that I have laid?
Will. Ay, or else think me as a villain.   90
Greene. And rather than you shall want, I'll help myself.
Mosby. You, Master Greene, shall single Franklin forth
　　And hold him with a long tale of strange news,
　　That he may not come home till suppertime.
　　I'll fetch Master Arden home; and we, like friends,   95
　　Will play a game or two at tables here.
Alice. But what of all this? How shall he be slain?
Mosby. Why, Black Will and Shakebag, locked within the
　　countinghouse,
　　Shall, at a certain watchword given, rush forth.
Will. What shall the watchword be?   100
Mosby. 'Now I take you'—that shall be the word.
　　But come not forth before in any case.
Will. I warrant you. But who shall lock me in?
Alice. That will I do; thou'st keep the key thyself.
Mosby. Come, Master Greene, go you along with me.—   105
　　See all things ready, Alice, against we come.
Alice. Take no care for that; send you him home.
　　And, if he e'er go forth again, blame me.
　　　　　　　　　　　　　　　　Exeunt MOSBY *and* GREENE.
　　Come, Black Will, that in mine eyes art fair;
　　Next unto Mosby do I honour thee.   110
　　Instead of fair words and large promises
　　My hands shall play you golden harmony.
　　How like you this? Say, will you do it, sirs?
Will. Ay, and that bravely, too. Mark my device:
　　Place Mosby, being a stranger, in a chair,   115

---

96. *tables*] the dice-board for the game of backgammon. (Also at lines 154, 165.2 and 219.)

98. *countinghouse*] private room used as a business office.

101. *Now . . . you*] i.e. now I put you out of the game (by capturing all your pieces).

106. *against*] by the time that, in anticipation of the moment when.

107. *Take . . . for*] don't worry about.

him] Arden.

112.] i.e. I'll give you money.

114. *bravely*] splendidly.

115–16.] Chairs, unusual even in wealthy houses, were normally reserved for the head of the household, but were offered as a courtesy to guests.

And let your husband sit upon a stool,
That I may come behind him cunningly
And with a towel pull him to the ground,
Then stab him till his flesh be as a sieve.
That done, bear him behind the Abbey,   120
That those that find him murdered may suppose
Some slave or other killed him for his gold.
Alice. A fine device! You shall have twenty pound,
And, when he is dead, you shall have forty more;
And, lest you might be suspected staying here,   125
Michael shall saddle you two lusty geldings.
Ride whither you will, to Scotland or to Wales;
I'll see you shall not lack where'er you be.
Will. Such words would make one kill a thousand men!
Give me the key. Which is the countinghouse?   130
Alice. [*Giving key*] Here would I stay and still encourage you,
But that I know how resolute you are.
Shakebag. Tush! You are too faint-hearted; we must do it.
Alice. But Mosby will be there, whose very looks
Will add unwonted courage to my thought   135
And make me the first that shall adventure on him.
Will. Tush, get you gone! 'Tis we must do the deed.
When this door opens next, look for his death.
                              [*Exeunt* WILL *and* SHAKEBAG.]
Alice. Ah, would he now were here, that it might open!
I shall no more be closed in Arden's arms,   140
That like the snakes of black Tisiphone
Sting me with their embracings. Mosby's arms
Shall compass me; and, were I made a star,
I would have none other spheres but those.
There is no nectar but in Mosby's lips!   145
Had chaste Diana kissed him, she like me
Would grow lovesick and from her wat'ry bower
Fling down Endymion and snatch him up.
Then blame not me that slay a silly man
Not half so lovely as Endymion.   150

                    Here enters MICHAEL.

Michael. Mistress, my master is coming hard by.
Alice. Who comes with him?

---

141. *Tisiphone*] one of the Furies, an avenger of crime against kin. Alice's use of
the reference is ironic: the stinging of Tisiphone's snakes is more usually seen as the
stirrings of conscience.
   143. *compass*] encompass.
   150. *Endymion*] a handsome man loved by the moon goddess, Diana (line 146).
See Intro., pp. 49–50.

Michael. Nobody but Mosby.

Alice. That's well, Michael. Fetch in the tables; and, when thou hast
    done, stand before the countinghouse door.   155

Michael. Why so?

Alice. Black Will is locked within to do the deed.

Michael. What? Shall he die tonight?

Alice. Ay, Michael.

Michael. But shall not Susan know it?   160

Alice. Yes, for she'll be as secret as ourselves.

Michael. That's brave! I'll go fetch the tables.

Alice. But, Michael, hark to me a word or two:
    When my husband is come in, lock the street door;
    He shall be murdered or the guests come in.   165

                  Exit MICHAEL [*and re-enters shortly*
                            with the tables].

        Here enters ARDEN *and* MOSBY.

Husband, what mean you to bring Mosby home?
Although I wished you to be reconciled,
'Twas more for fear of you than love of him.
Black Will and Greene are his companions,
And they are cutters and may cut you short;   170
Therefore, I thought it good to make you friends.
But wherefore do you bring him hither now?
You have given me my supper with his sight.

Mosby. Master Arden, methinks your wife would have me gone.

Arden. No, good Master Mosby, women will be prating.—   175
    Alice, bid him welcome; he and I are friends.

Alice. You may enforce me to it if you will,
    But I had rather die than bid him welcome.
    His company hath purchased me ill friends,
    And therefore will I ne'er frequent it more.   180

Mosby. [*Aside*] Oh, how cunningly she can dissemble!

Arden. Now he is here, you will not serve me so.

Alice. I pray you be not angry or displeased;
    I'll bid him welcome, seeing you'll have it so.—
    You are welcome, Master Mosby. Will you sit down?   185

      [MOSBY *sits down in chair facing the countinghouse door.*]

Mosby. I know I am welcome to your loving husband,

---

165. *or*] ere, before.

168. *fear of you*] (1) fear for your welfare; (2) hatred of you.

170. *cutters*] cutthroats.

173.] i.e. (1) the sight of Mosby takes my appetite away; (2) the sight of Mosby
is enough sustenance for me.

182.] Now that Mosby is actually here, I trust and insist that you will not disobey
my wishes.

But for yourself you speak not from your heart.
Alice. And if I do not, sir, think I have cause.
Mosby. Pardon me, Master Arden; I'll away.
Arden. No, good Master Mosby.   190
Alice. We shall have guests enough though you go hence.
Mosby. I pray you, Master Arden, let me go.
Arden. I pray thee, Mosby, let her prate her fill.
Alice. The doors are open, sir; you may be gone.
Michael. [*Aside*] Nay, that's a lie, for I have locked the doors.   195
Arden. Sirrah, fetch me a cup of wine; I'll make them friends.

                          [*Exit* MICHAEL.]

And, gentle Mistress Alice, seeing you are so stout,
You shall begin. Frown not; I'll have it so.
Alice. I pray you meddle with that you have to do.
Arden. Why, Alice, how can I do too much for him   200
Whose life I have endangered without cause?

       [*Re-enter* MICHAEL *with wine.*]

Alice. 'Tis true; and, seeing 'twas partly through my means,
I am content to drink to him for this once.

                        [*She toasts Mosby.*]

Here, Master Mosby! And, I pray you, henceforth
Be you as strange to me as I to you.   205
Your company hath purchased me ill friends,
And I for you, God knows, have undeserved
Been ill spoken of in every place;
Therefore, henceforth frequent my house no more.
Mosby. I'll see your husband in despite of you.—   210
Yet, Arden, I protest to thee by heaven,
Thou ne'er shalt see me more after this night.
I'll go to Rome rather than be forsworn.
Arden. Tush, I'll have no such vows made in my house.
Alice. Yes, I pray you, husband, let him swear;   215
And, on that condition, Mosby, pledge me here.
Mosby. Ay, as willingly as I mean to live.   [*He and Alice drink.*]
Arden. Come, Alice, is our supper ready yet?
Alice. It will by then you have played a game at tables.
Arden. Come, Master Mosby, what shall we play for?   220

---

   197. *stout*] stubborn.
   198. *begin*] i.e. drink a toast to Mosby first.
   199.] Please mind your own business.
   205.] Be as distant to me as I am to you (with the ironic understanding that they are equally passionate to one another).
   207. *undeserved*] undeservedly.
   219. *by then*] by the time.

Mosby. Three games for a French crown, sir, an please you.
Arden. Content.   [*He sits down on stool opposite Mosby.*]
                         Then they play at the tables.

[*Re-enter* WILL *and* SHAKEBAG *from behind Arden.*]

Will. [*Aside*] Can he not take him yet? What a spite is that!
Alice. [*Aside*] Not yet, Will. Take heed he see thee not.
Will. [*Aside*] I fear he will spy me as I am coming.   225
Michael. [*Aside*] To prevent that, creep betwixt my legs.
Mosby. One ace, or else I lose the game.   [*He throws the dice.*]
Arden. Marry, sir, there's two for failing.
Mosby. Ah, Master Arden, 'Now I can take you.'
                         Then Will pulls him down with a towel.
Arden. Mosby! Michael! Alice! What will you do?   230
Will. Nothing but take you up, sir, nothing else.
Mosby. There's for the pressing iron you told me of.
                              [*He stabs Arden.*]
Shakebag. And there's for the ten pound in my sleeve.
                              [*He stabs him.*]
Alice. What, groans thou?—Nay, then, give me the weapon!—
      Take this for hind'ring Mosby's love and mine.   235
                              [*She stabs him.*]
Michael. Oh, mistress!   [*Arden dies.*]
Will. Ah, that villain will betray us all.
Mosby. Tush, fear him not; he will be secret.
Michael. Why, dost thou think I will betray myself?
Shakebag. In Southwark dwells a bonny northern lass,   240
      The widow Chambley. I'll to her house now;
      And, if she will not give me harborough,
      I'll make booty of the quean even to her smock.
Will. Shift for yourselves; we two will leave you now.
Alice. First lay the body in the countinghouse.   245
                    Then they lay the body in the countinghouse.
Will. We have our gold. Mistress Alice, adieu;

---

223. *take him*] i.e. capture his pieces, put him out of the game (as at line 104).
228. *for failing*] to prevent failing.
231. *take you up*] settle matters for you (with wordplay on *take you* in line 229).
232. *pressing iron*] Compare 1.315 where Arden taunts Mosby for having been a tailor. In the source, Mosby attacks Arden with his pressing iron.
233.] i.e. And there's for the ten pound reward which I will get for murdering you.
240. *Southwark*] a southern suburb of London through which runs the main road from Kent.
242. *harborough*] harbour, shelter.
243.] I'll rob the whore right down to her underwear.

Mosby, farewell; and, Michael, farewell too.
                              Exeunt [WILL *and* SHAKEBAG].

                    Enter SUSAN.

Susan. Mistress, the guests are at the doors.   [*Knocking heard.*]
     Hearken! They knock. What, shall I let them in?
Alice. Mosby, go thou and bear them company.   *Exit* MOSBY.   250
     And, Susan, fetch water and wash away this blood.
                    [*Exit* SUSAN, *returns with pail of water*
                              and begins washing the floor.]
Susan. The blood cleaveth to the ground and will not out.
Alice. But with my nails I'll scrape away the blood.
                    [*She tries to scrape away the stain.*]
     The more I strive, the more the blood appears!
Susan. What's the reason, Mistress, can you tell?   255
Alice. Because I blush not at my husband's death.

                    Here enters MOSBY.

Mosby. How now, what's the matter? Is all well?
Alice. Ay, well, if Arden were alive again!
     In vain we strive, for here his blood remains.
Mosby. Why, strew rushes on it, can you not?   260
     This wench doth nothing. [*To Susan*] Fall unto the work.
Alice. 'Twas thou that made me murder him.
Mosby.   What of that?
Alice. Nay, nothing, Mosby, so it be not known.
Mosby. Keep thou it close, and 'tis unpossible.
Alice. Ah, but I cannot. Was he not slain by me?   265
     My husband's death torments me at the heart.
Mosby. It shall not long torment thee, gentle Alice.
     I am thy husband; think no more of him.

                    Here enters ADAM FOWLE *and* BRADSHAW.

Bradshaw. How now, Mistress Arden? What ail you weep?
Mosby. Because her husband is abroad so late.   270
     A couple of ruffians threat'ned him yesternight,
     And she, poor soul, is afraid he should be hurt.
Adam. Is 't nothing else? Tush, he'll be here anon.

                    Here enters GREENE.

Greene. Now, Mistress Arden, lack you any guests?
Alice. Ah, Master Greene, did you see my husband lately?   275

---

260. *rushes*] strewn on the floor (in order to cover the blood).
269. *What . . . weep?*] What ails you that you weep?

Greene. I saw him walking behind the Abbey even now.

Here enters FRANKLIN.

Alice. I do not like this being out so late.—
Master Franklin, where did you leave my husband?
Franklin. Believe me, I saw him not since morning.
Fear you not; he'll come anon. Meantime,   280
You may do well to bid his guests sit down.
Alice. Ay, so they shall.—Master Bradshaw, sit you there;
I pray you be content, I'll have my will.—
Master Mosby, sit you in my husband's seat.
[*Mosby sits down on the chair, the guests on stools.*]
Michael. [*Aside*] Susan, shall thou and I wait on them?   285
Or, an thou say'st the word, let us sit down too.
Susan. [*Aside*] Peace! We have other matters now in hand.
I fear me, Michael, all will be bewrayed.
Michael. [*Aside*] Tush, so it be known that I shall marry thee in the
morning, I care not though I be hanged ere night. But to   290
prevent the worst I'll buy some ratsbane.
Susan. [*Aside*] Why, Michael, wilt thou poison thyself?
Michael. [*Aside*] No, but my mistress, for I fear she'll tell.
Susan. [*Aside*] Tush, Michael, fear not her; she's wise enough.
Mosby. Sirrah Michael, give 's a cup of beer.—   295
Mistress Arden, here's to your husband.   [*He offers a toast.*]
Alice. My husband!
Franklin. What ails you, woman, to cry so suddenly?
Alice. Ah, neighbours, a sudden qualm came over my heart;
My husband's being forth torments my mind.   300
I know something's amiss; he is not well,
Or else I should have heard of him ere now.
Mosby. [*Aside*] She will undo us through her foolishness.
Greene. Fear not, Mistress Arden; he's well enough.
Alice. Tell not me; I know he is not well.   305
He was not wont for to stay thus late.—
Good Master Franklin, go and seek him forth,
And, if you find him, send him home to me,
And tell him what a fear he hath put me in.
Franklin. [*Aside*] I like not this; I pray God all be well.—   310
I'll seek him out and find him if I can.
Exeunt FRANKLIN, MOSBY, *and* GREENE.
Alice. [*Aside*] Michael, how shall I do to rid the rest away?

---

283. *I'll . . . will*] I insist.
288. *bewrayed*] revealed.
291. *ratsbane*] rat poison, arsenic.

Michael. [*Aside*] Leave that to my charge; let me alone.—
　　'Tis very late, Master Bradshaw,
　　And there are many false knaves abroad,　　　　　　　315
　　And you have many narrow lanes to pass.
Bradshaw. Faith, friend Michael, and thou sayest true.
　　Therefore I pray thee light 's forth and lend 's a link.
Alice. Michael, bring them to the doors, but do not stay;
　　You know I do not love to be alone.　　　　　　　320
　　　　　　　　　　　Exeunt BRADSHAW, ADAM, *and* MICHAEL.
　　Go, Susan, and bid thy brother come.
　　But wherefore should he come? Here is nought but fear.
　　Stay, Susan, stay, and help to counsel me.
Susan. Alas, I counsel? Fear frights away my wits.
　　　　　　　　　　Then they open the countinghouse door
　　　　　　　　　　　　　　and look upon Arden.
Alice. See, Susan, where thy quondam master lies,　　　325
　　Sweet Arden, smeared in blood and filthy gore.
Susan. My brother, you, and I shall rue this deed.
Alice. Come, Susan, help to lift his body forth,
　　And let our salt tears be his obsequies.
　　　　　　　　　　　　[*They bring forth his body.*]

　　　　　　Here enters MOSBY *and* GREENE.

Mosby. How now, Alice, whither will you bear him?　　330
Alice. Sweet Mosby, art thou come? Then weep that will;
　　I have my wish in that I joy thy sight.
Greene. Well, it 'hoves us to be circumspect.
Mosby. Ay, for Franklin thinks that we have murdered him.
Alice. Ay, but he cannot prove it for his life.　　　335
　　We'll spend this night in dalliance and in sport.

　　　　　　　Here enters MICHAEL.

Michael. Oh, mistress, the mayor and all the watch
　　Are coming towards our house with glaives and bills!
Alice. Make the door fast; let them not come in.
Mosby. Tell me, sweet Alice, how shall I escape?　　340

---

318. *light 's forth*] i.e. light us forth, light us on our way.
link] torch (to take along in the dark).
319. *bring*] escort.
325. *quondam*] former.
329. *obsequies*] funeral prayers.
331. *weep that will*] let those weep who want to.
332. *joy*] enjoy.
333. *'hoves*] behoves.
335. *for his life*] if his life depended on it.
338. *glaives and bills*] broadswords and halberds.

Alice. Out at the back door, over the pile of wood,
    And for one night lie at the Flower-de-Luce.
Mosby. That is the next way to betray myself.
Greene. Alas, Mistress Arden, the watch will take me here
    And cause suspicion where else would be none.   345
Alice. Why, take that way that Master Mosby doth;
    But first convey the body to the fields.

> *Then they* [MOSBY, GREENE, SUSAN, *and* MICHAEL]
>   *bear the body into the fields* [*and then return*].

Mosby. Until tomorrow, sweet Alice, now farewell;
    And see you confess nothing in any case.
Greene. Be resolute, Mistress Alice; betray us not,   350
    But cleave to us as we will stick to you.

> *Exeunt* MOSBY *and* GREENE.

Alice. Now let the judge and juries do their worst;
    My house is clear, and now I fear them not.
Susan. As we went, it snowèd all the way,
    Which makes me fear our footsteps will be spied.   355
Alice. Peace, fool! The snow will cover them again.
Susan. But it had done before we came back again. [*One knocks.*]
Alice. Hark, hark, they knock! Go, Michael, let them in.

> [*Michael opens the door.*]

> *Here enters the* Mayor *and the* Watch.

    How now, Master Mayor, have you brought my husband
        home?
Mayor. I saw him come into your house an hour ago.   360
Alice. You are deceived; it was a Londoner.
Mayor. Mistress Arden, know you not one that is called Black Will?
Alice. I know none such. What mean these questions?
Mayor. I have the Council's warrant to apprehend him.
Alice. [*Aside*] I am glad it is no worse.—   365
    Why, Master Mayor, think you I harbour any such?
Mayor. We are informed that here he is;
    And, therefore, pardon us, for we must search.
Alice. Ay, search, and spare you not, through every room.
    Were my husband at home, you would not offer this.   370

> *Here enters* FRANKLIN [*with a hand-towel and knife*].

---

343. *next*] quickest.
347.2. into the fields] i.e. offstage. The stage direction is understood from the
dialogue.
357. *done*] stopped snowing.
361. *a Londoner*] a reference left over from the source. In Holinshed, Alice invites
two London grocers to dinner after the murder.

Master Franklin, what mean you come so sad?
Franklin. Arden, thy husband and my friend, is slain.
Alice. Ah, by whom? Master Franklin, can you tell?
Franklin. I know not, but behind the Abbey
    There he lies murdered in most piteous case.   375
Mayor. But, Master Franklin, are you sure 'tis he?
Franklin. I am too sure; would God I were deceived!
Alice. Find out the murderers; let them be known.
Franklin. Ay, so they shall. Come you along with us.
Alice. Wherefore?
Franklin.   Know you this hand-towel and this knife?   380
Susan. [*Aside*] Ah, Michael, through this thy negligence
    Thou hast betrayèd and undone us all.
Michael. [*Aside*] I was so afraid I knew not what I did.
    I thought I had thrown them both into the well.
Alice. [*To Franklin*] It is the pig's blood we had to supper.   385
    But wherefore stay you? Find out the murderers.
Mayor. I fear me you'll prove one of them yourself.
Alice. I one of them? What mean such questions?
Franklin. I fear me he was murdered in this house
    And carried to the fields, for from that place   390
    Backwards and forwards may you see
    The print of many feet within the snow.
    And look about this chamber where we are,
    And you shall find part of his guiltless blood;
    For in his slipshoe did I find some rushes,   395
    Which argueth he was murdered in this room.
Mayor. Look in the place where he was wont to sit.—
    See, see! His blood! It is too manifest.
Alice. It is a cup of wine that Michael shed.
Michael. Ay, truly.   400
Franklin. It is his blood, which, strumpet, thou hast shed.
    But if I live, thou and thy complices
    Which have conspired and wrought his death shall rue it.
Alice. Ah, Master Franklin, God and heaven can tell
    I loved him more than all the world beside.   405
    But bring me to him; let me see his body.
Franklin. [*Pointing to Michael and Susan*] Bring that villain and
    Mosby's sister too;
    And one of you go to the Flower-de-Luce,
    And seek for Mosby, and apprehend him too.   *Exeunt.*

---

395. *slipshoe*] slipper.
399. *shed*] spilt. (But also ironically appropriate to the *shedding* of blood.)

[15]

Here enters SHAKEBAG *solus.*

Shakebag. The widow Chambley in her husband's days I kept;
    And, now he's dead, she is grown so stout
    She will not know her old companions.
    I came thither, thinking to have had
    Harbour as I was wont,   5
    And she was ready to thrust me out at doors.
    But, whether she would or no, I got me up;
    And, as she followed me, I spurned her down the stairs,
    And broke her neck, and cut her tapster's throat;
    And now I am going to fling them in the Thames.   10
    I have the gold; what care I though it be known?
    I'll cross the water and take sanctuary.   *Exit* SHAKEBAG.

[16]

Here enters the Mayor, MOSBY, ALICE, FRANKLIN,
    MICHAEL, *and* SUSAN[, *guarded by the* Watch].

Mayor. See, Mistress Arden, where your husband lies.
    Confess this foul fault and be penitent.
Alice. [*Leaning over the body*] Arden, sweet husband, what shall I
        say?
    The more I sound his name, the more he bleeds.
    This blood condemns me and in gushing forth   5
    Speaks as it falls and asks me why I did it.
    Forgive me, Arden; I repent me now;
    And, would my death save thine, thou shouldst not die.
    Rise up, sweet Arden, and enjoy thy love,
    And frown not on me when we meet in heaven!   10
    In heaven I love thee though on earth I did not.
Mayor. Say, Mosby, what made thee murder him?
Franklin. Study not for an answer; look not down.
    His purse and girdle found at thy bed's head

15.1. *kept*] kept as a mistress.
2. *stout*] proud, haughty.
8. *spurned*] kicked.
12. *sanctuary*] i.e. protection in one of designated areas of a church or a royal palace. Shakebag would not have had to cross the water to find sanctuary in Southwark since the Mint was in that area.

16.4–6.] alluding to the popular superstition that a corpse bled anew in the presence of its murderer.
13. *Study . . . answer*] do not try to think up a response.
14. *girdle*] belt.

Witness sufficiently thou didst the deed.   15
It bootless is to swear thou didst it not.
Mosby. I hired Black Will and Shakebag, ruffians both,
    And they and I have done this murd'rous deed.
    But wherefore stay we? Come and bear me hence.
Franklin. Those ruffians shall not escape. I will up to London and   20
    get the Council's warrant to apprehend them.   *Exeunt.*

[17]

Here enters WILL.

Will. Shakebag, I hear, hath taken sanctuary;
    But I am so pursued with hues and cries
    For petty robberies that I have done
    That I can come unto no sanctuary.
    Therefore must I in some oyster-boat   5
    At last be fain to go aboard some hoy,
    And so to Flushing. There is no staying here.
    At Sittingburgh the watch was like to take me;
    And, had I not with my buckler covered my head and run full
    blank at all adventures, I am sure I had ne'er gone further than   10
    that place, for the constable had twenty warrants to apprehend
    me; besides that, I robbed him and his man once at Gadshill.
    Farewell, England; I'll to Flushing now.   *Exit* WILL.

[18]

Here enters the Mayor, MOSBY, ALICE, MICHAEL,
SUSAN, *and* BRADSHAW, [*led by the* Watch].

Mayor. [*To the Watch*] Come, make haste, and bring away the
    prisoners.
Bradshaw. Mistress Arden, you are now going to God,
    And I am by the law condemned to die
    About a letter I brought from Master Greene.
    I pray you, Mistress Arden, speak the truth: 5

---

16. *bootless*] useless.

17.6. *hoy*] small boat plying along the coast and across the English Channel.
7. *Flushing*] in Holland.
8. *Sittingburgh*] Sittingbourne, a town on the road between Faversham and London.
like to] about to.
10.] and run full tilt without heeding the consequences.
12. *Gadshill*] a hill on the London–Rochester road, famous for highway robberies.

Was I ever privy to your intent or no?
Alice. What should I say? You brought me such a letter,
But I dare swear thou knewest not the contents.
Leave now to trouble me with worldly things,
And let me meditate upon my Saviour Christ,   10
Whose blood must save me for the blood I shed.
Mosby. How long shall I live in this hell of grief?
Convey me from the presence of that strumpet.
Alice. Ah, but for thee I had never been strumpet.
What cannot oaths and protestations do   15
When men have opportunity to woo?
I was too young to sound thy villainies,
But now I find it and repent too late.
Susan. [*To Mosby*] Ah, gentle brother, wherefore should I die?
I knew not of it till the deed was done.   20
Mosby. For thee I mourn more than for myself,
But let it suffice I cannot save thee now.
Michael. [*To Susan*] And if your brother and my mistress
Had not promised me you in marriage,
I had ne'er given consent to this foul deed.   25
Mayor. Leave to accuse each other now,
And listen to the sentence I shall give:
Bear Mosby and his sister to London straight,
Where they in Smithfield must be executed;
Bear Mistress Arden unto Canterbury,   30
Where her sentence is she must be burnt;
Michael and Bradshaw in Faversham must suffer death.
Alice. Let my death make amends for all my sins.
Mosby. Fie upon women!—this shall be my song.
But bear me hence, for I have lived too long.   35
Susan. Seeing no hope on earth, in heaven is my hope.
Michael. Faith, I care not, seeing I die with Susan.
Bradshaw. My blood be on his head that gave the sentence!
Mayor. To speedy execution with them all!   *Exeunt.*

18.6. *privy to*] in on the secret of.
17. *sound*] sound out, measure the depth of.
29. *Smithfield*] the site of a meat market, outside the city walls to the east of London; it was a regular place for executions.

[Epilogue]

Here enters FRANKLIN.

Franklin. Thus have you seen the truth of Arden's death.
   As for the ruffians, Shakebag and Black Will,
   The one took sanctuary and, being sent for out,
   Was murderèd in Southwark as he passed
   To Greenwich, where the Lord Protector lay.   5
   Black Will was burnt in Flushing on a stage;
   Greene was hanged at Osbridge in Kent;
   The painter fled, and how he died we know not.
   But this above the rest is to be noted:
   Arden lay murdered in that plot of ground   10
   Which he by force and violence held from Reede,
   And in the grass his body's print was seen
   Two years and more after the deed was done.
   Gentlemen, we hope you'll pardon this naked tragedy
   Wherein no filèd points are foisted in   15
   To make it gracious to the ear or eye;
   For simple truth is gracious enough
   And needs no other points of glozing stuff.   [*Exit.*]

FINIS.

---

3. *The one*] the former, Shakebag.
sent for out] i.e. summoned out of the church on some pretext.
6. *stage*] scaffold.
7. *Osbridge*] Ospringe, a village in Kent on the pilgrims' road to Canterbury.
15. *filèd points*] smoothly polished points of rhetoric, elaborate decoration.
18. *glozing*] specious, wordy.

A WOMAN KILLED
WITH KINDNESS

[*DRAMATIS PERSONAE*

SIR FRANCIS ACTON.
SIR CHARLES MOUNTFORD.
SUSAN, *sister to Sir Charles.*
JOHN FRANKFORD.
ANNE, *wife to Frankford and sister to Sir Francis.*
WENDOLL, }
CRANWELL, } *Frankford's friends.*
MALBY, *friend to Sir Francis.*
OLD MOUNTFORD, *uncle to Sir Charles.*
TYDY, *cousin to Sir Charles.*
SANDY, *former friend to Sir Charles.*
RODER, *former tenant to Sir Charles.*
SHAFTON, *false friend to Sir Charles.*
NICHOLAS, }
JENKIN, } *servants to Frankford.*
SPIGGOT, *butler to Frankford.*
SISLY MILK-PAIL, *servingwoman to Frankford.*
ROGER BRICKBAT, }
JACK SLIME, } *country fellows.*
JOAN MINIVER, }
JANE TRUBKIN, } *country wenches.*
ISBEL MOTLEY, }
Sheriff.
Keeper of the Prison.
Sergeant.
Officers, Falconers, Huntsmen, Coachman, Carters, Musicians,
    Servants, Servingwomen, Children.

SCENE: YORKSHIRE.]

The Prologue

I come but like a harbinger, being sent
To tell you what these preparations mean.
Look for no glorious state; our Muse is bent
Upon a barren subject, a bare scene.
We could afford this twig a timber-tree,   5
Whose strength might boldly on your favours build;
Our russet, tissue; drone, a honey-bee;
Our barren plot, a large and spacious field;
Our coarse fare, banquets; our thin water, wine;
Our brook, a sea; our bat's eyes, eagle's sight;   10
Our poet's dull and earthy Muse, divine;
Our ravens, doves; our crow's black feathers, white.
    But gentle thoughts, when they may give the foil,
    Save them that yield, and spare where they may spoil.

---

1. *harbinger*] messenger.

3. *glorious state*] grand splendour.

5–12.] The Prologue employs a number of antitheses (twig/tree, drone/bee, raven/dove etc.) to apologize for the inadequacy of the author's play by invoking, through stage language and gesture, a richer scene than can be literally presented.

5. *afford*] wish.

this twig] It is possible that the actor is carrying the twig on stage with him. It is unlikely to be placed on stage since the opening scene is an interior.

7. *russet*] coarse cloth, associated with country people, and often used as a metaphor for plain-speaking honesty.

tissue] fine cloth often interwoven with gold, used as a metaphor for luxury.

13. *gentle thoughts*] i.e. the audience's appreciation of the play.

when . . . foil] when they could knock (the play) flat (as in wrestling).

14. *spoil*] vanquish, lay waste.

A Woman Killed with Kindness

[I]

Enter MASTER JOHN FRANKFORD, SIR FRANCIS ACTON,
MISTRESS [ANNE] ACTON, SIR CHARLES MOUNTFORD,
MASTER MALBY, MASTER WENDOLL, *and*
MASTER CRANWELL.

Sir Francis. Some music there! None lead the bride a dance?
Sir Charles. Yes, would she dance 'The Shaking of the Sheets';
  But that's the dance her husband means to lead her.
Wendoll. That's not the dance that every man must dance,
  According to the ballad.
Sir Francis.   Music ho!
                   [Music. Sir Francis takes Anne by the hand.]   5
  By your leave, sister—by your husband's leave
  I should have said—the hand that but this day
  Was given you in the church I'll borrow.—Sound!
  This marriage music hoists me from the ground.
Frankford. Ay, you may caper, you are light and free;   10
  Marriage hath yoked my heels. Pray then pardon me.
Sir Francis. I'll have you dance too, brother.
Sir Charles.   Master Frankford,
  You are a happy man, sir; and much joy
  Succeed your marriage mirth, you have a wife
  So qualified and with such ornaments   15
  Both of the mind and body. First, her birth
  Is noble, and her education such
  As might become the daughter of a prince.
  Her own tongue speaks all tongues, and her own hand
  Can teach all strings to speak in their best grace   20

1.1. *the bride*] Anne, just married to Frankford.
  2. *The Shaking . . . Sheets*] a popular tune and a ballad, particularly appropriate
for a joke about wedding nights.
  4. *the dance . . . dance*] i.e. the dance of death, according to proverbial lore.
  6–9.] Sir Francis invites Anne Frankford to dance.
  11. *Marriage . . . heels*] Frankford jokes about being hampered by his marriage.
  14. *Succeed*] follow upon.
  15. *qualified*] endowed with fine qualities.
  20.] i.e. can play music admirably.

From the shrill treble to the hoarsest bass.
To end her many praises in one word,
She's beauty and perfection's eldest daughter,
Only found by yours, though many a heart hath sought her.
Frankford. But that I know your virtues and chaste thoughts,   25
I should be jealous of your praise, Sir Charles.
Cranwell. He speaks no more than you approve.
Malby. Nor flatters he that gives to her her due.
Anne. I would your praise could find a fitter theme
Than my imperfect beauty to speak on.   30
Such as they be, if they my husband please, *Heinrichel*
They suffice me now I am married. *only he is*
His sweet content is like a flattering glass, *when*
To make my face seem fairer to mine eye; *happy, can*
But the least wrinkle from his stormy brow *she be*   35
Will blast the roses in my cheeks that grow.
Sir Francis. A perfect wife already, meek and patient.
How strangely the word 'husband' fits your mouth,
Not married three hours since, sister. 'Tis good;
You that begin betimes thus must needs prove   40
Pliant and duteous in your husband's love.—
Godamercies, brother, wrought her to it already?
'Sweet husband', and a curtsey the first day!
Mark this, mark this, you that are bachelors
And never took the grace of honest man,   45
Mark this against you marry, this one phrase:
'In a good time that man both wins and woos
That takes his wife down in her wedding shoes.'
Frankford. Your sister takes not after you, Sir Francis.
All his wild blood your father spent on you;   50
He got her in his age when he grew civil.

---

24. *Only . . . yours*] claimed now by your heart alone.
25. *But*] were it not.
27. *approve*] test, make proof of.
28. *Nor flatters he*] nor does any person flatter.
31. *they*] my imperfect beauties.
42. *Godamercies*] an exclamation of surprise; a contraction of 'god have mercy'.
wrought] shaped.
45.] and have never assumed the honourable estate of husband.
46. *against*] in anticipation of the time when.
48.] that subdues his wife right from the start of marriage. The expression 'takes down' is from falconry, meaning to make the bird fly down.
50.] Your father exhausted all his unruliness in you. (The image refers to the ejaculation of semen, seen as connected to blood in humours theory.)
51. *got*] begot.
civil] civilized; as opposed to 'wild'.

All his mad tricks were to his land entailed,
And you are heir to all; your sister, she
Hath to her dower her mother's modesty.
Sir Charles. Lord, sir, in what a happy state live you!   55
This morning, which to many seems a burden
Too heavy to bear, is unto you a pleasure.
This lady is no clog, as many are;
She doth become you like a well-made suit
In which the tailor hath used all his art,   60
Not like a thick coat of unseasoned frieze
Forced on your back in summer. She's no chain
To tie your neck and curb you to the yoke,
But she's a chain of gold to adorn your neck.
You both adorn each other, and your hands   65
Methinks are matches. There's equality
In this fair combination; you are both scholars,
Both young, both being descended nobly.
There's music in this sympathy; it carries
Consort and expectation of much joy,   70
Which God bestow on you, from this first day,
Until your dissolution—that's for aye.
Sir Francis. We keep you here too long, good brother Frankford.
Into the hall! Away, go, cheer your guests!
What, bride and bridegroom both withdrawn at once?   75
If you be missed, the guests will doubt their welcome
And charge you with unkindness.
Frankford.   To prevent it,
I'll leave you here, to see the dance within.
Anne. And so will I.
Sir Francis.   To part you it were sin.
                  [*Exeunt* FRANKFORD *and* ANNE.]
Now gallants, while the town musicians   80
Finger their frets within, and the mad lads
And country lasses, every mother's child

---

52. *entailed*] made part of his estate's inheritance.

56. *This morning*] i.e. the wedding morning.

56–7. *to . . . bear*] Sir Charles insists on the unusualness of Frankford's happiness, suggesting that marriage is more commonly seen as a burden on male freedom.

58. *clog*] hindrance.

61. *unseasoned frieze*] coarse woollen cloth, inappropriate for the warm season.

65–6. *your . . . matches*] you match one another perfectly, especially in the hands you exchanged in marriage.

70. *Consort*] (1) harmony; (2) companionship.

75. *withdrawn*] in a room away from the public chamber where the dancing is taking place.

81. *frets*] divisions on the fingerboard of a lute.

With nosegays and bride-laces in their hats,
Dance all their country measures, rounds, and jigs,
What shall we do? Hark, they are all on the hoigh!   85
They toil like mill-horses, and turn as round—
Marry, not on the toe. Ay, and they caper,
But without cutting. You shall see tomorrow
The hall floor pecked and dinted like a millstone,
Made with their high shoes; though their skill be small,   90
Yet they tread heavy where their hobnails fall.
Sir Charles. Well, leave them to their sports. Sir Francis Acton,
I'll make a match with you: meet me tomorrow
At Chevy Chase, I'll fly my hawk with yours.
Sir Francis. For what? For what?
Sir Charles.   Why, for a hundred pound.   95
Sir Francis. Pawn me some gold of that.
Sir Charles. [*Putting down money*]   Here are ten angels;
I'll make them good a hundred pound tomorrow
Upon my hawk's wing.
Sir Francis.   'Tis a match, 'tis done.
Another hundred pound upon your dogs,
Dare you, Sir Charles?
Sir Charles.   I dare. Were I sure to lose   100
I durst do more than that. Here's my hand,
The first course for a hundred pound.
Sir Francis.   A match.
Wendoll. Ten angels on Sir Francis Acton's hawk;
As much upon his dogs.
Cranwell. I am for Sir Charles Mountford; I have seen   105
His hawk and dog both tried. What, clap you hands?
Or is 't no bargain?
Wendoll.   Yes, and stake them down.

---

83. *bride-laces*] lace ribbons given as favours at weddings.
85. *on the hoigh*] excited; boisterous.
86. *as round*] going heavily in circles like horses powering a mill.
87–8. *caper . . . cutting*] jump without turning in the correct manner.
89–90. *pecked . . . shoes*] marked with dents from hob-nailed boots. Millstones gradually became marked with the pressure from individual grains of corn as it was milled.
94. *Chevy Chase*] an area of forest and open ground used for hunting. It was the scene of a famous border skirmish.
96. *Pawn*] pledge.
angels] gold coins with the image of the archangel Michael standing on a dragon.
102. *course*] a contest between dogs in which they are released when the game is running. The winner is judged on points as well as speed.
106. *clap you hands?*] will you shake hands to confirm an agreement?
107. *stake . . . down*] deposit money as a stake on the result of the contest.

Were they five hundred they were all my own.

Sir Francis. Be stirring early with the lark tomorrow;
I'll rise into my saddle ere the sun   110
Rise from his bed.

Sir Charles.   If there you miss me, say
I am no gentleman; I'll hold my day.

Sir Francis. It holds on all sides. Come, tonight let's dance.
Early tomorrow let's prepare to ride;
We had need be three hours up before the bride.   [*Exeunt.*] 115

[2]

> *Enter* NICHOLAS *and* JENKIN, JACK SLIME, ROGER
> BRICKBAT, *with country* Wenches, *and two or*
> *three Musicians.*

Jenkin. Come, Nick, take you Joan Miniver to trace withal; Jack
Slime, traverse you with Sisly Milk-pail; I will take Jane
Trubkin, and Roger Brickbat shall have Isbel Motley. And now
that they are busy in the parlour, come, strike up, we'll have a
crash here in the yard.   5

Nicholas. My humour is not compendious. Dancing I possess not,
though I can foot it; yet since I am fall'n into the hands of Sisly
Milk-pail, I assent.

Jack. Truly, Nick, though we were never brought up like serving
courtiers, yet we have been brought up with serving creatures,   10
ay, and God's creatures too, for we have been brought up to
serve sheep, oxen, horses, and hogs, and such like; and though
we be but country fellows, it may be in the way of dancing we
can do the horse-trick as well as servingmen.

Roger. Ay, and the crosspoint, too.   15

Jenkin. Oh, Slime, oh, Brickbat, do not you know that comparisons
are odious? Now we are odious ourselves, too; therefore there
are no comparisons to be made betwixt us.

---

112. *hold my day*] keep my appointment.

2.1–3. *Nick . . . Motley*] The servants' names indicate their comic status.
1. *trace*] dance.
2. *traverse*] dance forward and back.
5. *crash*] general term for merrymaking.
6. *humour*] disposition, mood.
compendious] all-encompassing.
7. *foot it*] i.e. do rustic country dancing.
14. *horse-trick*] obscure; not recorded as a dance step. This may refer to a
dancing horse.
15. *crosspoint*] a dance step.

Nicholas. I am sudden, and not superfluous;
   I am quarrelsome, and not seditious;   20
   I am peaceable, and not contentious;
   I am brief, and not compendious.
   Slime, foot it quickly. If the music overcome not my melan-
   choly, I shall quarrel; and if they suddenly do not strike up, I
   shall presently strike thee down.   25
Jenkin. No quarrelling, for God's sake! Truly, if you do, I shall set
   a knave between you.
Jack. I come to dance, not to quarrel. Come, what shall it be?
   'Rogero'?
Jenkin. 'Rogero'? No. We will dance 'The Beginning of the World'.   30
Sisly. I love no dance so well as 'John, Come Kiss Me Now'.
Nicholas. I, that have ere now deserved a cushion, call for 'The
   Cushion Dance'.
Roger. For my part, I like nothing so well as 'Tom Tyler'.
Jenkin. No, we'll have 'The Hunting of the Fox'.   35
Jack. 'The Hay', 'The Hay'! There's nothing like 'The Hay'.
Nicholas. I have said, I do say, and I will say again—
Jenkin. Every man agree to have it as Nick says.
All. Content.
Nicholas. It hath been, it now is, and it shall be—   40
Sisly. What, Master Nich'las, what?
Nicholas. 'Put on Your Smock o' Monday'.
Jenkin. So the dance will come cleanly off. Come, for God's sake
   agree of something. If you like not that, put it to the musicians,
   or let me speak for all, and we'll have 'Sellenger's Round'.   45
All. That, that, that!
Nicholas. No, I am resolved thus it shall be:
   First take hands, then take you to your heels.
Jenkin. Why, would you have us run away?
Nicholas. No, but I would have you shake your heels.—   50
   Music, strike up!

   They dance; Nicholas, dancing, speaks stately and scurvily,
       the rest after the country fashion.

Jenkin. Hey! Lively, my lasses! Here's a turn for thee!   [*Exeunt.*]

---

19. *sudden*] brief.
24. *suddenly*] immediately.
27. *knave*] male servant. (Jenkins is referring to himself.)
29–45.] The titles listed are of well-known dances and popular tunes.
32. *deserved a cushion*] i.e. earned the right to some luxury.
33. *Cushion Dance*] an old-fashioned round country dance.
43. *will . . . off*] will be neatly performed (with a pun on the idea of taking off a
woman's *smock* or undergarment, playing on the name of the tune).
51.1–2.] The actors ad lib during the dancing. Jenkin's final line (52) acts as a cue
to end the scene.

[3]

> *Wind horns. Enter* SIR CHARLES, SIR FRANCIS, MALBY,
> CRANWELL, WENDOLL, Falconers, *and* Huntsmen.

Sir Charles. So! Well cast off. Aloft, aloft! Well flown!
    Oh, now she takes her at the souse, and strikes her
    Down to the earth, like a swift thunderclap.
Wendoll. She hath struck ten angels out of my way.
Sir Francis. A hundred pound from me.
Sir Charles.   What, falconer?   5
Falconer. At hand, sir.
Sir Charles. Now she hath seized the fowl, and 'gins to plume her.
    Rebeck her not; rather stand still and check her.
    So! Seize her jets, her jesses, and her bells.
    Away!   10
Sir Francis. My hawk killed, too.
Sir Charles.   Ay, but 'twas at the querre,
    Not at the mount like mine.
Sir Francis.   Judgement, my masters.
Cranwell. Yours missed her at the ferre.
Wendoll. Ay, but our merlin first had plumed the fowl,
    And twice renewed her from the river, too.   15
    Her bells, Sir Francis, had not both one weight,
    Nor was one semitone above the other;
    Methinks these Milan bells do sound too full,
    And spoil the mounting of your hawk.
Sir Charles.   'Tis lost.
Sir Francis. I grant it not. Mine likewise seized a fowl   20
    Within her talons, and you saw her paws
    Full of the feathers; both her petty singles
    And her long singles gripped her more than other.

3.1. *cast off*] unhooding and releasing the hawk from the falconer's wrist.

2. *she . . . souse*] the hawk swoops straight down from above after the quarry has risen from the ground.

4.] i.e. She has lost me ten angels in a bet. On *angels*, see 1.96.

7. *'gins to plume*] begins to pluck off the feathers.

8.] Don't startle her; reassure her by chirping to her.

9. *jets . . . bells*] parts of the hawk's harness.

11. *at the querre*] before the fowl has risen from the ground: cf. *at the mount* (line 12), after the quarry has risen.

13. *at the ferre*] on the far side of the river, or perhaps 'at the high point'.

14. *merlin*] a kind of small hawk.

15. *renewed . . . river*] had driven her from the river by a fresh attack.

16–17.] Wendoll is accusing Sir Francis of infringing the rules of the contest.

18. *Milan bells*] bells made of silver and thought to be superior.

22–3. *petty singles, long singles*] outer and middle claws.

The terrets of her legs were stained with blood,
Not of the fowl only; she did discomfit   25
Some of her feathers, but she brake away.
Come, come, your hawk is but a rifler.
Sir Charles.   How?
Sir Francis. Ay, and your dogs are trindle-tails and curs.
Sir Charles. You stir my blood!
You keep not a good hound in all your kennel,   30
Nor one good hawk upon your perch.
Sir Francis.   How, knight?
Sir Charles. So, knight? You will not swagger, sir?
Sir Francis. Why, say I did?
Sir Charles. Why, sir, I say you would gain as much by swagg'ring
As you have got by wagers on your dogs;   35
You will come short in all things.
Sir Francis. [*Drawing his sword*]   Not in this!
Now I'll strike home.
Sir Charles.   Thou shalt to thy long home,
Or I will want my will.
Sir Francis. All they that love Sir Francis, follow me!
Sir Charles. All that affect Sir Charles draw on my part.   40
Cranwell. On this side heaves my hand.
Wendoll.   Here goes my heart.
They divide themselves.

Sir Charles, Cranwell, Falconer, and Huntsman fight against
Sir Francis, Wendoll, his Falconer, and Huntsman, and Sir
Charles hath the better, and beats them away, killing both of Sir
Francis his men. [Exeunt all except Sir Charles.]

Sir Charles. My God! What have I done? What have I done?
My rage hath plunged into a sea of blood,
In which my soul lies drowned. Poor innocents,

---

24. *terrets*] Q's 'terrials' is otherwise virtually unknown and probably an error for 'terrets', leather loops used to attach the bells to a hawk's leg.

26. *she*] the fowl.

27. *a rifler*] a hawk that only gets hold of its quarry's feathers and so does not make a proper catch. Sir Francis is complaining that Sir Charles's hawk did not secure its prey properly.

28. *trindle-tails*] curly-tailed (and hence low-bred) dogs.

32. *swagger*] bluster.

37. *long home*] i.e. the grave (picking up *home*, all the way, from Sir Francis's speech).

38. *want my will*] not get what I want.

40. *affect*] favour.

41.4. *both*] Q1's '*one*' appears to be an error; see 3.48 and 4.48.

44–5. *innocents . . . answer*] dead men for whose deaths I will have to give an account. (Also in line 52.) Q1's 'innocent' appears to be an error.

For whom we are to answer! Well, 'tis done,   45
And I remain the victor. A great conquest,
When I would give this right hand, nay, this head,
To breathe in them new life whom I have slain.
Forgive me, God! 'Twas in the heat of blood,
And anger quite removes me from myself.   50
It was not I, but rage, did this vile murder;
Yet I, and not my rage, must answer it.
Sir Francis Acton he is fled the field,
With him all those that did partake his quarrel,
And I am left alone, with sorrow dumb,   55
And in my height of conquest, overcome.

                    Enter SUSAN.

Susan. Oh, God, my brother wounded among the dead!
    Unhappy jest that in such earnest ends!
    The rumour of this fear stretched to my ears,
    And I am come to know if you be wounded.   60
Sir Charles. Oh, sister, sister, wounded at the heart.
Susan. My God forbid!
Sir Charles. In doing that thing which He forbade,
    I am wounded, sister.
Susan.   I hope not at the heart.
Sir Charles. Yes, at the heart.
Susan.   Oh, God! A surgeon there!   65
Sir Charles. Call me a surgeon, sister, for my soul;
    The sin of murder, it hath pierced my heart,
    And made a wide wound there; but for these scratches,
    They are nothing, nothing.
Susan.   Charles, what have you done?
    Sir Francis hath great friends, and will pursue you   70
    Unto the utmost danger of the law.
Sir Charles. My conscience is become my enemy,
    And will pursue me more than Acton can.
Susan. Oh, fly, sweet brother!
Sir Charles.   Shall I fly from thee?
    What, Sue, art weary of my company?   75
Susan. Fly from your foe.
Sir Charles.   You, sister, are my friend,
    And, flying you, I shall pursue my end.

---

54. *partake his quarrel*] fight on his side.
56.1. *SUSAN*] Q1's '*Iane*' seems in error; also in speech prefixes and line 75.
70. *great*] powerful.
71. *danger*] penalty.

Susan. Your company is as my eyeball dear;
 Being far from you, no comfort can be near.
 Yet fly to save your life. What would I care   80
 To spend my future age in black despair,
 So you were safe? And yet to live one week
 Without my brother Charles, through every cheek
 My streaming tears would downwards run so rank
 Till they could set on either side a bank,   85
 And in the midst a channel; so my face
 For two salt water brooks shall still find place.
Sir Charles. Thou shalt not weep so much, for I will stay
 In spite of danger's teeth. I'll live with thee
 Or I'll not live at all. I will not sell   90
 My country and my father's patrimony,
 No, thy sweet sight, for a vain hope of life.

    Enter Sheriff *with Officers.*

Sheriff. Sir Charles, I am made the unwilling instrument
 Of your attach and apprehension.
 I am sorry that the blood of innocent men   95
 Should be of you exacted. It was told me
 That you were guarded with a troop of friends,
 And therefore I come armed.
Sir Charles.   Oh, master Sheriff,
 I came into the field with many friends,
 But, see, they all have left me; only one   100
 Clings to my sad misfortune, my dear sister.
 I know you for an honest gentleman;
 I yield my weapons and submit to you.
 Convey me where you please.
Sheriff.   To prison, then,
 To answer for the lives of these dead men.   105
Susan. Oh, God! Oh, God!
Sir Charles.   Sweet sister, every strain
 Of sorrow from your heart augments my pain.
 Your grief abounds and hits against my breast.
Sheriff. Sir, will you go?
Sir Charles.   Even where it likes you best. [*Exeunt.*]

78.] Your company is as dear to me as eyesight itself.
84. *rank*] profusely, abundantly.
92. *No*] not even.
94. *attach and apprehension*] arrest.
108. *abounds*] overflows.
109. *likes*] pleases.

[4]

Enter MASTER FRANKFORD *in a study.*

Frankford. How happy am I amongst other men
    That in my mean estate embrace content!
    I am a gentleman, and by my birth
    Companion with a king; a king's no more.
    I am possessed of many fair revenues,   5
    Sufficient to maintain a gentleman.
    Touching my mind, I am studied in all arts,
    The riches of my thoughts, and of my time
    Have been a good proficient. But the chief
    Of all the sweet felicities on earth,   10
    I have a fair, a chaste, and loving wife,
    Perfection all, all truth, all ornament,
    If man on earth may truly happy be,
    Of these at once possessed, sure I am he.

Enter NICHOLAS.

Nicholas. Sir, there's a gentleman attends without   15
    To speak with you.
Frankford.   On horseback?
Nicholas.   Ay, on horseback.
Frankford. Entreat him to alight; I will attend him.
    Knowest thou him, Nick?
Nicholas.   I know him; his name's Wendoll.
    It seems he comes in haste; his horse is booted
    Up to the flank in mire, himself all spotted   20
    And stained with plashing. Sure he rid in fear
    Or for a wager. Horse and man both sweat;
    I ne'er saw two in such a smoking heat.
Frankford. Entreat him in; about it instantly.   [*Exit* NICHOLAS.]
    This Wendoll I have noted, and his carriage   25
    Hath pleased me much by observation;
    I have noted many good deserts in him—
    He's affable and seen in many things,

4.0.1. *in a study*] refers to the opening in the rear wall of the stage. See Intro.,
p. 7. Or it could mean 'in meditation'.
  2. *mean*] offering a just balance between wealth and poverty.
  9. *good proficient*] profitable enough.
  15. *attends without*] who is waiting outside.
  17. *attend him*] see him.
  19. *booted*] covered in mud, as if wearing boots.
  21. *plashing*] splashing.
  24. *about it*] get on with it.
  28. *seen*] taken notice of.

Discourses well, a good companion,
And though of small means, yet a gentleman   30
Of a good house, somewhat pressed by want. '
I have preferred him to a second place *✓ second to Anne?*
In my opinion and my best regard.

        Enter WENDOLL, MISTRESS [ANNE] FRANKFORD,
                and NICHOLAS.

Anne. Oh, Master Frankford, Master Wendoll here
   Brings you the strangest news that e'er you heard.   35
Frankford. What news, sweet wife? What news, good Master
   Wendoll?
Wendoll. You knew the match made 'twixt Sir Francis Acton
   And Sir Charles Mountford.
Frankford.   True, with their hounds and hawks.
Wendoll. The matches were both played.
Frankford.   Ha! And which won?
Wendoll. Sir Francis, your wife's brother, had the worst   40
   And lost the wager.
Frankford.   Why, the worse his chance;
   Perhaps the fortune of some other day
   Will change his luck.
Anne.   Oh, but you hear not all.
   Sir Francis lost, and yet was loath to yield.
   In brief, the two knights grew to difference,   45
   From words to blows, and so to banding sides,
   Where valorous Sir Charles slew in his spleen
   Two of your brother's men—his falconer
   And his good huntsman, whom he loved so well.
   More men were wounded, no more slain outright.   50
Frankford. Now trust me, I am sorry for the knight.
   But is my brother safe?
Wendoll.   All whole and sound,
   His body not being blemished with one wound.
   But poor Sir Charles is to the prison led,
   To answer at th' assize for them that's dead.   55
Frankford. I thank your pains, sir. Had the news been better,
   Your will was to have brought it, Master Wendoll.

---

31. *a good house*] a well-known family and ancestry.
32. *preferred*] recommended, promoted.
second] presumably after Anne.
45. *grew to difference*] began to quarrel.
46. *banding sides*] forming hostile parties.
47. *Where*] whereupon.
57.] You would have brought the news more willingly.

Sir Charles will find hard friends; his case is heinous,
And will be most severely censured on.
I am sorry for him. Sir, a word with you: 60
I know you, sir, to be a gentleman
In all things, your possibilities but mean;
Please you to use my table and my purse—
They are yours.

Wendoll.   Oh, Lord, sir, I shall never deserve it.

Frankford. Oh, sir, disparage not your worth too much;   65
You are full of quality and fair desert.
Choose of my men which shall attend on you,
And he is yours. I will allow you, sir,
Your man, your gelding, and your table, all
At my own charge; be my companion.   70

Wendoll. Master Frankford, I have oft been bound to you
By many favours; this exceeds them all
That I shall never merit your least favour.
But when your last remembrance I forget,
Heaven at my soul exact that weighty debt!   75

Frankford. There needs no protestation, for I know you
Virtuous, and therefore grateful.—Prithee, Nan,
Use him with all thy loving'st courtesy.

Anne. As far as modesty may well extend,
It is my duty to receive your friend.   80

Frankford. To dinner! Come, sir, from this present day
Welcome to me for ever. Come, away.
            [*Exeunt* MASTER FRANKFORD, WENDOLL, *and* ANNE.]

Nicholas. I do not like this fellow by no means;
I never see him but my heart still earns.
Zounds! I could fight with him, yet know not why;   85
The devil and he are all one in my eye.

                    Enter JENKIN.

---

58. *hard friends*] unsympathetic friends.
59. *censured on*] judged.
62. *possibilities*] resources.
   mean] slender. (Cf. line 2.)
66. *quality and fair desert*] natural gifts and attributes which will be recognized by other gentlemen. See Intro., pp. 42–3.
69.] Your personal servant, a horse, and food.
73. *That*] so that.
77. *Nan*] diminutive of Anne.
78. *Use*] treat.
84. *earns*] grieves.
85. *Zounds*] by his (God's) wounds. (An oath.)

Jenkin. Oh, Nick, what gentleman is that comes to lie at our house?
My master allows him one to wait on him, and I believe it will
fall to thy lot.

Nicholas. I love my master—by these hilts I do—   90
But rather than I'll ever come to serve him,
I'll turn away my master.

Enter SISLY.

Sisly. Nich'las, where are you, Nich'las? You must come in,
Nich'las, and help the young gentleman off with his boots.

Nicholas. If I pluck off his boots, I'll eat the spurs,   95
And they shall stick fast in my throat like burrs.   *Exit.*

Sisly. Then, Jenkin, come you.

Jenkin. 'Tis no boot for me to deny it. My master hath given me a
coat here, but he takes pains himself to brush it once or twice a
day with a holly wand.   100

Sisly. Come, come, make haste, that you may wash your hands
again and help to serve in dinner.   [*Exit.*]

Jenkin. [*To the audience*] You may see, my masters, though it be
afternoon with you, 'tis but early days with us, for we have not
dined yet. Stay but a little; I'll but go in and help to bear up the   105
first course and come to you again presently.   *Exit.*

[5]

Enter MALBY *and* CRANWELL.

Malby. This is the sessions day. Pray, can you tell me
How young Sir Charles hath sped? Is he acquit,
Or must he try the law's strict penalty?

Cranwell. He's cleared of all, 'spite of his enemies,
Whose earnest labours was to take his life;   5
But in this suit of pardon he hath spent

---

87. *lie*] reside.

90. *by these hilts*] by the hilt of my dagger. (An oath.)

92.] I'll dismiss my master from my service. (A comic inversion of the usual
relationship.)

98. *boot*] avail (with a pun).

99–100. *he takes . . . wand*] i.e. he often thrashes my coat (with me in it).

104. *early days*] forenoon, before the regular dinner hour at noon or so. The play
was taking place in the afternoon. See Intro., p. 12.

105–6. *bear . . . course*] serve the first course of the dinner.

5.1. *sessions day*] i.e. day of the court hearing.

2. *sped*] prospered.

3. *try*] suffer.

6. *suit of*] lawsuit seeking.

All the revenues that his father left him,
And he is now turned a plain countryman,
Reformed in all things. See, sir, here he comes.

Enter SIR CHARLES *and his* Keeper.

Keeper. Discharge your fees, and you are then at freedom.   10
Sir Charles. [*Offering money*] Here, master Keeper, take the poor
      remainder
    Of all the wealth I have. My heavy foes
    Have made my purse light, but, alas, to me,
    'Tis wealth enough that you have set me free.
Malby. God give you joy of your delivery!   15
    I am glad to see you abroad, Sir Charles.
Sir Charles. The poorest knight in England, Master Malby.
    My life hath cost me all the patrimony
    My father left his son. Well, God forgive them
    That are the authors of my penury.   20

Enter SHAFTON.

Shafton. Sir Charles, a hand, a hand! At liberty?
    Now by the faith I owe, I am glad to see it.
    What want you? Wherein may I pleasure you?
Sir Charles. Oh me! Oh, most unhappy gentleman!
    I am not worthy to have friends stirred up   25
    Whose hands may help me in this plunge of want.
    I would I were in heaven, to inherit there
    Th' immortal birthright which my Saviour keeps
    And by no unthrift can be bought and sold;
    For here on earth, what pleasures should we trust?   30
Shafton. To rid you from these contemplations,
    Three hundred pounds you shall receive of me—
    Nay, five, for fail. Come, sir, the sight of gold
    Is the most sweet receipt for melancholy
    And will revive your spirits. You shall hold law   35

---

8. *plain countryman*] i.e. not a gentleman, because no longer a landowner. See
Intro., pp. 42–3.
9. *Reformed*] made over.
10. *Discharge your fees*] pay for the services you received in prison.
16. *abroad*] i.e. out of prison.
21. *a hand*] here's my hand.
23. *want*] lack.
26. *plunge*] point of being overwhelmed.
29. *unthrift*] spendthrift.
33. *for fail*] just in case.
34. *receipt*] recipe.
35–6. *hold . . . With*] take to court.

With your proud adversaries. Tush, let Frank Acton
Wage with knighthood-like expense with me,
And he will sink, he will. Nay, good Sir Charles,
Applaud your fortune and your fair escape
From all these perils.
Sir Charles.   Oh, sir, they have undone me.   40
Two thousand and five hundred pound a year
My father at his death possessed me of,
All which the envious Acton made me spend,
And notwithstanding all this large expense
I had much ado to gain my liberty;   45
And I have now only a house of pleasure,
With some five hundred pounds, reserved
Both to maintain me and my loving sister.
Shafton. [*Aside*] That must I have; it lies convenient for me.
If I can fasten but one finger on him,   50
With my full hand I'll gripe him to the heart.
'Tis not for love I proffered him this coin,
But for my gain and pleasure.—Come, Sir Charles,
I know you have need of money; take my offer.
Sir Charles. Sir, I accept it, and remain indebted   55
Even to the best of my unable power.—
Come, gentlemen, and see it tendered down.   *Exeunt.*

[6]

Enter WENDOLL, *melancholy.*

Wendoll. I am a villain if I apprehend
But such a thought; then to attempt the deed—
Slave, thou art damned without redemption!
I'll drive away this passion with a song.
A song! Ha, ha! A song, as if, fond man,   5
Thy eyes could swim in laughter when thy soul
Lies drenched and drownèd in red tears of blood.
I'll pray, and see if God within my heart
Plant better thoughts. Why, prayers are meditations,
And when I meditate—oh, God, forgive me—   10

---

46. *house of pleasure*] summerhouse.
51. *gripe*] squeeze.
56. *unable*] weak.
57. *tendered down*] agreed upon, paid.

6.1. *apprehend*] perceive, conceive.
3. *Slave*] wretch.
5. *fond*] foolish.

It is on her divine perfections.
I will forget her; I will arm myself
Not to entertain a thought of love to her;
And when I come by chance into her presence,
I'll hale these balls until my eyestrings crack   15
From being pulled and drawn to look that way.

> *Enter over the stage* FRANKFORD, *his wife* [ANNE],
> *and* NICHOLAS[, *and exeunt*].

Oh, God, oh, God, with what a violence
I am hurried to my own destruction!
There goest thou the most perfect'st man
That ever England bred a gentleman;   20
And shall I wrong his bed?—Thou God of thunder,
Stay in Thy thoughts of vengeance and of wrath,
Thy great, almighty and all-judging hand,
From speedy execution on a villain—
A villain and a traitor to his friend.   25

> *Enter* JENKIN [*behind*].

Jenkin. Did your worship call?
Wendoll. [*Not noticing Jenkin*] He doth maintain me, he allows me
      largely
      Money to spend—
Jenkin. [*Aside*] By my faith, so do not you me; I cannot get a cross
      of you.   30
Wendoll. My gelding and my man.
Jenkin. [*Aside*] That's Sorrel and I.
Wendoll. This kindness grows of no alliance 'twixt us—
Jenkin. [*Aside*] Nor is my service of any great acquaintance.
Wendoll. I never bound him to me by desert—   35
      Of a mere stranger, a poor gentleman,
      A man by whom in no kind he could gain!

---

15. *I'll . . . balls*] I will drag away these eyeballs from looking at her.
eyestrings] muscles or tendons thought to attach the eye to the brain. They were
thought to crack at death or loss of sight.
16.1. over the stage] i.e. crossing from one upstage door to the other.
19. *thou*] Wendoll addresses Frankford rhetorically.
22. *Stay in*] rein in, hold back.
25.1. Enter *JENKIN*] The clown's comic asides undercut the melodrama of
Wendoll's speech. See Intro., pp. 12–13.
27. *largely*] generously.
29. *cross*] coin, originally with a cross stamped on the side.
33. *alliance*] kinship. See Intro., pp. 41–2.
34.] i.e. Nor does my service lead to any recognition.
35. *desert*] deserving.
37. *kind*] manner.

He hath placed me in the height of all his thoughts,
Made me companion with the best and chiefest
In Yorkshire. He cannot eat without me,   40
Nor laugh without me. I am to his body
As necessary as his digestion,
And equally do make him whole or sick.
And shall I wrong this man? Base man! Ingrate!
Hast thou the power straight with thy gory hands   45
To rip thy image from his bleeding heart?
To scratch thy name from out the holy book
Of his remembrance, and to wound his name
That holds thy name so dear, or rend his heart
To whom thy heart was joined and knit together?   50
And yet I must. Then, Wendoll, be content;
Thus villains, when they would, cannot repent.

Jenkin. [*Aside*] What a strange humour is my new master in! Pray
    God he be not mad. If he should be so, I should never have any
    mind to serve him in Bedlam. It may be he is mad for missing   55
    of me.
Wendoll. [*Seeing Jenkin*] What, Jenkin! Where's your mistress?
Jenkin. Is your worship married?
Wendoll. Why dost thou ask?
Jenkin. Because you are my master, and if I have a mistress I would   60
    be glad like a good servant to do my duty to her.
Wendoll. I mean where's Mistress Frankford?
Jenkin. Marry, sir, her husband is riding out of town, and she went
    very lovingly to bring him on his way to horse. Do you see, sir,
    here she comes, and here I go.   65
Wendoll. Vanish.   [*Exit* JENKIN.]

                Enter MISTRESS [ANNE] FRANKFORD.

Anne. You are well met, sir. Now in troth my husband,
    Before he took horse, had a great desire
    To speak with you. We sought about the house,
    Halloed into the fields, sent every way,   70
    But could not meet you; therefore he enjoined me
    To do unto you his most kind commends.
    Nay, more, he wills you, as you prize his love

48–50. *name . . . heart*] The play on literal and metaphorical meanings of 'name'
and 'heart' suggest the complexity of Wendoll's view of identity.
    52. *when*] even when.
    55. *Bedlam*] Bethlehem hospital, London's most famous institution for the
insane.
    64. *bring . . . horse*] accompany him to his horse.
    72. *commends*] greetings; compliments.

Or hold in estimation his kind friendship,
To make bold in his absence, and command   75
Even as himself were present in the house;
For you must keep his table, use his servants,
And be a present Frankford in his absence.
Wendoll. I thank him for his love.
  [*Aside*] Give me a name, you whose infectious tongues   80
Are tipped with gall and poison! As you would
Think on a man that had your father slain,
Murdered thy children, made your wives base strumpets,
So call me, call me so! Print in my face
The most stigmatic title of a villain   85
For hatching treason to so true a friend!
Anne. Sir, you are much beholding to my husband;
  You are a man most dear in his regard.
Wendoll. I am bound unto your husband and you too.
  [*Aside*] I will not speak to wrong a gentleman   90
Of that good estimation, my kind friend.
I will not! Zounds, I will not! I may choose,
And I will choose. Shall I be so misled?
Or shall I purchase to my father's crest
The motto of a villain? If I say   95
I will not do it, what thing can enforce me?
Who can compel me? What sad destiny
Hath such command upon my yielding thoughts?
I will not. Ha! Some fury pricks me on;
The swift Fates drag me at their chariot wheel   100
And hurry me to mischief. Speak I must—
Injure myself, wrong her, deceive his trust.
Anne. Are you not well, sir, that you seem thus troubled?
  There is sedition in your countenance.
Wendoll. And in my heart, fair angel, chaste and wise: 105
I love you. Start not, speak not, answer not.
I love you—nay, let me speak the rest.
Bid me to swear, and I will call to record
The host of heaven.
Anne.   The host of heaven forbid
  Wendoll should hatch such a disloyal thought!   110

---

  85. *stigmatic*] infamous (lit. bearing a stigma).
  87. *beholding*] beholden, indebted.
  91. *estimation*] reputation.
  94. *purchase . . . crest*] add to my father's coat of arms. 'Purchase' suggests an attribute not acquired by inheritance.
  104. *sedition*] treason, discord.
  108. *to record*] to note it down.

Wendoll. Such is my fate; to this suit I was born,
    To wear rich Pleasure's crown or Fortune's scorn.
Anne. My husband loves you.
Wendoll.   I know it.
Anne.   He esteems you
    Even as his brain, his eyeball, or his heart.
Wendoll. I have tried it.   115
Anne. His purse is your exchequer, and his table
    Doth freely serve you.
Wendoll.   So I have found it.
Anne. Oh, with what face of brass, what brow of steel,
    Can you unblushing speak this to the face
    Of the espoused wife of so dear a friend?   120
    It is my husband that maintains your state;
    Will you dishonour him? I am his wife
    That in your power hath left his whole affairs;
    It is to me you speak?
Wendoll.   Oh, speak no more!
    For more than this I know and have recorded   125
    Within the red-leaved table of my heart.
    Fair, and of all beloved, I was not fearful
    Bluntly to give my life into your hand,
    And at one hazard all my earthly means.
    Go, tell your husband; he will turn me off,   130
    And I am then undone. I care not, I—
    'Twas for your sake. Perchance in rage he'll kill me.
    I care not—'twas for you. Say I incur
    The general name of villain through the world,
    Of traitor to my friend—I care not, I.   135
    Beggary, shame, death, scandal, and reproach—
    For you I'll hazard all. What care I?
    For you I'll live, and in your love I'll die.
Anne. You move me, sir, to passion and to pity.
    The love I bear my husband is as precious   140
    As my soul's health.
Wendoll.   I love your husband too,
    And for his love I will engage my life.
    Mistake me not, the augmentation
    Of my sincere affection borne to you
    Doth no whit lessen my regard of him.   145

---

115. *tried it*] put it to the test, experienced it.
126. *red-leaved table*] notebook with red pages (because of the blood in his heart).
127–9. *I . . . means*] I have not been afraid to put my life in your hands and by the same action risk all my earthly means.

I will be secret, lady, close as night,
And not the light of one small glorious star
Shall shine here in my forehead to bewray
That act of night.
Anne. [Aside]   What shall I say?
My soul is wand'ring and hath lost her way.   150
[To him] Oh, Master Wendoll, oh!
Wendoll.   Sigh not, sweet saint,
For every sigh you breathe draws from my heart
A drop of blood.
Anne.   I ne'er offended yet;
My fault, I fear, will in my brow be writ.
Women that fall not quite bereft of grace   155
Have their offences noted in their face.
I blush and am ashamed. Oh, Master Wendoll,
Pray God I be not born to curse your tongue,
That hath enchanted me. This maze I am in
I fear will prove the labyrinth of sin.   160

          Enter NICHOLAS [behind].

Wendoll. The path of pleasure and the gate to bliss,
     Which on your lips I knock at with a kiss.   [He kisses her.]
Nicholas. [Aside] I'll kill the rogue.
Wendoll. Your husband is from home, your bed's no blab—
     Nay, look not down and blush.
                    [Exeunt WENDOLL and ANNE.]
Nicholas.   Zounds, I'll stab.   165
Ay, Nick, was it thy chance to come just in the nick?
I love my master, and I hate that slave;
I love my mistress, but these tricks I like not.
My master shall not pocket up this wrong;
I'll eat my fingers first. [Drawing his dagger] What say'st thou,
     metal?   170
Does not the rascal Wendoll go on legs
That thou must cut off? Hath he not hamstrings
That thou must hock? Nay, metal, thou shalt stand

---

146. close] secret.
148. bewray] reveal.
164. blab] tale bearer.
166. in the nick] in the nick of time (playing on the name Nick).
169. pocket up] submit to.
170. I'll . . . first] The exact meaning of this phrase is obscure. It might refer to the practice of biting one's thumb in an obscene accusation of cuckoldry; it might refer to pushing one's fist in one's mouth as a means of keeping silent.
173. hock] cut, so as to disable.
173-4. stand . . . say] back me up (as in a fight).

To all I say. I'll henceforth turn a spy,
And watch them in their close conveyances.   175
I never looked for better of that rascal
Since he came miching first into our house.
It is that Satan hath corrupted her,
For she was fair and chaste. I'll have an eye
In all their gestures. Thus I think of them: 180
If they proceed as they have done before,
Wendoll's a knave, my mistress is a &c.   *Exit.*

[7]

Enter [SIR] CHARLES *and* SUSAN.

Sir Charles. Sister, you see we are driven to hard shift
    To keep this poor house we have left unsold.
    I am now enforced to follow husbandry,
    And you to milk; and do we not live well?
    Well, I thank God.
Susan.   Oh, brother, here's a change,   5
    Since old Sir Charles died, in our father's house.
Sir Charles. All things on earth thus change, some up, some down;
    Content's a kingdom, and I wear that crown.

Enter SHAFTON *with a* Sergeant.

Shafton. Good morrow, good morrow, Sir Charles. What, with
        your sister
    Plying your husbandry?—Sergeant, stand off.—   10
    You have a pretty house here, and a garden,
    And goodly ground about it. Since it lies
    So near a lordship that I lately bought,
    I would fain buy it of you. I will give you—
Sir Charles. Oh, pardon me; this house successively   15
    Hath 'longed to me and my progenitors
    Three hundred year. My great-great-grandfather,

---

175. *close conveyances*] secret dealings.
177. *miching*] sneaking, pretending poverty.
182. *&c*] The rhyme indicates that the missing word is 'whore'. The word is
commonly printed in the drama of this period, so there is no question of censorship.
Heywood's texts often use '&c' to indicate ad libbing (see Intro., p. 12). The actor
could insinuate this with a gesture to the audience which could express a range of
emotion from anger to regret.

7.1. *hard shift*] desperate expedient.
3. *husbandry*] farming.
8.1. a *Sergeant*] an arresting officer.
13. *lordship*] estate, manor.

He in whom first our gentle style began,
Dwelt here, and in this ground increased this molehill
Unto that mountain which my father left me.   20
Where he the first of all our house begun,
I now, the last, will end and keep this house,
This virgin title never yet deflowered
By any unthrift of the Mountfords' line.
In brief, I will not sell it for more gold   25
Than you could hide or pave the ground withal.
Shafton. Ha, ha! A proud mind and a beggar's purse.
Where's my three hundred pounds, beside the use?
I have brought it to an execution
By course of law. What, is my money ready?   30
Sir Charles. An execution, sir, and never tell me
You put my bond in suit? You deal extremely.
Shafton. Sell me the land and I'll acquit you straight.
Sir Charles. Alas, alas! 'Tis all trouble hath left me
To cherish me and my poor sister's life.   35
If this were sold, our names should then be quite
Razed from the bead-roll of gentility.
You see what hard shift we have made to keep it
Allied still to our own name. This palm you see
Labour hath glowed within; her silver brow,   40
That never tasted a rough winter's blast
Without a mask or fan, doth with a grace
Defy cold winter and his storms outface.
Susan. Sir, we feed sparing, and we labour hard,
We lie uneasy, to reserve to us   45
And our succession this small plot of ground.
Sir Charles. I have so bent my thoughts to husbandry
That I protest I scarcely can remember
What a new fashion is, how silk or satin

---

18. *gentle style*] entitlement to gentility.
28.] Shafton demands back from Charles the money he seemed to give him freely
at 5.32, together with the interest (*use*). See Intro., p. 43.
29. *brought . . . execution*] prepared a warrant to seize your goods in payment.
32. *put . . . suit*] put my bond in force in a court of law.
34. *'Tis . . . me*] The land is all that my troubles have left me.
37. *bead-roll*] list.
39. *palm*] i.e. palm of the hand.
40. *Labour . . . within*] i.e. has been made red with labour.
her silver brow] Susan's pale complexion.
42. *mask or fan*] used by ladies to protect their delicate complexions from the
elements.
44. *feed sparing*] eat sparingly.
45. *lie uneasy*] sleep uncomfortably (on hard, cheap bedding).

Feels in my hand. Why, pride is grown to us   50
A mere, mere stranger. I have quite forgot
The names of all that ever waited on me;
I cannot name ye any of my hounds,
Once from whose echoing mouths I heard all the music
That e'er my heart desired. What should I say?   55
To keep this place I have changed myself away.

Shafton. [*To the Sergeant*] Arrest him at my suit. [*To Sir Charles*]
        Actions and actions
Shall keep thee in perpetual bondage fast.
Nay, more, I'll sue thee by a late appeal
And call thy former life in question.   60
The keeper is my friend; thou shalt have irons,
And usage such as I'll deny to dogs.—
Away with him!

Sir Charles. You are too timorous; but trouble is my master,
And I will serve in him truly.—My kind sister,   65
Thy tears are of no force to mollify
This flinty man. Go to my father's brother,
My kinsmen and allies, entreat them from me
To ransom me from this injurious man
That seeks my ruin.

Shafton.   Come, irons, irons, away!   70
I'll see thee lodged far from the sight of day.

                              Exeunt. [SUSAN *remains.*]

        Enter [SIR FRANCIS] ACTON *and* MALBY [*behind*].

Susan. My heart's so hardened with the frost of grief
Death cannot pierce it through. Tyrant too fell!
So lead the fiends condemnèd souls to hell.

Sir Francis. Again to prison? Malby, hast thou seen   75
A poor slave better tortured? Shall we hear
The music of his voice cry from the grate,
'Meat for the Lord's sake'? No, no, yet I am not
Throughly revenged. They say he hath a pretty wench
Unto his sister; shall I, in mercy sake   80

---

56. *changed . . . away*] changed my way of life utterly.
57. *Actions*] lawsuits.
59. *sue . . . appeal*] prosecute you on a recent criminal charge.
61. *keeper*] prison keeper, gaoler.
64. *timorous*] dreadful, terrible. Or, Sir Charles may address this to Susan.
73. *fell*] deadly, fierce.
77. *grate*] grating of a prison from which prisoners would beg for food.
79. *Throughly*] thoroughly.
80. *Unto*] as, for.

To him and to his kindred, bribe the fool
To shame herself by lewd, dishonest lust?
I'll proffer largely, but, the deed being done,
I'll smile to see her base confusion.

Malby. Methinks, Sir Francis, you are full revenged   85
For greater wrongs than he can proffer you.
See where the poor sad gentlewoman stands.

Sir Francis. Ha, ha! Now I will flout her poverty,
Deride her fortunes, scoff her base estate;
My very soul the name of Mountford hates.   90
But stay, my heart! Oh, what a look did fly
To strike my soul through with thy piercing eye?
I am enchanted; all my spirits are fled,
And with one glance my envious spleen struck dead.

Susan. [*Seeing them*] Acton, that seeks our blood!   *Runs away.*

Sir Francis.   O chaste and fair!   95

Malby. Sir Francis, why, Sir Francis, zounds, in a trance?
Sir Francis, what cheer, man? Come, come, how is 't?

Sir Francis. Was she not fair? Or else this judging eye
Cannot distinguish beauty.

Malby.   She was fair.

Sir Francis. She was an angel in a mortal's shape,   100
And ne'er descended from old Mountford's line.
But soft, soft, let me call my wits together.
A poor, poor wench, to my great adversary
Sister, whose very souls denounce stern war
One against other. How now, Frank, turned fool   105
Or madman, whether? But no master of
My perfect senses and directest wits.
Then why should I be in this violent humour
Of passion and of love, and with a person
So different every way and so opposed   110
In all contractions and still-warring actions?
Fie, fie, how I dispute against my soul!
Come, come, I'll gain her, or in her fair quest
Purchase my soul free and immortal rest.   *Exeunt.*

---

81. *fool*] innocent, i.e. Susan.
82. *dishonest*] unchaste.
84. *base confusion*] degrading ruin.
94. *envious spleen*] malicious anger.
102. *soft, soft*] wait a minute.
104. *whose very souls*] i.e. Sir Charles's and mine.
106. *whether?*] which of the two?
107. *directest wits*] keenest intelligence.
111. *contractions*] dealings.
113–14. *or . . . rest*] or in the attempt to find and have her, die and go to heaven.

[8]

> *Enter 3 or 4* Servingmen [*including* SPIGGOT *the Butler and*
> NICHOLAS], *one with a voider and a wooden knife to take away all,*
> *another the salt and bread, another the tablecloth and napkins,*
> *another the carpet.* JENKIN *with two lights after them.*

Jenkin. So, march in order and retire in battle 'ray. My master and
the guests have supped already; all's taken away. Here, now
spread for the servingmen in the hall. Butler, it belongs to your
office.

Spiggot. I know it, Jenkin. What do you call the gentleman that   5
supped there tonight?

Jenkin. Who, my master?

Spiggot. No, no, Master Wendoll, he is a daily guest; I mean the
gentleman that came but this afternoon.

Jenkin. His name is Master Cranwell. God's light! Hark, within   10
there, my master calls to lay more billets on the fire. Come,
come! Lord, how we that are in office here in the house are
troubled! One spread the carpet in the parlour and stand ready
to snuff the lights; the rest be ready to prepare their stomachs.
More lights in the hall there! Come, Nich'las.   15

> [*Exeunt.* NICHOLAS *remains.*]

Nicholas. I cannot eat, but had I Wendoll's heart
I would eat that; the rogue grows impudent.
Oh, I have seen such vile, notorious tricks,
Ready to make my eyes dart from my head!
I'll tell my master, by this air I will;   20
Fall what may fall, I'll tell him. Here he comes.

> *Enter* FRANKFORD, *as it were brushing the crumbs from his*
> *clothes with a napkin, and newly risen from supper.*

Frankford. Nich'las, what make you here? Why are not you
At supper in the hall there with your fellows?

Nicholas. Master, I stayed your rising from the board
To speak with you.

Frankford.   Be brief, then, gentle Nich'las.   25
My wife and guests attend me in the parlour.

8.0.2. voider] tray or basket used for clearing the table. See Intro., p. 19.
0.4. carpet] heavy tablecover of tapestry. Carpets were not laid on the floor in
this period. Also line 13.
10. *God's light*] by God's light (an oath).
11. *billets*] logs.
14. *stomachs*] appetites.
21. *Fall . . . fall*] No matter what may befall.
24. *stayed*] waited for.
26. *attend*] wait for.

Why dost thou pause? Now, Nich'las, you want money,
And unthrift-like would eat into your wages
Ere you have earned it. Here's, sir, half a crown;
                              [*Offering money*]
Play the good husband, and away to supper.   30
Nicholas. [*Aside*] By this hand, an honourable gentleman. I will not
   see him wronged. [*To him*] Sir, I have served you long; you
   entertained me seven years before your beard. You knew me,
   sir, before you knew my mistress.
Frankford. What of this, good Nich'las?   35
Nicholas. I never was a make-bate or a knave;
   I have no fault but one—I am given to quarrel,
   But not with women. I will tell you, master,
   That which will make your heart leap from your breast,
   Your hair to startle from your head, your ears to tingle. 40
Frankford. What preparation's this to dismal news?
Nicholas. 'Sblood, sir, I love you better than your wife—
   [*Frankford threatens him.*] I'll make it good.
Frankford. Thou art a knave, and I have much ado
   With wonted patience to contain my rage   45
   And not to break thy pate. Thou art a knave;
   I'll turn you with your base comparisons
   Out of my doors.
Nicholas. Do, do.
   There's not room for Wendoll and me too   50
   Both in one house. Oh, master, master,
   That Wendoll is a villain.
Frankford. [*Striking him*]   Ay, saucy!
Nicholas. Strike, strike, do strike! Yet hear me. I am no fool;
   I know a villain when I see him act
   Deeds of a villain. Master, master, that base slave   55
   Enjoys my mistress and dishonours you.
Frankford. Thou hast killed me with a weapon whose sharpened
       point
   Hath pricked quite through and through my shivering heart.
   Drops of cold sweat sit dangling on my hairs
   Like morning's dew upon the golden flowers,   60
   And I am plunged into a strange agony.

---

28. *unthrift-like*] like a spendthrift.
30. *Play . . . husband*] be a good manager of your possessions.
33. *entertained me*] took me into your service.
before your beard] before you came to adulthood.
36. *make-bate*] trouble-maker.
42. *'Sblood*] by God's blood (an oath).
43.] i.e. I'll explain what I mean.
56. *Enjoys*] enjoys sexually.

What didst thou say? If any word that touched
His credit or her reputation,
It is as hard to enter my belief
As Dives into heaven.

Nicholas.   I can gain nothing;   65
They are two that never wronged me. I knew before
'Twas but a thankless office, and perhaps
As much as my service or my life is worth.
All this I know; but this and more,
More by a thousand dangers could not hire me   70
To smother such a heinous wrong from you.
I saw, and I have said.

Frankford. [*Aside*] 'Tis probable; though blunt, yet he is honest.
Though I durst pawn my life, and on their faith
Hazard the dear salvation of my soul,   75
Yet in my trust I may be too secure.
May this be true? Oh, may it? Can it be?
Is it by any wonder possible?
Man, woman, what thing mortal may we trust
When friends and bosom wives prove so unjust?   80
[*To Nicholas*] What instance hast thou of this strange report?

Nicholas. Eyes, eyes.

Frankford. Thy eyes may be deceived, I tell thee,
For, should an angel from the heavens drop down
And preach this to me that thyself hast told,   85
He should have much ado to win belief,
In both their loves I am so confident.

Nicholas. Shall I discourse the same by circumstance?

Frankford. No more. To supper, and command your fellows
To attend us and the strangers. Not a word;   90
I charge thee on thy life, be secret then,
For I know nothing.

Nicholas. I am dumb, and now that I have eased my stomach
I will go fill my stomach.

Frankford.   Away, begone!   *Exit* [NICHOLAS].

---

65. *Dives*] the rich man sent to hell in the parable of Dives and Lazarus (Luke, 16.19–31). The story was often represented on the tapestries and painted cloths decorating houses.

I . . . nothing] i.e. I have nothing to gain by telling you this.

73. *he*] Nicholas.

74. *their faith*] Wendoll and Anne's honesty.

88. *circumstance*] detailed instances.

90. *strangers*] visitors.

92. *I know nothing*] I will act as though I'd heard nothing.

93. *eased my stomach*] relieved myself of the burden of this knowledge. (Cf. the modern expression 'got it off my chest'.)

She is well born, descended nobly;   95
Virtuous her education; her repute
Is in the general voice of all the country
Honest and fair; her carriage, her demeanour
In all her actions that concern the love
To me her husband, modest, chaste, and godly.   100
Is all this seeming gold plain copper?
But he, that Judas that hath borne my purse,
And sold me for a sin—Oh God, oh God,
Shall I put up these wrongs? No, shall I trust
The bare report of this suspicious groom   105
Before the double gilt, the well-hatched ore
Of their two hearts? No, I will loose these thoughts;
Distraction I will banish from my brow
And from my looks exile sad discontent.
Their wonted favours in my tongue shall flow;   110
Till I know all, I'll nothing seem to know.—
Lights and a table there! Wife, Master Wendoll,
And, gentle Master Cranwell—

Enter MISTRESS [ANNE] FRANKFORD, MASTER WENDOLL, MASTER
    CRANWELL, NICHOLAS, *and* JENKIN, *with cards, carpet, stools,*
                    and other necessaries.

Oh, you are a stranger, Master Cranwell, you,
And often balk my house; faith, you are a churl.   115
Now we have supped, a table and to cards.
Jenkin. A pair of cards, Nich'las, and a carpet to cover the table.
    Where's Sisly with her counters and her box? Candles and
    candlesticks there! [*Enter* SISLY *and a* Servingman *with counters*
    and candles.] Fie, we have such a household of serving creatures!   120
    Unless it be Nick and I, there's not one amongst them all can
    say 'boo' to a goose. [*To Nicholas*] Well said, Nick.
        They spread a carpet, set down lights and cards.   [Exeunt all the
                                Servants except NICHOLAS.]

---

102. *Judas*] In St John's Gospel (13.29), Judas, the betrayer of Christ to the Jews,
carries the disciples' money bag.
106. *double gilt*] twice gilded (with a pun on 'guilt').
well-hatched] richly engraved.
107. *loose*] rid myself of. Perhaps Q1's 'loose' means 'lose'.
110. *wonted*] usual.
115. *balk*] pass by.
faith] in faith (a mild oath).
churl] peasant, ill-mannered person (said jokingly).
117. *pair*] pack.
118. *counters . . . box*] for the game of backgammon.
122. *Well said*] Well done.

Anne. Come, Master Frankford, who shall take my part?

Frankford. Marry, that will I, sweet wife.

Wendoll. No, by my faith, sir, when you are together I sit out; it   125
must be Mistress Frankford and I, or else it is no match.

Frankford. I do not like that match.

Nicholas. [*Aside*] You have no reason, marry, knowing all.

Frankford. 'Tis no great matter, neither.—Come, Master Cranwell,
shall you and I take them up?   130

Cranwell. At your pleasure, sir.

Frankford. I must look to you, Master Wendoll, for you will be
playing false—nay, so will my wife, too.

Nicholas. [*Aside*] Ay, I will be sworn she will.

Anne. Let them that are taken playing false forfeit the set.   135

Frankford. Content. [*Aside*] It shall go hard but I'll take you.

Cranwell. Gentlemen, what shall our game be?

Wendoll. Master Frankford, you play best at noddy.

Frankford. You shall not find it so. [*Aside*] Indeed you shall not!

Anne. I can play at nothing so well as double ruff.   140

Frankford. If Master Wendoll and my wife be together, there's no
playing against them at double hand.

Nicholas. I can tell you, sir, the game that Master Wendoll is best at.

Wendoll. What game is that, Nick?

Nicholas. Marry, sir, knave out of doors.   145

Wendoll. She and I will take you at lodam.

Anne. Husband, shall we play at saint?

Frankford. [*Aside*] My saint's turned devil! [*To her*] No, we'll none
of saint.
You're best at new-cut, wife. [*Aside*] You'll play at that!

Wendoll. If you play at new-cut, I am soonest hitter of any here, for   150
a wager.

Frankford. [*Aside*] 'Tis me they play on. Well, you may draw out,
For all your cunning; 'twill be to your shame.
I'll teach you at your new-cut a new game.
[*To them*] Come, come.   155

---

123. *take my part*] be my partner, be on my side.

124. *Marry*] an oath, from 'by the Virgin Mary'.

128.] There is double entendre in all the exchanges in this part of the scene,
especially in the names of the card games.

130. *take them up*] take them on.

136. *It . . . but*] unless things go against me.

138. *noddy*] (1) a card game; (2) a fool. The pun was commonplace.

140. *double ruff*] a card game similar to whist; the emphasis is on 'double'.
Compare line 142, *double hand*.

146, 147, 149. *lodam, saint, new-cut*] card games.

150. *hitter*] scorer of points in the game (with sexual double entendre continuing
from *new-cut*).

152. *draw out*] choose your cards so as to lose your game.

Cranwell. If you cannot agree upon the game, to post and pair.
Wendoll. We shall be soonest pairs, and my good host,
    When he comes late home, he must kiss the post.
Frankford. Whoever wins, it shall be to thy cost.
Cranwell. Faith, let it be vide-ruff, and let's make honours.   160
Frankford. If you make honours, one thing let me crave:
    Honour the king and queen; except the knave.
Wendoll. Well, as you please for that. Lift who shall deal.
Anne. The least in sight. What are you, Master Wendoll?
Wendoll. [*Cutting the cards*] I am a knave.
Nicholas. [*Aside*]   I'll swear it.
Anne. [*Cutting*]   I a queen.   165
Frankford. [*Aside*] A quean, thou shouldst say. [*To them*] Well,
    the cards are mine.
    They are the grossest pair that e'er I felt.
Anne. Shuffle, I'll cut. [*Aside*] Would I had never dealt!
Frankford. [*Misdealing*] I have lost my dealing.
Wendoll.   Sir, the fault's in me.
    This queen I have more than my own, you see.   170
    Give me the stock.   [*He deals.*]
Frankford.   My mind's not on my game.
    [*Aside*] Many a deal I have lost, the more's your shame.
    [*To them*] You have served me a bad trick, Master Wendoll.
Wendoll. Sir, you must take your lot. To end this strife,

---

156. *post and pair*] a card game.
158. *kiss the post*] be shut out. (Frankford, coming home late, will find his own
door shut against him.)
160. *vide-ruff*] a game like *double ruff* in line 140, with similar punning.
make honours] ?name the highest cards.
162. *except*] exclude, refuse to honour.
the knave] third face card in a pack, also known as 'the jack'. Here, implicitly,
Wendoll.
163. *Lift . . . deal*] Cut for the deal.
164. *The least in sight*] The lowest card when we cut the deck to choose the
dealer.
166. *A quean*] a loose woman.
the cards are mine] (1) I am the dealer; (2) I have the lowest card, and am thus
trumped by the *knave* and the queen (*quean*).
167. *grossest pair*] (1) thickest or most dog-eared pack; (2) most outrageous
couple.
168. *dealt*] (1) dealt the cards; (2) dealt sexually with Wendoll.
169. *lost my dealing*] (1) misdealt the cards; (2) lost in the deal regarding my wife.
170.] (1) In your misdealing you gave me a queen more than I should have; (2)
I have a woman not belonging to me.
171. *stock*] cards not yet dealt out.
173. *trick*] (1) hand of cards; (2) nasty deception.

I know I have dealt better with your wife.   175
Frankford. [*Aside*] Thou hast dealt falsely, then.
Anne. What's trumps?
Wendoll. Hearts. Partner, I rub.
Frankford. [*Aside*] Thou robb'st me of my soul, of her chaste love;
    In thy false dealing thou hast robbed my heart.   180
    Booty you play; I like a loser stand,
    Having no heart, or here or in my hand.
    [*To them*] I will give o'er the set; I am not well.
    Come, who will hold my cards?
Anne. Not well, sweet Master Frankford?   185
    Alas, what ail you? 'Tis some sudden qualm.
Wendoll. How long have you been so, Master Frankford?
Frankford. Sir, I was lusty and I had my health,
    But I grew ill when you began to deal.—
    Take hence this table.

        [*The Servants enter and remove the table, cards, &c.*]

                    Gentle Master Cranwell,   190
    You are welcome; see your chamber at your pleasure.
    I am sorry that this megrim takes me so
    I cannot sit and bear you company.—
    Jenkin, some lights, and show him to his chamber.
                            [*Exeunt* CRANWELL *and* JENKIN.]
Anne. [*To a Servant*] A nightgown for my husband, quickly there!   195

            [*Enter a Servant with a gown, and exit.*]

    It is some rheum or cold.
Wendoll.   Now, in good faith,
    This illness you have got by sitting late
    Without your gown.
Frankford.   I know it, Master Wendoll.
    Go, go to bed, lest you complain like me.

---

178. *rub*] take all the cards in one suit. Frankford plays on the homonym, 'rob',
in the next line.
181. *Booty you play*] You join with a partner to defeat another player.
182. *or here . . . hand*] either in my breast or in my hand of cards.
183. *give . . . set*] give up the game.
186. *qualm*] (1) nausea; (2) sinking heart.
188. *lusty*] vigorous.
191. *see . . . pleasure*] retire to your room whenever you wish.
192. *megrim*] migraine, headache.
195. *nightgown*] dressing gown.

come to accept to wha
the fact to
is happening

Wife, prithee, wife, into my bedchamber.   200
The night is raw and cold and rheumatic.
Leave me my gown and light; I'll walk away my fit.
Wendoll. Sweet sir, good night.
Frankford. Myself, good night.   [*Exit* WENDOLL.]
Anne.   Shall I attend you, husband?
Frankford. No, gentle wife, thou'lt catch cold in thy head;   205
Prithee, begone, sweet. I'll make haste to bed.
Anne. No sleep will fasten on mine eyes, you know,
Until you come.
Frankford.   Sweet Nan, I prithee, go.   *Exit* [ANNE].
[*To Nicholas*] I have bethought me; get me by degrees
The keys of all my doors, which I will mould   210
In wax, and take their fair impression,
To have by them new keys. This being compassed,
At a set hour a letter shall be brought me,
And when they think they may securely play,
They are nearest to danger. Nick, I must rely   215
Upon thy trust and faithful secrecy.
Nicholas. Build on my faith!
Frankford.   To bed then, not to rest.
Care lodges in my brain, grief in my breast.   *Exeunt.*

[9]

Enter SIR CHARLES HIS SISTER [SUSAN], OLD MOUNTFORD,
SANDY, RODER, *and* TYDY.

Old Mountford. You say my nephew is in great distress.
Who brought it to him but his own lewd life?
I cannot spare a cross. I must confess
He was my brother's son; why, niece, what then?
This is no world in which to pity men.   5
Susan. I was not born a beggar, though his extremes
Enforce this language from me; I protest
No fortune of mine could lead my tongue

---

201. *rheumatic*] conducive to head colds.
204. *Myself*] my other self, my alter ego (including the sense both of 'my dearest friend' and 'the man who replaces me sexually').
212. *compassed*] achieved, encompassed.

9.0.1. CHARLES HIS] Charles's.
2. *lewd*] wicked (not necessarily sexual).
3. *a cross*] a coin. The figure of a cross was often stamped on the reverse side of a coin.
confess] admit.

To this base key. I do beseech you, uncle,
For the name's sake, for Christianity,   10
Nay, for God's sake, to pity his distress.
He is denied the freedom of the prison,
And in the hole is laid with men condemned;
Plenty he hath of nothing but of irons,
And it remains in you to free him thence.   15
Old Mountford. Money I cannot spare; men should take heed.
He lost my kindred when he fell to need.   *Exit.*
Susan. Gold is but earth; thou earth enough shalt have
When thou hast once took measure of thy grave.—
You know me, Master Sandy, and my suit.   20
Sandy. I knew you, lady, when the old man lived;
I knew you ere your brother sold his land.
Then you were Mistress Sue, tricked up in jewels;
Then you sung well, played sweetly on the flute;
But now I neither know you nor your suit.   *[Exit.]*   25
Susan. You, Master Roder, was my brother's tenant;
Rent-free he placed you in that wealthy farm
Of which you are possessed.
Roder.   True, he did;
And have I not there dwelt still for his sake?
I have some business now, but without doubt   30
They that have hurled him in will help him out.   *Exit.*
Susan. Cold comfort still.—What say you, cousin Tydy?
Tydy. I say this comes of roisting, swagg'ring.
Call me not cousin; each man for himself!
Some men are born to mirth and some to sorrow;   35
I am no cousin unto them that borrow.   *Exit.*
Susan. O Charity, why art thou fled to heaven,
And left all things on this earth uneven?
Their scoffing answers I will ne'er return,
But to myself his grief in silence mourn.   40

Enter SIR FRANCIS *and* MALBY.

---

9. *base*] (1) vile, low; (2) bass (as in music).
10. *the name's sake*] i.e. the family name.
12. *the freedom . . . prison*] Those with money could move freely about the prison.
13. *the hole*] the worst part of the prison.
19. *took . . . grave*] i.e. measured your grave by lying in it, dead.
21. *the old man*] the Mountford who was father to Sir Charles and Susan, and brother to the Old Mountford in this scene.
33. *roisting*] boisterous revelling.
39. *return*] i.e. report to Sir Charles.

Sir Francis. She is poor; I'll therefore tempt her with this gold.
    Go, Malby, in my name deliver it,
    And I will stay thy answer.
Malby. [*To Anne*] Fair mistress, as I understand your grief
    Doth grow from want, so I have here in store   45
    A means to furnish you: a bag of gold
    Which to your hands I freely tender you.   [*He offers money.*]
Susan. I thank you, heavens; I thank you, gentle sir!
    God make me able to requite this favour.
Malby. This gold Sir Francis Acton sends by me,   50
    And prays you &c.
Susan. Acton! Oh, God, that name I am born to curse.
    Hence, bawd; hence, broker! See, I spurn his gold;
    My honour never shall for gain be sold.   [*She starts to leave.*]
Sir Francis. Stay, lady, stay!
Susan.   From you I'll posting hie,   55
    Even as the doves from feathered eagles fly.   [*Exit.*]
Sir Francis. She hates my name, my face—how should I woo?
    I am disgraced in everything I do.
    The more she hates me and disdains my love,
    The more I am rapt in admiration   60
    Of her divine and chaste perfections.
    Woo her with gifts I cannot, for all gifts
    Sent in my name she spurns. With looks I cannot,
    For she abhors my sight. Nor yet with letters,
    For none she will receive. How then? How then?   65
    Well, I will fasten such a kindness on her
    As shall o'ercome her hate and conquer it.
    Sir Charles, her brother, lies in execution
    For a great sum of money; and, besides,
    The appeal is sued still for my huntsman's death,   70
    Which only I have power to reverse.
    In her I'll bury all my hate of him.
    Go seek the keeper, Malby; bring me to him.—
    To save his body, I his debts will pay;
    To save his life, I his appeal will stay.   *Exeunt.*   75

---

43. *stay*] await.
45. *in store*] in abundance.
51. *&c*] indicates either adlibbing or whispering or that Anne cuts off Malby's speech.
53. *broker*] dealer (in sexual exchange).
55. *posting hie*] leave hurriedly.
68. *lies in execution*] is imprisoned.
70.] further prosecution (against Sir Charles) is pending in connection with my huntsman's death. One huntsman and one falconer were killed; see 4.48–9.
73. *keeper*] keeper of the prison.

[10]

> *Enter* SIR CHARLES *in prison, with irons; his feet bare,*
> *his garments all ragged and torn.*

Sir Charles. Of all on the earth's face most miserable,
 Breathe in this hellish dungeon thy laments,
 Thus like a slave ragg'd, like a felon gyved.
 O unkind uncle! O my friends ingrate,
 That hurls thee headlong to this base estate!   5
 Unthankful kinsmen! Mountfords all too base,
 To let thy name lie fettered in disgrace!
 A thousand deaths here in this grave I die.
 Fear, hunger, sorrow, cold—all threat my death
 And join together to deprive my breath.   10
 But that which most torments me, my dear sister
 Hath left to visit me, and from my friends
 Hath brought no hopeful answer; therefore I
 Divine they will not help my misery.
 If it be so, shame, scandal, and contempt   15
 Attend their covetous thoughts, need make their graves!
 Usurers they live, and may they die like slaves!

> *Enter* Keeper.

Keeper. Knight, be of comfort, for I bring thee freedom
 From all thy troubles.
Sir Charles.   Then I am doomed to die;
 Death is the end of all calamity.   20
Keeper. Live! Your appeal is stayed, the execution
 Of all your debts discharged, your creditors
 Even to the utmost penny satisfied,
 In sign whereof your shackles I knock off.

> [*The irons are removed.*]

 You are not left so much indebted to us   25
 As for your fees; all is discharged, all paid.

10.1–3.] Sir Charles apostrophizes himself as the most miserable of men, condemned now to breathe out or utter in this hellish prison his sad laments, thus
chained and reduced to ragged poverty like a slave or felon.
 4. *ingrate*] ungrateful.
 9. *threat*] threaten.
 12. *left*] ceased.
 14. *Divine*] guess.
 16. *need . . . graves*] may want and poverty drive them to their graves.
 17. *Usurers*] a general term for the covetous.
 21–2. *Your . . . discharged*] The proceedings against you are halted, all your debts
are paid.
 25–6. *You . . . fees*] You do not even owe us the usual fees for living in prison.

Go freely to your house or where you please;
After long miseries embrace your ease.
Sir Charles. Thou grumblest out the sweetest music to me
That ever organ played. Is this a dream?   30

                    [*The Keeper stands aside.*]

Or do my waking senses apprehend
The pleasing taste of these applausive news?
Slave that I was, to wrong such honest friends,
My loving kinsmen and my near allies!
Tongue, I will bite thee for the scandal breath   35
Against such faithful kinsmen; they are all
Composed of pity and compassion,
Of melting charity and of moving ruth.
That which I spake before was in my rage;
They are my friends, the mirrors of this age,   40
Bounteous and free. The noble Mountfords' race
Ne'er bred a covetous thought or humour base.

                    Enter SUSAN.

Susan. I can no longer stay from visiting
My woeful brother! While I could, I kept
My hapless tidings from his hopeful ear.   45
Sir Charles. Sister, how much am I indebted to thee
And to thy travail!
Susan.   What, at liberty?
Sir Charles. Thou seest I am, thanks to thy industry.
Oh, unto which of all my courteous friends
Am I thus bound? My uncle Mountford, he   50
Even of an infant loved me; was it he?
So did my cousin Tydy; was it he?
So Master Roder, Master Sandy too.
Which of all these did this high kindness do?
Susan. Charles, can you mock me in your poverty,   55
Knowing your friends deride your misery?
Now I protest I stand so much amazed
To see your bonds free and your irons knocked off
That I am rapt into a maze of wonder,
The rather for I know not by what means   60

---

32. *applausive*] worthy of applause, agreeable.
35. *scandal breath*] scandalous utterance.
38. *ruth*] loving kindness.
40. *the mirrors . . . age*] persons in whom the age can see itself reflected at its best.
47. *travail*] exertions, labour.
51. *of an infant*] since I was a child.
57. *protest*] declare.

This happiness hath chanced.

Sir Charles.   Why, by my uncle,
  My cousins, and my friends. Who else, I pray,
  Would take upon them all my debts to pay?

Susan. Oh, brother, they are men all of flint,
  Pictures of marble, and as void of pity   65
  As chasèd bears. I begged, I sued, I kneeled,
  Laid open all your griefs and miseries,
  Which they derided—more than that, denied us
  A part in their alliance, but in pride
  Said that our kindred with our plenty died.   70

Sir Charles. Drudges too much! What did they? Oh, known evil:
  Rich fly the poor as good men shun the devil.
  Whence should my freedom come? Of whom alive,
  Saving of those, have I deserved so well?
  Guess, sister, call to mind, remember me.   75
  These I have raised, these follow the world's guise,
  Whom, rich in honour, they in woe despise.

Susan. My wits have lost themselves; let's ask the keeper.

Sir Charles. Gaoler!

Keeper. [*Approaching*] At hand, sir.   80

Sir Charles. Of courtesy resolve me one demand:
  What was he took the burden of my debts
  From off my back, stayed my appeal to death,
  Discharged my fees, and brought me liberty?

Keeper. A courteous knight, one called Sir Francis Acton.   85

Susan. Acton!

Sir Charles. Ha! Acton! Oh, me, more distressed in this
  Than all my troubles! Hale me back,
  Double my irons, and my sparing meals
  Put into halves, and lodge me in a dungeon   90
  More deep, more dark, more cold, more comfortless!
  By Acton freed! Not all thy manacles

---

65. *Pictures*] statues.
66. *chasèd*] tormented (as in the sport of bear-baiting).
67. *Laid open*] laid before them in detail.
69. *A part . . . alliance*] membership of their family.
70. *kindred*] family connection.
71. *Drudges*] people involved in mean servile labour. Sir Charles implies that his kinsmen's meanness is a sign of servility. See Intro., pp. 43–5.
75. *remember*] remind.
76. *These . . . raised*] these persons whom I have socially elevated.
guise] fashion.
77.] despising, in their wealth and high social status, those who are in woe.
82. *What was he*] who was it that.
88. *Hale*] drag.

Could fetter so my heels as this one word
Hath thralled my heart, and it must now lie bound
In more strict prison than thy stony gaol.   95
I am not free; I go but under bail.
Keeper. My charge is done, sir, now I have my fees;
As we get little, we will nothing leese.   *Exit.*
Sir Charles. By Acton freed, my dangerous opposite!
Why, to what end? Or what occasion? Ha!   100
Let me forget the name of enemy
And with indifference balance this high favour. Ha!
Susan. [*Aside*] His love to me! Upon my soul, 'tis so;
That is the root from whence these strange things grow.
Sir Charles. Had this proceeded from my father, he   105
That by the law of nature is most bound
In offices of love, it had deserved
My best employment to requite that grace.
Had it proceeded from my friends, or him,
From them this action had deserved my life—   110
And from a stranger more, because from such
There is less execution of good deeds.
But he, nor father, nor ally, nor friend,
More than a stranger, both remote in blood
And in his heart opposed my enemy,   115
That this high bounty should proceed from him—
Oh, there I lose myself. What should I say,
What think, what do, his bounty to repay?
Susan. You wonder, I am sure, whence this strange kindness
Proceeds in Acton. I will tell you, brother: 120
He dotes on me and oft hath sent me gifts,
Letters, and tokens; I refused them all.
Sir Charles. I have enough; though poor, my heart is set
In one rich gift to pay back all my debt.   *Exeunt.*

his sister

---

94. *thralled*] captured, imprisoned.
98.] since we prison keepers earn little we won't give anything up (i.e. by taking
Sir Charles back into custody and so losing the fee which Acton has paid).
102. *indifference*] impartiality.
balance] weigh.
109. *him*] my father.
110. *my life*] my lifelong commitment.
111–12. *because . . . deeds*] because strangers do not owe me anything in return
for good deeds done to them. See Intro., pp. 43–5.
115. *opposed*] set up as.
117. *lose myself*] am lost, cannot understand what is happening.

[11]

> *Enter* FRANKFORD, *and* NICHOLAS *with keys,*
> *and a letter in his* [*Frankford's*] *hand.*

Frankford. This is the night, and I must play the touch,
To try two seeming angels. Where's my keys?
Nicholas. They are made according to your mould in wax.
I bade the smith be secret, gave him money,
And there they are. [*He gives keys.*] The letter, sir.   5
Frankford. True, take it; there it is.   [*He gives a letter.*]
And when thou seest me in my pleasant'st vein
Ready to sit to supper, bring it me.
Nicholas. I'll do 't; make no more question but I'll do 't.   *Exit.*

> *Enter* MISTRESS [ANNE] FRANKFORD, CRANWELL, WENDOLL,
> *and* JENKIN.

Anne. Sirrah, 'tis six o'clock already struck.   10
Go bid them spread the cloth and serve in supper.
Jenkin. It shall be done, forsooth, mistress. Where is Spiggot the
butler to give us out salt and trenchers?   [*Exit.*]
Wendoll. We that have been a-hunting all the day
Come with preparèd stomachs.—Master Frankford,   15
We wished you at our sport.
Frankford. My heart was with you, and my mind was on you.—
Fie, Master Cranwell, you are still thus sad.—
A stool, a stool! Where's Jenkin, and where's Nick?
'Tis suppertime at least an hour ago.   20
What's the best news abroad?
Wendoll.   I know none good.
Frankford. [*Aside*] But I know too much bad.

> *Enter* [SPIGGOT *the*] *Butler and* JENKIN *with a tablecloth,*
> *bread, trenchers, and salt*[, *then exeunt*].

Cranwell. Methinks, sir, you might have that interest
In your wife's brother to be more remiss
In this hard dealing against poor Sir Charles,   25

---

11. 1. *play the touch*] act as a touchstone (to test my wife's mettle).

2. *seeming angels*] (1) seemingly virtuous persons; (2) false coins (continuing the metaphor of testing for counterfeit money).

13. *trenchers*] wooden plates.

21. *abroad*] in the outside world.

23–5. *you . . . Sir Charles*] you might have enough influence with your wife's brother to urge him to be more lenient in his harsh dealing with Sir Charles.

Who, as I hear, lies in York Castle, needy,
And in great want.

Frankford. Did not more weighty business of my own
Hold me away, I would have laboured peace
Betwixt them with all care; indeed I would, sir.   30

Anne. I'll write unto my brother earnestly
In that behalf.

Wendoll.   A charitable deed,
And will beget the good opinion
Of all your friends that love you, Mistress Frankford.

Frankford. That's you, for one; I know you love Sir Charles,   35
[*Aside*] And my wife too, well.

Wendoll.   He deserves the love
Of all true gentlemen; be yourselves judge.

Frankford. But supper, ho!—Now as thou lovest me, Wendoll—
Which I am sure thou dost—be merry, pleasant,
And frolic it tonight. Sweet Master Cranwell,   40
Do you the like. Wife, I protest, my heart
Was ne'er more bent on sweet alacrity.
Where be those lazy knaves to serve in supper?

Enter NICHOLAS.

Nicholas. [*Giving a letter*] Sir, here's a letter.

Frankford. Whence comes it? And who brought it?   45

Nicholas. A stripling that below attends your answer,
And as he tells me it is sent from York.

Frankford. Have him into the cellar; let him taste
A cup of our March beer. Go, make him drink.
[*He reads the letter.*]

Nicholas. I'll make him drunk, if he be a Trojan.   [*Exit.*]   50

Frankford. My boots and spurs! Where's Jenkin? God forgive me,
How I neglect my business. Wife, look here;
I have a matter to be tried tomorrow
By eight o'clock, and my attorney writes me
I must be there betimes with evidence,   55
Or it will go against me. Where's my boots?

Enter JENKIN *with boots and spurs.*

Anne. I hope your business craves no such dispatch
That you must ride tonight.

Wendoll. [*Aside*]   I hope it doth.

---

42. *alacrity*] speed (in getting on with dinner and a jovial evening).
49. *March beer*] the first brew of the season to be ready.
50. *a Trojan*] a good fellow.
57. *dispatch*] urgency.

Frankford. God's me! No such dispatch?
 Jenkin, my boots. Where's Nick? Saddle my roan,   60
 And the gray dapple for himself. [*Exit* JENKIN.]
         Content ye,
 It much concerns me.—Gentle Master Cranwell
 And Master Wendoll, in my absence use
 The very ripest pleasure of my house.
Wendoll. Lord, Master Frankford, will you ride tonight? 65
 The ways are dangerous.
Frankford.   Therefore will I ride
 Appointed well, and so shall Nick, my man.
Anne. I'll call you up by five o'clock tomorrow.
Frankford. No, by my faith, wife, I'll not trust to that;
 'Tis not such easy rising in a morning   70
 From one I love so dearly. No, by my faith,
 I shall not leave so sweet a bedfellow
 But with much pain. You have made me a sluggard
 Since I first knew you.
Anne.   Then if you needs will go
 This dangerous evening, Master Wendoll,   75
 Let me entreat you bear him company.
Wendoll. With all my heart, sweet mistress.—My boots there!
Frankford. Fie, fie, that for my private business
 I should disease my friend and be a trouble
 To the whole house!—Nick!   80
Nicholas. [*Appearing at the door*] Anon, sir.
Frankford. Bring forth my gelding. [*Exit* NICHOLAS.]
 [*To Wendoll*]   As you love me, sir,
 Use no more words.—A hand, good Master Cranwell.
Cranwell. Sir, God be your good speed.
Frankford. Good night, sweet Nan; nay, nay, a kiss and part. 85
         [*He kisses her.*]
 [*Aside*] Dissembling lips, you suit not with my heart. [*Exit.*]
Wendoll. [*Aside*] How business, time, and hours all gracious prove
 And are the furtherers to my newborn love!
 I am husband now in Master Frankford's place
 And must command the house. [*To Anne*] My pleasure is 90
 We will not sup abroad so publicly,
 But in your private chamber, Mistress Frankford.
Anne. [*To Wendoll*] Oh, sir, you are too public in your love,

---

59. *God's me*] God's my life (an oath).
61. *Content ye*] rest assured. (Said to Anne and Wendoll.)
67. *Appointed*] equipped, armed.
79. *disease*] dis-ease; cause inconvenience to.

And Master Frankford's wife—
Cranwell.   Might I crave favour,
  I would entreat you I might see my chamber;   95
  I am on the sudden grown exceeding ill
  And would be spared from supper.
Wendoll. [*Calling*]   Light there, ho!—
  See you want nothing, sir, for if you do,
  You injury that good man, and wrong me too.
Cranwell. I will make bold. Good night.   [*Exit.*]
Wendoll.   How all conspire   100
  To make our bosom sweet and full entire!
  Come, Nan, I prithee let us sup within.
Anne. Oh, what a clog unto the soul is sin!
  We pale offenders are still full of fear;
  Every suspicious eye brings danger near,   105
  When they whose clear heart from offence are free
  Despise report, base scandals to outface,
  And stand at mere defiance with disgrace.
Wendoll. Fie, fie, you talk too like a Puritan.
Anne. You have tempted me to mischief, Master Wendoll; 110
  I have done I know not what. Well, you plead custom;
  That which for want of wit I granted erst
  I now must yield through fear. Come, come, let's in.
  Once o'er shoes, we are straight o'er head in sin.
Wendoll. My jocund soul is joyful above measure;   115
  I'll be profuse in Frankford's richest treasure.   *Exeunt.*

[12]

      Enter SISLY, JENKIN, [SPIGGOT *the*] *Butler*,
         and other Servingmen.

Jenkin. My mistress and Master Wendoll, my master, sup in her
  chamber tonight. Sisly, you are preferred from being the cook
  to be chambermaid. Of all the loves betwixt thee and me, tell
  me what thou thinkest of this.

---

  99. *injury*] in jure.
  103. *clog*] hindrance.
  106. *When*] whereas.
  107.] despise rumour, thus confronting low scandal-mongering.
  108. *mere*] absolute.
  111. *you plead custom*] you urge that we continue as before.
  112. *erst*] at first.
  114.] Once we first start getting our feet wet, we're soon in over over heads.
  116. *profuse*] lavish, immoderate.

  12.2. *preferred*] promoted.

Sisly. Mum. There's an old proverb, 'When the cat's away the   5
mouse may play'.

Jenkin. Now you talk of a cat, Sisly, I smell a rat.

Sisly. Good words, Jenkin, lest you be called to answer them.

Jenkin. Why, 'God make my mistress an honest woman'. Are not
these good words? 'Pray God my new master play not the knave   10
with my old master.' Is there any hurt in this? 'God send no
villainy intended, and if they do sup together, pray God they do
not lie together. God keep my mistress chaste and make us all
His servants.' What harm is there in all this? Nay, more, here
is my hand; thou shalt never have my heart unless thou say   15
'Amen'.

Sisly. 'Amen, I pray God', I say.

Enter Servingmen.

Servant. My mistress sends that you should make less noise, to lock
up the doors, and see the household all got to bed. You, Jenkin,
for this night are made the porter, to see the gates shut in.   20

Jenkin. Thus by little and little I creep into office. Come to kennel,
my masters, to kennel; 'tis eleven o'clock already.

Servant. When you have locked the gates in, you must send up the
keys to my mistress.

Sisly. Quickly, for God's sake, Jenkin; for I must carry them. I am   25
neither pillow nor bolster, but I know more than both.

Jenkin. To bed, good Spiggot; to bed, good honest serving-
creatures, and let us sleep as snug as pigs in pease-straw.

Exeunt.

[13]

Enter FRANKFORD *and* NICHOLAS.

Frankford. Soft, soft. We have tied our geldings to a tree
Two flight-shoot off, lest by their thund'ring hooves
They blab our coming back. Hear'st thou no noise?

---

5. *Mum*] Either a generalized noise of sceptical musing, 'Hmm', or an abbreviation of 'keep mum', meaning 'keep it a secret'.

8.] Speak charitably, Jenkin, in case you have to answer to your superiors.

21. *creep into office*] gradually progress through the ranks of the servants. Closing
up the house was the job of an upper servant.

25. *them*] i.e. the keys.

25–6. *I . . . both*] i.e. I am neither (my mistress's) pillow nor bolster, but I know
more than both (what goes on in her bed).

28. *pease-straw*] stalks and leaves of the pea plant used as fodder and bedding.

13.2. *flight-shoot*] lengths achieved by a lightly feathered 'flight arrow' specially
designed for long range.

Nicholas. Hear? I hear nothing but the owl and you.
Frankford. So; now my watch's hand points upon twelve,   5
    And it is dead midnight. Where are my keys?
Nicholas. Here, sir.   [*He gives keys.*]
Frankford. This is the key that opes my outward gate,
    This is the hall door, this my withdrawing chamber.
    But this, that door that's bawd unto my shame,   10
    Fountain and spring of all my bleeding thoughts,
    Where the most hallowed order and true knot
    Of nuptial sanctity hath been profaned:
    It leads to my polluted bedchamber,
    Once my terrestrial heaven, now my earth's hell,   15
    The place where sins in all their ripeness dwell.—
    But I forget myself. Now to my gate.
Nicholas. It must ope with far less noise than Cripplegate, or your
    plot's dashed.
Frankford. So, reach me my dark-lantern to the rest.   20
    Tread softly, softly.
Nicholas.   I will walk on eggs this pace.
Frankford. A general silence hath surprised the house,
    And this is the last door. Astonishment,   *he keeps*
    Fear, and amazement play against my heart,   *delaying*
    Even as a madman beats upon a drum.   25
    Oh, keep my eyes, you heavens, before I enter,
    From any sight that may transfix my soul!
    Or if there be so black a spectacle,
    Oh, strike mine eyes stark blind! Or if not so,
    Lend me such patience to digest my grief   30
    That I may keep this white and virgin hand
    From any violent outrage or red murder!
    And with that prayer I enter.   [*Exit.*]
Nicholas. Here's a circumstance!
    A man may be made cuckold in the time   35

---

9. *withdrawing chamber*] a private room attached to a public one.

17. *gate*] The exact relationship between the 'outward gate', the 'last door' (line 23), and the doors on the stage is complex. See Intro., pp. 11–12.

18. *Cripplegate*] one of the northern gates of London.

20. *dark-lantern*] a lantern with a slide to focus and conceal the light.

to the rest] either (1) to the rest of the gates, or (2) in addition to the other equipment.

21. *I will . . . pace*] At this soft, slow pace, I could walk on eggs without breaking them.

22. *surprised*] overcome.

31. *virgin*] having never shed blood.

35–6. *A man . . . about it*] Nicholas fears that Frankford's delay is leaving enough time for the lovers to cuckold him.

That he's about it. An the case were mine
As 'tis my master's—'sblood, that he makes me swear!—
I would have placed his action, entered there;
I would, I would.

[*Enter* FRANKFORD.]

Frankford. Oh, Oh!   40
Nicholas. Master! 'Sblood, master, master!
Frankford. Oh me unhappy! I have found them lying
    Close in each other's arms, and fast asleep.
    But that I would not damn two precious souls
    Bought with my Saviour's blood and send them laden   45
    With all their scarlet sins upon their backs
    Unto a fearful Judgement, their two lives
    Had met upon my rapier.
Nicholas. 'Sblood, master, have you left them sleeping still? Let me
    go wake them.   50
Frankford. Stay, let me pause awhile.
    Oh, God, oh, God, that it were possible
    To undo things done, to call back yesterday!
    That Time could turn up his swift sandy glass
    To untell the days and to redeem these hours,   55
    Or that the Sun
    Could, rising from the west, draw his coach backward,
    Take from the account of time so many minutes,
    Till he had all these seasons called again,
    Those minutes and those actions done in them,   60
    Even from her first offence, that I might take her
    As spotless as an angel in my arms!
    But oh, I talk of things impossible
    And cast beyond the moon. God give me patience,
    For I will in to wake them.   *Exit.*   65
Nicholas. Here's patience perforce!
    He needs must trot afoot that tires his horse.

Enter WENDOLL, *running over the stage in a nightgown* [*and exit*],
    he [FRANKFORD] *after him with his sword drawn; the* Maid *in*
    her smock stays his hand and clasps hold on him. He pauses awhile.

---

36. *An*] if.
37. *'sblood . . . swear*] by God, he makes me angry.
38. *placed his action*] made the move he needed to make.
44–8.] If Frankford had killed Anne and Wendoll before they had a chance to
repent, according to traditional theology, their souls would have gone to hell.
55. *untell*] undo the counting of.
59. *called*] recalled.
64. *beyond the moon*] in the impossible translunary realm.
66. *perforce*] of necessity (as the proverb in the next line illustrates).

Frankford. I thank thee, maid; thou like the angel's hand
    Hast stayed me from a bloody sacrifice.—
    Go, villain, and my wrongs sit on thy soul   70
    As heavy as this grief doth upon mine!
    When thou record'st my many courtesies
    And shalt compare them with thy treacherous heart,
    Lay them together, weigh them equally,
    'Twill be revenge enough. Go, to thy friend   75
    A Judas. Pray, pray, lest I live to see
    Thee, Judas-like, hanged on an elder tree.

he has been the ultimate trader [handwritten marginal note]

    Enter MISTRESS [ANNE] FRANKFORD *in her smock, nightgown,*
        and night attire.

Anne. [*Kneeling*] Oh, by what word, what title, or what name
    Shall I entreat your pardon? Pardon! Oh,
    I am as far from hoping such sweet grace   80
    As Lucifer from heaven. To call you husband—
    Oh me most wretched, I have lost that name;
    I am no more your wife.
Nicholas.   'Sblood, sir, she swoons.
Frankford. Spare thou thy tears, for I will weep for thee;
    And keep thy countenance, for I'll blush for thee.   85
    Now I protest I think 'tis I am tainted,
    For I am most ashamed, and 'tis more hard
    For me to look upon thy guilty face
    Than on the sun's clear brow. What wouldst thou speak?
Anne. I would I had no tongue, no ears, no eyes,   90
    No apprehension, no capacity.
    When do you spurn me like a dog? When tread me
    Under your feet? When drag me by the hair?
    Though I deserve a thousand thousand fold
    More than you can inflict, yet, once my husband,   95
    For womanhood—to which I am a shame,
    Though once an ornament—even for His sake
    That hath redeemed our souls, mark not my face
    Nor hack me with your sword, but let me go
    Perfect and undeformèd to my tomb.   100

68–9. *thou . . . sacrifice*] like the angel who stayed Abraham's hand when he was about to sacrifice his son Isaac (Genesis, 22.11–12). See Intro., p. 12.

70. *villain*] Wendoll (whom Frankford apostrophizes after Wendoll's abrupt departure).

75–6. *to . . . Judas*] having been a Judas to your friend. (Judas, who betrayed Jesus, was the type of a traitor. After Jesus had been captured and executed, Judas hanged himself. See Matthew, 26.14, 27.5.)

77. *elder tree*] traditionally the tree on which Judas hanged himself.

I am not worthy that I should prevail
In the least suit, no, not to speak to you,
Nor look on you, nor to be in your presence.
Yet as an abject this one suit I crave;
This granted, I am ready for my grave.   105

realizes what she has done.

Frankford. My God with patience arm me! Rise, nay, rise,
And I'll debate with thee. Was it for want
Thou played'st the strumpet? Wast thou not supplied
With every pleasure, fashion, and new toy—
Nay, even beyond my calling?

Anne.   I was.   110

Frankford. Was it then disability in me,
Or in thine eye seemed he a properer man?

Anne. Oh, no!

Frankford.   Did I not lodge thee in my bosom?
Wear thee here in my heart?

Anne.   You did.

Frankford. I did indeed; witness my tears I did—   115
Go bring my infants hither.

                [*Exit* Maid *and return with two* Children.]
                    Oh, Nan, oh, Nan,
If either fear of shame, regard of honour,
The blemish of my house, nor my dear love
Could have withheld thee from so lewd a fact,
Yet for these infants, these young, harmless souls,   120
On whose white brows thy shame is charactered
And grows in greatness as they wax in years—
Look but on them and melt away in tears.—
Away with them, lest, as her spotted body   *tainted*
Hath stained their names with stripe of bastardy,   125
So her adult'rous breath may blast their spirits
With her infectious thoughts. Away with them!

                [*Exeunt* Maid *and* Children.]

Anne. In this one life I die ten thousand deaths.

Frankford. Stand up, stand up. I will do nothing rashly.
I will retire awhile into my study,   130
And thou shalt hear thy sentence presently.   *Exit.*

---

104. *abject*] castaway.

110. *calling*] rank, station in life.

116 SD. *Children*] There seems to have been no time in the play for two children
to have been born, but plays often foreshorten time dramatically. See Intro., p. 13.

119. *fact*] deed.

121. *charactered*] written in characters like a brand.

125. *stripe*] like the 'bend sinister', a slash across a coat of arms, indicating
bastardy.

Anne. [*Rising*] 'Tis welcome, be it death. Oh me, base strumpet,
    That, having such a husband, such sweet children,
    Must enjoy neither! Oh, to redeem my honour
    I would have this hand cut off, these my breasts seared,   135
    Be racked, strappadoed, put to any torment;
    Nay, to whip but this scandal out, I would hazard
    The rich and dear redemption of my soul.
    He cannot be so base as to forgive me,
    Nor I so shameless to accept his pardon.   140
    [*To the audience*] O women, women, you that have yet kept
    Your holy matrimonial vow unstained,
    Make me your instance! When you tread awry,
    Your sins like mine will on your conscience lie.

        Enter SISLY, SPIGGOT, *all the* Servingmen, *and*
            JENKIN, *as newly come out of bed.*

All. O mistress, mistress, what have you done, mistress?   145
Nicholas. 'Sblood, what a caterwauling keep you here!
Jenkin. Oh Lord, mistress, how comes this to pass? My master is
    run away in his shirt, and never so much as called me to bring
    his clothes after him.
Anne. See what guilt is! Here stand I in this place,   150
    Ashamed to look my servants in the face.

        Enter MASTER FRANKFORD *and* CRANWELL,
            whom seeing she falls on her knees.

Frankford. My words are registered in heaven already.
    With patience hear me: I'll not martyr thee
    Nor mark thee for a strumpet, but with usage
    Of more humility torment thy soul   155
    And kill thee even with kindness.
Cranwell.   Master Frankford—
Frankford. Good Master Cranwell—woman, hear thy judgement:
    Go make thee ready in thy best attire,   *wont call by*
    Take with thee all thy gowns, all thy apparel;   *her name*

---

136. *racked*] tortured by being stretched on the rack.
    strappadoed] subjected to a form of torture in which the victim's hands are are
tied with a rope behind the back, the rope is attached to a pulley and s/he is then
hoisted above the ground and left to hang.
    137. *to . . . out*] alluding to the belief that evil can be exorcized from the body by
whipping.
    143. *instance*] example.
    146. *keep you*] do you keep up.
    148. *shirt*] nightshirt.
    152.] Frankford is saying that he has made his judgement with the help of prayer
and so registered his intentions with God.

Leave nothing that did ever call thee mistress,   160
Or by whose sight being left here in the house
I may remember such a woman by.
Choose thee a bed and hangings for a chamber,
Take with thee everything that hath thy mark,
And get thee to my manor seven mile off,   165
Where live. 'Tis thine; I freely give it thee.
My tenants by shall furnish thee with wains
To carry all thy stuff within two hours;
No longer will I limit thee my sight.
Choose which of all my servants thou likest best,   170
And they are thine to attend thee.
Anne.   A mild sentence.
Frankford. But as thou hop'st for heaven, as thou believ'st
Thy name's recorded in the Book of Life,
I charge thee never after this sad day
To see me, or to meet me, or to send   175
By word, or writing, gift, or otherwise
To move me, by thyself or by thy friends,
Nor challenge any part in my two children.
So farewell, Nan, for we will henceforth be
As we had never seen, ne'er more shall see.   180
Anne. How full my heart is in my eyes appears;
What wants in words, I will supply in tears.
Frankford. Come, take your coach, your stuff; all must along.—
Servants and all make ready, all be gone!—
It was thy hand cut two hearts out of one.   [*Exeunt.*]   185

[14]

> *Enter* SIR CHARLES, *gentlemanlike, and* [SUSAN]
> *his sister, gentlewomanlike.*

Susan. Brother, why have you tricked me like a bride?
Bought me this gay attire, these ornaments?

---

163. *hangings*] curtains for a bed.
164. *thy mark*] (1) laundry mark indicating your ownership; (2) the mark of your disgrace.
167. *by*] nearby.
wains] waggons.
169. *limit . . . sight*] allow you to remain within my sight.
173. *Book of Life*] record of those who will inherit eternal life: see Revelation, 20.12.
178. *challenge*] lay claim to.
180. *As . . . seen*] as if we had never seen each other.
185.] It was your hand's action that cut our joint heart in two.

14.1. *tricked*] dressed up.

Forget you our estate, our poverty?
Sir Charles. Call me not brother, but imagine me
　　Some barbarous outlaw or uncivil kern,　　　　　　　　　5
　　For, if thou shut'st thy eye and only hear'st
　　The words that I shall utter, thou shalt judge me
　　Some staring ruffian, not thy brother Charles.
　　Oh, Susan!
Susan. Oh, brother, what doth this strange language mean?　　10
Sir Charles. Dost love me, sister? Wouldst thou see me live
　　A bankrupt beggar in the world's disgrace
　　And die indebted to my enemies?
　　Wouldst thou behold me stand like a huge beam
　　In the world's eye, a byword and a scorn?　　　　　　　15
　　It lies in thee of these to acquit me free,
　　And all my debt I may outstrip by thee.
Susan. By me? Why, I have nothing, nothing left;
　　I owe even for the clothes upon my back;
　　I am not worth, &c.
Sir Charles.　　　　　　　Oh, sister, say not so.　　　　　20
　　It lies in you my downcast state to raise,
　　To make me stand on even points with the world.
　　Come, sister, you are rich. Indeed you are,
　　And in your power you have, without delay,
　　Acton's five hundred pound back to repay.　　　　　　　25
Susan. Till now I had thought you loved me. By mine honour—
　　Which I had kept as spotless as the moon—
　　I ne'er was mistress of that single doit
　　Which I reserved not to supply your wants.
　　And do you think that I would hoard from you?　　　　　30
　　Now by my hopes in heaven, knew I the means
　　To buy you from the slavery of your debts,
　　Especially from Acton, whom I hate,
　　I would redeem it with my life or blood.
Sir Charles. I challenge it, and, kindred set apart,　　　　35

---

5. *kern*] Irish warrior; thought of as wild and uncivilized.
8. *staring*] wild-eyed.
14–15. *beam . . . eye*] an obstruction in the world's vision: as in the Sermon on the Mount, Matthew, 7.3: 'And why seest thou the mote that is in thy brother's eye and perceivest not the beam that is in thine own eye?'
20. *&c*] indicates that Charles interrupts.
22. *on even points*] in the right relationship.
27. *spotless . . . moon*] conflating two images for virginity: purity without blemish and Diana the moon goddess who was also an emblem of chastity.
28. *doit*] the smallest imaginable sum of money; actually a small Dutch coin worth half a farthing.
35.] I take up your offer, and setting aside all family feeling.

Thus ruffian-like I lay siege to your heart.
What do I owe to Acton?
Susan. Why, some five hundred pounds, toward which I swear
    In all the world I have not one denier.
Sir Charles. It will not prove so. Sister, now resolve me: 40
    What do you think—and speak your conscience—
    Would Acton give might he enjoy your bed?
Susan. He would not shrink to spend a thousand pound
    To give the Mountfords' name so deep a wound.
Sir Charles. A thousand pound! I but five hundred owe;   45
    Grant him your bed, he's paid with interest so.
Susan. Oh, brother!
Sir Charles.   Oh, sister! Only this one way,
    With that rich jewel you my debts may pay.
    In speaking this my cold heart shakes with shame,
    Nor do I woo you in a brother's name,   50
    But in a stranger's. Shall I die in debt
    To Acton, my grand foe, and you still wear
    The precious jewel that he holds so dear?
Susan. My honour I esteem as dear and precious
    As my redemption.
Sir Charles.   I esteem you, sister,   55
    As dear for so dear prizing it.
Susan.   Will Charles
    Have me cut off my hands and send them Acton?
    Rip up my breast, and with my bleeding heart
    Present him as a token?
Sir Charles.   Neither, sister.
    But hear me in my strange assertion: 60
    Thy honour and my soul are equal in my regard,
    Nor will thy brother Charles survive thy shame.
    His kindness like a burden hath surcharged me,
    And under his good deeds I stooping go,
    Not with an upright soul. Had I remained   65
    In prison still, there doubtless I had died;
    Then unto him that freed me from that prison
    Still do I owe that life. What moved my foe
    To enfranchise me? 'Twas, sister, for your love!
    With full five hundred pounds he bought your love.   70

---

39. *denier*] another type of small sum; from a French coin worth one-twelfth of a sou.

48. *rich jewel*] i.e. virginity; see Intro., pp. 44–5.

63.] Acton's kindness in releasing me from prison has placed an overwhelming obligation on me. See Intro., pp. 44–5.

69. *enfranchise*] set at liberty.

And shall he not enjoy it? Shall the weight
Of all this heavy burden lean on me,
And will not you bear part? You did partake
The joy of my release; will you not stand
In joint bond bound to satisfy the debt?   75
Shall I be only charged?
Susan.   But that I know
These arguments come from an honoured mind,
As in your most extremity of need,
Scorning to stand in debt to one you hate—
Nay, rather would engage your unstained honour   80
Than to be held ingrate—I should condemn you.
I see your resolution, and assent;
So Charles will have me, and I am content.
Sir Charles. For this I tricked you up.
Susan.   But here's a knife,
To save mine honour, shall slice out my life.   85
Sir Charles. I know thou pleasest me a thousand times
More in that resolution than thy grant.
[*Aside*] Observe her love: to soothe it to my suit,
Her honour she will hazard, though not lose;
To bring me out of debt, her rigorous hand   90
Will pierce her heart. Oh, wonder, that will choose,
Rather than stain her blood, her life to lose!
[*To her*] Come, you sad sister to a woeful brother,
This is the gate; I'll bear him such a present,
Such an acquittance for the knight to seal   95
As will amaze his senses and surprise
With admiration all his fantasies.

Enter [SIR FRANCIS] ACTON *and* MALBY.

Susan. Before his unchaste thoughts shall seize on me,
'Tis here shall my imprisoned soul set free.
Sir Francis. [*To Malby*] How? Mountford with his sister hand in
hand?   100

---

75. *In . . . bound*] sharing the contract with me. See Intro., pp. 44–5.
80. *engage*] make available for the transaction.
86–7.] Susan's decision to kill herself after Acton has taken her virginity pleases
Charles more than the agreement to give up her body to pay his debts.
88. *to soothe . . . suit*] to cajole her honour to comply with my request.
89.] Susan will risk her honour by giving way to Sir Charles's demand, but will
keep it by killing herself.
95. *acquittance*] document of release.
97. *admiration*] astonishment. Also in line 102.
fantasies] powers of imagination.
99. *'Tis here*] i.e. the knife is here that.

What miracle's afoot?
Malby.   It is a sight
  Begets in me much admiration.
Sir Charles. [*To Sir Francis*] Stand not amazed to see me thus
    attended.
  Acton, I owe thee money, and, being unable
  To bring thee the full sum in ready coin,   105
  Lo! for thy more assurance here's a pawn,
  My sister, my dear sister, whose chaste honour
  I prize above a million. Here—nay, take her;
  She's worth your money, man; do not forsake her.
Sir Francis. [*Aside*] I would he were in earnest.   110
Susan. Impute it not to my immodesty.
  My brother, being rich in nothing else
  But in his interest that he hath in me,
  According to his poverty hath brought you
  Me, all his store, whom, howsoe'er you prize   115
  As forfeit to your hand, he values highly,
  And would not sell, but to acquit your debt,
  For any emperor's ransom.
Sir Francis. [*Aside*]   Stern heart, relent!
  Thy former cruelty at length repent!
  Was ever known in any former age   120
  Such honourable wrested courtesy?
  Lands, honours, lives, and all the world forgo
  Rather than stand engaged to such a foe!
Sir Charles. Acton, she is too poor to be thy bride,
  And I too much opposed to be thy brother.   125
  There, take her to thee. If thou hast the heart
  To seize her as a rape or lustful prey,
  To blur our house that never yet was stained,
  To murder her that never meant thee harm,
  To kill me now whom once thou saved'st from death,   130
  Do them at once on her; all these rely
  And perish with her spotted chastity.
Sir Francis. You overcome me in your love, Sir Charles.
  I cannot be so cruel to a lady
  I love so dearly. Since you have not spared   135
  To engage your reputation to the world,

---

106. *pawn*] pledge, security for a debt.
121. *wrested*] distorted, forced.
127. *lustful prey*] prey to your lust.
128. *blur*] stain.
131. *rely*] rely on.

Your sister's honour which you prize so dear,
Nay, all the comforts which you hold on earth,
To grow out of my debt, being your foe,
Your honoured thoughts, lo, thus I recompense: 140
Your metamorphosed foe receives your gift
In satisfaction of all former wrongs.
This jewel I will wear here in my heart,
And, where before I thought her for her wants
Too base to be my bride, to end all strife   145
I seal you my dear brother, her my wife.
Susan. You still exceed us. I will yield to fate, ⎫
    And learn to love where I till now did hate. ⎭
Sir Charles. With that enchantment you have charmed my soul
    And made me rich even in those very words.   150
    I pay no debt, but am indebted more;
    Rich in your love, I never can be poor.
Sir Francis. All's mine is yours; we are alike in state.
    Let's knit in love what was opposed in hate.
    Come, for our nuptials we will straight provide,   155
    Blessed only in our brother and fair bride.   *Exeunt.*

[15]

            Enter CRANWELL, FRANKFORD, *and* NICHOLAS.

Cranwell. Why do you search each room about your house,
    Now that you have dispatched your wife away?
Frankford. Oh, sir, to see that nothing may be left
    That ever was my wife's. I loved her dearly,
    And when I do but think of her unkindness   5
    My thoughts are all in hell, to avoid which torment
    I would not have a bodkin or a cuff,
    A bracelet, necklace, or rebato wire,
    Nor anything that ever was called hers
    Left me by which I might remember her.   10
    Seek round about.
Nicholas. [*Finding a lute*] 'Sblood, master, here's her lute flung in
    a corner.
Frankford. Her lute! Oh, God, upon this instrument

---

141. *metamorphosed*] transformed.
144. *for her wants*] because of her poverty.
146. *seal*] endorse, ratify (as on a legal document).
147. *exceed us*] i.e. go beyond us in status and in generosity.

15.5. *unkindness*] (1) hurtful behaviour; (2) unnatural behaviour.
7. *bodkin*] ornamental hair-pin.
8. *rebato wire*] used to support the elaborate ruffs worn by rich women.

Her fingers have run quick division,
Sweeter than that which now divides our hearts.   15
These frets have made me pleasant, that have now
Frets of my heartstrings made. Oh, Master Cranwell,
Oft hath she made this melancholy wood,
Now mute and dumb for her disastrous chance,
Speak sweetly many a note, sound many a strain   20
To her own ravishing voice, which being well strung,
What pleasant, strange airs have they jointly sung!—
Post with it after her.—Now nothing's left;
Of her and hers I am at once bereft.
Nicholas. I'll ride and overtake her, do my message,   25
    And come back again.   [*Exit with the lute.*]
Cranwell.   Meantime, sir, if you please,
    I'll to Sir Francis Acton and inform him
    Of what hath passed betwixt you and his sister.
Frankford. Do as you please. How ill am I bestead
    To be a widower ere my wife be dead!   [*Exeunt.*]   30

[16]

> *Enter* MISTRESS [ANNE] FRANKFORD, *with* JENKIN,
> *her maid* SISLY, *her* Coachman, *and three* Carters.

Anne. Bid my coach stay. Why should I ride in state,
    Being hurled so low down by the hand of fate?
    A seat like to my fortunes let me have:
    Earth for my chair, and for my bed a grave.
Jenkin. Comfort, good mistress; you have watered your coach with   5
    tears already. You have but two mile now to go to your manor.
    A man cannot say by my old Master Frankford, as he may say
    by me, that he wants manors, for he hath three or four, of which
    this is one that we are going to.
Sisly. Good mistress, be of good cheer. Sorrow, you see, hurts you   10
    but helps you not. We all mourn to see you so sad.
Carter. Mistress, I spy one of my landlord's men
    Come riding post; 'tis like he brings some news.

---

14. *run quick division*] played a rapid melody.
16–17. *frets . . . Frets*] stops on a lute's sounding board . . . fretting, scolding.
19. *for . . . chance*] because of her misfortune.
23. *Post*] hurry.
29. *bestead*] treated.

16.7. *by*] about.
8. *manors*] (1) estates; (2) manners. (Q1: 'maners'). See *Roaring Girl*, 2.1.62
and n.
13. *post*] speedily.
like] likely.

Anne. Comes he from Master Frankford, he is welcome;
  So are his news, because they come from him.   15

Enter NICHOLAS.

Nicholas. [*Handing her the lute*] There!
Anne. I know the lute. Oft have I sung to thee;
  We both are out of tune, both out of time.
Nicholas. Would that had been the worst instrument that e'er you
  played on. My master commends him to ye; there's all he can   20
  find that was ever yours. He hath nothing left that ever you
  could lay claim to but his own heart—and he could afford you
  that. All that I have to deliver you is this: he prays you to forget
  him, and so he bids you farewell.
Anne. I thank him; he is kind and ever was.—   25
  All you that have true feeling of my grief,
  That know my loss, and have relenting hearts,
  Gird me about, and help me with your tears
  To wash my spotted sins. My lute shall groan;
  It cannot weep, but shall lament my moan.   [*She plays.*]   30

Enter WENDOLL [*behind*].

Wendoll. Pursued with horror of a guilty soul
  And with the sharp scourge of repentance lashed,
  I fly from my own shadow. O my stars!
  What have my parents in their lives deserved
  That you should lay this penance on their son?   35
  When I but think of Master Frankford's love
  And lay it to my treason, or compare
  My murd'ring him for his relieving me,
  It strikes a terror like a lightning's flash
  To scorch my blood up. Thus I, like the owl,   40
  Ashamed of day, live in these shadowy woods
  Afraid of every leaf or murmuring blast,
  Yet longing to receive some perfect knowledge
  How he hath dealt with her. [*He sees Anne.*] O my sad fate!
  Here, and so far from home, and thus attended!   45
  O God, I have divorced the truest turtles
  That ever lived together and, being divided
  In several places, make their several moan;

---

14. *Comes he*] if he comes.
37. *lay*] compare.
38. *murd'ring him*] i.e. destroying his happiness.
43. *perfect*] correct.
46. *turtles*] turtledoves.
48. *several moan*] separate lament.

She in the fields laments and he at home.
So poets write that Orpheus made the trees   50
And stones to dance to his melodious harp,
Meaning the rustic and the barbarous hinds,
That had no understanding part in them;
So she from these rude carters tears extracts,
Making their flinty hearts with grief to rise   55
And draw down rivers from their rocky eyes.

Anne. [*To Nicholas*] If you return unto your master, say—
Though not from me, for I am all unworthy
To blast his name so with a strumpet's tongue—
That you have seen me weep, wish myself dead.   60
Nay, you may say too—for my vow is passed—
Last night you saw me eat and drink my last.
This to your master you may say and swear,
For it is writ in heaven and decreed here.

Nicholas. I'll say you wept; I'll swear you made me sad.   65
Why how now, eyes? What now? What's here to do?
I am gone, or I shall straight turn baby too.

Wendoll. [*Aside*] I cannot weep; my heart is all on fire.
Cursed be the fruits of my unchaste desire!

Anne. Go break this lute upon my coach's wheel,   70
As the last music that I e'er shall make—
Not as my husband's gift, but my farewell
To all earth's joy; and so your master tell.

Nicholas. If I can for crying.

Wendoll. [*Aside*]   Grief, have done,
Or like a madman I shall frantic run.   75

Anne. You have beheld the woefullest wretch on earth,
A woman made of tears. Would you had words
To express but what you see. My inward grief
No tongue can utter, yet unto your power
You may describe my sorrow and disclose   80
To thy sad master my abundant woes.

50–3.] The interpretation of the myth of Orpheus as social allegory, in which the trees and stones which moved to his music were a figure for the lower classes, was common in Renaissance handbooks of mythology.

52. *hinds*] country people.

56. *rocky*] i.e. hard, unrelenting.

59. *blast*] (1) wither, blight; (2) proclaim.

61. *passed*] made.

67. *I am gone . . . too*] i.e. I must leave before I burst into tears.

78. *but*] only.

79. *unto your power*] as far as you are able.

Nicholas. I'll do your commendations.
Anne.   Oh, no.
    I dare not so presume; nor to my children.
    I am disclaimed in both; alas, I am.
    Oh, never teach them, when they come to speak,   85
    To name the name of mother; chide their tongue
    If they by chance light on that hated word;
    Tell them 'tis nought, for when that word they name,
    Poor, pretty souls, they harp on their own shame.
Wendoll. [*Aside*] To recompense her wrongs, what canst thou do?   90
    Thou hast made her husbandless and childless too.
Anne. I have no more to say. Speak not for me,
    Yet you may tell your master what you see.
Nicholas. I'll do 't.   *Exit.*
Wendoll. [*Aside*] I'll speak to her and comfort her in grief.   95
    Oh, but her wound cannot be cured with words.
    No matter though, I'll do my best good will
    To work a cure on her whom I did kill.
Anne. So, now unto my coach, then to my home,
    ⎰So to my deathbed, for from this sad hour   100
    I never will nor eat, nor drink, nor taste
    Of any cates that may preserve my life;
    I never will nor smile, nor sleep, nor rest;
    But when my tears have washed my black soul white,
    Sweet Saviour, to Thy hands I yield my sprite.   105
Wendoll. [*Coming forward*] Oh, Mistress Frankford—
Anne.   Oh, for God's sake, fly!
    The devil doth come to tempt me ere I die.
    My coach! This fiend, that with an angel's face
    Courted mine honour till he sought my wrack,
    In my repentant eyes seems ugly black.   110
    Exeunt all [*except* WENDOLL *and* JENKIN], *the* Carters *whistling.*
Jenkin. What, my young master that fled in his shirt! How come you
    by your clothes again? You have made our house in a sweet
    pickle, have you not, think you? What, shall I serve you still or
    cleave to the old house?
Wendoll. Hence, slave! Away with thy unseasoned mirth;   115
    Unless thou canst shed tears, and sigh, and howl,

---

    82. *do your commendations*] present your compliments and best wishes.
    84. *disclaimed in both*] disowned by husband and children, having lost all claim of
legitimacy.
    90. *thou*] i.e. Wendoll.
    102. *cates*] food, delicacies.
    105. *sprite*] spirit.
    109. *wrack*] ruin.

Curse thy sad fortunes, and exclaim on fate,
Thou art not for my turn.
Jenkin. Marry, an you will not, another will; farewell and be hanged!
Would you had never come to have kept this coil within our   120
doors! We shall ha' you run away like a sprite again.   [*Exit.*]
Wendoll. She's gone to death, I live to want and woe—
Her life, her sins, and all upon my head,
And I must now go wander like a Cain
In foreign countries and remoted climes,   125
Where the report of my ingratitude
Cannot be heard. I'll over, first to France,
And so to Germany and Italy,
Where, when I have recovered, and by travel
Gotten those perfect tongues, and that these rumours   130
May in their height abate, I will return;
And I divine, however now dejected,
My worth and parts being by some great man praised,
At my return I may in court be raised.   *Exit.*

[17]

Enter SIR FRANCIS, SIR CHARLES, CRANWELL, [MALBY,] *and* SUSAN.

Sir Francis. Brother, and now my wife, I think these troubles
Fall on my head by justice of the heavens
For being so strict to you in your extremities;
But we are now atoned. I would my sister
Could with like happiness o'ercome her griefs   5
As we have ours.
Susan. You tell us, Master Cranwell, wondrous things
Touching the patience of that gentleman,
With what strange virtue he demeans his grief.
Cranwell. I told you what I was witness of;   10
It was my fortune to lodge there that night.

---

118. *for my turn*] useful for what I want.
119. *an . . . another will*] i.e. if you won't get away from here, we will leave you.
120. *kept this coil*] stirred up this trouble.
124. *Cain*] the first murderer, who killed his brother Abel and was condemned to wander the world (Genesis, 4.2).
125. *remoted climes*] distant places.
130–1. *Gotten . . . abate*] learned those foreign languages perfectly, and so that these rumours, now at their height, might die down.
132. *divine*] predict.

17.4. *atoned*] made one, reconciled.
8. *that gentleman*] i.c. Frankford.
9. *demeans*] reduces, mitigates.

Sir Francis. Oh, that same villain Wendoll! 'Twas his tongue
    That did corrupt her; she was of herself
    Chaste and devoted well. Is this the house?
Cranwell. Yes, sir, I take it here your sister lies.   15
Sir Francis. My brother Frankford showed too mild a spirit
    In the revenge of such a loathèd crime;
    Less than he did, no man of spirit could do.
    I am so far from blaming his revenge
    That I commend it; had it been my case,   20
    Their souls at once had from their breasts been freed.
    Death to such deeds of shame is the due meed.

Enter JENKIN *and* SISLY.

Jenkin. Oh, my mistress, my mistress, my poor mistress!
Sisly. Alas that ever I was born! What shall I do for my poor
    mistress?   25
Sir Charles. Why, what of her?
Jenkin. Oh, Lord, sir, she no sooner heard that her brother and his
    friends were come to see how she did, but she for very shame of
    her guilty conscience fell into a swoon, and we had much ado to
    get life into her.   30
Susan. Alas, that she should bear so hard a fate!
    Pity it is repentance comes too late.
Sir Francis. Is she so weak in body?
Jenkin. Oh, sir, I can assure you there's no hope of life in her, for she
    will take no sustenance. She hath plainly starved herself, and   35
    now she is as lean as a lath. She ever looks for the good hour.
    Many gentlemen and gentlewomen of the country are come to
    comfort her.

Enter MISTRESS [ANNE] FRANKFORD *in her bed.*

Malby. How fare you, Mistress Frankford?
Anne. Sick, sick, oh, sick! Give me some air, I pray you.   40
    Tell me, oh, tell me, where's Master Frankford?
    Will not he deign to see me ere I die?
Malby. Yes, Mistress Frankford; divers gentlemen,
    Your loving neighbours, with that just request
    Have moved and told him of your weak estate,   45

---

    14. *devoted well*] faithful to her marriage vows; pious.
    36. *a lath*] a thin, narrow strip of wood used as the groundwork on which to
fasten the slates or tiles of a roof, or the plaster of a wall or ceiling.
    the good hour] i.e. the hour of her death.
    38.1.] a common form of stage direction: the bed is pushed out from the discovery space. See Intro., p. 10.
    45. *moved*] taken action, moved him.

Who, though with much ado to get belief,
Examining of the general circumstance,
Seeing your sorrow and your penitence,
And hearing therewithal the great desire
You have to see him ere you left the world,   50
He gave to us his faith to follow us,
And sure he will be here immediately.
Anne. You half revived me with those pleasing news.
Raise me a little higher in my bed.
Blush I not, brother Acton? Blush I not, Sir Charles?   55
Can you not read my fault writ in my cheek?
Is not my crime there? Tell me, gentlemen.
Sir Charles. Alas, good mistress, sickness hath not left you
Blood in your face enough to make you blush.
Anne. Then sickness, like a friend, my fault would hide.   60
Is my husband come? My soul but tarries
His arrive and I am fit for heaven.
Sir Francis. I came to chide you, but my words of hate
Are turned to pity and compassionate grief;
I came to rate you, but my brawls, you see,   65
Melt into tears, and I must weep by thee.

Enter FRANKFORD.

Here's Master Frankford now.
Frankford. Good morrow, brother; good morrow, gentlemen.
God, that hath laid this cross upon our heads,
Might, had He pleased, have made our cause of meeting   70
On a more fair and a more contented ground;
But He that made us made us to this woe.
Anne. And is he come? Methinks that voice I know.
Frankford. How do you, woman?
Anne. Well, Master Frankford, well; but shall be better,   75
I hope, within this hour. Will you vouchsafe,
Out of your grace and your humanity,
To take a spotted strumpet by the hand?
Frankford. [*Taking her hand*] That hand once held my heart in
faster bonds
Than now 'tis gripped by me. God pardon them   80

---

46. *Who*] i.e. Frankford.
get belief] be convinced.
47. *Examining of*] considering.
51. *faith*] promise.
62. *arrive*] arrival.
65. *rate*] scold.

That made us first break hold!

Anne.   Amen, amen!
Out of my zeal to heaven, whither I am now bound,
I was so impudent to wish you here,
And once more beg your pardon. O good man,
And father to my children, pardon me.   85
Pardon, oh, pardon me! My fault so heinous is
That if you in this world forgive it not,
Heaven will not clear it in the world to come.
Faintness hath so usurped upon my knees
That kneel I cannot; but on my heart's knees   90
My prostrate soul lies thrown down at your feet
To beg your gracious pardon. Pardon, Oh, pardon me!

Frankford. As freely from the low depth of my soul
As my Redeemer hath forgiven His death
I pardon thee. I will shed tears for thee,   95
Pray with thee, and in mere pity
Of thy weak state I'll wish to die with thee.

All. So do we all.

Nicholas. [*Aside*] So will not I;
I'll sign and sob, but, by my faith, not die.   100

Sir Francis. O Master Frankford, all the near alliance
I lose by her shall be supplied in thee.
You are my brother by the nearest way;
Her kindred hath fallen off, but yours doth stay.

Frankford. Even as I hope for pardon at that day   105
When the great Judge of Heaven in scarlet sits,
So be thou pardoned. Though thy rash offence
Divorced our bodies, thy repentant tears
Unite our souls.

Sir Charles.   Then comfort, Mistress Frankford!
You see your husband hath forgiven your fall.   110
Then rouse your spirits and cheer your fainting soul.

Susan. [*To Anne*] How is it with you?

Sir Francis. [*To Anne*]   How do you feel yourself?

Anne. Not of this world.

Frankford. I see you are not, and I weep to see it.
My wife, the mother to my pretty babes,   115
Both those lost names I do restore thee back,
And with this kiss I wed thee once again.   [*He kisses her.*]

94.] i.e. as Jesus has forgiven mankind for killing him.
96. *mere*] simple, pure.
104.] although she will cease to be my kindred when she dies, your kinship will
remain.

Though thou art wounded in thy honoured name,
And with that grief upon thy deathbed liest,
Honest in heart, upon my soul, thou diest.   120
Anne. Pardoned on earth, soul, thou in heaven art free!
Once more thy wife dies, thus embracing thee.   [*She dies.*]
Frankford. New married and new widowed. Oh, she's dead,
And a cold grave must be our nuptial bed.
Sir Charles. Sir, be of good comfort, and your heavy sorrow   125
Part equally amongst us; storms divided
Abate their force, and with less rage are guided.
Cranwell. Do, Master Frankford; he that hath least part
Will find enough to drown one troubled heart.
Sir Francis. Peace with thee, Nan.—Brothers and gentlemen,   130
All we that can plead interest in her grief,
Bestow upon her body funeral tears.
Brother, had you with threats and usage bad
Punished her sin, the grief of her offence
Had not with such true sorrow touched her heart.   135
Frankford. I see it had not; therefore on her grave
I will bestow this funeral epitaph,
Which on her marble tomb shall be engraved.
In golden letters shall these words be filled:
'Here lies she whom her husband's kindness killed.'   140

FINIS.

---

131. *interest*] personal involvement.
139. *golden letters*] engraved letters filled in with gold.

The Epilogue

An honest crew, disposèd to be merry,
Came to a tavern by and called for wine.
The drawer brought it, smiling like a cherry,
And told them it was pleasant, neat, and fine.
    'Taste it', quoth one. He did so. 'Fie!' quoth he,   5
    'This wine was good; now 't runs too near the lee.'

Another sipped, to give the wine his due,
And said unto the rest it drunk too flat.
The third said it was old, the fourth too new.
'Nay', quoth the fifth, 'the sharpness likes me not.'   10
    Thus, gentlemen, you see how in one hour
    The wine was new, old, flat, sharp, sweet, and sour.

Unto this wine we do allude our play,
Which some will judge too trivial, some too grave.
You as our guests we entertain this day   15
And bid you welcome to the best we have.
    Excuse us, then; good wine may be disgraced
    When every several mouth hath sundry taste.

Epilogue. 2. *by*] nearby.
3. *drawer*] tapster.
4. *neat*] unadulterated.
6. *lee*] sediment.
13. *allude*] refer to, compare.
18. *several*] individual.